WHEN THE WAR CAME HOME

WHEN THE WAR CAME HOME

The Ottomans' Great War and the

Devastation of an Empire

YİĞİT AKIN

STANFORD UNIVERSITY PRESS
STANFORD, CALIFORNIA

Stanford University Press
Stanford, California

Printed in the United States of America on acid-free, archival-quality paper

Library of Congress Cataloging-in-Publication Data

Names: Akın, Yiğit, 1975– author.
Title: When the war came home : the Ottomans' Great War and the devastation of an empire / Yiğit Akın.
Description: Stanford, California : Stanford University Press, 2018. | Includes bibliographical references and index.
Identifiers: LCCN 2017026478 (print) | LCCN 2017027781 (ebook) | ISBN 9781503604995 (ebook) | ISBN 9781503603639 (cloth : alk. paper) | ISBN 9781503604902 (pbk. : alk. paper)
Subjects: LCSH: World War, 1914–1918—Social aspects—Turkey. | Turkey—History—Ottoman Empire, 1288–1918.
Classification: LCC D524.7.T8 (ebook) | LCC D524.7.T8 A35 2018 (print) | DDC 940.3/56—dc23
LC record available at https://lccn.loc.gov/2017026478

For Zülâl

CONTENTS

ACKNOWLEDGMENTS

Many people have contributed to the writing of this book. It is a pleasure for me to acknowledge my gratitude to all of them. I am indebted to Carter V. Findley for his unfailing support for this project and his willingness to share his expertise in Ottoman history; to Jane Hathaway for her continued support from the very beginning and for many helpful suggestions along the way; and to David L. Hoffman, who not only offered incisive recommendations, but also introduced me to the rich world of Russian/Soviet history.

Several institutions generously provided funding for the research and writing of this book. I would like to thank the School of Liberal Arts, History Department, and Newcomb College Institute at Tulane University, the College of Charleston, and the Hoover Institution. In 2012–13, I had the great fortune to be a postdoctoral fellow at EUME (Europe in the Middle East–The Middle East in Europe) Program at the Wissenschaftskolleg zu Berlin. George Khalil, the academic coordinator of the program, Ulrike Freitag, the director of the Zentrum Moderner Orient, and Nora Lafi all deserve special thanks.

This project has also benefited from the gracious assistance provided by the personnel of various archives and libraries: the Prime Ministry Ottoman Archives (Istanbul), the National Archives (London), the United States National Archives (College Park, Maryland), the Hoover Library and Archives (Palo Alto, California), Izmir National Library, Istanbul Beyazıt Library, Istanbul Atatürk Library, the William Oxley Thompson Library at Ohio State, and the Howard-Tilton Memorial Library at Tulane.

I would like to thank everyone at Tulane's History Department for friendship, guidance, and intellectual generosity, including Emily Clark, Felipe Cruz, Brian DeMare, Katie Edwards, Lupe Garcia, Blake Gilpin, Karissa Haugeberg, Andy Horowitz, Kris Lane, Jana Lipman, Liz McMahon, Marline Otte, Linda Pollock, Sam Ramer, Randy Sparks, and Justin Wolfe.

I have discussed many ideas in this book with my friends, colleagues, and mentors. They have generously spared their time to listen to me, shared their knowledge, read drafts, and provided invaluable suggestions. I thank them all: Mustafa Aksakal, Ayhan Aktar, Ebru Aykut, Mehmet Beşikçi, Erdem Çıpa, Lerna Ekmekçioğlu, Özge Ertem, Benjamin Fortna, Chris Gratien, Christy Gruber, Sophia Horowitz, Nurçin İleri, Nazan Maksudyan, Charalampos Minasidis, Devi Mays, Can Nacar, Nilay Özok Gündoğan, Andrew Patrick, Fuat Şen, Elizabeth Thompson, Nicole Van Os, Ali Yaycıoğlu, and Seçil Yılmaz.

Over the years, I have spent many hours with Emre Sencer discussing politics, culture, food, and spirits, as well as history. Kyle Heatherly read everything I wrote and made much-appreciated suggestions and stylistic comments, which greatly contributed to this book. For their continued friendship, I'd like to thank them both.

At Stanford University Press, I am grateful to my editor Kate Wahl, Tim Roberts, Peter Dreyer, and Micah Siegel for making the publishing process such a smooth and pleasurable experience.

My parents have always supported my pursuit of an academic career in history. I cannot possibly thank them enough for their understanding and ceaseless love and support. I wish my father too could see the product of these long years abroad. I am also thankful to Ayşe and Halil Fazlıoğlu, whose warmth and support have been second to none. I would like to acknowledge the gracious help of my sister-in-law, Müge Fazlıoğlu, who has always been with us in times of both grief and joy. My brother Altuğ has always shared my enthusiasm and been a constant source of encouragement from many different cities around the world.

Most of all I am grateful to Zülâl for her comments, her presence, her constant encouragement, and for keeping my spirits high and positive during the completion of this book. This work would not have been as enjoyable if she were not beside me, and life would not be as colorful. I dedicate this book to her with love.

WHEN THE WAR CAME HOME

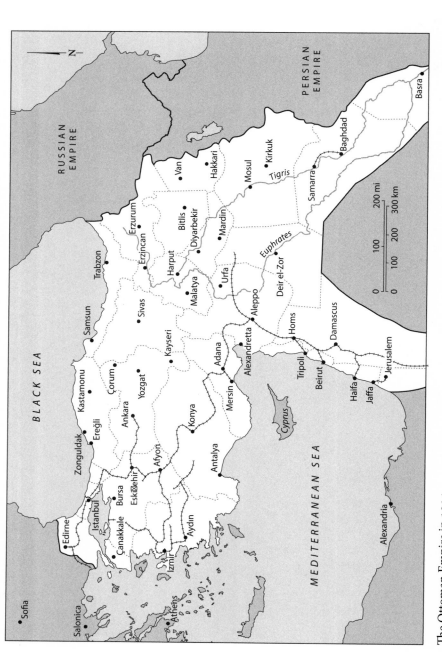

The Ottoman Empire in 1914

Note: The provinces of Hijaz and Yemen are not shown.

INTRODUCTION

Yaşar Kemal, a leading figure of modern Turkish literature, was a renowned bard in his native southern Anatolian Çukurova. In the late 1930s, he wandered from village to village, singing his ballads to peasants. During these visits, he also listened to villagers' songs and collected laments and ballads from them. The laments about World War I surprised him the most: they told of conscripted boys, widowed brides, orphaned children, dissolved families, unattended fields, and destroyed lives. Taken together, they recounted the experiences of the Ottoman people who had been embroiled in a long and dreadful conflict. Kemal was astonished by both the multitude and ubiquity of these accounts. More than two decades had passed since the war's end, yet in every village he visited he heard women's laments about it.[1]

Folklorists, teachers, local intellectuals, and amateur researchers have collected similar accounts of the traumatic experiences of World War I from various communities of the former Ottoman Empire.[2] These songs and laments provide an invaluable glimpse into a society at war, illuminating how the Ottomans experienced, perceived, and remembered the conflict. Most important, they offer alternative narratives to official renderings of the war, which emphasized its political, military, and religious meanings. War is described in these accounts as carnage that includes blood, tears, fear, pain, and sorrow, but not heroism and pride. One of them poignantly addresses the sultan:

Topların güllesi ne yaman geldi.   How frightfully came the cannonballs.
Kapandı kulaklar, hep sağır oldu.   Ears closed, all went deaf.

| Gövdeler yaralı, gömlek kan doldu. | Bodies wounded, shirts covered in blood. |
| Askerin kanını gör padişahım![3] | See the soldier's blood, O my Sultan! |

The war is viewed in these songs and laments through the prism of the family and the individual, rather than that of empire and religion. They condemn the war as a disaster that left behind hundreds of thousands of widows and orphans. The suffering and bereavement of families torn apart are at the forefront:

Anan duyar bacın ağlar.	Your mother listens, your sister cries.
Ak gelinler karalar bağlar.	White-clad brides don black.
Hep kapandı büyük evler	All the big houses are shut.
Kaldı koca karıyınan.[4]	Only old folk remain.

Inspired by the poignancy of these accounts, this book explores the wartime experiences that left such deep and painful marks on the collective memory of the Ottoman people. It offers a broad view of how the Great War affected Ottoman society, tracing the new socioeconomic and cultural realities that the war created in the form of mass conscription, a state-controlled economy, widespread shortages, population movements, ethnic cleansing, and death. It examines how the Ottomans interpreted, wrestled with, and adapted to these new wartime realities. In short, this book tells the story of a society caught up in "the seminal catastrophe of the twentieth century."[5]

The Ottomans' Great War

World War I spanned four years, from 29 October 1914 to 30 October 1918, for the Ottoman Empire. The hope of regaining the territories lost in the previous decades and achieving full economic and political independence brought the Ottomans into the war. More important, the realization by the Unionists (members of the ruling Committee of Union and Progress, CUP) that the war would eventually extend to the Ottoman Empire, and that the empire could not survive such a massive conflict on its own, drove them into a search for an alliance with one of the power blocs in Europe.[6] The CUP government signed a secret alliance treaty with Germany on 2 August 1914, and that same day declared general mobilization. After three months of armed neutrality, the Ottomans entered the war on the side of the Central Powers.

Over the next four years, the Ottomans would fight a multi-front war against the Entente. They confronted the Russians in the Caucasus and eastern Anatolia; engaged with British imperial and French forces at the Dardanelles; fought the British in Mesopotamia, Palestine, and the Suez Canal zone; and conducted military operations in Persia. Ottoman troops also saw combat in the European theaters of war, supporting the empire's wartime allies against their adversaries in Galicia, Macedonia, and Romania. To the surprise of both its allies and its enemies, the Ottoman army proved to be more resilient than many had expected. Although its size and strength diminished significantly over the four years of fighting due to both high casualty and desertion rates, the imperial army remained at war until the final month of World War I. Throughout the war, Ottoman forces tied down large enemy contingents in the Middle East, diverting them from European theaters of the conflict. The Ottomans also fought successful battles and scored remarkable victories, such as the defense of the Dardanelles in 1915 and the siege at Kut-al-Amara, south of Baghdad, and surrender of a 13,000-strong British Indian division in 1916. These victories, however, were not enough to win the war.[7]

World War I took a heavy toll on the Ottomans in terms of human and material losses. At the beginning of the Great War, the population of the Ottoman Empire was estimated to be around 19 million in its core provinces. Out of the 2.9 million civilians mobilized into the armed forces, the empire would suffer some 750,000 fatalities from combat and disease by the war's end. Another 750,000 soldiers were wounded, and some 250,000 ended up in foreign captivity.[8] This gigantic loss of human capital had enormous social, economic, and demographic consequences for the home front population, as well as for the states established in the region following the demise of the Ottoman Empire. Even a decade after the war had ended, in some former provinces of the empire over 30 percent of adult women were widows.[9]

World War I required the most comprehensive mobilization of men and resources in the long history of the empire. Mobilizing such a massive army and keeping it on the battlefields for four long years was not an easy task for the Ottomans. Fighting against militarily and economically more advanced adversaries compelled the CUP government to adopt a series of wartime policies that would lead to dramatic changes in the way the Ottoman state functioned. To enable it to fight the war effectively over such a long period of time and across such a broad geographic expanse, these policies extended the state's capacity of intervention into the distant corners of the empire to extract men and resources to a degree never seen before.

The war thus intensified the interaction between the Ottoman state and its citizens, a process that had already been under way since at least the mid-nineteenth century due to the empire's centralizing reforms. The war, however, created new forms of interaction, affecting an even larger swath of society. More Ottoman subjects than ever before now came into continuous contact with the government, its policies, its representatives, and its discourses. Agents of the Ottoman state made demands on its people with increasing frequency and intensity, whether in the form of a draft through a progressively tighter and ever-expanding net of conscription, the requisitioning of grain and other possessions, the impressment of farm animals into military service, the compulsory procurement of agricultural products at low prices and with paper currency, the involuntary billeting of troops at private homes, forced employment in transportation, agriculture, and construction, or deportation and forced relocation. And these encounters usually entailed coercion and outright physical violence. Few aspects of Ottoman subjects' lives remained untouched by the war. Along with defeats on the battlefield, it was the destructiveness of these wartime policies and encounters that led to the disintegration of the empire.

War, Civilians, and the State

World War I has been called a "total" war—but this is a contentious and elusive concept for historians.[10] Rather than offering an all-embracing, clear-cut definition, recent literature emphasizes several key factors that contributed to the growing "totality" of warfare between the mid-nineteenth and mid-twentieth centuries.[11] First, due to industrial and technological advancements, the deadliness of wars increased exponentially. Second, the scope of war aims expanded. Limited goals, such as territorial gains, came to be regarded as insufficient, with the complete destruction of the enemy becoming the only acceptable outcome for the belligerents. Third, the line separating combatants from noncombatants blurred, as civilians became legitimate targets through strategic bombing campaigns, naval blockades, and other wartime measures. Simultaneously, the involvement of civilians became politically, economically, and ideologically essential for the belligerents to sustain their war efforts. Warring governments called upon the increasingly predominant sentiments of nationalism to mobilize their populations and to secure their contributions to the war effort. Fourth, wars during this period also became more global in scope, involving more belligerents who fought simultaneously in different theaters of conflict and in coalitions. Considering all these dynamics, World War I was unprecedented with respect to previous conflicts.[12]

As a belligerent of the Great War, the Ottoman Empire suffered from the dramatically heightened level of lethality and expanded scope of war. Fighting a multi-front war and contending with multiple enemies at once placed an enormous burden on the empire's human and material resources. Casualty rates on the battlefields surpassed anything that had occurred before. Naval bombardments by the Entente Powers frequently targeted the empire's coastal towns and civilian vessels, instilling continuous fear in the home-front population. Aerial strategic bombing, especially in the second half of the war, had a considerably unsettling psychological effect on the empire's urban centers, including its capital city, Istanbul. More critical for the Ottomans, the blockade of the Straits (the Dardanelles and the Bosporus) and the empire's coasts disrupted established patterns of economic and social life and signaled the erosion of the boundary between combatants and noncombatants. The blockade figured prominently in the wartime suffering of the empire's people, most notably in the great famine in Syria between 1915 and 1918.[13]

The Unionists were not passive observers of the colossal changes taking place in the conduct of warfare. They actively sought to adapt to the new and shifting circumstances they found themselves in, striving to overcome the socioeconomic and military challenges that beset the empire. This process in turn contributed to the growing totalization of war for the Ottoman people. Four interrelated factors influenced the CUP governments' policies and played a prominent role in shaping the wartime experience: the empire's infrastructural deficiencies, which curtailed its ability to wage a full-scale modern war; its lack of access to global resources and the exigency of having to fight the war within its borders; its recent, disastrous war experience immediately predating World War I; and, finally, the Unionists' perception of the war as an opportunity to redesign the empire demographically. The interweaving of these four factors rendered the Ottoman experience of World War I not only different from that of the empire's previous wars, but also considerably distinct from the experiences of other World War I belligerents.

Totalizing tendencies in World War I and the wartime transformation and expansion of state apparatuses were not unique to the Ottoman Empire; all of the belligerents experienced them in one way or another.[14] What makes the Ottoman case so interesting and important for comparison is the empire's lack of the necessary "infrastructure" for such a wartime transformation.[15] The Ottoman political and military elites tried to conduct this first truly industrial war of history without a significant industrial base, effective transportation network, sound financial structure, developed agricultural economy, or extensive demographic resources. Of all the Great War's belligerents, the Ottoman

Empire was among the least prepared to engage in such a massive conflict. The absence or inadequacy of these key components of modern warfare did not, however, mean that the war's impact on Ottoman society would be less than totalizing.[16] On the contrary, the Unionists' determination to enhance the empire's war-making capacity coupled with the difficulty of realizing this goal with the readily available human and material resources led to excessively coercive policies. More than in any previous Ottoman war, the success of the imperial army on the battlefields came to depend upon obtaining resources from the home front.

The Unionists' decision to persist with fighting the war despite the empire's infrastructural deficiencies had far-reaching consequences for its citizens, including the ones who were not directly engaged in the fighting. Measures in two particular areas, soldiering and provisioning, constituted the backbone of the CUP's wartime policies. The Unionists correctly perceived the regulation of these two areas to be of critical importance in harnessing the empire's resources toward the war effort and therefore to sustaining the war. As the conflict swallowed up the empire's human, animal, and material resources, military and civilian authorities were compelled to seek new and increasingly aggressive ways of extracting those resources from Ottoman society. Serious manpower shortages led to the imposition of conscription on ever-younger and -older sections of the empire's male population as well as on groups that had previously been exempt from service. In provisioning, policies were directed towards creating a more intrusive and centralized structure, which culminated in the army's complete takeover of the provisioning system. Both sets of policies caused significant dislocation and proved devastating to the majority of the Ottoman population.

These policies, however, did not run a straight and unbroken course, nor did they go unchallenged. Constraints of various kinds affected their implementation and hampered their efficiency. For instance, operating under various circumstances and facing distinct challenges, different levels of the bureaucracy did not always cooperate with one another. Similarly, relations between military and civilian authorities, which were fraught with tension, often led to serious disagreements and scrambles over scarce resources. Furthermore, the effectiveness of the Unionists' wartime policies was also limited by their inherent contradictions. Conscription, for instance, usually meant depriving the provisioning system of much-needed labor. Last but not least, these policies also met with resistance from ordinary Ottoman citizens themselves. When state officials tried to intervene in daily civilian life and implement the government's policies, ordinary Ottomans contended with the state by playing different levels of government against one another, resisting regulations, and seeking both legal and illegal ways to evade the obligations imposed upon them.

The second factor that increased the war's totalizing impact on the Ottomans was the empire's inability to acquire the necessary resources to sustain the war effort from outside its borders. The Entente's access to colonies, dominions, and overseas markets that could replenish depleted ranks and material resources gave it a significant advantage over the Central Powers.[17] Anglo-French naval superiority enabled the deployment of hundreds of thousands of imperial troops from Australia, New Zealand, India, and North and West Africa in various theaters of war, including Mesopotamia, Palestine, and the Dardanelles. Hundreds of thousands of laborers from China, Vietnam, India, and African colonies were similarly employed by the British and French armies behind the lines.[18] At the same time, the Entente imposed increasingly rigorous naval blockades to isolate the Central Powers from overseas trade and undermined their access to international financial markets. Both policies had a devastating impact on the Ottoman population. To be sure, the Ottomans benefited from a wartime alliance with Germany and Austria-Hungary, which provided financial, military, technical aid to the empire.[19] For human and other material resources, however, they had to rely entirely on the people and resources of the empire itself.

The Ottomans did not benefit from the territories they occupied either. The bulk of their fighting took place within the boundaries of their own empire, with the imperial army facing multiple enemies on Ottoman lands. There were two exceptions to this. In February 1918, Ottoman forces crossed the line of the armistice signed with Russia in the aftermath of the Bolshevik Revolution and occupied parts of Caucasia, including the important oil center of Baku.[20] Similarly, at several points throughout the war, Ottoman troops conducted military operations in Persia, fighting British and Russian forces and occupying strategic territories there. Nevertheless, in both instances, the scope of the occupation was limited and the duration was short. The empire derived few economic and political benefits from its "occupation regimes," which might have mitigated the strains on Ottoman society at the expense of those people living under occupation.[21]

Not only were the Unionists' expansionist dreams never realized, but the Ottomans saw significant portions of their own lands come under enemy control. From early 1916 onwards, the Russian army occupied large swathes of eastern Anatolia. In Mesopotamia, British imperial forces advanced slowly northwards, despite several major setbacks, such as the siege of Kut-al-Amara, and managed to capture the fertile lands of lower Mesopotamia, including Baghdad, by mid-1917. In Palestine, the British advance was slower yet steady. By the end of 1917, British forces were in control of southern Palestine, including the symbolically important city of Jerusalem. Thus, during the second half of the war, the Ottomans found it increasingly difficult to extract human and material resources from the empire's shrinking holdings.

The third factor that influenced the Ottoman experience of World War I was the profound impact the recent and tragic Balkan War experiences had on the Unionists' psyche and policies. Throughout the Second Constitutional Period (1908–1918), the Ottoman Empire had faced constant wars and internal rebellions with only brief intervals of peace and tranquility. While provincial revolts in Albania, Syria, and the Yemen between 1910 and 1912 had sapped the empire's military energy, its war with the Italians in 1911 resulted in the loss of the last Ottoman provinces in Africa. None of these events, however, proved to be as disastrous for the Ottomans as the Balkan Wars of 1912–13. The abrupt and humiliating defeat at the hands of four smaller Balkan states forced the Porte to relinquish most of its territories in Europe. Still, the Balkan Wars were much smaller in scope and shorter in duration than World War I, and they paled in comparison to its deadliness. Nonetheless, the loss of these provinces, which had been under Ottoman rule for centuries, had profound repercussions for Ottoman politics, society, and culture.[22] The intrusiveness that characterized the Unionists' Great War policies owed a great deal to this previous military experience.

The Balkan Wars had two major formative influences on the Unionists. First, their unexpected defeat in the First Balkan War revealed the changing nature of warfare and allowed them to draw important lessons from it. The Balkan Wars, as the historian Richard Hall has observed, "introduced an age of modern warfare, encompassing mass armies, machines, and entire civilian populations."[23] The Unionists felt the burning urgency of the need to adapt to these new circumstances. More critically, however, the Ottoman experience of the Balkan Wars showed how the need for imperial strength was defeated by the inadequacy of the means available to achieve it. This realization was the major stimulant to military reforms as well as to the reshaping of Ottoman politics and civil society, which prepared the empire to withstand the ordeal of the Great War.

Second, raising the specter of imperial collapse, the Balkan Wars led the Unionists to view the future in apocalyptic terms. More than ever, war for them became a question of life or death, as another defeat would certainly spell the end of the empire. The Unionists were thus plagued by the fear that the next war would again catch them unprepared. These concerns would guide their wartime policies over the next four years. When they declared the military mobilization in August 1914, the Unionists were determined to rally all available resources to the war effort and eliminate any threats, real or perceived, to the survival of the empire. While this determination enhanced the empire's war-making capacity, it also contributed to the totalization of the conflict for the Ottoman people. As the setbacks over the course of the war deepened their sense of urgency, the Unionists did not hesitate to push Ottoman society beyond the "limits of the possible." For millions of Ottomans throughout the empire, "limits of the possible" meant losing their only breadwinner in the household, their only farm animal, and their last scrap of grain. By the end of the war, virtually every family, village, and neighborhood would be touched by its terrible effects.

The fourth and final factor that enhanced the war's totalizing impact on the Ottoman people was the Unionist policies of reshaping the empire's social structure and economy. During World War I, the CUP government engaged in a process of demographically redesigning Ottoman society through various means, ranging from assimilation to annihilation. In addition to soldiering and provisioning, demographic engineering thus became another major set of policies that ensured thorough and frequent intrusion into people's lives. The forced deportation and resettlement of Ottoman Armenians is the best-known of these demographic engineering policies.

Fearing that the Armenians living in Ottoman territories might collaborate with the Russian enemy and organize a rebellion that would jeopardize the Ottoman war effort, the government in 1915 decided to deport them to the provinces of Der Zor and Mosul. The deportations, which were carried out in an extremely brutal manner, swept up Armenians from all regions of the empire, even those who lived far from the war zone in eastern Anatolia, and from all walks of life. Tens of thousands of deported civilians were slaughtered on their march by tribal units, Kurdish and Turkish irregulars, and armed gangs. Under the extremely harsh weather and road conditions, many of them died from starvation and exhaustion before reaching their final destinations. The properties of deported Armenians were confiscated by the government and auctioned off, a process by which the wealth that had been accumulated by Armenians was transferred to Muslims. Without any doubt, the Armenians were subject to the utmost cruelty during the war, which led to the virtual disappearance of a population with one of the longest histories in the region and the near destruction of their tangible and intangible heritage.[24]

The war had provided the sociopolitical and military context in which the CUP government could execute its large-scale demographic engineering projects. This, however, does not mean that the Unionists were waiting for an opportune moment to realize their long-planned dream of creating an ethnically homogeneous Turkish nation-state out of a multi-ethnic empire, and that World War I presented them with such a historic opportunity. In the early months of the conflict, the army and the government first resorted to limited security measures to eliminate perceived threats to the empire's war effort. In its initial phase, the Unionists' treatment of Armenians resembled other belligerents' treatment of their own "domestic others." These policies, which originated from the concern that ethnic others might sympathize and collaborate with the enemy and engage in treacherous activities, reflected "the historic shift in the nature of warfare between the French Revolution and World War I from war between small professional armies to war between mobilized nations, in which some ethnic groups were defined as the nation while others were stigmatized as the 'enemy within.'"[25] After a certain point, however, the Unionists' objectives transcended the original limited goals and became more comprehensive in scope, total in intent, and future-oriented in outlook. In this regard, the destructiveness of the Unionists' demographic engineering policies distinguished the Ottomans' wartime experience from that of many other belligerents.[26] The disaster that befell Ottoman Armenians was particularly unmatched in its extent and lethality.

Legitimacy Deficit

By the end of World War I, having lost millions of its former subjects and most of its Arab provinces, the Ottoman Empire had been reduced to Anatolia. More important, perhaps, the social capital of the region had been depleted by military casualties, ethnic cleansing, population movements, epidemics, and hunger. Defeats on the battlefield and harsh and intrusive wartime policies had completely discredited the Unionist regime in the eyes of most Ottoman subjects. For many, however, it was not only the Unionists who had lost their legitimacy. The war also delegitimized the whole idea of empire in ways that prepared various ethno-religious communities for new political projects that would aspire to be everything that the empire had not been.

From the very beginning, the Unionists had fought an uphill battle to justify the empire's war effort to the Ottoman people. The disastrous defeat in the First Balkan War had brought about widespread war-weariness and a general decline in morale, while evoking deep concerns about the imperial army's fighting capacity. Ottomans from all walks of life and ethno-religious backgrounds thus met the declaration of mobilization in August 1914 with a deep sense of apprehension. Unprecedented levels of conscription, which covered groups that had previously been exempt, ruthless requisitioning, and the imposition of a harsh martial law exacerbated those feelings even further. The CUP government attempted to dispel people's anxiety and win their consent by portraying the empire as the victim of Entente aggression, casting the mobilization and war as defensive efforts. In the face of violent and unjust attacks, as the official rhetoric proclaimed, the government found itself in a position of defending the empire's honor, borders, and official religion. All Ottoman subjects, regardless of their social class, age, and gender, were now under the obligation to share in the sacrifice and contribute to the war effort.

As the war continued, the heavy-handed execution of wartime policies, the material and emotional damages they generated, and the government's inability to alleviate the war's impact deepened the Unionists' crisis of legitimacy. With battlefield casualties mounting, inflation skyrocketing, the value of Ottoman paper currency plummeting, agricultural production declining, and food shortages becoming widespread, people throughout the empire grew increasingly disillusioned and alienated from the state. Determined to continue the war, however, the government and the army persisted with their draconian policies, adopting an even more intrusive position in the face of looming defeat, a contracting pool of resources, and an increasingly uncooperative population. Although the prolongation of the conflict and persistence of the regime's extraction policies required popular consent, the Unionists failed to secure it. The solutions they adopted fell short of persuading people to accept the material and emotional sacrifices they incurred.

This lack of popular consent is perhaps most apparent in the large number of soldiers who eventually refused to fight. Especially in the last two years of the war, desertion rates soared and the imperial army gradually melted away.[27] An increasingly large number of soldiers came to interpret the war through the prism of the individual and the family rather than in terms of empire and religion. The hardships and deprivation the troops suffered and concern for family at home drained the ordinary soldier's will and motivated him to desert, while on the home front, civilians became increasingly resistant to official wartime policies and refused to make further sacrifices. People came to see the war as an unnecessary, if not reckless, adventure launched without their consent by an irresponsible cadre of politicians. In tandem with deteriorating social conditions, the increasing encroachment of the state apparatus on people's lives strained the legitimacy of the Ottoman state and intensified pressure on the government and military command. This loss of legitimacy presented a sharp challenge to the state's authority and capacity to maintain social and cultural integration.

The war thus delegitimized the whole Ottoman order in the eyes of many of the empire's subjects. In this sense, the wartime experience was the final nail in the coffin of Ottomanism, an ideological and political direction adopted by the Unionists to maintain the integrity of the empire's various ethno-religious communities. Following an initial period of euphoria and enthusiasm in the aftermath of the Constitutional Revolution of 1908, hopes generated by the Unionists' promises of equality, justice, and brotherhood among all ethno-religious communities were dashed after 1909.[28] Initial optimism was gradually replaced by fear and distrust of the Unionists. The experiences of the Balkan Wars and the CUP's increasingly antagonistic stance towards non-Muslim Ottomans dealt another blow to Ottomanism. Yet, despite their strained relations with the Unionists, both Muslim and non-Muslim minorities continued to imagine themselves as part of the Ottoman Empire, seeking to achieve varying degrees of autonomy within the broader Ottoman framework.

World War I marked the end of these endeavors and destroyed the foundations of intercommunal coexistence. The wartime policies adopted by the CUP government and the wartime encounters stemming from these policies irretrievably alienated the empire's non-Muslim and non-Turkish minorities from the very idea of the empire. Their wartime experiences did not turn members of these minorities into die-hard nationalists overnight. But they made them exceedingly receptive to alternative political formulations outside of the Ottoman framework. In this sense, the war accelerated "the ongoing process of the definition of modern national identit[ies]."[29] Separatist tendencies, which until the war had been embraced only by small, marginal groups within these communities, became more popular and influential. The new international context that had emerged in the war's aftermath and greater emphasis on the right of self-determination lent strong impetus to these tendencies.[30]

The strains of war and the destructiveness of the Unionists' wartime policies also challenged the Ottoman Turks' moral and emotional bonds with the empire. Many Ottoman Turks came to see the state again through the prism of the individual and the family. It sent their sons, husbands, and fathers to fight in far-off provinces and foreign countries, requisitioned their meager harvests, and in many cases impressed their only farm animal into army service. And yet, it did not extend help when they needed it most. Although this widespread discontent did not evolve into a revolutionary movement, the situation on the ground was exceptionally fragile in the six months between the end of World War I in October 1918 and the landing of Greek forces in Smyrna/Izmir in May 1919. Only the return of surviving Armenians with the backing of the Entente Powers, the Greek occupation of western Anatolia, and the French occupation of southern Anatolia would persuade them to acquiesce to another mobilization, this time for the Turkish War of Independence.

***

In 1940, an elderly peasant from Sarıkamış, İhsan Dayı, made an unexpected observation in his interview with an ethnographer: despite the general increase in their wealth over the previous decades, people in his village were discontented with their lives. For those expecting him to cite a contemporary source for this discontent, the interviewee's answer must have been quite surprising: "The Great War spoiled things for everyone. For four years, people suffered a lot of misery. Now, they cannot forget it, no matter how hard they try. Before the war, our weddings would last all week. Since the war, weddings have lost all their joy."³¹ Even after more than two decades, memories of World War I still haunted people who had lived through that period. İhsan Dayı's fellow villagers were certainly not alone in how they felt. This book is an attempt to understand the wartime experiences that left such deep and unhealed scars.

1 FROM THE BALKAN WARS TO THE GREAT WAR

On 12 November 1912, in a rare, emotional entry in his colossal diary, Cavid Bey described his feelings about the fall of Salonika, the birthplace of the Young Turk Revolution, to Greek forces three days earlier: "Between sleeping and waking I think of Greek and Bulgarian flags flying over the harbor of Salonika. I want to believe that this is a vision; I cannot consider it as a matter of fact. Is this the reason we strove to save this country from the foreigners' yoke? Did we launch the constitutional regime [meşrutiyet] to attain this conclusion? Where did the meşrutiyet, instituted to save Rumelia [i.e., European provinces of the empire, which prior to the war included Epirus, Thrace, and Macedonia], deliver us in the hands of the greedy and the betrayers? A Turkey without Rumelia, an Ottoman government without Salonika. How unbelievable and unbearable!"[1] The pain that this leading Unionist politician poured into the pages of his diary was not solely felt by him. The humiliating defeat during the First Balkan War and the subsequent loss of most of the empire's remaining Balkan provinces deeply shocked the Ottoman political elite and traumatized Ottoman society. That all this took place in a remarkably short span of time only deepened the agony, which had no parallel in the empire's modern history.

Historians have long noted the importance of the Balkan Wars as a harbinger of the general conflagration that would occur a year later. Against the historical background of the events surrounding the Balkan War crisis, political and military tensions built up in Europe, which would soon erupt in worldwide conflict.[2] Beyond their broad international repercussions, however, the Balkan Wars also had a strong formative influence on participating nations. The wars' outcomes affected dramatic shifts in belligerent countries' political, social, and cultural landscapes, while wartime experiences triggered new concerns and deepened already existing prejudices. How belligerent societies and their political elites perceived the Balkan War crisis and responded to it would have a profound impact on these societies' experience of World War I. The Ottoman Empire was no exception.

Vanquished at the hands of four small neighboring states, the Ottomans were gripped by an overwhelming sense of existential crisis, leading to an extensive, heated debate about the possible causes of the disaster that had befallen the empire. This process of self-questioning did not remain confined to military matters. The Ottoman army's defeat highlighted broader sociopolitical and cultural issues and precipitated an all-encompassing search for a new type of society.[3] The questions raised and the answers arrived at in this process would be crucial in shaping Ottoman policies during World War I.

The Balkan War experiences evoked a dramatically heightened sense of vulnerability among the Unionists, which stemmed from three closely interrelated sources. First, the Unionists emerged out of the war with a deep conviction that the empire's defeat was rooted in overall political and military weaknesses. Partial and palliative measures implemented since the beginning of the Constitutional Revolution had been unable to ward off the disaster. Second, the war revealed plainly and forcefully that the empire had been pushed into diplomatic isolation by the European powers. At critical moments during the war, they favored the Balkan allies' claims and left the Porte to contend for itself. In the Unionists' minds, there was little reason to believe that things would be different in coming years. They believed that in a future crisis they should be able to count on the empire's own strength first and foremost. Third, the Unionists were convinced that the first two conditions generated a discernibly enhanced political energy among the empire's Muslim and non-Muslim minorities, encouraging decentralizing tendencies. In the highly emotional climate of the Balkan Wars' aftermath, these three sources of vulnerability became inseparably fused in the Unionists' minds and bred a deep sense of urgency. If the empire was to be preserved, sweeping measures would have to be put in place to mitigate these vulnerabilities. The very survival of the empire would depend on the Unionists' performance in implementing those measures. Those measures and policies, however, would have far-reaching implications for the Ottoman people's relationship with the state.

The Ottoman Defeat in Detail

The First Balkan War began on 8 October 1912, with Montenegro's declaration of war on the Ottoman Empire. Within a couple of days, Bulgaria, Greece, and Serbia joined Montenegro and declared war on the Ottomans. The quick turn of events had caught the Porte underprepared. Merely two weeks after the declaration of mobilization, the Ottoman army had to enter the war. The Balkan armies' advance through Ottoman territories was swift and devastating. By the time of the ceasefire on 3 December 1912, the Ottoman army had withdrawn to the Çatalca Line, only forty kilometers from the empire's capital, Istanbul/Constantinople, lost almost all of its provinces in Europe, and surrendered thousands of soldiers and tons of military matériel. Three fortified cities, Yanya/Ioannina, İşkodra/Scutari/Shkodër, and Edirne/Adrianople, continued to be defended under difficult conditions. The Ottoman army's performance in this first phase of the war was horrendous. Strategic blunders, logistical malfunctions, failure of the supply and sanitary systems, lack of general coordination, widespread disorder, poor weather conditions, and the low quality of manpower all contributed to the army's collapse.[4] Pitched against more capable and better-motivated forces, Ottoman troops panicked and fled in the face of the looming defeat. A young Arab Ottoman officer, Jafar al-Askari, described the situation as such: "When finally the army halted to camp two or three miles from Kirk-Kilisse [Kırklareli in eastern Thrace], a doom-stricken scene like the Day of Judgment lay all around: soldiers shivering from the bitter cold, animals mired in mud—the beasts hauling the artillery were wallowing and stumbling chest-deep in it—and men crying out for their units like lambs bleating for their mothers."[5] "It would take an [Émile] Zola to describe" the Ottoman troops' traumatic rout, another contemporary wrote.[6]

Two months of prolonged negotiations in London did not yield an agreement between the fighting parties, and hostilities resumed on 3 February 1913. This second phase of the conflict lasted until mid-April. Ottoman Rumelia's three fortress cities fell, but the imperial army held the Çatalca Line. The fall to the Bulgarians of Edirne, the empire's second capital, was a particularly staggering blow to the Unionists, who had just come to power in a coup d'état in January 1913. Pressure from the Great Powers and the specter of losing Istanbul compelled the CUP government to sign the Treaty of London on 30 May 1913, which officially ended the First Balkan War. The treaty terms stipulated the surrender of all Ottoman provinces in Europe to the west of the Enos-Midia line, including Edirne. The allies' victory was complete and resounding. Reflecting the agony and anger overwhelming Unionists and non-Unionists alike, Baban-zade İsmail Hakkı declared in an editorial in the Unionist daily *Tanin* that there had been no disaster in Ottoman history even remotely comparable to the recent cataclysm: "Never have the Ottomans and Muslims been subjected to such disgrace, massacres, and cruelties." He proposed that May 30th henceforth be a day of mourning, writing: "Had our religion permitted it, I would have begged for a law that would oblige all Ottomans to dress in black. . . . We will carry that blackness in our hearts until the day we get our revenge."[7]

An unexpected opportunity for revenge in fact presented itself within a few weeks' time. Disputing over the territories they had won, the victors of the First Balkan War, formerly united by their hostility to the empire, now embarked on the bloody struggle among themselves that would come to be known as the Second Balkan War. Seizing the opportunity presented by Bulgaria's preoccupation with its erstwhile allies, the Ottoman forces staged a surprise attack, recapturing Edirne and most of eastern Thrace. These gains partially restored the CUP's much tarnished prestige and injected a degree of self-confidence into its leadership.

Nevertheless, the overall price that the Ottomans had to pay was staggering. The empire's humiliating defeat forced the government to relinquish most of its territory in Europe, home to nearly four million inhabitants. It also precipitated the migration of hundreds of thousands of Muslim refugees, under deplorable conditions, from their homes in the Balkans to Anatolia and other Ottoman provinces. The areas where battles were fought, particularly in Thrace, were almost totally devastated. The war also exacted a heavy toll on the Ottoman army; of 340,000 soldiers, at least 50,000 died in battle and 75,000 died from disease. An additional 100,000 men were wounded, while 115,000 ended up in captivity.[8] The war also depleted the army's stocks of weapons, ammunition, artillery, equipment, and animals. A list of surrendered items prepared by Mahmut Şevket Pasha, the grand vizier of the post-coup regime, included 500,000 rifles, 700 pieces of artillery, 20,000 horses, 40,000 other draft animals, 30,000 tents, and 100,000 uniforms, worth a total of more than 15 million lira.[9] The overall cost of the war put enormous pressure on the already frail Ottoman fiscal structure and added considerably to the empire's indebtedness.

The discrepancy between the unrealistically heightened popular expectations of victory and the imperial army's deplorable performance on the battle-field aggravated the shock of defeat. The Ottoman press almost unanimously greeted the coming of the war with excitement. The Unionist daily *Tanin* was not alone when it wrote that in the face of the approaching war, "a joy and enthusiasm that had not been seen for years suffused the streets of Istanbul."[10] Public opinion in the empire perceived the Balkan allies' challenge to Ottoman authority and demands for greater autonomy as scandalous and unacceptable. Irrespective of political opinion, everyone was equally outraged by the Balkan nations' impertinence, and calls to teach them a lesson abounded.[11] Exasperation and anger were voiced not only in the newspapers but also in the streets. Reporting on a massive pro-war rally in Sultanahmet square, *Tanin* wrote that thousands of participants chanted, "Long live the nation; long live the war."[12]

Excitement about the war was accompanied by a gross underestimation of the enemy. People from all walks of life expected that the imperial army would easily triumph over its Balkan enemies. Newspapers voiced utterly unrealistic ambitions of capturing Sofia, Belgrade, and Athens in a short span of time and without much resistance. An observer noted that Bulgarians were mocked with the term "milkman" (*sütçü*), alluding to a common occupation among them.[13] In addition to entrenched derogatory perceptions, what helped foster the sense of Ottoman superiority was a deeply felt yet misguided conviction that the Ottoman army was much better prepared for a war than its adversaries. The confidence in the army's invincibility and its fighting prowess was particularly remarkable in the Unionist press, but could also be found in non-Unionist journals and newspapers. For instance, a cartoon published by a major satirical magazine, *Cem*, showed Nazım Pasha, the commander in chief of the army, leaning over a ticket counter conversing with the seller:

—I'll be traveling to Sofia, Belgrade, [Montenegro's historic capital] Cetinje, [and] Athens. I want to buy a ticket.

—Are you alone?

—No, me and my guys, for now, 700,000–800,000 of them.[14]

This misapprehension mostly arose from the transformation that the army underwent under the Unionists in the first three years after the Constitutional Revolution. "At no time in the past few centuries has [the empire] had a more perfect army with regards to military equipment, munitions, science, preparation, and combat . . . . [and Ottoman troops] have never fought under more suitable conditions," *Cenin* asserted at the start of the war.[15] Many ordinary people apparently shared these sentiments. A German resident of the capital related people's enthusiasm about the war to this belief in the army's superior fighting capabilities.[16] Warnings about the unpreparedness of the army fell on deaf ears amid the patriotic frenzy. Abdullah Pasha, one of the most knowledgeable officers, had warned the cabinet, the grand vizier, and other politicians that the army was not even powerful enough to defeat Bulgaria, let alone an alliance of the four Balkan states.[17] The next few weeks proved him right.

The Impact of the War

Dreams of Ottoman flags flying over the Balkan capitals were soon shattered by the collapse of the army in under two months. The public enthusiasm at the outbreak of the war quickly gave way to bewilderment and despair. People from all walks of life were not only reminded of the empire's vulnerability and its army's inefficiency, they also realized that the war had a direct material impact on their own everyday lives and communities. Civilians were by no means spared the horrors of the conflict. On the contrary, modern warfare necessitated unprecedented levels of direct and indirect contributions from the civilian population, while simultaneously exposing them to previously unknown levels of violence.

The fact that the Balkan Wars were fought in such a close proximity to the imperial capital made their impacts all the more tangible and visible. On a daily basis the inhabitants of Istanbul came across wounded soldiers arriving from battlefields, many of them exhausted, half-clad, and wretched.[18] They became concerned about the cholera outbreak among the troops and worried about the possibility of its spreading to the city. They experienced a slowdown of the economy, suffered from soaring prices, and faced occasional shortages.[19] They witnessed the plight of Muslim refugees passing every day through the streets of the capital with their carts and oxen by the thousands. They saw them living outdoors, in schoolyards, mosques, and train stations, begging on the streets, and queuing in front of municipal bakeries and soup kitchens. They heard stories of the unfortunate refugee women and girls who had been forced into prostitution. This was the first time since the 1877–78 Russo-Ottoman War that Istanbulites found war at their own doorstep.

The war's impact was also felt well beyond the capital. Young men everywhere were called up to join the ranks. The extraction of these men from the agrarian economy and consequent labor shortages affected the harvest season of 1912 and especially of 1913. Additional war taxes imposed by the government compounded the negative impact of conscription. Especially in the northwestern provinces of the empire, people had to bear the burden of surrendering their animals and transport vehicles to requisitioning officers. The war disrupted economic activity throughout the empire, albeit to varying degrees.[20] While some provinces suffered significantly from the war, others escaped its worst effects. Nevertheless, people's purchasing power diminished almost everywhere as prices increased. Even provinces as far removed from the war zone as Damascus and Aleppo witnessed popular demonstrations triggered by the increase in bread prices.[21] The salaries of civil servants went unpaid for months, prompting distrust and resentment of the government.[22] The misery of soldiers' destitute families was particularly disheartening everywhere. Although the Balkan Wars lasted less than a year and the scope of mobilization was much more limited than that of August 1914, conscription could easily push a soldier's family into poverty. An American missionary in Antep noted: "There is much suffering among the Turks, in the city and the surrounding villages, where the bread-winners have been taken. In such cases the Christians help each other, but among the Moslems there is cold, hunger, and suffering beyond description."[23]

Besides conscription and economic slowdown, refugees served as a reminder of the war's ugly face. Many Ottomans learned about the devastation caused by the war through the refugees who were settled among them. From the outset, the government aimed to prevent refugees from being concentrated at specific locations by sending them to the interior of the country. After settling a certain numbers of refugees in major towns along the Anatolian railroad, the government distributed the newly arriving refugees to nearby villages. Each village was allotted a few refugee families. According to a Red Cross report, this policy was "carried out most thoroughly and the many hundreds of villages from one to two hours to two or three days distance from the railroad have almost all received their quota of unfortunates to care for, an exception having [been] made for the Christian villages, few if any of the latter having been thus called upon."[24] These refugees, whose maintenance was now entrusted to village communities, brought with them their stories of expulsion, atrocities, and suffering. These stories, along with the stories of returning soldiers, might have played a significant role in politicizing the villages along ethno-religious lines. And they also served as vivid reminders of the potential consequences of war and of the Ottoman state's inability to shield its citizens from its ravages.

Soon, the scope of the refugee problem exceeded the government's initial arrangements of distribution and relocation around the Anatolian railroad line. While tens of thousands of refugees passed through Istanbul into Anatolia, the government also arranged for the shipment of thousands others to port towns of various sizes. Izmir, Antalya, Mersin, Alexandretta, Tripoli, Beirut, and Samsun all received their shares. From these entry points, they were usually sent to the interior and resettled.[25] The government's policy of sending refugees to various parts of the empire made the inhabitants of even the most distant provinces aware of their misery and its causes. The locals did not, however, welcome the refugees everywhere. In Arab provinces, for instance, they were perceived as pawns of the CUP's long-term demographic/political project and thus stirred significant discontent.[26]

Reshaping Politics

While people throughout the empire were coping with the hardships of the war, the political landscape underwent a dramatic change. In January 1913, the Unionists seized power in a coup d'état and forced the cabinet led by Kamil Pasha to resign, blaming his government for improper conduct of the war and the surrender of the Balkan provinces, including Edirne.[27] The coup led to the formation of a new government led by Mahmut Şevket Pasha and composed of prominent Unionists and some independent politicians. The decision to make Mahmut Şevket Pasha grand vizier was a risky one for the CUP. Although he was a prestigious military and political figure who was able to give the coup much-needed legitimacy, he was also one of the few people who had the authority to keep the Unionists in check. His distaste for the extreme members of the Committee was well known within political and military circles. Until his assassination six months later, he strove to carry out a policy relatively independent of the CUP and managed to curb the Unionists' ambitions to a certain extent.

Despite their differences, however, the Unionists and Mahmut Şevket Pasha concurred in the belief that the previous governments had failed to put all available resources at the army's disposal. Moreover, they firmly believed that this hesitation and inability to do so had severely hampered the Ottoman war effort. This prompted the new government to adopt a more coercive stance towards society and implement new measures to exercise state power in more direct and diversified ways. These measures included the expansion of the scope of the mobilization and conscription of new cohorts of soldiers, the implementation of a new taxation policy (*tekalif-i harbiye*) and requisitioning, and the ruthless suppression of any opposition to the war effort. For the Unionists, the threats posed to the very existence of the empire were dire enough to necessitate such radical changes.

Mahmut Şevket Pasha's assassination in June 1913 gave the CUP an invaluable pretext to assert greater influence in political life and tighten its grip on society. Following the assassination, the Unionists deported some five hundred political opponents, including many journalists, politicians, and military officers, to Sinop and other cities. They also purged state officials who were known for their anti-Unionist views. Several non-Unionist organizations were dissolved, and a number of newspapers and periodicals were shuttered. By granting the cabinet the authority to close down newspapers that would imperil "the internal and external security of the state," amendments to the Press Law restricted the freedom of press even further.[28] Through these and several other measures, the CUP largely eliminated any potential threat to its hold on political power. As the British ambassador observed, the Unionists were now "firmer in the saddle than they have ever been before."[29] The words of a famous journalist and CUP opponent, Refik Halid [Karay], corroborate the ambassador's observations. Before the Unionists came to power, he wrote, the opposition was a surviving, yet crippled and sick, body. Following the Bab-ı Ali coup, however, "it became a corpse [ceset]," and after Mahmut Şevket Pasha's assassination, "it turned into a carcass [leş]."[30] Pacifying political opposition in such a swift and effective way was another reflection of the deepened sense of urgency among the Unionists. A political system riven by ceaseless conflicts and tensions would only detract from implementing the measures they deemed necessary to save the empire.

Later in 1914, the Unionists further reinforced their hold on the political scene by securing a vast majority in the parliamentary elections. The elections, especially in the provinces, were held under the close scrutiny of local CUP clubs, which used every means at their disposal to ensure the election of candidates approved by the Committee. In the words of the British consul in Aleppo, what took place was a "nomination, and not [an] election."[31] As a result, the new parliament was mostly composed of devoted Unionists and local dignitaries chosen by the CUP. This decisive majority meant that Unionist policies would face few challenges from the parliament in the years that followed.

A less well known, but perhaps more important change concerned the internal structure of the CUP. The 1913 party congress issued new bylaws to reorganize the relationship between the party headquarters and local branches. According to these new regulations, the central committee would appoint executive secretaries to the provinces (katib-i mesuls), who would act as the highest-ranking representatives of the party at the local level and maintain direct communication between the party center and the local CUP braches.[32] This change was clearly aimed at imposing stricter control over local branches and bringing them closer into line with the CUP's political orientation. At the same time, by appointing executive secretaries, the CUP intended to forge closer relationships among the party center, local branches, patriotic civil society organizations, and local population. As evidenced by the Navy League campaigns of the following year, this new organizational structure helped to spread patriotic messages and mobilize popular support.

The Unionists knew full well that the politicized officers within the army had more potential than their civilian counterparts to undermine the CUP regime. Changes to the military establishment thus proved to be equally critical in consolidating the CUP's hold on political life. In January 1914, Enver Bey assumed the posts of the war minister and the chief of staff, dissolved the Supreme Military Council (Askeri Şura), and enacted wide-ranging reforms within the army. His appointment to the ministry could be seen as the fulfillment of the Unionists' long-held desire to raise a war minister "of their own," instead of relying on a prestigious yet non-Unionist figure such as Mahmud Şevket or Ahmed İzzet Pashas.[33] But Enver's appointment was also a critical milestone whereby military decision-making would come to take absolute precedence over civilian concerns. In the post–Balkan War era, military considerations would frequently overrule political, economic, and even moral ones. In the face of the empire's existential crisis, "military necessity" provided such a powerful justification for any act that no one dared argue against it.

Enver, now Pasha, started to implement his policies by forcing hundreds of high-ranking elderly officers to retire and dismissing many others whom he perceived as heavily involved in politics, unsuccessful, or incapable of keeping up with recent developments in the military profession. The purge was foreshadowed by heavy criticism in the Unionist press directed at the senior ranks in the army and underlining their responsibility in the Balkan War defeat.[34] The elimination of these officers from the ranks marked a critical turning point for the rejuvenation of the Ottoman army.[35] Enver Pasha's purge put an end to the established principle of seniority within the army, bringing a younger generation of Unionist officers into positions of responsibility. "No hope for the future could be placed in men who, by the brilliance of their uniforms, by their rank, and by the names they bore, deceived their country into thinking that it possessed an army," *Tanin* declared, expectedly lauding the purge as an essential step in infusing a much-needed reformist, youthful spirit into the military system. The operation, according to the newspaper, ushered in a new era for the Ottoman army, an era of "tight discipline and continuous training and work." The Ottoman army, the newspaper announced, would henceforth place the utmost emphasis on capacity and merit as well as on effort and zeal.[36] Almost a year later, during the height of the Gallipoli campaign, Enver Pasha still sounded content with the purge when he remarked to an American journalist: "That step has made the Ottoman army what it is to-day. I have not the slightest use for the incompetent, the unfit, the weak, the hesitating, the evaders, the shirkers, the pleasure-seekers. I am obliged to thrust them out of my way, and so far, I am glad to say, I have not lacked the courage to do that."[37]

Reshaping Civil Society

The conflict in the Balkans prompted reconsideration of the civilian population's role in war by the Ottoman political elite. Warfare on this scale and intensity clearly required both material and immaterial support from society. The deplorable situation of Ottoman finances in particular enhanced the need for such support. More unnerving were reports about other belligerents indicating that they had successfully integrated broad segments of their civilian populations into the governments' war efforts. Once they came to power in the aftermath of the Bab-ı Ali coup, the Unionists sought to similarly reinvigorate the patriotic spirit. The initial enthusiasm aroused by the conflict, they noted, had not survived the war's subsequent disastrous impacts. In the face of demoralizing defeats and mounting human and material costs, the popular willingness to sustain the war effort wore thin. The Society of National Defense (Müdafaa-i Milliye Cemiyeti) thus grew out of the Unionists' search for means to rekindle patriotic sentiment throughout the empire.

The CUP's call for the inaugural meeting of the Müdafaa-i Milliye Society in February 1913 underlined the unprecedented nature of the ordeal and the sense of urgency it provoked, declaring: "The Ottoman Empire, in its 600-year-long existence, has never encountered a situation such as the one that it has been subjected to over the past three months. Today our fatherland is in danger." It called on people to renounce personal interests and strive to save the fatherland.[38] The Müdafaa-i Milliye Society emphasized the unity of the empire and was intended to provide a direct link between its civilian population and the soldiers on the front. This idea of interdependency between the soldier and the civilian, between the front and the home constituted the main thrust of its public discourse. Increasingly common rhetoric asserted that the defense of the fatherland was civilians' responsibility too. In emergencies such as the Balkan Wars, the active participation of and sacrifices by the civilian population were required: "A more important duty than the one that falls upon the army rests on your shoulders both in this world and the next," the Müdafaa-i Milliye Society proclaimed in the summer of 1913.[39]

In close collaboration with local state authorities and CUP clubs, the Müdafaa-i Milliye Society quickly created an extensive network of local branches throughout the empire. Its activities were concentrated in areas such as organizing and supplying volunteer battalions, providing care for the wounded and sick soldiers, setting up hospitals, and collecting donations to support refugees. To mobilize Ottoman patriotism, the Society also waged an intensive propaganda campaign. It sent "guidance committees" (irşad heyetleri) to provinces, organized well-publicized lectures and sermons, asked for the help of local dignitaries to spread its message, and published frequent notices in newspapers and journals. Renowned clerics and local religious figures played a significant role in its campaign. "How could we remain untouched as if we have not heard of the atrocities, the tragedies when the enemies are assaulting our religion and our citizens with their utmost monstrosity?" asked the mufti of Trabzon, encouraging his fellow townsmen to do their best for the Society.[40] The office of chief religious authority (şeyhülislam) also became involved in patriotic mobilization and encouraged Muslims' active participation in the war effort.[41] As a result, during the post-coup period, patriotic propaganda took on a distinctively religious tone and the conflict came to be framed increasingly in religious terms.

This was a radical change from the war's earlier days when the use of religious discourse within the public and political spheres was quite minimal. Neither the Unionists—who were the opposition since July 1912—nor their opponents had then sought to portray the war in strictly religious terms.[42] Official declarations, speeches, and newspaper articles consciously refrained from casting the conflict as a Christian–Muslim struggle, presumably to allay the fears of Ottoman non-Muslims. On the contrary, both the government and the CUP tried to create the illusion of a harmoniously unified nation that had overcome all political and ethno-religious differences. Newspapers highlighted Ottoman non-Muslims' contributions to the war effort and their willingness to protect the fatherland just like their Muslim brethren. Massive war meetings in early October saw non-Muslim speakers addressing the audience. The CUP meeting's speakers included the Greek Emmanouil Emmanouilidis, the Bulgarian Pançe Doref, the Armenian Hagop Boyaciyan, and the Wallachian Besarya Efendis, all former members of the Ottoman parliament, as well as Dr. Garabed Pashayan, representing the Armenian Revolutionary Federation.[43] The Armenian journalist Diran Kelekyan, editor of the newspaper *Sabah*, declared at the meeting organized by the Freedom and Accord Party (Hürriyet ve İtilaf Fırkası), that the natural frontier of the Ottoman Empire was the Danube.[44]

Portraying the conflict in religious terms was indeed regarded as unacceptable and morally repugnant by the Ottoman public. When the Balkan nations declared their ultimate aim as saving Ottoman Christians from the Muslim yoke, *Cenin* condemned this call as fanatical and utterly dangerous.[45] In its editorial, *Sabah* similarly insisted that the current conflict was entirely political and certainly not a religious one.[46] During the early days of the war, the CUP Central Committee issued circulars emphasizing the importance of solidarity among the empire's ethno-religious communities and calling on the party's members to support the government in its efforts to strengthen this solidarity.[47] The appearance of intense religious rhetoric after the Unionists came to power in early 1913 thus marked a critical turning point, reflecting their realization of religion's power to mobilize the masses.

The Müdafaa-i Milliye Society played the most prominent role in arousing patriotic sentiments, but was not the only venue of civil society activism. The dramatically intensified patriotic remobilization opened up more opportunities for broader sections of Ottoman society, especially middle- and upper-class women, to get involved in civil society activities. At around the same time as the establishment of the Müdafaa-i Milliye Society, Ottoman women held two remarkable mass meetings where they discussed alternative ways of supporting the government's renewed war effort. According to local newspapers, as many as 5,000 women attended the meetings. At the instigation of the feminist novelist Halide Edip Hanım, the attendees resolved to send telegrams to the Ottoman army as well as to European queens to ask them to intervene to save Balkan Muslims from massacres. Over the following months, Ottoman women were actively involved in supporting the CUP government's war effort.[48] This fiercely patriotic campaign, comprised of broad sections of the society, distinguished the Balkan Wars from earlier Ottoman wars.

Although it is difficult to assess the direct contribution of these activities to the Ottoman war effort, this experience would later prove invaluable during World War I. Such intense activism led to the establishment of a vast network of local branches of patriotic civil society organizations, which would be revitalized in under two years. These outfits developed relations with broader segments of their local populations and spread religiously colored patriotic sentiment beyond educated circles. From the very beginning, this local civil society activism was coordinated by local CUP organizations and the Ottoman state's local representatives. All of these actors gained immense experience in patriotic activism and mastered methods to secure and maintain contributions from people. This emphasis on civilians' patriotic mobilization was a clear sign that the Unionists had come to perceive the management of the home front as an integral part of the broader war effort.

Reshaping the Military

Of all the perceived causes of the empire's vulnerability, it was the military's enfeeblement that evoked the deepest sense of urgency among the Unionists. The First Balkan War had not only taken a heavy toll in dead, wounded, and captured and depleted the army's stocks of weapons, ammunition, artillery, equipment, and animals. Perhaps more important, the empire's crushing defeat had also exposed the overall malfunctioning of the Ottoman military system. In the war's aftermath, the empire's dwindling ability to deal with its enemies elevated the issue of military capacity into a mainstream concern. "The best friend of a government is its own power," a leading intellectual wrote in 1913: "Words, however, are not sufficient to be powerful. . . . Power consists solely in the army's and navy's actual fighting capacity, in their unfailing preparedness and readiness for war."[49] The months immediately following the Balkan Wars thus confronted the Unionists with the daunting task of reforming the Ottoman military system. They wanted to make sure that the empire would have the largest possible pool of thoroughly prepared, motivated, and reliable troops at its disposal the next time it fought its adversaries.

From the earliest days of the Constitutional Era, the army occupied a privileged place in the CUP's policies and rhetoric. The Unionists, many of whom were soldiers themselves, sought to change the long-standing negative image of military service by recasting the army as the protector of the fatherland, defender of the revolution, and the facilitator of the constitutional principle of "the unity of elements" (*ittihad-ı anasır*). Military service came to be praised as a civic duty that every man was expected to fulfill of his own free will. In the aftermath of the revolution, the army received considerable attention and investment from the Unionist governments and underwent a series of major transformations, reflecting the ideological and practical concerns of the new regime. These changes most notably included the abolition of a number of exemptions, including those granted to non-Muslims, students of religious seminaries, and the residents of the capital.[50]

Nevertheless, for most people, the sociopolitical meaning of military service remained unchanged. Despite the new emphasis on the virtues of serving in the army and its link to modern citizenship, this relationship remained tenuous, if not totally absent. Many continued to see military service as an intrusive disruption to the life of the conscript, his family, and his community, and not a necessary part of his civic obligations. The oppressive nature and rigors of army life rendered the burdens laid upon the conscript's shoulders difficult to bear. Military service in the Ottoman Empire also had an unmistakable class dimension. The well-to-do usually found their way out of the service, either through paying the exemption fee or using legal and illegal loopholes to be exempted on health, education, marital, or occupational grounds. As a result, the ranks of the enlisted were mostly filled by lower-class men from rural communities. For their families, conscription primarily meant the loss of a son, husband, or father to a distant duty on the far-off frontiers of the empire. In a predominantly agricultural economy, the conscription of young men deprived rural families of a principal source of labor. These negative popular sentiments about compulsory military service were perhaps best summarized in an Anatolian saying that when somebody became a soldier, "his money loses value, his wife is widowed" (askere gidenin parası pul karısı dul olur).[51] Conscripts typically acted out their frustration with compulsory military service by evading the draft, emigrating, or deserting. On occasion, however, they also expressed their resentment in open protest, usually in the form of local mutinies, which generally led to their discharge after an overly extended period of service.

The Balkan Wars laid bare these and other problems that had overwhelmed the Ottoman military system. For many, who remained beyond the immediate Unionist circles, the reforms predating the war failed to substantially improve the army's fighting capacity. Despite the major overhaul the army had undertaken, they claimed, there was still a lack of officers, properly trained soldiers, sanitary services, and logistical support. The Unionists agreed with some of these observations. What set apart their reasoning about the causes of the defeat, however, was their unequivocal emphasis on the empire's unrealized military potential. The real weakness of the Ottoman military, according to this view, did not primarily lie in organizational problems or the material deficiencies of the army. During the war, they claimed, Ottoman soldiers were actually better equipped than their Bulgarian, Greek, and Serbian counterparts. The infantry had the weapons it needed and did not suffer from lack of ammunition. The Ottoman forces had also outgunned their opponents. At the war's outbreak, the Ottoman army had more field guns than the four enemy armies put together, and much of the same was true of machine guns. Based on this material superiority, the Unionists argued, the Ottoman army actually entered the First Balkan War in better shape than it had ever been before.[52]

But why then had it been so ingloriously defeated? The real problem, according to the Unionists, lay in the inefficient Ottoman military system, which had failed to harness the empire's full potential and take advantage of its demographic superiority. Despite the fact that the Ottoman population outnumbered that of the Balkan allies combined by a 2-to-1 ratio, the empire had still lost the war. Even more disheartening for the Unionists was the comparison of mobilization ratios. While the Ottomans mobilized only 4.3 percent of their entire population, the Bulgarians, Greeks, Serbians, and Montenegrins mustered 8.6, 6.9, 5.0, and 15.0 percent of their populations, respectively: "Montenegrins are three times more altruistic than we are, Bulgarians are twice as patriotic. Even the merchant [*tüccar*] Greeks, who shun military service, are more self-sacrificing than us." This, *Tanin* declared, was like "a dark stain branded on the foreheads of all Ottomans."[53]

According to the Unionists, it was primarily the still-existing exemptions from military service that stood in the way of taking military advantage of the empire's demographic superiority. Unless those exemptions were abolished, or at least severely restricted, the next conflict would end just like the First Balkan War, but this time with even more dreadful consequences. This line of reasoning on military exemptions was further reinforced by a general consensus about Ottoman soldiers' abysmal lack of preparation. For many observers, Ottoman and non-Ottoman alike, the Balkan Wars displayed the fighting prowess, skill, and training of the soldiers in the Balkan armies, especially Bulgarian soldiers, while exposing acute problems in the wartime performance of Ottoman conscripts. The Unionist leaders shared the view that the army's regular cadres were relatively well prepared for the conflict. The reserves (*redif*s), however, which made up the bulk of wartime Ottoman troops, were conspicuously ill-prepared for any war, much less one against armies of well-trained and better-motivated soldiers. Normally, the reserves were supposed to be summoned periodically for training during peacetime and would bring infantry divisions up to mobilization strength during wars. In early October 1912, when they were hastily called up, however, the reserves responded poorly to the mobilization order. And when they finally did join the ranks, it became quite clear that they had received little to none of the military training required by modern warfare.[54] Their lack of basic military skills occasionally reached absurd levels. Eyewitness reports mentioned reservists who did not know how to use their weapons at all, who tried to shoot with the rifle butts on their foreheads or bellies, or who attempted to load their rifles through the muzzle of the gun.[55] Unfamiliar with the concept of military discipline, they refused to obey orders from their officers and acted individually or in small bands. Fear of punishment proved insufficient to keep them fighting. When pitted against a strong, fast, and capable enemy, they panicked and deserted by the thousands. The conscription of large numbers of these virtually untrained men also had deleterious effects on the regular troops, and therefore on the overall fighting capacity of the army.

Peacetime preparation was a principle that Unionist officers had long accepted. The Balkan Wars had shown them, however, that the price a country had to pay for its unpreparedness had become much costlier. Rendering armies more formidable and the battles more destructive, modern warfare enhanced the necessity of war readiness and made the lack of it a fatal mistake. For the Unionists, the primary causes of the problem of unpreparedness were, again, the exemptions from military service. Granting exemptions to a substantial number of military-age men and assigning them directly to the reserves meant that they received only a cursory peacetime training, if any at all. In stark contrast, the superior performance on the battlefield of the troops of the empire's Balkan enemies was attributed to the universality and efficiency of their all-embracing conscription systems. The Serbian army, according to an Ottoman observer, was an efficient force because it left no one without training.[56] Another officer wrote with appreciation that the Bulgarian people did not resort to circumventing conscription. Irrespective of profession or social status, all were obligated to perform active military service: "Everyone, every individual is a soldier. Be he the prime minister's son, he is still a soldier."[57] For these and other observers, the Ottoman army's defeat clearly indicated the superiority of the Balkan states' tight, efficient, and comprehensive recruiting systems. The defeat thus revealed above all else the burning need for a stronger and wider net of conscription. Only a truly universal system of conscription would enable the army to exploit all of the empire's available manpower.

Based on these observations, the Unionists responded to the shock of the

Balkan Wars with a comprehensive plan for military reform. The main goal of this massive reorganization was to revive the Ottoman army after the grave losses it had endured and to turn it into an effective fighting force capable of defending the empire against external and internal threats. Enver Pasha framed the reform as an act of self-defense, telling the press unambiguously that his intention was to counteract the aggressive intentions of the Balkan countries: "I clearly intend to keep in check the aggrandizement of our small neighbors, who are never satisfied."[58] Under his leadership, the entire military system and army organization underwent a dramatic process of transformation and reorganization. From the purge of high-ranking officers mentioned earlier to the creation of new military units and the elimination of old ones, the introduction of new training schemes, the preparation of new campaign and mobilization plans, the formation of paramilitary youth organizations, and finally the abolition of the infamous reserve system, the Unionist leadership tackled a series of problems that had been plaguing the Ottoman military.[59]

The most crucial component of military reform proved to be the enactment in May 1914 of the new Law of Military Obligation (Mükellefiyet-i Askeriye Kanun-ı Muvakkatı), which required all male Ottoman citizens aged twenty one, Muslim and non-Muslim alike (excluding the members of the Ottoman dynasty), to perform military service, and also permitted the conscription of nineteen- and twenty-year-olds in wartime.[60] The priority of the military reformers was to improve the quality of conscripts by passing the highest possible number of eligible males through the increasingly rigorous military system. The new conscription law aimed to do this by shortening the active military service period in the infantry from three years to two, thereby increasing the number of recruits drafted at each call.[61] More important, the new law completely abolished the exemptions permitted to those who were the sole breadwinners of their households (*muins*), limited the waiver of active service granted in return for an exemption fee (*bedel*) to peacetime, and severely restricted the exemption of government officials, religious functionaries, and students in universities and high schools. The new legislation thus extended the reach of conscription to an unprecedented degree, even before World War I started.[62]

The new Law of Military Obligation of 1914 marked a critical milestone in the universalization of military service in the Ottoman Empire. Through this law, the leaders of the Unionist regime sought to raise a more effective mass army for a future conflict, which they saw as both imminent and inevitable. A circular published by the central committee of the CUP in June 1914 stressed this point, portraying the new law of conscription as essential to the survival of the empire. The circular commended the new law for requiring that each and every able-bodied Ottoman man serve in the military and regarded it as an important step towards the creation of the "armed nation" (*millet-i müsellaha*).[63] The abolition of exemptions from military service, according to the circular, was at the core of the new legislation. It harshly criticized the outdated Law of Conscription of the Abdülhamid era for exempting a significant portion of potential recruits from serving in the last conflict, while the Bulgarians had mobilized everyone: rich and poor, educated and illiterate, and students and nonstudents alike. Even Bulgarian women were employed in transportation. By eliminating these exemptions, the new law would allow the Ottoman Empire to develop an equally formidable fighting force.[64]

In significantly extending the scope of conscription, the Law of Military Obligation of 1914 provided an efficient legal tool for officials to intervene on the home front to extract men for the army. The new law, however, also attracted severe criticism from various social and political groups throughout the empire. Deputies from the Arab provinces, for instance, conveyed the anger of their people, "bordering on rebellion," to Enver Pasha, who adamantly refused any revisions to the law, stating, "We are on the verge of a general war, and I can in no way retract the law."[65] Similarly, the World Congress of the Armenian Revolutionary Federation (ARF) held in Erzurum in July 1914 passed a resolution harshly criticizing the new measures regarding military service. "Accepting that everyone should fulfill his duty to serve his country," the World Congress opposed the conscription of the sole breadwinners of their families and proposed that Christians be drafted only up to the age of thirty-one.[66] The Armenian Patriarch Zaven Efendi raised similar criticisms, saying: "Today, the issue that concerns our people most is the new Law of Military Obligation's extension of military service to everyone regardless of the conscript's status as sole breadwinner of his family. I hope the cries of widows who are in need of bread and especially those of orphans will inspire mercy in the parliament and the ministers and that the law will be revised as necessary."[67] These concerns and criticisms, not surprisingly, fell on deaf ears. When the next mobilization was ordered in August 1914, the empire's people would have to deal with a dramatically expanded conscription net.

Religion and the Ottoman Army

While the Ottoman system of conscription became stricter and more comprehensive, the ideological discourse that surrounded the army and military service underwent a similarly dramatic change, again as a response to the Balkan War experiences. The official rhetoric that the army served as the symbol and the facilitator of the Ottoman brotherhood was abandoned for good. Just as Islamic tones had assumed new significance in propaganda aimed at home-front civilians, the wartime governments also adopted a deeply religious discourse to rouse soldiers' bellicose feelings. Two factors played a critical role in helping the Ottoman officials to overcome their reservations about the use of religious rhetoric: (1) the obvious lack of motivation among the majority of Ottoman recruits; and (2) the enemies' extensive use of religion to motivate their own soldiers and home-front populations.

Although they disagreed on many other points, both Unionist and non-Unionist observers shared the view that Ottoman soldiers, especially the reservists, had shown no eagerness to fight in the most recent conflict. Critics lamented the disappearance of age-old Ottoman bravery and military virtues that the ordinary soldier supposedly possessed.[68] In stark contrast, the success and resilience of the enemy was attributed to the individual conscript's patriotism and enthusiasm to fight. For many, the Ottoman soldiers' conspicuous lack of commitment to fight indicated their unwillingness or inability to identify with the abstract notions of "nation" and "fatherland."[69] Along with the lack or proper military training, this lack of identification with the imperial cause led to disheartening confusion and partial disintegration of the army at the very beginning of the war. In the face of this deepening military crisis, the Kamil Pasha government saw the arousal of a religious spirit as the only way to overcome the problem of soldier motivation. Less than a month into the war, the office of the Şeyhülislam, the empire's highest Muslim religious authority, called upon all members of the clergy to "practice jihad" by visiting the front lines and stoking soldiers' religious passions.[70] Preachers, students of religious seminaries, and other religious functionaries were accordingly sent to the front to incite soldiers' religious sentiments.[71]

Upon their return from the front, two of these preachers, Elhac Ahmed Tahir and Mustafa Necati wrote about their observations of the army for the daily İkdam.[72] They claimed that a series of material shortcomings, including a lack of transportation vehicles and munitions shortages, were certainly contributing to the Ottoman army's failure. However, the two preachers also pointed to the weaknesses of the soldiers' religious devotion as a major cause of the disaster. While in the past soldiers in the army had prayed together five times a day and preachers had lectured to them about the virtues of martyrdom on a regular basis, these practices had been ignored in recent years under the CUP leadership. The "motivation to die for the nation" (*vatan için ölmek hissi*) had been used as a substitute for religious motivation. For these and many other observers, the efforts to transcend soldiers' traditional religious affiliations and create a new martial spirit based solely on the love of the fatherland proved to be a complete failure. This new sense of patriotic devotion was not embraced by most of the soldiers and remained alien to them. The preachers' unsparing criticism was clearly directed at the CUP and its policy of seeking to unite all Ottoman subjects around a common, secular notion of the fatherland.

For their part, the Unionists never acknowledged openly that they had prematurely adopted secular patriotism. However, they too realized clearly that these ideas had failed to animate soldiers on the battleground, which left religious symbols and rhetoric as the only available means for maintaining soldiers' commitment. In that sense, the Balkan War experiences convinced the Unionists of the power of religion as a motivating factor for the ordinary soldier.[73] Enver Pasha's appointment to the War Ministry was thus accompanied by a discernible emphasis on religion. In his short message to the army, the new minister stated explicitly that he did not believe "an army without religion would be successful." He ordered every member of the army, Christian or Muslim, to carry out the requirements of his religion.[74] In a similar vein, Cemal Pasha, who had been appointed commander of the First Army Corps in Istanbul, underlined the importance of religion in his first message to his troops. But, unlike Enver Pasha, he did feign a persistent belief in an Ottomanist spirit: "An army, whose religious feelings are weak, cannot fulfill its duty towards the fatherland. Therefore the First Army Corps' ties to the religion of Islam should be strengthened."[75] Publication of both statements in the press suggested that the Unionists were simultaneously aiming to make broader sections of the Ottoman population aware of the army's renewed emphasis on religion.

The Balkan War experiences also convinced the CUP of the value of religious homogeneity in the army. Mixing Muslim recruits with non-Muslims proved to be crippling for the former's motivation. Some officers noted that Muslim soldiers questioned the rationale of fighting together in the same ranks with Christians.[76] On the other hand, the war revealed to the Unionists the non-Muslims' failure to fully commit themselves to protecting the empire.

Non-Muslims, the Unionists argued, either remained indifferent to the empire's ordeal and did not contribute to the war effort, or defected to the enemy.[77] Their presence in the army ranks was therefore deemed unnecessary, if not outright detrimental, to victory. Even during the war, many of these soldiers were sent to labor battalions and employed behind the front.

In the aftermath of the Balkan Wars, one of the leading Unionist ideologues, Hüseyin Cahid, assessed non-Muslims' wartime performance in his column in *Tanin*. Following the Constitutional Revolution of 1908, Cahid argued, the Unionists conceived of military service as a means to effect a positive change in society by forging a new bond among all the empire's peoples regardless of their ethno-religious background. They hoped that the barracks "would constitute the strongest foundation of Ottomans' unity." These expectations, however, did not materialize, as many non-Muslims refused to put up with the difficulties of the military life and deserted abroad. "We cannot blame them," wrote Cahid, "[m]ilitary life is difficult. Especially for the elements [*anasır*] who had never served in the army. . . . It requires a strong attachment to the fatherland. Obviously, not enough time has passed since the revolution for the non-Muslims to develop such an attachment."[78]

Even though his tone was mild, Hüseyin Cahid's editorial was one of the most explicit signs of the Unionists' departure from their earlier Ottomanist policies. It likely reflected a broader consensus among the Unionist leadership. For the CUP, extending mandatory military service to non-Muslims had always been a central pillar of Ottomanism and a negation of the Hamidian regime. Enrolling collectively in the defense of the fatherland and sacrificing for the greater good of the empire was thought to be the most efficient way to transcend ethno-religious divisions.[79] Although the implementation of the process on the ground met with several obstacles, the Unionists, at least on paper, stuck to the idea until the Balkan Wars. By adopting a new approach to the military service of non-Muslims as a response to Balkan War experiences, however, they drew a bold line between them and the Muslim citizens of the empire. Religious affiliation came to be the key variable determining this distinction. The dual process of Islamicization—namely, the conviction that religion was the prime motivator of Ottoman soldiers and non-Muslims' exclusion from the fighting ranks—would contribute to the CUP government's decision to wage the next war in the name of all Muslims and to condemn non-Muslims to hard labor, persecution, and death.

The Great Powers and the Ottoman Empire

The Balkan Wars brought to light the terrifying reality of the Ottoman Empire's political and military weaknesses. For the Unionists, however, this was not the only source of the empire's increasingly manifest vulnerabilities. The Balkan Wars and their aftermath also revealed that the European powers' sympathy lied firmly with the Ottomans' enemies. From the very beginning of the war, they had openly favored the Balkan allies' cause, pressured the Ottomans to accept insufferable terms, and shut their eyes to the misery of hundreds of thousands of Muslims. In a future confrontation with its enemies, the Unionists were convinced, the Porte would face a similarly unsympathetic, if not outright antagonistic, front of European powers. This mind-set, which by no means was confined to the political and intellectual elites, would guide Ottoman public opinion on the eve of World War I.

This sense of abandonment and injustice became gradually entrenched through four critical junctures of the Balkan War crisis. The first of these came very early in the war. With the outbreak of the hostilities, the Great Powers declared that they would uphold the status quo in the Balkans and would not let any belligerent benefit territorially, whatever the outcome of the conflict might be.[80] Widespread expectations about a decisive Ottoman victory prompted them to adopt this posture. In the face of the Balkan armies' swift progress, however, the European governments quickly abandoned their prewar position for just the opposite stance: under these new circumstances, they claimed, it had become impossible to preserve the political status quo any further, and belligerents should adjust to the new situation. The Ottoman reaction was one of indignation and loathing.[81]

Later in January 1913, when the Ottomans sat at the negotiation table with their enemies in London, the Great Powers intervened to pressure the Porte to accept conditions of peace that included ceding the Aegean islands and Edirne to the Balkan allies. The Ottomans had actually gone to London with heightened expectations that the powers would favor the claims of the famous Anglophile Kamil Pasha's government and moderate the allies' excessive demands. The joint note of January 17 presented by the Great Powers to the Porte, advising the immediate surrender of Edirne to the Balkan allies and referring of the future of the islands question to them, therefore came as a shock. If the Porte would not listen to their "advice," the powers threatened not to intervene in the case that the hostilities resumed, and to refuse any request for financial aid in the future. Apart from the alliance of four Balkan states, the daily İkdam wrote, "we are also against a bloc of opposition composed of all European Great Powers."[82] The Porte responded to the note by partially accepting the allies' demands, but refusing to cede Edirne and the islands, a proposal they summarily rejected. The resumption of hostilities led to the fall of Edirne to the Bulgarians and the signing of the humiliating peace treaty in London in May 1913.

For many Ottomans, the Europeans' hostile stance against the empire was further confirmed during the Second Balkan War. The Great Powers objected to the Ottomans' recapture of Edirne in the summer of 1913 and pressured the Porte to comply with the Treaty of London. The Unionists in particular, who had been in power since January of that same year, felt deeply frustrated at the powers' partiality and anti-Ottomanism. An editorial in *Tanin* on 8 August 1913, perfectly captured the Unionists' anger and resentment: "Once again to our detriment, we have painfully experienced that no good or faithfulness [*vefa*] would come to us from Europe. We have understood that it was not only the Balkan states allied against the Ottoman Empire, but also all European states. . . . We were at war, not only with the Balkan states, but with the whole of Europe, perhaps not materially but morally."[83] This time, however, the CUP felt confident enough to resist the Great Powers' pressure and did not return Edirne to the Bulgarians.

Ottoman public opinion unanimously blamed the Great Powers, but mostly Great Britain, for turning a blind eye to the misery of hundreds of thousands of Muslims in Rumelia. While celebrating the Balkan allies' victories, the press claimed, Europeans showed no concern for the atrocities committed by their armies against Muslims, including the mass murder of civilians, the rape of women, and the destruction of personal property and places of worship. Newspapers were full of graphic details of these atrocities, as well as an outpouring of anger against Europeans' silence about them. "There is no one in Europe," *İkdam* declared, "who has witnessed [these atrocities] and been saddened by them."[84] Many Ottoman citizens saw Europeans as so callous or self-centered that they disregarded the sufferings of anyone other than their co-religionists. Had Ottoman troops "been accused of the half of what is set out in this document there would have been a howl of protest from one end of Europe to the other." For Ottoman public opinion, this European indifference, if not condoning, only emboldened the Balkan allies in their unrestrained conduct of war against civilians.[85]

The last blow to the Unionists came during the Aegean islands crisis that followed the war. As it constituted such a thorny issue between the fighting parties, the solution to the "islands question" had been entrusted to the Great Powers during the peace negotiations between the Ottoman Empire and Greece. In December 1913, much to the dismay of the Ottomans, Great Britain recommended that the Greeks retain all the islands they had occupied during the war. The other members of the Triple Entente and Triple Alliance accepted the British proposal for the settlement of the islands' fate. These islands included Chios and Mytilene, which were predominantly inhabited by Greeks, yet lie only ten miles off the Anatolian coast. The Ottomans' hopes that Great Britain would support the Porte's claims and safeguard its interests were once again shattered. Despite the Porte's vigorous protests, the islands were not restored to the Ottoman Empire. The Great Powers' decision outraged the Ottomans, reinforcing their feeling of emasculation and victimhood. "Once again idealists like us, who, still in this age, believe in the notions of right and justice have been greatly disappointed. . . . Being feeble is a fault. Today justice means power," read the editorial of *Tanin*.[86] "All our efforts are in vain," *İkdam* wrote, "Violating our rights has, it appears, become a clause in international law. All this is the sad manifestation of the principle that the Crescent cannot stay where the Cross has once entered."[87]

Even though the sentiment of injustice was firmly entrenched in the Unionists' minds, it did not preclude them from searching for ways to cultivate good relations with European governments. It was mostly the CUP's fear of political isolation and, perhaps more important, the empire's acute financial distress that prompted the Unionists to bite their tongues. In early 1914, the government found itself in such abysmal conditions that officials' salaries were months in arrears. Raising a large army and maintaining it on a war footing for more than a year had depleted the empire's already limited financial reserves. To close the deficit in the imperial budget, the government imposed new burdens on taxpayers, including a 25 percent increase in income (*temettü*) and cattle (*ağnam*) taxes.[88] But these were far from sufficient. The Unionists knew well that European financial markets constituted the only source of fresh loans. Such a grave situation mandated diplomatic caution and amiable relations. Between the end of the Balkan War and World War I, they negotiated with several European governments and reached agreements over port and railroad concessions, granted contracts for a number of construction projects, invited a German military mission to reform the army, appointed French and British advisors to several ministries, and resolved long-standing border disputes. Through these attempts the Porte hoped to maneuver the empire out of political isolation and financial dire straits. Nevertheless, mistreatment at the hands of the Great Powers left a deep imprint on the Unionists as well as the broader Ottoman public. During World War I, the CUP would skillfully evoke those buried sentiments to construct a convincing war narrative.

A New Imperial Configuration

In a curious entry in his diary on 2 July 1913, the Unionist minister of finance, Cavid Bey, who was in Paris negotiating a new loan from French banks, noted a letter he had received from Istanbul. He frequently exchanged letters with other leading Unionists regarding his activities abroad, as well as recent developments in the Ottoman capital. The letter from Istanbul informed him about an important decision that had been made by the Central Committee: the CUP would henceforth pursue an "Islamic politics" (İslam siyaseti). The new policy, however, would not be written down, but would be kept in mind by the Unionist leaders.[89] Neither in this entry nor in the remainder of his diary did Cavid Bey give a detailed explanation about what exactly was meant by the notion of "Islamic politics." From later developments, however, one can surmise that it referred to a new imperial configuration based predominantly on the empire's Muslim elements, specifically Turks and Arabs.

The letter Cavid Bey received implied a change in the Unionist policies of managing ethno-religious difference in the empire. The Unionist leaders were fully cognizant of the enhanced political energy among the empire's Muslim and non-Muslim minorities in the aftermath of the Balkan Wars. The CUP government's apparent inability to counteract its enemies and forestall territorial losses gave rise to widespread skepticism among Greeks, Armenians, Kurds, Arabs, and others about the future of the empire.[90] The empire's disintegration and collapse seemed imminent to many of them. The Unionists followed the growth of this sentiment with mounting concern that it might soon translate into full-fledged separatist aspirations, especially if the minority claims found European backing. Their deep distrust in European powers only aggravated the Unionists' concerns. It was these concerns that dictated a new approach to ethno-religious relations in the empire.

The new direction that the CUP adopted was not towards abandoning the Ottomanist ideology in favor of Turkism or Turkish nationalism, as was commonly assumed. The new strategy, evolved over time and in response to internal and external pressures, was far more complex. It comprised two fundamental components: neutralizing autonomist/decentralist tendencies through

political and administrative measures, and revamping Ottomanism based on
the unity and primacy of the two largest Muslim communities of the empire,
Turks and Arabs. The Balkan Wars, according to the Unionists, had brought
the empire to the brink of collapse. Having lost the European provinces, the
Ottomans now had to withdraw to Anatolia and the Arab provinces. The defeat
and humiliation shook the foundations of the state, Hüseyin Cahid wrote in a
Tanin editorial on 15 November 1913. These did not, however, inflict serious
damage on its "real source of life." On the contrary, the losses and suffering
even replenished it:

> To be able to hold on to Rumelia, we were wrecking Anatolia. The Ottoman
> state resembled a creature devouring a part of its body to extend its life a little
> longer. We were continually sacrificing [the people of] Anatolia to retain various
> non-Muslim elements who fought [us] in Rumelia and were determined never
> to submit to Ottomanism and, in their determination, received encouragement
> and support from neighboring states.

Since the end of the war, this situation, which had undermined the power of
the Ottoman state, no longer applied. Henceforth, the brotherhood between
Turks and Arabs would constitute "a new life and a new hope" for the empire
and provide a moral basis (*manevi istinadgah*) for the Islamic world as well.[91]

In line with this new spirit, the Unionists launched a new policy towards
the empire's Arab provinces and took some critical steps to moderate their
centralizing policies and to appease existing tensions between the CUP and
its decentralist/reformist Arab critics.[92] In view of the increasingly vocal au-
tonomist claims and intensifying foreign machinations, the Unionists saw the
compromise as an efficient way of defusing separatist aspirations and countering pro-British and pro-French inclinations among the Arabs. Unlike with
the non-Muslim minorities of the empire, the Unionists thought that such a
compromise was still possible with the Arabs, especially Muslim Arabs. After
all, most of them harbored suspicions of the intentions of Great Britain and
France in Arab provinces and expressed their desire to pursue provincial reforms within the Ottomanist framework.[93] The Unionists reached out to this
group of Arab intellectuals and politicians and drew up a compromise agreement with them.

The compromise included measures regarding some of the long-standing
demands voiced by the Arab decentralists: introduction of regional military
service; institution of Arabic as the medium of instruction in elementary and

secondary schools (along with a promise to extend this clause to higher education in the future); the requirement of proficiency in Arabic as well as in Turkish for local civil servants; the appointment of second-level functionaries by
provincial administrations; and the appointment of judges and other judicial
functionaries from among these locally-selected officials.[94] The Unionist press
announced the agreement with much fanfare. The agreement between Turks
and Arabs, *Tanin* wrote, would surely eliminate certain misunderstandings between them and symbolize the unshakable solidarity between "the two great
nations of the East and two great brothers of religion."[95] The reference to Islam
was unmistakable. The new understanding between Turks and Arabs signaled
a new future for the Islamic world, which "had been sunk in misery and con-
tempt [*zillet*] for centuries," another Unionist wrote.[96]

Although the government was not inclined to concede full autonomy to
local administrations, and therefore fell short of satisfying the more fervent
decentralists, the compromise measures still marked a dramatic shift away
from the CUP's centralist policies. Until the Balkan War crisis, the Unionists
had vehemently opposed any proposals that would diminish the imperial center's authority over the provinces. This change did not escape the attention of
foreign observers. In his annual report of 1913, the British ambassador to the
Porte summed up his observations as follows: "The disastrous centralization
policy of the Government which succeeded the Hamidian regime, involving
the forcible Turkification of provinces differing widely in race, customs, and
religion, appears to have now been abandoned."[97] By addressing some of the
long-standing Arab demands for greater autonomy and administrative reform,
the Unionists managed to contain the decentralist movement's growing energy,
prevent the internationalization of the "Arab Question," and maintain the men-
tal and political ties of the majority of Arabs with the empire. The World War I
years would see the scrapping of these policies under Cemal Pasha's strict rule
and the rupture of the Arabs' ties with the empire, eventually leading many of
them to contemplate full independence.

The conspicuous criticism of non-Muslims in Hüseyin Cahid's lines bears on
the question of how Ottoman non-Muslim minorities would fit into this new
imperial configuration. For the Unionists, the Balkan War experience highlighted the government's failure to persuade non-Muslims to identify with the
empire. At best, they remained uninterested in the empire's fate; at worst, they
implicitly and occasionally explicitly extended their sympathy and support to

the Balkan allies' war efforts. This criticism was particularly directed against the Ottoman Greeks, but other non-Muslim groups were not totally exempted from it. In the eyes of the Unionists, the Balkan Wars showed that the process of "Greekization" of the Ottoman Greeks had long been completed. For decades, Greece had gradually been increasing its influence over the empire's Greeks, especially through education. This process had accelerated after the 1908 Revolution, when the Greek community's leadership passed from the Church to a secular, urban, middle-class elite.[98] The victories of the Balkan Wars thus struck a particularly powerful chord of patriotism among the Ottoman Greeks. These sentiments were presumably not embraced by all Greeks of the empire, let alone by all non-Muslims. However, the deep sense of urgency among the Unionists led them, on the one hand, to exaggerate the non-Muslims' overall impact on the war effort. On the other hand, it prompted them to expand these relatively limited sentiments to all the empire's ethno-religious communities. In the Unionists' minds, significant socioeconomic and political differences within these communities were blurred as the paths of the empire's Muslims and non-Muslims diverged.

The Unionists' alienation from the Ottoman Greeks was also determined by one important conclusion that they drew from the Balkan Wars: the interdependence of military performance and demographic realities. Many firsthand accounts by Ottoman officers described the difficulties of conducting a military campaign where the local populations' sympathies lay with the enemy. Local people informed the Ottomans' enemies about troop movements, provided logistical support to enemy soldiers, and even robbed or fired on Ottoman soldiers who were separated from their battalions.[99] They also occasionally joined regular or irregular enemy forces. Greek, Bulgarian, and Serbian irregulars, fighting along with the regular armies, waged effective guerrilla warfare against the Ottomans. They guided regular troops through unfamiliar regions, ambushed smaller units, and hit supply lines, effectively wearing down the Ottoman army. The rugged, wooded territory only increased their efficiency. On several occasions, their presence denied the Ottomans freedom of movement and operation. Under pursuit they could easily disappear into the local population and avoid retribution. The very nature of these bands blurred the distinctions between the enemy army and the local population, in effect strengthening the Unionists' propensity to categorize entire communities as disloyal if not outright hostile to the empire.

In the war's aftermath, these perceptions prompted a systematic policy of un-mixing in the Ottoman Empire. The Unionists came out of the war convinced of the need to alter the demographic structure of strategically sensitive regions. In this regard, the Porte concluded a peace treaty with Bulgaria, which was followed by a treaty of reciprocal population exchange concerning the ethnic Bulgarians and Bulgarian Muslims of eastern Thrace. The treaty affected some 50,000 Ottoman Bulgarians and some 50,000 Muslims who had already emigrated during the wars.[100] The presence of a large Greek population on the western coast of Anatolia, however, was a bigger source of anxiety for the Unionists, and the reason for their adoption of a much more virulent tone against Greece. The Unionists' nightmare of the conflation of a foreign power and a sympathetic local population materialized during the crisis over the Aegean islands. As mentioned, the question of the Aegean islands remained unresolved during the peace negotiations of the Balkan Wars. Both sides, but especially the Ottomans, reluctantly agreed to entrust the resolution of the problem to the Great Powers. From the very beginning, however, the Unionists claimed that the islands were a natural extension of Anatolia and indispensable to its security.[101] Using these islands, they claimed, Greece could easily extend its influence over Anatolian Greeks living on the coastal areas or, in the case of war, land troops in Anatolia. So long as the islands remained in the possession of Greece, the argument went, western Anatolian provinces would be in constant danger.

In the words of the grand vizier Said Halim Pasha, the islands posed a "vital question" (*mesele-i hayatiye*) for the Ottomans, and the empire could not renounce its sovereignty over them.[102] Writing in January 1914, Hüseyin Cahid demanded that Chios and Mytilene, the two closest islands off the west coast of Anatolia, be surrendered to the Ottomans for the sake of the future of the empire: "Otherwise, we know, as long as Greek propaganda is active there, it would hinder our rebuilding program in Anatolia."[103] The Ottoman ambassador to Athens, Galip Kemali Bey, similarly argued that any solution that did not return Chios and Mytilene to the empire was unacceptable to them: "Otherwise the Greek influence would without difficulty prevail over 400,000 Greeks living on the coast."[104]

Despite the signing of the peace treaty in November 1913, the relations between Greece and the Ottoman Empire underwent a steady deterioration after the Balkan Wars. The Great Powers' final decision to give the islands to Greece exacerbated relations between the two countries even further. At this point in time, the Unionists certainly did not rule out the possibility of a war with Greece and may have actually been willing to wage one.[105] This expectation underpinned most of their military and demographic policies following the end of the Balkan Wars. On the one hand, the Unionists organized a widespread and effective boycott of Greek businesses. In many places, local boycott committees led by the Unionists themselves urged their co-religionists to stop shopping at non-Muslim, but especially Greek, stores.[106] The momentum of grass-roots patriotism persisted, on the other hand, through an extensive fund-raising campaign for the navy. From the early years of the Constitutional Revolution, the demand for a strong navy had been a major pillar of the patriotic propaganda of the Unionists, but it gained a new urgency following the escalation in tensions with Greece. Members of the Navy League (Donanma Cemiyeti) and state officials regularly visited towns and villages to collect donations to purchase new battleships. Governmental employees were asked to contribute a month's salary to the Navy Fund. The Istanbul correspondent of the paper *The Near East* reported with awe: "Money is pouring in for the needs of the fleet with a rapidity that has surprised even the promoters of the patriotic movement in favour of the purchase of fresh units."[107] Two weeks later he was reporting that "Committees have been formed in every town, almost in every village, and there has been a very genuine response to the call for funds."[108] Both the boycott of Greek businesses and the navy campaign seemed to rejuvenate Ottoman public opinion.

More important, the Unionists embarked on a substantial demographic engineering campaign in the summer of 1914 on the Aegean coast. Their ultimate objectives were to create a new demographic reality on the ground and to eliminate any potential obstacles that would hinder the Ottoman fighting capacity if a war erupted with Greece. Bands under the direction of the clandestine paramilitary unit known as the Special Organization (Teşkilat-ı Mahsusa) expelled some 150,000 Anatolian Greeks from their historic homelands to the Greek islands and mainland Greece.[109] The intervention of foreign embassies did little to impede the process of de-Greekization of the Aegean coast. This expulsion was a calculated, centrally planned and orchestrated policy of terror with serious consequences. In some districts, such as Çesme and Urla, nearly the entire Greek population crossed over to the Greek islands or took refuge in Smyrna. Their properties were for the most part occupied by Muslim refugees from Rumelia. During this process, the Unionists observed the "effectiveness" of terror campaigns. The campaign against the Greeks persuaded them that it was possible to radically transform the demographic structure of a region and to neutralize a perceived threat with a relatively small number of men and in a short span of time. In addition, the government could still remain behind the curtain. These observations would guide them when they engaged in a much more disastrous campaign against the Ottoman Armenians a year later.

The growing estrangement between the Unionists and the Armenians was only indirectly related to the Balkan War crisis. At the heart of their alienation was the question of administrative and political reforms in the eastern provinces of the empire. Since the early months of the Constitutional Revolution, Ottoman Armenians had been repeatedly demanding the implementation of a series of reforms to remedy the problems of perpetual insecurity of Armenian communities, the policy of resettlement of refugees from the Balkans and the Caucasus to the region, and, most important, the restitution of Armenian lands that had been seized by local Kurds in previous decades. The Unionists' reluctance and inability to carry out the reforms and to enforce security and order in the region over the past four years had led to widespread pessimism among the Armenians.[110]

The Balkan War crisis and subsequent Ottoman setbacks revived Armenian hopes of finding receptive ears for their demands. The moment was ripe to raise the issue of reforms. "Today, the international political situation is not favorable for the Turks," a prominent Armenian political and literary figure, Krikor Zohrab, noted in his diary. "Therefore, it is a most appropriate time to talk with them. We will not be able to find such a perfect moment again."[111] Having been disappointed by the Unionists in the past, however, Armenians knew only too well that "talking with the Turks" alone would not mitigate their problems. For an effective and long-lasting solution, they had to find a way to get the Great Powers to put pressure on the Porte. In December 1912, the Armenian National Assembly, which was made up of the representatives of Armenian political parties, Armenian notables, and the clergy, took a fateful decision to convey the Armenians' demands to European governments. What made the Armenians' decision even more consequential was the fact that it was taken by the unanimous vote of all Armenian political parties and power holders, who had rarely agreed upon anything before then.[112] Despite several attempts over the ensuing months, the Unionists failed to exploit internal tensions among Armenians, something they had managed to do when they dealt with the Arabs.

The more important difference between the Arab and Armenian cases was the Unionists' failure to forestall the internationalization of the question of Armenian reforms. On the one hand, the Armenians' persistence in requesting Great Powers' supervision of the reforms and their continuous refusal of the Unionists' demands to solve the question through Ottoman-Armenian negotiations, and, on the other hand, the Great Powers', especially Russia's, readiness to play an active role in the process condemned the Unionists' efforts to failure. The CUP had already been deeply concerned about Russia's renewed interest in eastern Anatolia and its desire to increase its influence over Armenians and Kurds living in the region.[113] According to the Unionists, the internationalization of the reform question would undoubtedly pave the way for greater Russian hegemony in eastern Anatolia and presumably the creation of a fully autonomous regime under Russian auspices. Such a prospect was tantamount to the end of Ottoman sovereignty in the region. Therefore, they spent considerable energy to derail the process, albeit without much success. The internationalization of the Armenian question, as one historian put it, "is the central reason that the state-Armenian dynamic deteriorated as it did within the larger matrix of demographic change and territorial diminution of the late Ottoman Empire."[114]

The initial reform project was drafted by the reform committee selected by the Armenian National Assembly and submitted to André Mandelstam, the chief dragoman of the Russian Embassy, who, in turn, revised and distributed this draft project to the representatives of other Great Powers. What came to be known as the "Mandelstam Plan" proposed to organize six eastern provinces—Erzurum, Van, Bitlis, Diyarbekir, Harput, and Sivas—into one province and place it under the control of a Christian or European governor appointed by the sultan. The governor would enjoy considerable autonomy over the administrative, judiciary, and military affairs of the province. The provincial assembly would be composed of an equal number of Muslim and Christian members. The infamous Hamidiye Light Cavalry would be disbanded. Muslim refugees would not be allowed to settle in the province. The police and gendarmerie forces of the province would be recruited from the inhabitants of the province and half of them would be Christians. A special commission would be formed for the explicit purpose of investigating Armenian land losses and supervising the restitution process. Finally, the Great Powers would ensure the implementation of the reforms.[115] The Mandelstam Plan was met with furious reactions by the Great Powers, which interpreted the project as a means of direct Russian intervention in eastern Anatolia. Fearing that the increased Russian influence would jeopardize its own strategic and economic interests, Germany was particularly spurred into action by the plan. From that point on, Russia and Germany emerged as the main actors who would negotiate and work out a reform project that would be acceptable to the Great Powers, the Ottoman government, and the Armenians.[116]

In imposing reforms on the Ottoman Empire, the Great Powers, including Russia, neither intended to partition its territories nor to carve out a national homeland for the Armenians. They were fully aware that this would upset the precarious balance they had struck among themselves. But the Unionists perceived the Great Powers' intentions to be contrary to their own interests. The Balkan War experiences had completely eroded the credibility of the powers in the eyes of the Unionists. Especially after they had learned about the Mandelstam Plan, the Unionists' objection to foreign control became more vigorous. "No matter how subtle and gilded," Hüseyin Cahid wrote in a *Tanin* editorial, "once we detect European control [over the reform project], we will become its sworn enemy."[117] Even Cavid Bey, a relatively moderate member of the CUP, told the German undersecretary of state, Arthur Zimmermann, that they by no means wanted "a new Macedonia [to] come about in Anatolia."[118] The hardening of the Unionists' tone did not escape the attention of European diplomats. As the German ambassador to the Porte, Hans von Wangenheim, wrote: "The problem is that we don't have to negotiate with the Sultan or a personality of superior prestige . . . but with the Committee, that means a group which is ruled by ideas, not by personalities. At present the prevailing thought in the Committee is to have Turkey rather ruined than to continue to have it further under the political control of the Powers."[119]

In the meantime, the Unionists tried in vain to persuade the Armenians to renounce Great Power supervision over the reforms. Throughout 1913, leading members of the CUP gave interviews to major Armenian newspapers to persuade the Armenian public of their goodwill and determination to implement the desired reforms. They met several times with their Armenian counterparts, especially the Dashnaks (members of the Armenian Revolutionary Federation, the Dashnaksutiun), with whom they had closely cooperated in the past. Simultaneously, they conducted an intimidation campaign behind the scenes, threatening prominent Armenians, defacing churches, and boycotting Armenian merchants.[120] These efforts, however, failed to convince Armenians to forsake the supervision of the Great Powers and engage in direct negotiations with the Unionists. Over the years, the Unionists had made many promises that they could not or did not deliver. The Europeans' guarantee was therefore essential for the Armenians to ensure the implementation of the reforms. They also knew that by late 1913 they were closer than ever to securing such a guarantee. In December 1913, the Unionists finally agreed to meet all Armenian demands. In return, they asked them to issue a proclamation denouncing supervision by foreign powers. The response was again negative. Zohrab Efendi, who conveyed the Unionists' proposal to the Armenian leaders, wrote in his diary prophetically that the leadership's fateful decision would be fraught with disastrous ramifications: "The entire nation will suffer from the consequences [of the decision]."[121]

The outcome of the long and arduous process of negotiation among the Great Powers, the Ottomans, and Armenians was the Reform Act of 8 February 1914. Compared to the Mandelstam Plan, the final version of this agreement represented a significant achievement for the Unionists: The provinces would be grouped into two inspectorships instead of one. Trabzon, which had a large Muslim population, was added to the inspectorships, thereby diluting the proportional strength of the Armenians. The principle of proportional rather than equal representation was accepted for the provincial assemblies—except in the provinces of Van and Bitlis, where equal representation would be the rule. The two inspector-generals would be the subjects of smaller European powers, and would have extensive authority over the civic, judicial, and administrative branches of the provinces as well as the police and gendarmerie. The Hamidiye regiments would be absorbed into the army. The land question, the most critical issue for the Armenians, was left intentionally vague. The agreement stipulated that agrarian conflicts would be settled under the supervision of the inspector-generals. No commitment was made about the settlement of Muslim refugees in the region, the extension of the reforms to other Ottoman provinces, or the enforcement of the reforms by the Great Powers.[122]

The final version of the reform plan was considerably different from the one that had been drawn up by the Dashnaks and revised by Mandelstam. But it was still a grave blow for the Unionists even though they managed to obtain significant concessions. After all, they were forced to yield on the issue of foreign control. To save face and avoid any further damage to its already tarnished prestige, the CUP represented the reforms as a general set of measures aimed at the whole of Asia Minor. An article published in *Tanin* describing the reform package stated that Anatolia would be divided into six inspectorships and avoided mentioning any ethnic community by name.[123] In the following months, the Porte did everything it could to slow down the implementation of the reforms. The outbreak of war in Europe and the declaration of mobilization in the empire in early August offered the CUP government a perfect opportunity to shelve the reform project.

It is tempting to establish a direct connection between the Reform Act of 1914 and the annihilation of the Ottoman Armenians in 1915–16. Yet such a conclusion would be too deterministic. Certainly, the process widened the rift between the Unionists and the Armenians to such a degree that it became almost impossible to heal.[124] The process convinced the Unionists that the Armenians were firmly under the influence of Russia. Even the Dashnaks, with whom they had close personal relations, were irreversibly lost. "The events of 1913 had completely transformed the Talaat I had known," a leading Dashnak observed.[125] "We are living in terrible times. These Turks have totally changed, especially towards us," Zohrab Efendi exclaimed to one of his friends.[126] Complete mistrust and anger came to characterize the Unionists' attitude towards their Armenian counterparts. Still, there is a wide gap between the dramatically soured relations between the Unionists and the Armenians and the large-scale massacre of hundreds of thousands of people. The coming of the war in the fall, however, would create radically new conditions under which the Unionists' suspicions would evolve into destructive policies targeting a whole people.

Conclusions

At all levels of Ottoman society, defeat at the hands of four smaller Balkan armies was perceived as evidence of imperial decline and led to widespread demoralization. The Balkan Wars also showed the Ottomans that in this era, wars would lead not only to mass casualties on the battlefield but terrible consequences for the civilian population. They observed the misery of soldiers' families in their villages, felt the impact of extracted labor on the local economy, and suffered from unpaid salaries and increased prices on the home front. Furthermore, soldiers of the Balkan Wars returned to their homes with stories of the painfulness and brutality of everyday life under arms. All of these recent observations compounded the already negative image of military service, making the Ottomans extremely reluctant to engage in another conflict.

The disastrous Balkan War experiences nonetheless sharpened the Unionists' awareness of their own weaknesses and added a fresh burst of urgency to their concerns. The defeats revealed, above all else, the burning need for more efficient tools to mobilize the empire's human and material resources. The CUP government undertook a number of drastic measures regarding politics, the military, and society in a series of attempts to increase the empire's fighting capacity. As a result, the empire entered World War I much more experienced in how to penetrate society and mobilize its resources. In that sense, the lessons drawn from the Balkan Wars proved invaluable for the Ottoman political and military elites, contributing to their resilience in World War I.

The political and cultural atmosphere engendered by the Balkan Wars constituted the backdrop against which the next war would be unleashed. This backdrop was characterized by a tightened Unionist grip on the empire's political and social life, an expanded civil society network and centrally organized effort to reinvigorate the patriotic spirit, and a heavy use of religious rhetoric that came to replace more secular, Ottomanist discourses in civil society activism and the army. Politicizing ethno-religious differences, these developments contributed to the widening gulf between Muslim and non-Muslim Ottomans on the eve of World War I.

2 FROM THE FIELDS TO THE RANKS

After spending an enjoyable evening with his close friends, İhsan Bey awoke on the morning of 3 August 1914, to find his hometown, Harput, in eastern Anatolia, in a somber yet hectic mood. Gloom had fallen over the city. It did not take long for him to realize the source of this noticeable change. Like thousands of other towns and villages throughout the empire, Harput had been decorated overnight with bright-red posters depicting green flags, a gun, a saber, and a cannon. The message on the posters was plain and simple: "Mobilization is in effect. All soldiers to arms." (Seferberlik var. Asker olanlar silah altına.) This marked the second time in less than two years that the Ottoman government called its male citizens to arms. As İhsan Bey observed, people in Harput were "agitated, despondent, and dejected."[1] Like millions of Ottomans, they anticipated that the *seferberlik* (mobilization) would bring disruption to their lives. Few could conceive, however, just how disruptive the mobilization would be, and how deeply it would be etched into their personal and collective memories over the next four years and beyond.

The process of mobilization marked the first stage in turning of hundreds of thousands of Ottoman citizens into soldiers. The unexpected call threw their lives and the lives of their families into great disarray. The three months between the mobilization order and the empire's entry into the war also saw the first steps of dramatic changes in the way the Ottoman state functioned. The all-consuming needs of the army led to an unprecedented intervention by authorities on the home front. The widespread requisitioning of food and supplies, the appropriation of public buildings and private homes for quartering soldiers, the impressment of draught animals and vehicles into army service, the imposition of martial law, and severe restrictions on travel, assembly, and expression transformed urban centers and the countryside. Bitter memories of the last war and an overwhelming sense of urgency among the Unionists ensured that this process would entail a good dose of compulsion and violence. These social and economic disruptions would have deeply unsettling effects on millions on the home front.

The mobilization process was not confined, however, to military preparations and the expansion of state authority. Reflecting the fundamentally transformed character of warfare since the mid-nineteenth century, "wartime mobilization" had come to embody also the "mobilization of the imagination."[2] When a nation mobilizes for war, it does so "both imaginatively, through collective representations and the belief and value systems giving rise to these, and organizationally, through the state and civil society," the historian John Horne argues.[3] Like other belligerent governments in the Great War, the CUP government thus strove to craft a "war narrative" through which people could make sense of the war, the enemy, and their own role in the conflict. A convincing narrative was essential to justify the government's extensive preparations for war. Unlike other governments, however, the Unionists were demanding further sacrifices from a war-weary society that was still trying to recover, both materially and emotionally, from a disastrous defeat.

The Decision to Mobilize

Immediately after the first shots were fired on European battlefields, the Ottoman Empire declared "armed neutrality" (*müsellah bitaraflık*). In the meantime, the Unionist leaders had negotiated and concluded a secret alliance with Germany on 2 August 1914, and with Austria-Hungary three days later.[4] On the same day that it signed the alliance treaty with Germany, the government ordered the mobilization of the army and the navy, fearing that the rapidly escalating European conflict would eventually spread to Ottoman lands. The mobilization order officially covered all male Ottoman citizens between the ages of twenty and forty-five, regardless of ethnicity or religion, who were fit for service. Alongside the mobilization, the Porte also declared martial law throughout the empire and suspended the parliament and the senate.

The early and comprehensive mobilization was clearly the idea of the Ottoman military decision-makers. However, the decision was far from unanimous among the Unionists. Several members of the CUP cabinet objected to the idea of general mobilization on the grounds that such a comprehensive call to arms might provoke Russia and, worse, deplete the empire's already weak financial resources and lead to bankruptcy. "This state," the minister of finance, Cavid Bey, explained to the CUP's Central Committee, "does not have the capacity to keep eight hundred thousand soldiers under arms. They would go hungry and naked."[5] Nevertheless, the arguments of the military leadership won the day. Overruling any political or economic concerns, the need for military prepared-ness once again proved to be the most crucial factor in Ottoman decision-making. From their disastrously chaotic Balkan War experience, the military planners knew well that the Ottoman army would require substantial time to mobilize. The last time the army had gone to war—with its Balkan enemies—the mobilization order had been issued only two weeks earlier. As a result, the Ottoman forces were caught woefully undermanned and underprepared. The Unionists were determined not to make that mistake again.

The imperial army was far from ready to go to war in August 1914, even though it had taken some substantial steps towards recovery. Ambitious and comprehensive military reforms had not yet borne all of the anticipated fruits. For instance, the British director of military operations, Colonel Henry Wilson, who had visited the Çatalca lines and other battlefields in October 1913, noted in his diary that, "the Turkish army is *not* a serious modern army" and that it was "ill commanded, ill officered & in rags." The country, he observed, was poorly developed, with "[n]o roads, only single railways & very few of them, & in fact no sign of adaptation to Western thought & methods." He concluded bleakly: "I cannot think Turkey in Europe will survive another shaking."[6] Wil-son was not alone in his unfavorable assessments. Enver Pasha himself was painfully aware of the army's situation and the challenges an untimely conflict could pose for it. In March 1914, he explained to the cabinet that he would need at least five years of peace to prepare the army for a major war.[7] The mili-tary leadership's concerns about material and organizational problems were compounded by widespread skepticism about the fighting capacity of the aver-age Ottoman soldier. By mobilizing at the earliest possible moment and con-scripting an unprecedentedly high number of citizens, the military planners wanted to train a significant portion of the empire's men, acquaint them with military discipline, and give them more time to adjust to military life.

In addition to military concerns, two more factors influenced the Union-ists' decision to order an early and comprehensive mobilization. The first was the lack of regular and reliable population records and military rolls: it was uncertain how many people would respond to the general call-up, and whether that number would suffice to meet the army's wartime needs.[8] In the face of this uncertainty and immeasurable risk, calling up as many potential recruits as possible must have seemed to the high command to be the safest way to ensuring a sizable fighting force. Arguably, however, the more important consideration undergirding the Unionists' decision was the perilous state of the empire's finances. The amount of money that could be collected through exemption fees would partially mitigate the situation and help to meet the cost of mobilization. The government hoped to maximize this amount by calling up each and every male citizen who was liable for military service, including those whom the army high command deemed militarily "worthless."

"Oceans of Sorrow": Reactions to the Mobilization

The government announced the mobilization through newspapers, town criers, church bells, and colored posters. Local officials had placed these posters on the walls of government buildings, mosques, coffeehouses, and schools, and also sent them to village headmen for posting.[9] Criers and drummers everywhere called on all eligible men to present themselves at the nearest enlistment office within five days. Even in the provinces, where this method of public announcement had hitherto been unknown, it was used in this mobilization in hope of whipping up public enthusiasm.[10] On the contrary, however, the sound of the drums came to instill fear and anxiety as the harsh reality of impending war gradually set in. Yervant Odian was among those who recalled this prevailing feeling of trepidation: "Those drummers had become the bane of the lives of all the men of military age, and for their parents too. At all hours of the day, even at night, the ominous sound of the drums could suddenly be heard. Everyone, trembling with fear, would rush to the windows to listen."[11]

The scope of conscription was dramatically extended in August 1914 in comparison with the First Balkan War. By the time the mobilization was ordered, about 200,000 Ottoman soldiers (those born in 1891–93) were already in uniform.[12] In the countryside, the mobilization called up all Muslim males between the ages of twenty and forty-five, and all non-Muslim males between twenty and thirty-one. In Istanbul, the first mobilization order covered Muslim and non-Muslim males between the ages of twenty and thirty-one.[13] Yet a law issued immediately after the mobilization specifically stated that the inhabitants of the capital city and all non-Muslims between the ages of thirty-two and forty-five were also liable to serve.[14] Like everyone else, they were obliged to register at the enlistment offices. By late October 1914, when the government finally decided to declare war, the Ottoman state had managed to put a total of more than 800,000 men under arms, including soldiers employed in logistics, fortress garrisons, and coastal defenses.[15] In the words of the head of an enlistment office in a small Anatolian town, "except for the invalids and the elderly, no one remained outside the reach of conscription."[16] Perhaps not in that Anatolian town, but the initial recruitment even included some invalids in other places. "[M]any physical wrecks are now lying in the camps out of the city," a foreign resident of Istanbul noted, and a resident of Jerusalem similarly observed that "the invalid, deformed, and healthy are huddled together in squalid tents."[17]

From the very beginning, the Unionists were acutely aware of the difficulties that another mobilization would impose on society. The government thus faced the onerous task of justifying its decision to the Ottoman people. The Unionist press explained that the mobilization was a necessity required by circumstances entirely beyond the control of the CUP government. In the face of the deepening crisis in Europe, the Porte had to anticipate that the war might expand onto the empire's territory. "We all know what a huge burden it is for a country that emerged from a costly war less than a year ago to have to mobilize once again," *Tanin* said, lamenting "this heavy yet inevitable" necessity.[18] In these first days of the mobilization, the press underlined that the Porte's overriding objective was to maintain its neutrality at all costs. The government would strive not to get too entangled in European affairs, but military preparedness was needed to preserve the peace and that called for sacrifices by all Ottoman citizens.[19]

The rhetoric of potential threats posed by a distant war, however, could hardly arouse public enthusiasm for yet another cumbersome mobilization. For most people, military preparedness was a mere abstraction. They saw the mobilization, not as a necessary military precaution in the face of a looming conflict, but as a bitter reminder of the debacle of the First Balkan War. Many of them had a firm grasp of the realities of warfare and were in any case highly suspicious of the Ottoman army's war-making capacity. Thus, when the mobilization order was issued in early August, fear and anxiety, rather than enthusiasm and exuberance, were the predominant reactions throughout the empire.

In fact, the memories of the Balkan War mobilization were still so vivid that the government and the press felt compelled to underline the differences between the current mobilization and the preceding one. While disorder and chaos had characterized the mobilization for the First Balkan War, efficiency, speed, and order were the hallmarks of the current one. "The recent mobilization is taking place in a completely different way than all other previous mobilizations," *Tanin* wrote. "Everyone's place to report was specified in advance, everyone who was called up knew where to apply."[20] To counter the widespread sense of anxiety, the press also tried to create the image that people were responding to the call-up enthusiastically and were aware of the seriousness of their responsibility. Newspapers and journals published pictures of young men gathered around mobilization posters or leaving their hometowns and flocking cheerfully and confidently to the colors.[21] The Balkan War disasters, *İkdam* argued, had been caused by indolence and indifference to the defense of the fatherland. But the lesson has been learned, and this time mobilization was being met with "genuine delight and gratification."[22]

On the ground, however, the picture was very different. The mobilization was "characterized by a complete absence of enthusiasm, and differs in a marked degree from that which preceded the later war," a contemporary observer stated.[23] New conscripts had many reason to be concerned about the lot of their families in their absence, the soaring cost of living, shortages, the fate of their harvests, and the likelihood of their not being allowed to go back to their fields and reap their crops, which were already rotting. An aversion to military service and the gloomy memories of the recent disaster only deepened their concerns. "Can you realize what this means to the families dependent on the men?" asked an observer of mass mobilization in Adana province. "This is the most important time of the year, when the winter food stores are prepared, and next month the cotton-picking season starts, when great numbers take up this work to gain money for their rents and for the winter."[24] For hundreds of thousands of men like the Adana conscripts, the mobilization not only interfered with the long-established rhythm of agrarian life, but also prevented them from fulfilling their duties to their families.

Farewell ceremonies were therefore usually heart-rending scenes. Both the recruits and the people seeing them off knew there was little chance of their ever returning if war broke out. A soldier preparing to leave his relatives and his hometown described the prevailing mood in his diary: "The mountains are crying, the stones are crying, in short, the world is crying."[25] An Armenian observer in Şebinkarahisar wrote in similar vein:

The Turks of Karahissar who had been mobilized were also going. Their moments of parting were even sadder and more picturesque. Even drums and fifes were not enough to encourage the ranks of the departing. They were poorer than Armenians. Barely covering their nakedness under rags, they shouldered their military knapsacks, and said goodbye to their families at the limits of the city. Each Turk left behind one or more pallid wives from the harem who cried beneath their veils: *Allahaismarladim*, I have given you to Allah's keeping. *Ugurlar olsun*, may the best happen. My God, what oceans of sorrow.[26]

From time to time, anger and frustration also poured out at these farewell ceremonies. In Malatya, for instance, reacting to people shouting, "Long live the sultan!" (Padişahım çok yaşa!), an old woman said angrily: "Down with the Sultan! Those who left [for the front] never returned. He wiped out our people."[27] To avoid such disturbances and tragic scenes, some convoys of conscripts left at night, when martial law kept people indoors.[28]

In addition to the expanded scope of the age of recruitment, what made the mobilization for World War I exceptionally onerous were recent changes to policies regarding military service. Through the new Law of Military Obligation—enacted provisionally in May 1914, only a couple of months before the announcement of the mobilization—the Unionists had severely curtailed some exemptions from service and abolished some others entirely, such as the one granted to the sole breadwinners of their families. All these previously exempted groups were now required to fulfill their military obligations like all other conscripts, affecting tens of thousands of young men and their relatives. For many who had historically enjoyed the privilege of exemption, it was a shocking experience to find out that they were also being called up when the mobilization was ordered. And the fact that so many men from such a large age bracket were being called up simultaneously must have compounded this sense of distress.

Folkloric accounts vividly reflected this despondent mood. A folk song summarized the mobilization process with heart-rending simplicity:

Seferberlik oldu gelin dediler	"The mobilization is under way, join!" they said.
Üç günlük erzağın' alın dediler	"Bring three days of food!" they said.
Gidin Erzurum'da ölün dediler.	"Go to Erzurum and die there!" they said.[29]

Others used the metaphor of "spreading fire" to describe the mobilization. Instead of "joy," "feast," or "festival," they frequently preferred metaphors like "fire," "doomsday," or "flood" to describe the mass departure of young men for the army:

Gizli gelen tezkereyi açtılar.	They opened the secret memorandum.
Onbeşli'den kırkbeşli'ye seçtiler.	They picked [men] between 15 and 45.
Alemin üstüne ataş saçtılar.	They set the whole world ablaze.
Ne karalı günlere kaldık bu sene.	What horrible days we have endured this year.[30]

Such feelings were rarely recorded in postwar histories, yet they speak to the earth-shattering impact that the mobilization had on Ottoman society from early on.

Despite the evident lack of enthusiasm on the ground, the high turnout of draftees that the press emphatically described in the early days of mobilization was indeed a reality. Newspapers and official declarations attributed this interest to citizens' eagerness to join the ranks and to serve in the army to protect the empire against its enemies.[31] They failed to mention a draconian amendment to the Military Penal Law that might have been the prime mover behind the rush to the enlistment offices, which mandated severe punishments of those who did not enlist or who deserted. Under the new law, men who did not show up at recruitment centers within ten days of having received the draft order without a valid excuse would be liable to capital punishment. Those who deserted and failed to return within seven days would also be sentenced to death. In addition, the law sentenced to prison anyone who facilitated such crimes or was negligent or lenient in the application of these new provisions.[32] The empire had "secured such a large enlistment," Enver Pasha told U.S. Ambassador Henry Morgenthau, "because he makes a refusal to enlist a crime punished with death."[33]

People throughout the empire typically heard about the order of mobilization concurrently with the threat of execution for refusal to comply. The army's high command asked the army corps to expend every effort in announcing the provisions of this new amendment so as to expedite the mobilization process and to achieve the highest possible rate of participation.[34] Official proclamations and town criers who summoned people to recruitment offices to enlist announced that noncompliance would be severely punished.[35] "Those who do not come to the barracks within forty-eight hours and do not establish their presence . . . will be subject to investigation and their relatives punished instead of them," an official statement in *al-Ittihad al-Uthmani* read. "If they flee, they will be executed immediately upon arrest. As for those who report within the appointed time, they will be excused."[36] To make credible the threat, the governor of Baghdad proclaimed: "Those who deserted or did not obey the invitation to join the army . . . were, without loss of time, executed in Constantinople."[37]

Due mostly to this threat, the mobilization order brought unexpectedly high turnouts. Except for a few regions where the Ottoman state's authority was relatively weak, people throughout the empire rushed to the enlistment offices to register. The initial outpouring of men, however, exceeded the army's capability to enlist and organize them. As a result, confusion and disarray ensued. The sight of thousands of recruits flocking to town centers and recruiting stations, sometimes along with their wives, children, and fathers, astonished contemporary Ottoman observers, who write of the "stream of people,"[38] liken the recruiting stations to "disorderly marketplaces,"[39] and call the resulting situation "judgment day."[40] Muhammad Izzat Darwaza, a postal official in Nablus, described the first days of the mobilization as "an apocalypse, which appeared in the form of thousands of people from towns and villages all around the empire registering their names and receiving their documents in the enlistment offices within the space of a week."[41] The rosy picture of an orderly and efficient mobilization painted in the press hardly aligned with the realities on the ground.

The recruits' suffering, which for many of them would continue for four long years, began even before they officially became soldiers. Calling up all classes at once, the military authorities had not taken into consideration the enormous demands of sheltering and provisioning hundreds of thousands of men. Although they were ordered to take five days' worth of their own food with them,[42] in many places recruits had to wait much longer, sometimes weeks, to be enlisted. As all available inns, hotels, and other facilities in towns were already overflowing with recruits, those remaining had to stay wherever they could while waiting their turn to enroll and be assigned to their respective units. This lack of organization produced disheartening scenes of soldiers sleeping in the streets and mosque yards and seeking help from civilians.[43] Kazım Karabekir, then a major and head of the Bureau of Intelligence at the army's headquarters, recounts his mother's execration (*beddua*) of the authorities who had caused this suffering when she witnessed the lamentable condition of recruits sleeping in the yard of the Fatih Mosque.[44] These scenes must have deepened the suspicions already harbored among both recruits and the home front population that the Ottoman state was not ready for another conflict.

The authorities tried to curb this chaotic situation by imposing order by force. In districts where the number of enlisted recruits remained below the army's expectations or where the records of potential recruits in the enlistment offices were missing or incomplete, patrols went from house to house searching for men of draft age. On the streets and in public places, they asked for the necessary documentation proving exemption, the absence of which usually meant immediate detention and drafting.[45] In the words of a Jew from Baghdad, "the Turkish gendarmerie hunted us like wild animals and when we were caught they sent us to the *qishle* [barracks] and treated us like prisoners of war."[46] As a result of these harsh measures, the prevailing wave of fear and anxiety among conscripts and their families reached unprecedented heights. This fear and distress in turn led many eligible men to look for ways to avoid military service, to flee to areas where they thought they would be more secure,[47] or to emigrate abroad.[48]

Exemption from Military Service for the Well-Off

Among all the different ways of avoiding military service, payment of an exemption fee (*bedel-i nakdi*) proved to be the most common, at least for those who could afford to pay it. From the early days of the 1908 Revolution, the exemption fee had occupied the Unionists' agenda. The last political program of the CUP categorically opposed the practice of purchasing exemption and promised to abrogate it in favor of a new law that would require all male citizens to perform military service.[49] Accepted at the party's annual congress of 1913, this stance clearly reflected the impact of the First Balkan War on the Unionists. Despite this determination, however, the large sum collected each year from exemption payments prevented the Unionists from rescinding this long-established practice.[50] Nevertheless, the new Law of Military Obligation of 1914 limited the application of the practice to peacetime and made clear that the state would not accept exemption fees after the mobilization began.[51]

Much to the chagrin of military authorities, however, the dismal financial situation of the empire and the pressing needs of an impending war obliged the government to shelve this new policy in August 1914. Upon the proclamation of the mobilization, the government declared that it would accept exemption fees from citizens in lieu of military service. The exemption fee was set at thirty Ottoman gold lira. Combining this with the war tax and local taxes, it would reach forty-three lira. This amount had to be paid in a week following the promulgation of the law.[52] The state granted a limited, older class of non-Muslims (active reserves, *ihtiyats*) the right to purchase exemption first.[53] It was soon extended to the territorial reserves (*müstahfız*) of non-Muslims and finally to untrained (*gayri muallem*) Muslims who fell into either one of these two classes.[54]

From the very beginning, the military intended to accept exemption fees only from individuals and groups whom it deemed "less useful" for military purposes, most notably the Ottoman non-Muslims. As discussed in the previous chapter, the Balkan War experiences had convinced the military planners of the value of religious homogeneity in the army. Despite occasional statements otherwise, they harbored no illusions about a multi-faith army's potential for victory. The army's high command, as finance minister Cavid Bey's diary entries suggest, must have seriously contemplated limiting the option of paying the exemption fee only to non-Muslims. This was Henry Morgenthau's impression as well. When the ambassador asked Enver Pasha to make an exception for an embassy translator, he politely refused, saying, "Christians could buy themselves off, but not Moslems." "They want an entire[ly] Moslem army," Morgenthau wrote in his diary: "They think Christians caused their last defeat. They are getting more people than they want, and needing the money, as he said, they are glad to release Christians."[55] In several provinces, local administrators or army commanders explicitly told the Christians to pay the exemption fee rather than enlist. In Damascus, for instance, the governor publicly stated that "in case of Christians, the forty-three lira would be preferred, since money was needed." Upon the governor's statement, local Christians of all denominations held a meeting, discussed the issue, and voted not to pay the exemption fee but to serve. According to the U.S. consular agent, they did so out of the belief that "ultimately the Christian soldiers would not be actually taken because of their lack of patriotism and the expense of maintaining them."[56]

The army was reluctant to let Muslims benefit from the same law. Even when the high command eventually consented to allow Muslims to purchase exemption, it tried to keep the number of potential beneficiaries as low as possible by specifying a very short period for the payment of the fee and excluding individuals who had received three or more months of military training. By granting the right to Muslims from the very beginning, setting a longer period for payment, and, finally, excluding men who had received military training of six months or more (instead of three), Cavid Bey argued, the state could have gained five to six hundred thousand lira more from *bedel* payments. He criticized the military for continually asking for more money, while drying up all sources of revenue.[57]

Even though it was not expanded to everyone, the option to pay the exemption fee aroused a great deal of excitement among Ottoman citizens. In a letter to a friend, Rev. Henry Riggs, an American missionary in Harput, recounted the collective mood as follows: "There is, as I said, absolutely no enthusiasm over the war, so far as I have seen or heard. The only sign of enthusiasm is the enthusiasm to pay 'bedel' (military exemption tax), which has risen to white heat of late. It was announced that 'bedel' would be accepted only up to last evening, and the scramble to pay it would be ludicrous if it were not so pitiful."[58] As the fee constituted a significant amount of money, however, purchasing exemption from military service was not a realistic option for most. By the eve of the war, an estimate by the Istanbul Chamber of Commerce placed the monthly budget for a family of middle standing (*orta halli*) at 945 kuruş, or 8.75 lira.[59] The hefty sum required to pay the *bedel* then was almost equal to five months' household expenses for such a family. The situation was further aggravated as banks throughout the empire froze their lending activities and did not allow their customers to withdraw money. Even for the affluent segments of society, coming up with forty-three lira on such short notice was no easy feat. Emin Bey, a local notable and son of a landowner in Eskişehir in northwestern Anatolia, for instance, recorded in his diary that he had just barely put together the necessary amount by selling *beşibirlik*s (five-lira gold pieces kept for use as jewelry) that he had at home.[60] The desire to purchase the exemption put many who, unlike Emin Bey, did not have gold on hand at the mercy of usurers, leading many families to financial ruin.[61] The magnitude of the fee and the short deadline given for payment obliged many others to sell their wares and personal belongings, such as rugs, jewelry, and household items, at well below market prices to gather the necessary amount. A contemporary observer in Mardin described the extraordinary situation vividly: "The gold from the heads, and necks and wrists, is taken to the market and peddled like old iron, and no one will buy, doing anything and everything to raise money to pay exemption fees."[62] This unexpected flow of goods to the market lowered the prices of almost everything in the first days of the mobilization, although only fleetingly. In Syria, olive oil merchants were reported to be willing to sell their oil at any price, "provided the purchaser pays in cash." "Cash, however, is rare," the reporter continued, "the small amount of cash now on hand is reserved to be paid for exemptions from military service."[63] In other parts of the empire, the price of a bushel of wheat (about 36.5 kilograms) dropped as low as ten piasters, and barley to five or six piasters. One could buy a cow for one or two lira.[64]

Many, of course, could not even imagine paying such an amount under any circumstances. The exemption fee fueled resentment among the urban and rural poor, who could not afford to buy their way out of military service. The practice of *bedel* also contradicted the government's overarching discourse of "unity and equality in defense of the fatherland," crippling its rhetoric of equal distribution of sacrifice. Such complaints seeped even into official military records: "the rich were exempted from military service, as if it were a disastrous condition reserved for the poor," the Thirtieth Division's logbook noted. "Although a little financial benefit was achieved through the *bedel*, there is no doubt that the damage it did to morale was huge."[65] For many, such as the officers who kept these records, the Ottoman conscription system had an evident class bias.

Although official rhetoric deliberately refrained from mentioning the *bedel*, soldiers and their relatives seem to have been keenly aware of the inegalitarian nature of conscription embodied in the exemption fee, and they refused to remain silent on the issue, which became a recurrent theme in folkloric accounts:

Yolları var takırdan.	His roads are rough.
Karavanası bakırdan.	His mess kit is made of copper.
Zengin olan bedel verir.	The rich man buys exemption.
Hep ölen böyle fakirden.[66]	The poor man faces death.

None of these are perhaps more touching than a mother's lament that she could not do enough to free her son from the conscription net. She berates herself for not having had enough money to buy him out of military service:

Öyle deme kızım hatun.	Don't say that, my dear daughter.
Oğlum öldü kaldım yetim.	My son died, and I was left all alone.
Böyle olacağın' bilsem	If I had known this would happen
Alırdım oğlumu satın.[67]	I would have bought him out.

From the very outset of the war, then, the *bedel* inhibited the formation of a collective sense of sacrifice, serving as a constant reminder of the unequal distribution of the war's burden.

The Mobilization's Impact on Civilian Life

As the process of mobilization turned hundreds of thousands of Ottoman civilians into soldiers, it also affected the lives of the millions who depended on them. In the ten days between 1 and 10 August 1914, as an American missionary in Syria observed, the whole country was completely transformed: "There were no young men to be seen in the streets, shops were closed, business was paralyzed, and the anxious countenances of women and children already bespoke fear and anxiety as to where they should find their next meal."[68] The famous Orientalist Alois Musil noted similar negative effects in Baghdad: "The streets of the inner town, through which it was hard to move in 1912, gaped emptily. The shops were mostly closed, the coffeehouses only half filled, and the countrywomen who sold food in normal times were absent. . . . There was no longer any life in the town, formerly one of the busiest in the Orient."[69] The sheer scope of the call, uncertainties about the process itself, and, above all, the aggressive stance of the authorities led to a panic that swept across the empire's urban centers, ripping apart the routines of everyday life. Commercial activity dwindled, municipal services were hampered, and the first shortages occurred. The whole country, indeed, was completely transformed.

What accentuated the already deep sense of despair was financial chaos and distress. The panic in financial markets began when an alarmed public rushed to the banks to withdraw their savings and convert their paper currency into gold as soon as the news about the outbreak of the war in Europe reached major Ottoman cities. The unexpected run forced many banks to close their doors and suspend business for lack of capital on hand. A contemporary witness described the consternation in Istanbul as follows: "On the Monday morning an interesting spectacle could be seen on Pera's straight street. All the banks had shut their doors. The people, both men and women, crowded around the doors, shouted and demanded their money. Agitation, panic, and desperation were everywhere."[70] The gravity of the situation compelled the Porte to decree a moratorium on August 3rd, a measure that was not taken during the Balkan Wars.[71] The moratorium relieved the credit institutions from their obligations towards customers, allowing them to refuse requests for the reimbursement of deposits. However, its overall impact on the economy and society was quite damaging. The moratorium deepened the prevailing sense of uncertainty and led to an extreme shortfall of money in the market, bringing all economic activity to a standstill. Merchants, businessmen, and producers were hit hard by the shortages of credit. Big farmers could not hire labor they needed for the harvest.[72] Even the wealthiest families found themselves with very little cash on hand, which they desperately needed for an uncertain future and, more urgently, to pay the exemption fee for their sons.

Along with the economic recession, the rhythm of everyday life was disturbed by the lack of reliable information about current developments. Following the mobilization order, the CUP government took increasingly drastic steps to control the production and spread of information throughout the empire. Before the first week of the mobilization had ended, the government imposed strict censorship on the press—ostensibly to preserve military secrets. Newspapers were warned not to publish "even a single letter" on military movements, measures, or appointments.[73] In reality, however, the scope of the censorship was much broader. In addition to news about the army and the navy, the Unionists censored news regarding internal and foreign politics, the financial and commercial situation, sanitary conditions, and all other news that might excite people, even including the news about train and steamer accidents and fires.[74] The government also reserved the right to suspend or shut down any newspaper or journal that did not conform to the censorship regulations. The dailies were required to send examination copies to the censorship bureaus and were allowed to print only after the censors approved those copies.[75] News that might affect morale on the home front negatively concerned the government the most. The army headquarters declared that a specific bureau would provide daily updates about military affairs. Those who published or made statements concerning military issues outside of official statements would be arrested and sent to court-martial to be punished in the severest way possible.[76] Censorship of the press proved particularly effective in suppressing controversial news and opinions and, later in the war, in obscuring the losses suffered by the Ottoman forces and generally downplaying its horrors. The censorship regulations also attempted to control the flow of information within the empire. As long as the mobilization remained in effect, letters and telegrams were required to be sent unsealed and to be written in only Turkish, Arabic, French, or German.[77] The use of all other languages was strictly prohibited.

In addition to censorship, two other factors contributed to the tightness of information on the Ottoman home front. First, the outbreak of the war in Europe had severely hampered steamship lines, which were vital connections between the empire and the rest of the world. Communication with the Entente countries in particular was delayed and occasionally interrupted. Even in the early days of the mobilization, the Istanbul correspondent of *The Near East* likened the situation to living in a "besieged city."[78] Nevertheless, this early isolation was partial. The Dardanelles and Bosporus straits remained open to merchant shipping for two more months, despite intense military activity. In late September, however, as a result of the battleships crisis (a subject discussed below in more detail) the Ottoman navy and its German allies mined the Dardanelles, effectively closing it for military and civilian traffic until the end of the war.[79]

The Ottoman Empire's entry into the war shortly afterwards exacerbated the situation even further. The presence of the Entente navies in the Aegean Sea and the blockade of the eastern Mediterranean coast brought the heavy traffic through Ottoman port cities to a standstill. The blockade meant more than the cessation of imports and exports. These thriving socioeconomic centers of the empire were virtually cut off from the rest of the world. It meant the dramatic reversal of a trend that had prevailed over the past several decades, when numerous companies had established regular and frequent steamship services, international trade had flourished, and the empire's port cities had become intensely connected to Europe and beyond.[80] This process had brought prosperity and wealth to certain sections of these cities' populations. Especially for those who had benefitted from this trend, the war and the subsequent isolation of the empire from the rest of the world came as a devastating shock.

The second factor that curtailed the flow of information as well as other deliveries, such as cash remittances,[81] into the empire was the closure of foreign post offices, which had previously been operating under the protection of the capitulations (see pp. 74–77 below). Foreign post offices not only provided fast, efficient, and uncensored communication with European cities without the gaze of the Ottoman authorities. For the reading public, they were also major suppliers of foreign newspapers and journals. The abolition of the capitulations and the subsequent closure of foreign post offices therefore stripped this small yet influential group of people of their alternative sources of information. It is difficult to gauge the effectiveness of all these measures on the Ottoman people's access to news. But if the words of the Spanish consul in Jerusalem are any indication, they succeeded in keeping them in the dark: "What one truly has to admire is the success of the Turkish censorship, since no one, absolutely no one, knows a word about what is going on in the Dardanelles and in Europe. With no communications with our governments, we have to content ourselves with the news the Turks and Germans give us, and God knows if it's true."[82]

The Unionist leadership sought to keep a tight rein on the day-to-day flow of information about the war to the provinces.[83] Widely disseminated bulletins produced by the official news agency (Osmanlı Milli Telgraf Ajansı) were used for the purpose of informing town-dwellers of recent developments on the fronts. These bulletins, which included briefs about political, social, and cultural developments, as well as highly exaggerated news about the military victories of the Ottoman forces and their allies, were prepared by the army headquarters, sent to local state officials, printed locally, and sold cheaply. A typical bulletin read like this:

> Because of gifts from the German and Austrian emperors, The Red Crescent Society has decided to show its gratitude by presenting its gold medals to them. In Constantinople, a society of women, which has been formed to help the families of soldiers, has begun its work. The latest German reports give particulars of German successes in France. The French have been pushed north of the Aisne River, which is considered of great military importance. Even the French newspapers cannot hide the importance of this fact. During the 4 weeks since the French began their attacks in the offensive, they have had no success. In this period they have lost 150,000 men. The French public opinion is already discouraged. It is thought that the French can hold out only 3 months longer. On Turkish coins, instead of stamping "Minted in Constantinople," they will hereafter stamp "Minted in the capital of the Caliphate.[84]

The news bulletins were sold locally by street peddlers. Fevzi Güvemli, who was eleven years old when the war broke out, could not forget the peddler who sold these bulletins, which included news about the "terrific victories of the Germans." They cost ten *para*s each and were sold with wild enthusiasm.[85] The bulletins were also affixed to the walls and windows of governmental buildings, coffeehouses, and the local CUP clubs, and might as well have been read aloud at mosques, marketplaces, and squares. In the remote corners of the empire, these bulletins, along with the news telegrams published by the German Wolff Agency, were the only available source of information about the war, at least for the reading and listening public.[86] It is naturally difficult to assess their impact. People must have followed them with interest to quench their thirst for news about the war, especially during the early months of the conflict. They were at least influential enough to attract criticism from the Entente's representatives. In the words of the British vice-consul in Diyarbekir, "Every effort is made by the Committee here to keep the population in ignorance as to the real state of things. In the twice daily published 'Agence Ottomane,' Entente successes are never mentioned, while German or Austrian successes are not only exaggerated, but, I believe, even invented."[87] Although the impact of the bulletins gradually declined over the course of the war, they must have played an important role in shaping local public opinion during its initial phases.

The mobilization's immediate impacts were more visible in cities, but these were far from exclusively urban phenomena. The impacts on the countryside were equally damaging. The major problem there resulting from the mobilization was the removal of a considerable portion of the labor force from agricultural production during the high season. In many provinces, the mobilization interrupted the harvest, the most labor-intensive part of the growing process. The government's call and accompanying threat of capital punishment obliged hundreds of thousands of agricultural producers to abandon their crops and rush to town centers.[88] "All able-bodied men," wrote an observer of mobilization in the province of Aydın, "have been taken just at the time when they were most needed for the crops, for drying of the sultana grapes, and for the working of the figs."[89] Clarence Douglas Ussher, an American physician and missionary stationed in Van, vividly described the exodus of men and the abrupt cessation of farmwork in the early days of the mobilization: "Sickles lying in half-cut fields of grain, sheaves of wheat dropped on the way to the stack, and a little later weeping women with bags of bread or clothing on their backs running to overtake their men, who had been taken from the fields without time allowed them to secure necessary provisions from their homes or to say good-bye to their families. Conscription—for a war not yet declared."[90] The observations of Dr. Daniel Thom, a longtime missionary in Mardin, similarly indicate the most deplorable effects of the mobilization on agriculture:

> The government has robbed the city, and the country around, of its men, of its animals, of its money, leaving the threshing floors loaded down with a richer harvest than has ever been laid upon [them], to rot where they [the crops] are, for lack of men and beasts to tread them out and care for them. The millions that will be lost to the people and the Government cannot be estimated. Such a suicidal conduct of a government I have not seen, during this variegated life I have lived.[91]

The situation was more or less similar throughout the empire. The withdrawal of men from the countryside coupled with the requisitioning of a large number of draught animals practically brought agricultural work to a standstill. The crops, as a result, could not be reaped and a significant portion of the harvest was wasted. Sowing for the new season could only be carried out with difficulty. This turned out to be a gross and critical mistake on the part of the Unionist government, as the crop yield in 1914 was exceptionally good and might have to some extent compensated peasants for the losses occasioned in 1913 due to the Balkan Wars.[92] The army tried to correct its mistake by releasing older recruits and holding the commanders and officers of the enlistment offices responsible for organizing the harvesting of the fields belonging to the conscripts. Army headquarters ordered military units to give furloughs to 5 to 10 percent of soldiers so that they could help with the unfinished farmwork. These soldiers were usually sent to nearby regions within a day's walking distance.[93] The army corps were also allowed to bring in the harvest in their regions using draught animals and transport vehicles confiscated for military purposes.[94] Despite these measures, however, harvests throughout the empire were not completed, resulting in significant crop loss.

"Our Ships That We Could Never Forget:" British Confiscation of Ottoman Battleships

Amid the chaos of mobilization, an unexpected bit of news dropped like a bombshell onto Ottoman public opinion. Two battleships, purchased by the Porte and impatiently awaited by the Ottomans, would not be delivered as planned. Instead, they would be integrated into the British Royal Navy and retained by Britain for the period of the war. When the British decision was announced, Captain Rauf Bey and a contingent of Ottoman sailors had already arrived at the Armstrong shipyard at Newcastle upon Tyne to accept the delivery of one of the dreadnoughts, *Sultan Osman-ı Evvel*. They were forced to return to Istanbul with empty hands. In his telegram to Enver Pasha, Winston Churchill, the First Sea Lord of Admiralty, explained the act as one of military contingency: "I deeply regretted [the] necessity for detaining Turkish ships because I knew the patriotism with which the money had been raised all over Turkey. As a soldier you know what military necessity compels in war."[95] He promised to deliver the ships to the Ottoman Empire at the end of the war and pay compensation for the delay. Offended and humiliated, the Porte summarily rejected Churchill's proposal and denounced the British decision as constituting an arbitrary violation of the international law and protested energetically against it, but to no avail.

The two battleships had been purchased as part of the aggressive naval program the Unionists had pursued since the end of the Balkan Wars. The program aimed primarily to offset Greek naval power in the Aegean and to maintain naval superiority against the Russians in the Black Sea. With these goals in mind, in early 1914, the Ottoman government purchased a dreadnought, *Rio de Janeiro* (later renamed *Sultan Osman-ı Evvel*), which had originally been intended for Brazil and was nearing completion. It had earlier contracted for the construction of a dreadnought named *Reşadiye* by the British company Vickers in 1911.[96] The *Reşadiye* was scheduled for delivery in August 1914. Despite the weaknesses of imperial finances, the government also finalized its negotiations with the Armstrong-Vickers Group on the reorganization of naval dockyards and arsenals and the construction of a large floating dock in İzmit as part of the military rejuvenation efforts after the Balkan Wars. In April 1914, the Ottoman Ministry of Marine ordered an additional dreadnought (*Fatih Sultan Mehmed*, to be completed in 1916), two light cruisers, four destroyers, and two submarines from British shipyards. Six destroyers and two submarines were likewise ordered from the French Normand and Schneider shipyards.[97] Although the Greeks countered by ordering several battleships, with these new acquisitions the Ottoman navy seemed to be on the way to outpacing its rival in the Aegean and altering the power dynamic in the Black Sea. The seizure of the ships thus frustrated Ottoman plans for naval superiority.

Perhaps more significant, the seizure also deeply affected the public mood throughout the empire. Intense propaganda by the government and patriotic civil society organizations, most notably the Ottoman Navy League, had firmly convinced the public that the purchase of these two battleships meant the reversal of the long-standing trend of the empire's erosion of influence.[98] The British seizure dashed these hopes. What added to the Ottomans' frustration was the fact that a significant portion of the ships' cost, as Churchill mentioned in his letter, had been raised through public contributions. The massive scope of the campaign, the patriotic energy it had generated, and the popularity it had achieved were unparalleled in Ottoman history. These unique features of the campaign caused the empire's humiliation and despair to be felt at a much more personal level. For many, Great Britain had not only violated international law and wounded imperial honor, but had also stolen the small contributions they had made towards the purchase.

"No step could have exasperated the Turks more than [the internment of the ships]," the British military attaché to Istanbul recalled years later.[99] Exasperate them it did. The announcement of the retention caused an outburst of indignation in Ottoman urban centers and the countryside, giving birth to widespread anti-British sentiment throughout the empire. People from around the empire sent angry letters to the British embassy.[100] An Ottoman piaster (*kuruş*) was attached to one of them by a poor man, "in case the British should be so impoverished that they could do nothing better than steal ships bought with hard earned Turkish money."[101] In the third week of August, the British ambassador to the Porte wrote about "sentiments of violent hostility towards England which now pervade all classes."[102] The news spread like wildfire to Ottoman towns through the channels of the state bureaucracy, the press, local CUP branches, and civil society organizations. In Diyarbekir, the British vice-consul observed that, "indignation is intense among local Moslems against the reported British seizure of Ottoman war vessels building in Great Britain."[103] In Jaffa, there was "a great anti-British feeling among the Moslem population and sympathy is altogether German."[104] *The Near East*'s Izmir correspondent observed of the outpouring of patriotic sentiment in early September 1914: "At no time during the Italian or Balkan Wars has the anti-foreign feeling prevailing amongst the Turks been so pronounced as at present. This feeling has been caused primarily by the seizure of the Turkish Dreadnoughts."[105]

The seizure of the dreadnoughts provided a rare opportunity to the pro-war party among the Unionists to energize an entirely unenthusiastic and deeply worried population. They used the incident as a rallying point to win over the demoralized public and to justify the need for military preparedness.[106] Moreover, it contributed greatly to the Unionists' shaping of the broader contours of the Ottoman war narrative. From the very beginning, the Ottoman official wartime rhetoric persistently insisted that the Ottoman Empire was the victim of its enemies' unilateral aggression. The empire was being provoked, the Unionist-dominated press argued, by a series of events orchestrated by the Entente powers, which eventually compelled it to enter the war despite its strong intention to maintain strict neutrality and its desire to live in peace: doing so was a legitimate act of self-defense, rooted solely in the desire to protect the empire's boundaries and honor.[107] For the Unionists, this rhetoric of victimization was essential in convincing people of the worthiness of the Ottoman cause and encouraging them to support the government's war effort only months after the disastrous defeat in the Balkans.

The Ottoman narrative of victimization had two sides to it: it held the empire's enemies solely responsible for the looming catastrophe, and it convincingly cited incidents of the recent past to portray current developments as part of a historical continuum of victimization. European machinations had long sought to prevent the Ottoman Empire from acquiring military superiority. The heinous British seizure of the battleships reconfirmed Europeans' longstanding anti-Ottoman stance, which had been evident many times over the past two years.

The battleships crisis also gave the Unionists a unique opportunity to argue that the interests of the Ottoman Empire overlapped with those of all Muslims. They portrayed the seizure of the ships as an insult to the entire Muslim world. According to the press, Muslims living in various parts of the world genuinely shared the pain of it. "Seizing and hijacking these ships dashes the hopes of the Ottoman nation and the Muslim *umma*," *Sabah* declared.[108] "A thousand curses," Yunus Nadi invoked in an editorial for *Tasfir-i Efkar*: "The blow that the English struck first at the Ottomans and secondly at the entire Muslim world will generate great currents, like the great currents of the oceans. And no Englishman shall doubt that one day these currents will drown the Englishmen on the island of Britannia."[109] Beginning with the battleships crisis, the press employed religious imagery and vocabulary with increasing frequency. Direct and repeated use of religious references from early on demonstrates that the Unionists' had internalized the lessons of the Balkan Wars, and that they were determined to employ religion again in the service of patriotism.

While the Ottoman populace was still grappling with this shock, another naval incident further complicated the situation. On the evening of August 10th, Enver Pasha granted permission to two cruisers of the German Mittelmeerdivision, *Goeben* and *Breslau*, to pass through the straits. The two battleships had been chased by the British Mediterranean Squadron after bombarding French troopships and ports on the Algerian coast, and had managed to reach the Dardanelles.[110] The Entente powers immediately protested that the presence of the German battleships would compromise Ottoman neutrality. To defuse this pressure, the Porte declared that the cruisers had been purchased from Germany for 80 million marks and transferred to the Ottoman navy.[111] Upon their transfer, the *Goeben* was renamed the *Yavuz Sultan Selim,* while the *Breslau* became the *Midilli* (i.e., Mytilene, or Lesbos). The latter name was no coincidence; it indicated the Ottoman fixation on the adjacent Aegean islands.

The purchase of the ships replaced the two dreadnoughts interned by the British. The *Yavuz Sultan Selim* in particular had the capacity to tip the naval balance in the Black Sea towards the Ottomans. The incident proved to be crucial for another reason too: for the first time in a long while, a major European power was acting favorably towards the Ottomans in such a direct and evident manner. For the pro-German wing of the Unionists, this was a unique opportunity to drive the Ottoman public towards the Central Powers and to excite patriotic feelings against Great Britain. The press and other propaganda outlets almost unanimously presented the sale of the battleships as an honorable gesture by Germany and as a sign of German friendship towards the Porte. A flyer distributed and posted on street walls and coffeehouses in Damascus, for instance, read: "Great Britain's feeling towards Turkey may be seen by their seizure of our two Dreadnoughts and on the other hand Germany making us a gift of *Sultan Selim* and *Medelli* [*sic*]."[112] Along the same lines, *Tanin* dismissed the Entente's claims that the purchase constituted a violation of the Porte's neutrality and wrote that it was perfectly normal for Ottoman public opinion to have become favorably disposed towards the Germans because of this gesture.[113] The disappointment caused by the British retention of the battleships and the consequent outburst of anti-British feelings significantly contributed to the development of pro-German tendencies among both military and governmental officials as well as Ottoman Muslims in general.

Ottoman Abrogation of the Capitulations

In these turbulent days of the mobilization, the only other incident that energized Ottoman Muslims was the abrogation of capitulations by the CUP government. The capitulations were a series of historic treaty agreements between the Ottoman Empire and several European states that conferred extraterritorial status on the subjects of European states residing within the empire and gave them a number of judicial, fiscal, and economic privileges, including exemption from income tax, the right to trial in mixed courts, and legal protection by consulates. Foreign post offices throughout the empire also operated under the protection of the capitulations.

From the earliest days of the Constitutional Revolution, the capitulations and their abrogation had been high on the CUP's agenda. Unionist rhetoric repudiated the capitulations as a bundle of privileges that had been historically abused by the European powers at the expense of the empire. Capitulary rights, according to this view, not only undermined the Ottoman state's authority and violated its sovereignty, but also hampered the empire's economic and social development. The Unionists repeatedly attempted to renegotiate the capitulary concessions with the Great Powers, though these efforts met with little success. Even under seemingly impossible conditions, they insisted on the abolition or limitation of the capitulations. For instance, in its reply to the Great Powers' collective note during the height of the Balkan Wars in January 1913, the Unionist cabinet conceded to some of the requests, while demanding in return the closure of foreign post offices, the taxation of foreigners on the same conditions as Ottoman subjects, and an increase in customs duties by 4 percent.[114] Reflecting the heightened sensitivity about the empire's vulnerabilities in the aftermath of the Balkan Wars, the 1913 congress of the CUP adopted an even bolder stance regarding the capitulations. The second article of the new political program stated: "The CUP regards working towards the elimination of all fiscal and economic privileges enjoyed by foreigners . . . and all kinds of capitulations as the most sacred duty."[115] The outbreak of the war in Europe a year later provided the Unionists with a unique opportunity to do just that.

The Unionists' calculations were based on the expectation that the European powers could now no longer collectively restrain the Porte's policies. Seeking to seize the moment, they approached European governments to request the immediate abrogation of the capitulations, only to be rebuffed again.[116] Disappointed and infuriated, the Porte took a momentous decision on 9 September 1914, and declared that it had unilaterally abolished all capitulations, effective October 1st. That same day, Ottoman ambassadors notified foreign governments of the abrogation of the privileges and immunities associated with the capitulations: "Having thus freed itself from what was an intolerable obstacle to all progress in the Empire, the Imperial Government has adopted as basis of its relations with the other Powers the general principles of international law."[117] All the European powers, including Germany, with which the CUP leaders had recently signed treaty of alliance, reacted strongly to this announcement. Contrary to the Unionists' expectations, and regardless of the ongoing war among them, they responded to the Porte's decision in unison. "The impossible has been achieved," a British observer wrote: "The Porte, by a mere stroke of the pen, has revived, in Constantinople at least, no less an entity than the Concert of Europe, which was generally supposed to have died six weeks ago!"[118] Their protests, however, fell short of getting the CUP government back down. From 1 October 1914 on, foreigners residing within the borders of the empire would be fully subject to the laws applied to Ottoman citizens.

The Ottoman press hailed the government's decision as the harbinger of a new, prosperous, fully independent era for the empire. In a full-page illustration in *Tasfir-i Efkar*, a woman representing the empire pointed a young man representing future generations to the "economic and developmental" benefits of the abrogation of the capitulations, which included railroads, ports, industrial facilities, bountiful agriculture, battleships, zeppelins, and airplanes, all brought about by the abolition of foreign privileges.[119] Throughout the empire, the abrogation of the capitulations was greeted with great enthusiasm by the empire's Muslims and celebrated with fanfare.[120] Along with patriotic civil society organizations, the CUP and its local branches evidently backed these efforts. These celebrations took a form what the historian Mehmet Beşikçi calls "organized spontaneity."[121] Everywhere they began on the order and encouragement of local authorities. People were instructed to close their shops, decorate their dwellings with flags, and illuminate them at night. Daytime mass meetings were held either in main squares of towns or courtyards of major mosques, where local representatives of the CUP gave speeches about the capitulations. Participants then proceeded to government offices and the local headquarters of the CUP. In the evening, processions marched through the streets.

Given the prevailing intense anti-British sentiment, the Unionists' propaganda fell on receptive ears. The British consul in Izmir reported that the "Turkish population as a whole has naturally received the news of the intended abolition of the Capitulations with feelings of undisguised contentment, as it has been carefully explained to them by their newspapers and by word of mouth that this abolition means depriving the European of his vaunted superiority, making him equal of the Turk and lowering him from a vantage ground of which he had unfairly taken possession."[122] On 11 September 1914, an American missionary in Harput wrote in her line-a-day diary: "The Sultan's birthday is being celebrated, also the abrogation act, which pleases the Turks very much."[123] Of the various ethno-religious communities of the empire, it was the Muslims who celebrated the decision most enthusiastically. In Beirut, for instance, while the Muslims of the city rejoiced, the Christian population went into a state of alarm, and many of them fled the city.[124]

The Unionists' portrayal of the capitulations and their abrogation fit perfectly within the broader wartime narrative of Ottoman victimization, according to which the capitulations had more than anything else provided foreign governments with an effective means of intervening in the empire's domestic affairs. Over the past six years, the Unionists had done everything to solve the problem of the capitulations through peaceful negotiations in the hope that the European powers would appreciate the significance of the Constitutional Revolution and accept the Ottoman Empire into the ranks of civilized nations, the Unionist narrative ran. But the CUP's well-intentioned moves were constantly met by the Europeans with blatant arrogance and disrespect, if not outright hostility. Despite all of the assurances given about the safety of foreigners' lives and properties, European governments proved to be inordinately stubborn in upholding the capitulary privileges and refused to make any concessions. For the Unionists, this tenacity reflected broader European desires to perpetuate the Ottoman Empire's inferior status. What made things even worse was the fact that the European powers had abandoned capitulary privileges in former Ottoman provinces when they gained their independence, but refused to do so in the empire.

For the Unionists, the abrogation of the capitulations was key to fashioning the war narrative in increasingly Islamic terms. Just as the seizure of the battleships had been an egregious assault, not only on Ottoman citizens, but on all Muslims, the abrogation of the capitulations was a moment of salvation for Muslims around the world. September 10th would henceforth be celebrated as the most important holiday, not only of the Ottoman state, but of the entire Islamic community (*umma*), *Tasfir-i Efkar* declared.[125] A leaflet distributed by the Navy League in honor of the abrogation of the capitulations reflected these overtly religious overtones:

> The curse of the capitulations has been lifted. God is with us. Praise be to him. The soul of Muhammad is enlivened by the felicity of Islam today. Thousands of salutes to his holy tomb! Hail to the current government! It put an end to the greatest scourge in centuries. Gratitude and respect to them. . . . Muslims! New life calls for new deeds. Those who said that the scourge was our fault should tomorrow see the new Turkey in a new life. The new life is possible with moral and material strength. Citizens! As you rejoice at the end of the curse of the capitulations, don't forget that those whose interests have suffered will take action to attack us. Go to war with enthusiasm, practice charity with sacrifice![126]

European dominance over the imperial economy had provided benefits to non-Muslims while depriving the Muslims of the empire of these benefits. A good number of Ottoman non-Muslims had adopted foreign citizenship and benefitted from the privileges that the capitulations conferred. Ottoman Muslims in this sense were the true victims of the capitulations, the Unionists invoked. Their co-religionists in European colonies suffered under similar regulations. The CUP's decision thus represented the dawning of a new era for all Muslims, who would follow the Unionists and break free from their own shackles.

The Ottoman Empire Finally at War

On 2 August 1914, the day the Ottoman Empire signed its treaty of alliance with Germany, the German chief of staff, General Helmuth von Moltke, presented the foreign minister, Gottlieb von Jagow, with a long list of suggestions on how German foreign policy should be conducted given the current political situation. Moltke's remarks on the Ottoman Empire were plain and brief: "The alliance treaty with Turkey should be made public immediately. Turkey ought to *declare war on Russia as soon as possible*."[127] The Balkan War experiences, however, had taught the Unionists the importance of entering war at the most propitious moment. In line with those lessons, and much to the frustration of its allies, the Porte managed to delay the empire's entry into the war until late October. The Unionists skillfully maneuvered through the pressures coming from the Entente powers while driving a hard bargain with the Germans. Friedrich Kress von Kressenstein, a member of the German military mission in Istanbul, aptly described the Unionists' foot-dragging for three long months as a "masterpiece of Eastern diplomacy."[128]

After three months of mobilization, the pro-war party among the Unionists decided that the right moment had finally arrived. On the morning of October 29th, the Ottoman navy, now under the command of German Admiral Wilhelm Souchon, shelled the Russian ports of Odessa, Sevastopol, Novorossiysk, and Feodosia, sinking Russian commercial vessels in a surprise raid. Souchon was acting under explicit orders from Enver Pasha to "seek and destroy the Russian navy" in the Black Sea.[129] Although the attack fell short of fulfilling its intended objective of destroying the Russian Black Sea fleet, it nevertheless led to the rupture of relations between the Porte and the Allies. In the three months preceding the attack, the Russians had sought to keep the Ottomans out of the war.[130] For as much as they did not want to open another front, the unprovoked attack on their territory was too much to bear. In the first week of November, the Ottoman Empire was finally at war, first with Russia, and then with Great Britain and France.

Following the attack on Russian ports and ships, the Porte spent considerable energy vindicating Ottoman action and assigning the blame for the war to Russia. The Unionists were fully aware of the importance of depicting the Russians as the aggressor. In his private memo to Enver Pasha about Souchon's attack, the navy minister, Cemal Pasha, wrote that in any case, "it would be better to depict the Russians as the initial offender."[131] According to the Ottoman press, Russian battleships had attacked the Ottoman navy while it was engaged in routine naval exercises just outside the Bosporus. Despite recurring provocations by the Entente powers over the past three months, the press claimed, the Ottomans had so far stuck to the rules of international diplomacy and striven to avoid war. Their sincere wish to stay out of the conflict, however, was not respected, and the war was forced upon them. The newspaper reports describing the first clash between the Ottoman and Russian navies in the Black Sea thus perfectly epitomized the Unionists' victimization rhetoric.[132]

On November 12th, almost a week after the Triple Entente's declarations of war, Sultan Mehmed V declared war on the Entente powers in turn. The imperial declaration similarly emphasized that the hostility of the Entente armies had propelled the Ottoman Empire, which was "always subjected to sudden and unjust attacks," to abandon its long-held desire for peace.[133] Working to recover from the devastation wrought by the Balkan Wars and longing for peace and tranquility, as the official discourse asserted, the empire had been attacked by the Russian army in the Caucasus, by the Russian navy in the Black Sea, and by the British navy at Aqaba. The enemy had been lying in wait, ready to pounce at the slightest sign of weakness or vulnerability. The war had begun solely as a result of the Entente powers' "unmanly attacks."[134]

The official rhetoric that depicted the Ottoman Empire as defending itself against rapacious enemies served two basic purposes. First, the government and the army high command wanted to obscure the fact that it was actually the Ottoman navy that had attacked the Russians. Second, and more important, by deploying this rhetoric, the political and military elite sought to present a convincing argument to the war-weary Ottoman people that would energize them and enlist their support for a new war. Justifying the empire's entry into the war as a defensive act was thus crucial for the Unionist leadership's overall wartime strategy.

Depiction of the Ottoman Empire as a victim of Entente aggression clearly did not square, however, with the bellicose, religiously colored rhetoric of the Porte, the CUP, and the Ottoman press—which at this point, almost unanimously depicted the empire's struggle as that of the Muslim world as a whole. *Tanin*'s bombast was typical:

> We have acquiesced to these tortures so far not for the sake of our own insignificant lives, but because we are the only hope of a world of 300 million people. . . . Whenever we wanted to raise our heads, a shell exploded on our brains; whenever we wanted to straighten up, our wrists were broken. But finally the day has arrived! . . . From now on, we can no longer bear to hear the word "peace": Either them or us! . . . Yes, revenge! And we will take it from them![135]

With the declaration of jihad on November 14th, this rhetoric was heightened even further.[136] The press exalted the war as a just and holy war, which gave all Ottomans the duty, not only of defending the honor and borders of the empire, but also of fighting for the very existence of Islam. Defending the empire thus overlapped with the duty of defending the religion, a theme that would occupy a fundamental place in official Ottoman propaganda, at least throughout the first half of the war.[137] A quick victory over the hereditary foes both of the empire and of Islam, as numerous articles in the press maintained, would relieve the suffering of Muslims under the yokes of the Russian, British, and French empires. Thus, "among all the belligerents," *Türk Yurdu* wrote, "none is more righteous than the Ottomans."[138] "It has become a sacred duty for us," a leading Unionist intellectual and politician, Ahmet Ağaoğlu, wrote a year later, "to fight against the Entente, which currently rules ninety-eight percent of all Muslims through oppression and tyranny [*cebr ve zulm*], has caused the decline of all Muslim governments, and has decided to destroy the last two remaining Muslim states [i.e., the Ottoman Empire and Iran]."[139] Religious themes and imagery thus became inseparable components in the official war culture, and were commonly employed in Ottoman propaganda geared to both the soldiers on the battlefields and the civilian population on the home front.

Conclusions

İhsan Bey, introduced at the beginning of this chapter, wrote in retrospect, "as a matter of fact, the fall of Harput began on that ominous day [3 August 1914], the first day of drifting into a war with an uncertain outcome."[140] His observations certainly pertain to the rest of the empire as well. In all of the languages of the region, World War I itself and all the horrors that surrounded it were referred to in popular memory as *seferberlik*. As countless folklore accounts and oral and written testimonies reveal, people throughout the empire remembered the *seferberlik* as one of the most significant events in their personal, familial, and collective histories.[141] People who lived through it commonly remembered World War I as the "war of mobilization" (*seferberlik harbi*). The fact that it is the only war remembered in the region in conjunction with mobilization points to the unprecedented totality of this war's mobilization of the human and material resources of the empire.

In many respects, the three months between early August and late October 1914 when the empire was mobilized for war constituted an exceptional period in late Ottoman history. The Unionists' determination not to be caught unprepared for a war placed a heavy burden on the Ottoman people's shoulders. Resolved to prepare the greatest number of soldiers they could in a short amount of time, they conscripted hundreds of thousands of men, who swelled the imperial army's ranks, leaving their families and communities behind. In a predominantly rural society, this massive and unexpected loss of men to the army at the peak of the harvest season came as a devastating shock. That the empire entered the war with a significantly expanded conscription system compounded this shock even further. Almost overnight, tens of thousands of families found themselves deprived of their sole breadwinners. Yet this was only the prelude to the four long, grueling years of war that would soon follow.

The harshness of the mobilization process ensured that the Unionists faced serious legitimacy problems even before they entered the war. "The sense of the tragic,"[142] which a long period of peace and tranquility had almost extinguished in Europe, was very much alive in the Ottoman world—only a year before the European diplomatic crisis of July 1914 resulting from the assassination of Archduke Franz Ferdinand, presumed heir to the Austro-Hungarian throne, the Ottoman Empire had sustained a devastating military defeat. "When World War I came [after the war with Italy and the Balkan Wars]," the historian Erik Jan Zürcher observes, "it was therefore the third war in quick succession."[143] The Unionists had to fight an uphill battle to mobilize a war-weary society and legitimize the government's intrusive policies and strict measures. To this end, they molded a multilayered war narrative and sought to propagate it throughout the empire. This narrative was based on an increasingly bolder rhetoric of the Ottomans' victimization at the hands of the European powers, portraying the empire as the target of European assaults and injustice. The British confiscation of the Ottoman battleships and the abrogation of the capitulations provided invaluable ammunition for such rhetoric. They helped the Unionists to frame the war as defensive and invest it with a moral purpose.

As the mobilization proceeded on the ground, the Unionists' war narrative came to rely increasingly on religious imagery and vocabulary, a process that culminated in the Ottoman declaration of jihad in November 1914. In that sense, the jihad was declared not only to incite the Muslims living in the colonies of the empire's enemies against their colonial masters. Perhaps more important, framing the conflict in religious terms was meant to serve the Unionists' purposes of legitimizing the mobilization and the war to Ottoman people. Along with the imposition of strict security measures, these attempts maintained the Ottomans' acquiescence during the initial months of the conflict. The Unionists' wartime rhetoric, however, would eventually crumble under the pressures generated by a lengthy war and its ever-consuming demands, leading to a profound and ever-deepening crisis of legitimacy.

3 FILLING THE RANKS, EMPTYING HOMES

Ahmet, an eighteen-year-old peasant boy from a village near Konya in Central Anatolia, was among the military-age men who were called to gather at the village square when the order of mobilization reached his village in August 1914. After bidding a touching farewell to their families, the group hurried to the district center to register at the enlistment office. From there, the young recruits were sent to various fronts. Ahmet would eventually return to his village after seven years of fighting in World War I and subsequently the Turkish War of Independence. Only three of the twenty-one boys who left the village that August day made it back home. Ahmet was one of them. All three, however, returned with missing limbs as well as less obvious scars. Although he had lost one of his legs, Ahmet kept his spirits high: "I got back to my village with three legs [a leg and two crutches]. They [the villagers] accepted me as I was and married me to one of their daughters. Honestly, there were no other boys left in the village to marry daughters."[1]

Haim Nahmias, a Jew from Jerusalem, who had his own profitable business as a master shoemaker, was much older than Ahmet when he was called to the colors in 1917. Haim's wife had just passed away when he was conscripted, leaving him as their five children's sole caregiver. He had no option but to leave the children to his aging mother before embarking upon his military service. He did not see active combat during the war, but suffered from lack of proper food, hygiene, and shelter, as well as the cruelty of his superiors, long hours of labor, and a deep sense of isolation. By the end of the war, he managed to get back to his beloved hometown only to face the tragedy awaiting him there. Wartime difficulties and deprivation had exceeded his elderly mother's caregiving capacity: Two of his five children had died of starvation while he was away.[2]

For millions of Ottoman men like Ahmet and Haim, war above all meant conscription and endless military service, which entailed combat, injury, disease, hard labor, captivity, and possibly death. Enormous wartime casualties compelled the Ottoman government to hone the state's capacity to harness untapped sources of manpower. By continually amending existing laws, drafting new legislation, and resorting to extrajudicial methods of recruitment, the Unionists sought to cast the net of conscription as wide as possible. Given the duration, scale, and destructiveness of the conflict, this process would have devastating consequences for Ottoman society.

The Unionists, however, were quick to realize that their coercive strategies were insufficient to fill the ranks and keep an increasingly disillusioned population aligned with their war effort. As the war dragged on and became more destructive than anyone had anticipated, the Unionists devised a novel patriotic identity centered on the idealized image of the ordinary Ottoman soldier, Mehmetçik, "Little Mehmet," a figure comparable to the British Tommy Atkins or French *poilu*. Through the cult of the ordinary soldier, the CUP strove to convey the impression of a people that had overcome its internal divisions and unified behind the government in defense of imperial honor. Along with the new and more intrusive recruitment policies, the Unionists devoted considerable energy to utilizing this patriotic identity to produce consent.

The cult of Mehmetçik linked the battle- and home fronts in official propaganda, but managing the connection in the real world proved to be exceedingly difficult. Draftees devised a variety of escape strategies to untangle themselves from the net of conscription. During the war, conscription became a field of contestation in which various social actors actively participated. This chapter focuses on unique wartime relationships that emerged between the Ottoman state, its male subjects, and their relatives on the home front. Examining the state's policies on conscription and reactions to them, it explores the complexities of military conscription during World War I and its impact on Ottoman society.[3]

Early Problems of Soldiering during World War I

The three months of mobilization saw an unprecedented expansion of state authority over the civilian life. People throughout the empire found themselves

subjected to new and harsher restrictions and increasingly intrusive state policies. While all of these measures inflicted great hardships and disrupted everyday routines, compulsory military service affected them most profoundly. For
the military-age men, conscription brought about sudden and radical changes
in their lives. Their ties were severed with the civilian life, they were compelled
to adjust to an entirely different lifestyle, and, above all, a new and alien authority was imposed upon them. More disturbingly, that alien authority, the state,
came to play a direct role in controlling their lives and determining their fates.
For families and communities, the enforced absence of their male members
meant new physical and emotional challenges, many of which they were ill prepared to handle.

The process of turning hundreds of thousands of civilians into soldiers on
short notice required planning, organization, and resources that were painfully lacking in the Ottoman Empire. As a result, the initial difficulties caused
by the extensive and disorganized nature of the mobilization continued well
into the later months of 1914. The lives of the fresh recruits were miserable
even before they were sent to the battlefront. Since the army did not have a
sufficient number of buildings or even tents to adequately house hundreds of
thousands of men, soldiers were usually forced to sleep on the bare floor in
very crowded rooms, which quickly became breeding grounds for typhus, dysentery, and other diseases.[4] The confiscation of a large number of buildings
(especially those belonging to Entente citizens and institutions), mansions, and
private houses did not ease the problem. Once conscripted, learning whom to
obey and how to fight occupied most of the recruits' time. The vast majority of
them were illiterate villagers and some did not even speak the same language as
their officers.[5] Instilling military discipline, punctuality, and obedience in them
was not a simple task for their superiors, and usually included a heavy dose of
curses and beatings. Physical demands were extensive. Endless drills and hard
labor left many of them extremely weary. Anticipating long marches during
the war, army commanders tried to increase soldiers' stamina by pushing their
bodies to the limit. Unsurprisingly, many conscripts could not stand the grind-
ing routine of military life and strains associated with it.[6]

In addition to these hardships, recruits usually lacked proper uniforms and
footwear; their provisioning was inadequate; and their pay (needed especially
to buy tobacco) was always in arrears. At the beginning of the mobilization
(and throughout the war years), clothing thousands of soldiers on short notice
proved to be a daunting task for the military authorities.[7] As domestic produc-

tion failed to reach desired levels and imported material was appropriated for military units in and around Istanbul, some troops, especially those on the eastern front, had to prepare for war in ragged, multicolored uniforms and defective footwear.[8] A missionary who had observed the local conscription process in Van counted twenty-two sorts of material in the uniforms of a group of sixty soldiers.[9] Another missionary likened the recruits he saw in Antep in southeastern Anatolia more to refugees rather than to the soldiers of an army "[w]ithout uniforms, dirty and tired from the road, without weapons, possessed of a few lumber wagons and a group of ox-carts."[10] Even in the winter of 1914–15, some soldiers were still wearing their summer uniforms.[11] For high-ranking commanders, this lack of clothing and equipment prompted comparisons with the Balkan Wars. Like that of many of his colleagues, Hasan İzzet Pasha, then the commander of the Ottoman Third Army in eastern Anatolia, indulged in a certain amount of wishful thinking: "In the Balkan War, the equipment of the army and the clothing of the soldier were perfect. We lost the war then. Now, equipment is inadequate, and the soldiers' clothing is deplorable. God willing, we'll win."[12] Due largely to these unfavorable conditions, already in the first few weeks of mobilization, disease, and desertion began to take their toll on the Ottoman army.

The empire's underdeveloped network of railroads, poor condition of overland routes, and woefully insufficient number of motorized vehicles, locomotives, and railroad cars made walking the only option for many Ottoman soldiers to reach their destinations. Frequent, poorly planned, and sometimes completely unnecessary marches, which could amount to forty kilometers a day,[13] in horrible conditions, along with inadequate provisioning and accommodation en route, were bound to be detrimental to the strength of the military units. The troops, as a result, lost a significant part of their manpower on the move.[14] Many soldiers did not have proper clothing and boots, which made the long marches unbearable. Soldiers were usually not given sufficient food to keep them alive in the extreme weather and road conditions. Once they reached a provisioning station (*menzil noktası*), it was not uncommon for the station commander to refuse to supply them, instead sending them on to the next station.[15] Consequently, soldiers who were not strong enough fell ill or died, and many of them opted to desert their columns. When caught, they protested that conditions had forced them to do so. The U.S. consul in Baghdad reported in October 1914, for instance, that 1,600 men had returned to Baghdad from various stages on the march to Mosul. These men claimed that they were not deserters, but that they had received neither food nor proper treatment. According to the consul, they were "quite willing to continue their military service, but could not survive under the conditions they were forced to endure recently."[16]

Apart from the physical difficulties associated with the marches, soldiers' morale was also deeply affected by scenes they witnessed en route, especially refugees, wounded veterans making their way to the rear, and the fallen. On their way to the front, soldiers came into contact with hundreds of wounded veterans who had not received any assistance from the army. Moreover, many of them were attacked and robbed by brigands.[17] The heart-rending sight of these men sapped the motivation and discipline of soldiers marching forward to an uncertain fate. Recalling the sight of oxcarts transporting the corpses of dead soldiers back from the front, one young recruit exclaimed: "Gruesome, horrible scene! We were shocked. Who knows, perhaps [the fate of] those lying in front of us would be our future as well."[18] Desertion, in many cases, seemed the only viable option. The army attempted to address this problem of desertion en route by assigning more responsibility to unit leaders and threatening to court-martial them if they lost more than a certain percentage of their men on the way.[19] To forestall desertion, cordons of armed guards commonly surrounded troops on the march and at stopovers,[20] but soldiers still managed to find ways to desert their units.

Although desertions took place on a regular basis in these earlier stages of mobilization and war, the number did not alarm Ottoman military planners. The state's security infrastructure was still functioning relatively efficiently. The local military and civilian authorities were able to exert coercive control on the home front mostly with gendarmerie and police. Exact statistics are hard to come by, but, in the first months of the war, the likelihood of a deserter being caught and punished was not remote. Many were hunted down and sent back to their divisions. The vast number of conscripts reassured military planners. With hundreds of thousands of men under arms, the high command felt confident of the army's supply of manpower. This picture, however, was about to change soon with the massive Ottoman campaigns in the Caucasus and the Dardanelles.

The First Campaigns

The first radical attempts to widen the Ottoman conscription net came in the aftermath of the imperial army's disastrous campaigns in the winter months of

1914–15. Fighting against the Russians commenced in early November 1914 in eastern Anatolia, which quickly became the key front for the Ottoman high command. Launching a major offensive with three army corps, Enver Pasha planned to encircle the Russian units in the vicinity of Sarıkamış and inflict on them a crushing defeat similar to the one achieved by the German army in the battle of Tannenberg that August. Although he had initially professed military action to be impossible in eastern Anatolia before the spring, Enver changed his mind sometime around mid-November.[21] Encouraged by the early Ottoman successes enjoyed against the Russians under the command of Hasan İzzet Pasha and motivated by dreams of imperial glory in the Caucasus, he led the Third Army to almost complete destruction in an ill-conceived winter offensive. The increasing socioeconomic cost of maintaining a massive army on a war footing may have led Ottoman military planners to attempt this risky route to quick victory. Lack of well-organized, reliable lines of communications, difficult mountainous terrain, harsh climactic conditions, the overly ambitious nature of the Ottoman offensive, and poor generalship all contributed to what a military historian has called "a self-inflicted disaster."[22] By the time Enver Pasha left the front to return to the capital on 9 January 1915, only 10,000 of the 75,000 regular Ottoman soldiers were still under arms. Tens of thousands of others died in the mountains of northeastern Anatolia of cold, typhus, and starvation or were killed or captured by the Russian forces.[23] These were the Ottoman army's best troops in terms of training and health. Their loss was therefore a heavy, demoralizing blow, which considerably sapped the Ottomans' military energy.[24]

In the meantime, the massive Entente attack on the Dardanelles began in February 1915 and contributed significantly to the sense of urgency among the Ottoman political and military elites. Mounting a large-scale joint operation, British imperial and French forces aimed to force the straits, take Istanbul, compel the Unionist government to sue for peace, and secure a critical supply route to Russia.[25] As preparatory shelling by Entente warships increased, Ottoman commanders responded by hastily drawing troops from other fronts and effectively resisting the onslaught from March 1915 on. After countering the Entente's naval attack, they contained landings in coastal enclaves on several points of the Gallipoli peninsula. By the summer of 1915, the confrontation had developed into a bloody stalemate, which both sides tried to break at a cost of prohibitive casualty rates. By the end of the Gallipoli campaign in January 1916, there were tens of thousands of Ottoman casualties, but the Entente's onslaught had been successfully resisted.

The annihilation of three army corps on the Caucasus front, and the pressing need to strengthen the Gallipoli front had important repercussions for the Ottoman policy of conscription.[26] Along with drafting new classes of conscripts ahead of schedule, the Unionists tried to wrestle with the manpower problem by dragging groups and individuals who had so far remained exempt into the conscription net. The burning need to make up for the losses compelled the CUP government first gradually to bring in men between thirty-two and forty-five. They had already been called up in the countryside, but were not conscripted in Istanbul. In some provinces, men older than thirty-eight had been registered but temporarily released, to be mobilized in case of necessity.[27] Now they were called up and sent to the battlefronts.

On the other hand, the army's immediate solution to the decimation of regular units was to fill their ranks from local gendarmerie units. In some parts of the empire, gendarmes had already been employed in army units, albeit on a limited scale. The sense of urgency felt among the Unionists accelerated this process of transferring them to the army, a policy that proved detrimental to internal security.[28] With the wide-scale incorporation of trained gendarmes into the army, the state's ability to maintain order in the countryside weakened considerably. Requisitioning, the impressment of new recruits, and the pursuit of deserters were all hampered by the dwindling number of gendarmes. "Had the gendarmes remained in place, the deserters and those who had not reported for duty [*bakaya*] would not have outnumbered them by ten to one, public order would not have been disrupted, and everything the army wanted to accomplish would have been done in a timely manner," a contemporary observer wrote.[29] This policy also contributed to weakening of the army in the long run, "since too few gendarmes remained to pursue and capture the large number of deserters," Mehmet Beşikçi notes.[30]

As gendarmes were transferred to the army, the government responded to the diminution of internal security forces by extending conscription to those with any kind of familiarity with firearms (*silah istimaline kabiliyetli olanlar*). The provisional law enacted for this purpose allowed for the enlistment of young men of nineteen and twenty years of age, if they had not already been drafted, and of men over forty-five. These new conscripts would be employed "in the defense of borders and coasts and the maintenance of public order."[31] In the course of discussions of the law in the parliament, deputies rightly lambasted the lack of a fixed upper age limit and the abuses to which this uncertainty might lead. Many of them expressed their concerns that this regulation would leave the door open for the conscription of men aged fifty, sixty, or even seventy. This process in turn would negatively affect life on the home front since, in the absence of young men, these older men, along with women and children, were already obliged to do farmwork, provide transportation, and perform other duties.[32] To assuage these concerns, the army representative tried to assure the deputies that these men would not be sent to the battlefronts.

Yet these efforts to replenish the ranks of the army still fell short and led to two other, equally momentous decisions. First, less than six months into the war, the government was compelled to draft men below the regular age of conscription. In this regard, a drastic change in the law allowing eighteen-year-olds to be drafted was approved at the height of the Gallipoli fighting.[33] Second, the net of conscription was expanded to refugees, who had historically enjoyed periods of exemption from military service (as well as from several taxes) in the Ottoman Empire.[34] In line with the new Regulation for the Settlement of Refugees (İskan-ı Muhacirin Nizamnamesi) of 1913, the new law of conscription granted them exemption from military service for the first six years after their arrival in Ottoman territory. The sheer magnitude of casualties and the burning need for able-bodied men, however, compelled the Unionists to rescind this provision and make refugees liable for service immediately. The new legislation authorized the Ministry of War to draft those refugees who had already arrived, as well as those who would arrive during the course of the war if necessary.[35] The law reduced the six-year exemption period significantly and granted refugees only three months for settling and registration.[36] Although the law left the door open for the conscription of incoming refugees, given the desperation of those fleeing the advancing Russian army, the Ministry of War gave orders to exempt those who had migrated from lands invaded by the enemy.[37] The army high command primarily sought to conscript the tens of thousands of Muslim refugees who had fled to the Ottoman Empire during and after the Balkan Wars and were exempt from military service in accordance with the new law of conscription of 1914 and the regulation concerning the settlement of refugees.

The state's efforts to conscript refugees attracted considerable criticism from both deputies and senate members as well as from refugees themselves. Much to the annoyance of army representatives, Abdurrahman Şeref Efendi, a famous historian and a prominent member of the Ottoman Senate, likened the refugees' situation to that of the lamb that escapes the wolf but is slaughtered by the butcher.[38] Other members of the parliament and the senate argued that refugees had already become victims of the war, losing everything they once owned. As most of the refugee families had left their properties, businesses, and other sources of income behind, their survival depended mostly on the labor of the men, whose conscription would condemn their families to poverty and hunger.

Refugees themselves resisted the state's attempts to draft them in various ways, most commonly by extending their refugee status. After having settled in a region, refugees would not stay there long, instead joining other newly arrived groups and migrating to other parts of the empire. In this way, they could continually present themselves to authorities as newly arrived refugees and enjoy the three months' settling period of exemption from service. After this period was over, they would move to another location or destroy their registration documents to continue to evade military service. Although the authorities sent order after order to catch these refugees and hand them over to the recruiting stations, it turned out to be practically impossible to keep track of them.[39] As a partial solution, the army ordered the immediate conscription of refugees who had left their families in their native countries and came alone. They would not be granted even the three months' exemption.[40] Some other refugee groups who could not move freely from one location to another opted to remain in uninhabited areas and around swamps to hide the male members of their families.[41] Refugee army recruits resented conscription so strongly that British Intelligence identified them as invaluable sources of information, "always worth singling out."[42]

Although the Ottoman authorities, on the one hand, coped with serious difficulties in filling the depleted ranks of the army during the first year of the war, on the other hand, they paradoxically also contributed to depleting those ranks themselves. As noted earlier, the call for mobilization included all male subjects of the empire, irrespective of their ethno-religious identity. The recruitment of non-Muslim soldiers had always been a controversial issue for the Ottomans, however, and that fact had not changed since 1909, when their exemption from service was formally abolished.[43] Despite occasional calls for equality before the law and fellowship in carrying the burdens of protecting "the Ottoman nation," neither Muslims nor non-Muslims had shown much enthusiasm for the idea of serving together in the ranks.[44] During World War I, however, conscription became an equally great burden for Ottoman non-Muslims, who on the eve of the war constituted about 20 percent of the empire's population.

Even before the start of the war, the army high command seemed to be developing a strong sense of distrust of non-Muslim soldiers. In the first days of mobilization, the Ministry of Interior sent a circular to the provinces regarding the army's decision to employ non-Muslim soldiers in road construction.[45] This decision, however, was not intended to separate all non-Muslims from their units by sending them to labor battalions. There is evidence that the army began to disarm Armenian soldiers in eastern Anatolia and place them in labor battalions as early as October 1914.[46] But especially following its defeat on the Caucasus front, the army embraced a considerably more radical stance towards non-Muslim soldiers. Responding to rumors that increasing numbers of Armenians were voluntarily surrendering to the enemy or sharing secrets about Ottoman forces, in February 1915, the army high command decided to remove non-Muslims from active service and transfer them to labor battalions. Over the course of the war, some 100,000 soldiers were employed in labor battalions.[47]

Before being sent to labor battalions, the soldiers were disarmed and their uniforms were taken away. For many of them, this was a humiliating shock. Alexander Aaronsohn, a Jewish soldier from a small village named Zicron-Jacob south of Mount Carmel (today Haifa in northern Israel), recalls his feelings as follows: "I shall never forget the humiliation of that day when we, who, after all, were the best-disciplined troops of the lot, were first herded to our work of pushing wheelbarrows and handling spades, by grinning Arabs, rifle on shoulder."[48] In a similar vein, Khalil Sakakini, an Arab Orthodox Christian and a noted intellectual, recorded this feeling of humiliation in his diary: "Today a large number of Christians were recruited as garbage collectors to Bethlehem and Bait Jala. Each was given a broom, a shovel, and a bucket and they were distributed among the alleys of the town. Conscripts would shout at each home they passed, 'send us your garbage.' The women of Bethlehem looked out from their windows and wept. No doubt this is the ultimate humiliation. We have gone back to the days of bondage in Roman and Assyrian days."[49] The fear of being disarmed, the humiliation, and the increased sense of threat and foreboding led many non-Muslim soldiers to desert the labor battalions.[50]

The army usually employed labor battalions in paving new roads and constructing railroads and repairing old ones, cutting down trees for fuel for locomotives, transporting wood, ammunition, and other military provisions, and in several municipal services.[51] Ottoman authorities also used labor battalions especially in the Arab provinces of the empire for grandiose renovation projects in the cities of Beirut, Damascus, Jaffa, and Aleppo initiated by Cemal Pasha, the governor general of Greater Syria and the commander of the Fourth

Ottoman Army. War, in the words of the historian Salim Tamari, transformed these provinces "into one huge construction site" and these battalions provided the necessary free labor.[52] Many Anatolian towns also saw intense construction activity in which labor battalions were employed. Not surprisingly, non-Muslim soldiers in labor battalions suffered from extreme weather conditions, backbreaking work, undernourishment, and, finally, mistreatment at the hands of their guards. When the deportation of the Armenians began in April 1915, unarmed Armenian soldiers in labor battalions were "sitting ducks," Erik J. Zürcher writes. Especially in eastern Anatolia, they were either marched off to their deaths or killed by gendarmes and tribesmen.[53]

A Living Symbol of Ottoman Patriotism

The first Ottoman campaigns resulted in significant manpower loss, causing a dramatic expansion of the empire's conscription net. These turbulent months also taught the Unionists that modern conscript armies are held together by what the historian Dennis Showalter calls "a complex interface between front and home, military and civil society, incorporating varying combinations of compulsion, patriotism, and ideology."[54] As losses mounted on the battlefields and the war's impact became apparent on the home front, the Unionists found maintaining people's acquiescence increasingly difficult. Growing war-weariness, they rightly feared, might undermine the government's authority and social cohesion. Among other things, this concern gave rise to the "cult of the ordinary soldier." To overcome war-weariness and keep the populace supportive of or at least acquiescent to government's wartime policies, the Unionists went to great lengths to develop the cult and propagate it through the press, popular literature, songs, theater plays, speeches, and sermons. More so than in any prior Ottoman war, the ordinary soldier occupied a central place in official rhetoric during World War I.

It was no coincidence that the cult of the ordinary soldier developed in earnest during the height of the Gallipoli campaign. The escalating Dardanelles conflict once again confronted Istanbul, where painful memories of the Balkan Wars were still fresh, with the harsh reality of war. With casualty rates skyrocketing, medical facilities at the front were inadequate to care for soldiers who succumbed to injuries and disease, and thousands of them were transported back to Istanbul to be treated. Horse-drawn carts filled with wounded soldiers became common sights on the streets of the capital. "It is an awful sight nowadays to see the troops marching one side of the street hail [sic] and hearty, and being brought up wounded and in bad shape in carriages on the other side," U.S. Ambassador Morgenthau noted in his diary.[55] The flood of the wounded and the sick, however, quickly exceeded the capacity of the capital's medical facilities. Schools and other big buildings were converted into makeshift hospitals.[56] University and high school students were employed in the transportation of the wounded, and upper-middle- and upper-class women volunteered to take care of them at hospitals.[57] While the presence of these soldiers gave a boost to volunteer activity, it also served as a constant reminder of the war's brutality. Widespread rumors about the fate of the campaign and a thoroughly shaken belief in the Ottoman soldier's capabilities, based mostly on his Balkan War performance, caused a high degree of anxiety among Istanbulites. The presence of British submarines in the Sea of Marmara and widespread expectation that the Entente forces would soon destroy the Ottoman defenses and reach the capital only aggravated their concerns.[58] This continuous state of anxiety deeply affected the morale at the capital and prompted a good number of its inhabitants to send their families to Anatolia. Even high-ranking officers and statesmen made contingency plans to move to the interior in the event of the Entente navies attacking the capital. Entente bombardment caused a similar panic in Izmir, the second largest city of the empire.[59] Under these conditions, the Unionists realized, manipulating public opinion and maintaining home-front morale were of the utmost importance to sustain the war effort. The cult of ordinary soldier thus became an essential component of the official war culture.

Mehmetçik—Little Mehmed—the soldier who figured centrally in official propaganda was a man who was ready and eager to perform his historically monumental tasks. His foremost qualities were altruism, courage, modesty, and, most important, a sincere willingness to sacrifice in the name of the greater Ottoman cause. History assigned the ordinary soldier a momentous role: the fate of the six hundred-year-old empire, under attack by enemies from every direction, depended upon him. His performance on the battlefield would determine not only the future of the seat of the sultan and home of the caliph, but also the lives of millions of fellow Muslims. Aware of the fact that he was fighting for the very existence of the empire and defending the entire Islamic world, the soldier, as described in wartime propaganda, was determined to fight to the last drop of his blood. In the wake of the Ottoman victory at Gallipoli, Mehmetçik was glorified for fulfilling this historic duty of defeating the enemies of the Ottomans and Islam. In *Orduya Selam* [Hail to the Army], a

well-known poet of the era, Mehmed Emin Bey (Yurdakul), whom the literary historian Erol Köroğlu calls a "one-man propaganda army," addressed the
soldier as "the sword of God," writing: "Your chest spanned wide / protecting
the sultans' thrones / Your voice calling 'God is great' [*tekbir*] / answered the
cannon of the enemy."[60] This image of the soldier found its most distinguished
place in a poem written by Sultan Mehmed V Reşad himself to honor the de-
fenders of the throne, which was published in each and every newspaper and
magazine throughout the empire: "Yet, as divine assistance reached our army /
Each soldier turned into a steel-bodied fortress."[61]

The Ottoman soldier portrayed in the official propaganda was a man who
would voluntarily put the cause of the empire and religion above his own life
and be willing to leave his village and family behind and rush to the battlefront.
He eagerly undertook the most difficult duties, yet performed them skillfully.
He did not expect any reward or recognition in return and sometimes even rejected rewards if they were offered to him. The most effective way to highlight
the altruism of the ordinary soldier was to show that he prioritized his duty to
the empire over his attachment to his home, family, and loved ones. Zahir, the
hero of Faik Ali's play *Payitahtın Kapısında* [At the Gates of the Capital], tells
his fiancée before leaving for the front that he has found a love, a love for the
nation, for which he can leave her without thinking twice: "Don't be jealous of
this love. Share this feeling of mine sincerely. And love me less, much less than
the nation."[62] Similarly, in Ali Ekrem's famous poem *Şehid Oğlum* [My Martyred Son], the son's loyalty to the nation is so strong that he does not hesitate
to leave his own mother, who heartily embraces him: "'Mother,' he said, 'let me
go off to the war / Let me destroy the enemy of the nation / The nation is my
real mother, not you / I will not let the enemy trample my nation.'"[63]

Centered on the image of the ordinary soldier, the official rhetoric also prescribed certain roles for relatives who sent their fathers, sons, and husbands to
join the army. Parents, wives, and children were expected to carry on during
the war, which tore their male family members away from them, with great
pride and dignity. The message conveyed through propaganda was that they
should, first and foremost, encourage their sons and husbands to go to war,
fight bravely, and, if necessary, die a hero's death. Realizing that attachment
to family members might play a significant role in deterring young men from
answering the call, the Unionists sought to develop a wartime image of the supportive, encouraging family. In a poem published by Celal Sahir in *Türk Yurdu*
[Turkish Homeland], for instance, a wife called out to her husband: "Go, my

lion-hearted one, go and save the country / If you don't go, I won't shed fewer tears but more!"[64] In Sergeant Fahreddin's story, published in *Harp Mecmuası* [War Magazine], the prominent propaganda organ published by the Ministry of War, his son, Necmeddin, plays a similarly encouraging role. When he hears the drums announcing the mobilization, Necmeddin curiously asks his father, "Father! Our Sultan has declared war. This is why the drums are being played. Those who go to the army will become either a martyr or a *ghazi* [Muslim warrior]. . . . Dad, will you not become a martyr or a *ghazi* like them?"[65] Mehmed Emin repeated the same message in his poem *Ordunun Destanı* [Epic of the Army], exhorting young women to emulate their mothers and grandmothers: "And be like those who / Demanded [from their husbands] heroism and sacrifice" and admired them. "How happy is the woman who, / In her heart, suppresses deep sorrows that shake the soul / In the springtime of her life / Endures her inner woe for the nation."[66]

While emphasizing its supportive functions, official propaganda marginalized the suffering of the home-front population and shrouded it in an all-encompassing discourse of duty (*vazife*) and sacrifice (*fedakarlık*). Just as the soldier was expected to sacrifice his life for the sake of the empire, home-front civilians were expected to put the empire's survival above their own grief. Their duty in the war included, but was not limited to, the acceptance of privations and other difficulties with fortitude. Cenab Şahabettin, another famous poet of the era, wrote in *War Magazine* that even the capture of Constantinople by the Ottomans in 1453 had not required as great a sacrifice from the nation, yet "the nation has never seemed so willing to make such a sacrifice."[67] The popular press and propaganda literature included numerous accounts that strengthened this image of the family that would not hesitate to sacrifice its only breadwinner for the motherland. In a fictitious account, the soldier Hüseyin's mother reminds her son of their family tradition of heroism and altruism, and asks him to proudly take part in this tradition. Bidding farewell to her son, who is about to leave for the front, she exclaims, "Hüseyin! Your uncle fell in Şıpka [in the Russo-Ottoman War of 1877–78], your father in Dömeke [in the Greco-Ottoman War of 1897], and your brothers at Gallipoli eight months ago. You are all I have left! If the call to prayer coming from the minarets falls silent, if the candles in the mosques burn out, die and do not come back to [our] village."[68] In *Hail to the Army*, Mehmed Emin spoke for every woman and household when addressing the army: "Know that in this country every woman's / Last son is yours / Big or small, every household's / Last life is yours."[69] All necessary sacrifices to ensure victory for the Ottoman army should be made without hesitation. Families might endure wartime difficulties, but none of these mattered so long as the enemy was defeated and the empire and the religion survived.

The deployment of a rhetoric that featured the ordinary soldier and lauded the sacrifices on the war front was obviously intended to persuade people to adopt this idealized wartime code of behavior and to encourage similarly altruistic acts. This moral language became a means of regulating what the historians Jay Winter and Jean-Louis Robert call the "social relations of sacrifice."[70] The CUP elites, in conjunction with intellectuals and civil society organizations, promoted this imagery to boost patriotism and strengthen social cohesion, which, under the weight of mounting battlefield casualties and home-front privations, became increasingly vulnerable. They construed the key term in this wartime vocabulary, "sacrifice," as a metaphorical bridge holding the Ottoman people together by linking battlefronts with the rear.

Soldiers and the Home Front

If Mehmetçik figuratively represented the strong link between battlefront and home in official war propaganda, managing those connections in reality proved to be exceedingly difficult. Both soldiers and their relatives understood the war and the sacrifices it required noticeably differently from the official version. Their actions, writings, and other cultural products implicitly and explicitly negated the rhetoric of sacrifice, heroism, and resignation endorsed by the government. Rather than offering an opportunity to reveal the latent valor and heroism of the Ottoman soldier, the war meant unprecedented material and emotional burdens both for himself and for his family. The abstract concepts of protecting the empire and sacrificing one's own life in the name of this greater cause collided with the soldier's role as the head of the family and his essential duties of safeguarding his family members and providing for them. Folkloric accounts written by soldiers often reveal the profound concern they felt for their families on the home front and the pain of separation:

Möyünlü möyünsüz hepsini aldı.	[The army] took all the breadwinners.
Çoluğu çocuğu arada kaldı.	Their families were left out in the cold.
Sivas kolordusu sevkiyat oldu.	The Sivas army corps was ordered to the front.
Bugün Kızılırmak bulanık akar.	Today, the Kızılırmak flows muddy.
Nice koçyiğidin bendini yıkar.	It destroys many heroes' weirs.
Dizilmiş yavrular yollara bakar.[71]	Little ones are lined up, watching the roads.

The war, in many respects, expanded the horizons of the ordinary Ottoman soldier, took him, perhaps for the first time, out of his village or hometown, introduced him to new lands, people, and lifestyles, familiarizing him with new cultures, ideas, and concepts. Nevertheless, his attachment to his particular home region, his village, and his family continued to define who he was. He did everything in his capacity to maintain his ties with his family and community through channels including furloughs, letters, unauthorized visits, and friends. When on the march they passed close to their home regions, soldiers often sneaked off to their villages to visit their families, help out with the farmwork, and lend support or protection.[72] While some of these soldiers eventually returned to their units, some did not. In the words of a British prisoner who spent the last two years of war in captivity in Anatolia, Ottoman soldiers "were so drawn by ties of family and anxiety for the fate of their relations that they preferred the life of an outlaw near their homes to the uncertainty of awaiting news in distant Mesopotamia or Palestine."[73] Indeed, soldiers' concern for their families' well-being and security was among the most important reasons for desertion.[74] "I entered the service and served my sultan faithfully," shouted a soldier before he was taken to the gallows in Urfa. "I was hungry and naked in the army, and my family at home was destitute. Who could stand this? Let me tell you, if I could rise from the dead, if you were to treat me again the same way as a soldier, and if I knew that I'd be hanged, I'd still desert."[75] Apparently, he was speaking for many others as well.

Ottoman officials, and particularly the army's high command, were acutely aware of this fundamental link between the front and home. The Ministry of War consistently criticized the malfunctioning policies towards soldiers' families and expressed the army's concerns that these flaws would negatively affect the morale of soldiers "who entrusted their families to the protection of the state."[76] An investigation by the army into unceasing desertions that "cannot be prevented despite all manner of prosecutions and harsh penalties" disclosed that problems related to the assignment of women's pensions and their distribution were among the causes of desertion from the army's ranks. News that reached soldiers about the irregular disbursement of monthly payments, the negligence of revenue officers, and the unfair treatment of women based on personal enmities disturbed them, causing them to leave their posts to lend support to their families at home. The Minister of War asked the Ministry of Interior to take necessary measures to prevent the recurrence of such incidents. It was also decided that perpetrators would be tried in courts-martial upon the accusation of facilitating desertion (*firari teshil cürümüyle*).[77]

Ottoman authorities, however, were not the only ones observing the connectedness between the front and the home. The Entente powers similarly realized the emotional impact of propaganda on Ottoman soldiers in regard to their families' miserable situation on the home front. British planes dropped leaflets over Ottoman troops, depicting the desperate conditions their families had to deal with. "You run from one disaster to another with empty stomachs. The government did not leave any grain, stove, pots or pans in your villages. Your children fell into destitution, your homes into ruin. . . . If you don't pity yourself, show mercy to your children starving in your villages and to your women who sell their chastity due to poverty."[78] A Russian propaganda leaflet mentioned women and children who stormed into stores out of hunger. Some of these women were shot dead by the police.[79] "Do they [the Germans] give you bread?" read another leaflet, emphasizing the helplessness of the home-front population, "Do they help your families in your homeland? No! They care only about themselves. They never care about you. Nobody pays attention to the hunger and vulnerability of your families."[80] In a similar vein, another propaganda flyer asked: "Do you think that you fight for the welfare of the homeland and the family? Oh, you naïve soldiers! You fight for their total annihilation, but you are not aware of this fact." "As the war continues," the flyer stated, "the situation of children, wives, and elderly people will worsen and eventually you will perish due to starvation,"[81] pointing the soldiers to the conclusion that their fighting was directly related to (if not responsible for) their families' misery. It is difficult to assess the exact impact of the Entente propaganda on soldiers. But it did not escape a German officer's attention that, along with the material conditions at the front, it was especially this type of propaganda that stoked Ottoman soldiers' concerns and encourage them to desert from their units.[82]

Growing awareness of the interconnectedness of soldiers' war-making and life on the home front can also be observed in the Unionist press. Along with the relief policies directed at soldiers' family members, the Unionists resorted to various means, including propaganda, in hope of assuaging soldiers' concerns about their families. In accordance with this purpose, *Harp Mecmuası*, the Ottoman propaganda magazine widely disseminated among both civilians and soldiers, published several literary pieces on the experiences of soldiers' families on the home front. These texts were designed to create the impression that military service was a short interlude in a conscript's life, and that once he returned home from the battlefield, he would find his family and village unaffected by the war. In a poem by Manastırlı M. Hasib, for instance, the mother of Sergeant Hasan encourages her son to keep fighting bravely and updates him on what is going on in their village: "Do not worry, the community takes good care of us / Thank God, there is abundance of provisions and grain everywhere."[83] (Sen düşünme, millet bizi gözü gibi bakıyor / Bolluk şükür, zad zahire her taraftan akıyor.) Once again, however, folkloric accounts, presumably reflecting more authentic home-front experiences, painted a completely different picture. A mother of seven sons, for instance, who fell into destitution wrote:

Yaşıtlarını gördükçe	When I see boys your age
Günde bin kere ölüyom.	I die a thousand times a day.
Yedi oğlanın anasıyım	I am a mother of seven sons
Elden fitire alıyom.[84]	Yet I take alms from strangers.

Material hardships, however, were not the only source of vulnerability of soldiers' families at home. Along with extreme privations, hard work, and loss of family members, violence against women was a characteristic feature of everyday life on the Ottoman home front. As early as in January 1915, the Ministry of Interior sent a general circular to all provinces informing them that in some regions assaults were taking place on the families of soldiers who were "ready to sacrifice their lives on the borders in order to defend religion, chastity, and motherland." The minister of the interior ordered local administrators to do their best to prevent such unfortunate incidents and, if they occurred, to send the perpetrators to courts-martial immediately.[85] A couple of months later, a similar circular was sent to the provinces regarding encroachments on soldiers' properties that occurred during their absence. The Ministry reminded local officials that it was their duty to protect soldiers' estates and properties, which were entrusted to the care of the government, and urged them to take the necessary measures to prevent such incidents.[86]

Although violence affected almost every woman's life, especially those in the countryside, soldiers' families were one of the most vulnerable groups on the Ottoman home front. By August 1915, the Ministry of War had warned the Ministry of Interior that assaults on their families were adversely affecting soldiers' morale. Army officials seemed extremely concerned that the soldiers would become distracted by troubles at home. They recognized that unless the government took harsh measures to prevent these attacks, the war effort would be seriously compromised. Soldiers whose families were attacked either requested leave or deserted their units in order to go back to their villages, furnish protection against assailants, or take revenge. For these soldiers, military service was at odds with the duty of protecting the family. War, in this sense, led to the violation of the right of husbands to exclusive sexual access to their wives, hurt the honor of the family, and undermined masculine dominance. While fulfilling the duty of protecting the empire against the enemy, they found themselves unable simultaneously to protect their hearths and homes.

Alarmed by increasing desertion rates, the state came to assume the role of a "surrogate husband" that would protect the family and its honor in the absence of men. With the purpose of accelerating the process of trial and punishment, military tribunals were charged with the duty of prosecuting crimes against officers' and soldiers' relatives.[87] In a circular, the Ministry of War declared that the military tribunals would treat the attacks on military families as the equivalent of the serious offense of "undermining military strength" and mete out harsh punishments to those guilty of them. The increasing number of assaults on soldiers' families and their properties, however, gave a new sense of urgency for the government to take bolder measures. In September 1915, it enacted a draconian law to curb such assaults on soldiers' families. According to this provisional law, people who forcibly raped soldiers' wives, children, or other close relatives were to be summarily executed.[88] Despite these harsh measures, however, the state became increasingly unable to shield soldiers' families from sexual abuse and exploitation as the war progressed. Desertion, in that sense, became the soldier's response to the state's inability to protect his family and his determination to reassume that role.

After Gallipoli: A Desperate Search for New Recruits

Between February 1915 and January 1916, the Ottomans successfully defended the Dardanelles against the Entente troops, forcing the latter to withdraw. The defeat of the British and French forces affected the overall course of the war in several important ways, the discussion of which is beyond the scope of this book. It should be emphasized, however, that the cost of the Gallipoli campaign for the Ottoman Empire was huge. While the victory elevated the spirits of the people and boosted the self-confidence of the Unionists, it placed an enormous burden on the Ottomans in terms of manpower losses. A postwar Ottoman General Staff study put the number of casualties at 55,127 killed, 21,498 died of disease, and 174,684 wounded, sick, and missing, while Otto Liman von Sanders Pasha, commander of the Ottoman Fifth Army in Gallipoli, estimated that there were a total of 218,000 Ottoman casualties, 66,000 of whom were fatalities.[89] These figures became even more important when one considers that, in less than a year, this was a second major blow to the relatively well-trained segments of the army. In general, it would not be wrong to argue that the Gallipoli campaign drained the available pool of reserves to such a degree that the Ottoman army would never be able to overcome the shortage in manpower throughout the rest of the war. Even though the Entente powers could not reach their immediate objectives, "the Dardanelles operations . . . had the effect of permanently weakening the Turkish army as a striking force," the historians W. E. D. Allen and Paul Muratoff observe.[90]

From the early months of 1916 on, the Ottoman authorities were occupied with trying to recuperate from this costly victory and, at the same time, resist the enemy now advancing on two different fronts: in eastern Anatolia and Mesopotamia. The British advance towards Kut al-Amara and Baghdad obliged the Ottoman army to reinforce this front with thousands of new conscripts while simultaneously trying to tackle with the unexpected Russian winter offensive under the command of General Nikolai Yudenich. In the first half of 1916, the Third Ottoman Army in eastern Anatolia found itself defending an exceptionally wide front stretching from the Black Sea to Lake Van. By mid-February 1916, the Russians had already shattered the Ottoman defenses and captured Erzurum, forcing the Ottoman army to surrender thousands of prisoners. In the spring and summer of the same year, Yudenich's forces smashed what had remained of the Third Army, advanced deep into the Ottoman territory, and captured the major Ottoman cities of Trabzon and Erzincan. The Ottomans at this point seemed helpless to halt the Russian advance to the west. "Had the Russian revolution not happened," a historian of the Russian war effort observes, "the Army would have been well placed to bring the war against the Ottoman Empire to a triumphant conclusion."[91] The Russians, however, did not press ahead and fully exploit their gains. Nevertheless, the 1916 campaign wore down the already weakened Ottoman army even further. The Russians' 1916 campaign against the Third Army, according to a high-ranking Ottoman officer, inflicted the heaviest damage on the Ottoman forces in the war after Gallipoli.[92] Continuous drainage of Ottoman manpower in two consecutive war years would compel the Unionists into a desperate search for more men, imposing even heavier burdens on society.

The staggering human cost of the war so far and the increasingly fragile military situation did not, however, prevent the Ottoman High Command from taking a momentous decision that would deeply affect the management of the available manpower sources: the empire would contribute to the European campaigns of its allies. Enver Pasha and his advisors were convinced that the fate of the Great War would be decided on the Western Front, and that the Ottoman military should actively engage in battles there to tip the balance in favor of the empire's allies. Between the summer of 1916 and the spring of 1918, approximately 100,000 Ottoman soldiers were accordingly sent to Galicia, Romania, and Macedonia. These units were formed by selecting the best-trained soldiers available in the Ottoman army. They were equipped and clothed much better than their counterparts left behind.[93] The stiff opposition mounted by several high-ranking Ottoman and German officers on the grounds that the empire itself desperately needed these troops, did not suffice to alter this decision.[94]

To the opponents of the decision, the gravity of the situation on the ground could hardly be overstated: two years of continuous fighting had sorely depleted the ranks and elevated the manpower problem to crisis proportions. The government and army high command were indeed keenly aware of the situation and had attempted to fill the ranks by increasing the upper age limit for military service from forty-five to fifty in March 1916.[95] In its reasoning, the government maintained that the empire still had extensive sources of manpower to continue the war effort. The Law of Military Obligation in its current form did not, however, suffice to meet the needs of the army, which was fighting on several scattered fronts.[96] The law that increased the age limit particularly emphasized that the provisions would also cover individuals who had already performed military service and fulfilled their obligations. As discussed above, many of these men over forty-five had already been drafted into home and coast guard regiments. Now, with the new legislation, the military planners aimed to call up those who had managed to evade service.

As these efforts fell short of producing sufficient number of recruits, the Unionists turned to more drastic measures in the face of the growing manpower problem. A new provisional law enacted in October 1916 empowered the heads of enlistment offices to conscript those who were not liable according to their registered ages (*sinn-i mukayyed*) but were suitable for military service because of their personal physical characteristics.[97] By means of this law, as the army representative explained in the parliament, the state aimed to draft people who had either destroyed their identity cards, never registered, or registered late. The unreliability of population records and the generally accepted idea that Ottoman citizens customarily did not register their children until years after they were born underlay the government's move.[98]

As rumors about the government's decision spread, once again panic swept through the Ottoman home front like wildfire. Lifting established principles with the stroke of a pen, the government caused great concern and indignation among those potentially affected. The policy, as a high-ranking Ottoman officer later confessed, was implemented in a dreadful manner and opened doors for the utmost abuse.[99] With a new and unprecedentedly enhanced authority in their hands, security forces began to arrest men who looked strong enough to serve. The result was a veritable manhunt for able-bodied men on the home front. A contemporary recalled vividly the treatment of men over sixty who were still robust: "They seized these men by the collar and sent them to enlistment offices. They check their size, height, teeth. 'You are at most forty,' [they say]. 'A perfect soldier.'"[100] Fear especially in the empire's urban centers reached such an extent that healthy looking men did everything to avoid to be seen in public places. On the opposite end of the age spectrum, the panic was equally devastating, both for teenage boys and parents striving to save them from the draft. "Every effort was made by the Turkish mothers," observed the new American ambassador to the Porte, "to have their young men try to appear younger than they were so as not to be drafted. Boys of fifteen and sixteen looked grotesque in their children's costumes."[101]

This provisional law generated arguably the most heated discussions about conscription in the Ottoman parliament, which was usually quite compliant with the demands of the army and the government. Deputies from all over the empire demonstrated their eagerness to repeal it immediately. In no other meeting of the parliament during the war was the rejection of a law so fervently requested. Since the law had been in effect for some time on a provisional basis before it reached the parliament, deputies had witnessed the horrors it was creating on the ground.[102] Arguing that the law brought about the conscription of children fourteen and fifteen years of age, many of them demanded its immediate abrogation and the release of the conscripts who had been drafted by means of it. Given the abuses it encouraged, the Edirne deputy Faik Bey said, it should not be allowed to remain in effect even for a minute.[103] It absurdly called for "the determination of age through the [condition of the] body [*cüsse itibariyle sinn tayini*]," the Istanbul deputy Charalampidis Efendi protested.[104] Eventually, the parliament managed to defeat the bill, which would become one of only a few government proposals pertaining to soldiering ever rejected by the parliament during the war.[105]

Although the Unionist regime resorted to increasingly harsher draft policies, they proved inadequate to meet the army's ever-growing needs. The high number of casualties during the first two years of the war and the ever more threatening advance of Russian and British forces compelled the authorities to expand the resources of conscription. Towards the end of 1916, the Unionists calculated that they could raise only 300,000 more men, including the non-Muslims.[106] Entangled in an increasingly destructive war, the Ottoman High Command realized that the army was so depleted that it could not bear the burden of the few remaining exemptions any longer. As the new Law of Military Obligation had already eliminated many exemptions, the only sizable group of individuals who still enjoyed the privilege of not being drafted were those who could pay the exemption fee. Desperate in its search for new recruits, the government enacted a provisional law in October 1916 revoking the legislation that allowed for the purchase of exemption from military service. In its reasoning, the government openly stated that the level of human resources necessary to sustain the strength and order of the imperial army had diminished, and that this situation required the exploitation of all available reserves.[107]

The law annulled previous legislation on exemption fees and authorized the minister of war in case of urgent necessity to conscript those who had already bought exemption.[108] The fees they had paid would be reimbursed.[109] The calls from deputies in the parliament and senate members to exempt teachers, artisans, craftsmen, and, above all, farmers fell on deaf ears.[110] Once the government announced the law, which came to be known among the Ottoman people as the *redd-i bedel* (literally, "rejection of the exemption fee"), and summoned those who had paid exemption fees to enlistment offices, it caused great concern and displeasure, especially among merchants, businesspeople, and other well-to-do segments of the society. Worried about turmoil in the economic sphere, Enver Pasha felt compelled to publish a declaration in newspapers to reassure public opinion: "The government would never use this authority in a way that would instigate an economic crisis. It would provide sufficient time to those called up to make the necessary business arrangements in order to avoid any harm being inflicted on themselves, their families, and the nation."[111] Nevertheless, the decision to draft the *bedelci*s (those who had purchased their exemption from military service) dealt a staggering blow to commercial life in urban centers and brought economic activity almost to a standstill.[112]

By enacting this law, the CUP government clearly violated the contract set forth by the previous laws on exemption fee. Subjects from all over the empire who had already paid the exemption fee wrote to the Ministry of Interior and the parliament to protest and ask for the maintenance of the existing system on the grounds that their presence on the home front was crucial. In their petitions, people underlined the importance of their activities to the well-being of the empire and sought to obtain exemption from military service.[113] The many attempts in this direction were fruitless, however, leading people to contrive new ways of disentangling themselves from the net of conscription. Since the *bedel* was no longer an option, bribing conscription officials and physicians to obtain a draft deferment became the commonest ways to evade the draft.

Towards the End

The second half of World War I saw the weakening and eventual withdrawal of Russia from the conflict. The political turmoil and growing resentment against tsarist wartime policies led to regime change in March 1917. Tsar Nicholas II abdicated his throne, ending three centuries of Romanov rule, and a provisional government took office. The provisional government's fateful resolution to carry out Russia's obligations to its allies and to continue the war, however, met with widespread popular anger. As socioeconomic and political discontent grew, the Russian army gradually disintegrated. The new revolutionary situation left the government in disarray and propelled the Bolsheviks into power in November 1917. Opposed both to the tsarist government's imperialist designs and to the provisional government's decision to continue the war, the Bolsheviks sued for peace and took Russia out of the conflict. To the beleaguered Ottoman government, the dramatic breakdown of its archenemy came as a great relief.

The Ottomans, however, still had other reasons to worry. Between early December 1915 and late April 1916, Ottoman troops besieged Major General Charles Townshend's 6th (Poona) Division of the British Indian Army at Kut-al-Amara. Exhaustion of supplies, failure of the relief operations, logistical breakdowns, and Ottoman persistence forced Townshend to surrender with his 13,000 troops on 29 April 1916. The siege and subsequent humiliation, however, had spurred a radical reorganization of the British army on the Mesopotamian front. Reinforced with new troops and better logistics, it had recovered from the devastating defeat and become a formidable foe by late 1916. Despite the weeks-long fierce defense at Kut, Ottoman forces could not forestall the

British advance. Baghdad fell in March 1917, Tikrit in November 1917, and Kirkuk in May 1918.

On the Sinai/Palestinian front, the British army similarly turned the tables. In the two years between the first Ottoman attack on the Suez Canal and the British advance in early 1917, the British army had repulsed two Ottoman assaults into the Canal Zone, laid a water pipeline and constructed a railroad through the Sinai Peninsula to southern Palestine. The Ottoman army had successfully resisted the British attacks along the Gaza-Beersheba line until late October 1917, albeit at a high cost. The worn-down Ottoman troops could not hold out much longer. Gaza and Jaffa fell to the British in November and Jerusalem surrendered in December 1917. Following the loss of Baghdad, the fall of Jerusalem dealt a painful blow to the Unionists' already tarnished prestige, especially in the Arab provinces of the empire.[114]

During the second half of the war, the Ottomans also witnessed the gradual erosion of the imperial army. From a peak of around 800,000 combatants in November 1915, the army's strength dropped sharply: down to 400,000 in March 1917 and 275,000 in January 1918. By the time the Ottoman Empire's war effort collapsed in October 1918, there were fewer than 100,000 Ottoman combatants on the battlefields.[115] The army had lost a significant number of its forces to battlefield casualties, disease, and captivity. Desertion, in the meantime, had evolved into a mass phenomenon as the war's socioeconomic ravages became increasingly devastating.[116] Amid worsening conditions on both the battlefronts and the home front, men left their ranks in droves to save their lives and provide for their families. As a result, desertion rates climbed to unprecedented levels. By the end of 1917, Otto Liman von Sanders estimated the number of deserters to be roughly 300,000.[117] According to General Hans von Seeckt, Friedrich Bronsart von Schellendorff's successor as chief of staff of the Ottoman army, this number had reached 450,000 by the end of the war.[118]

In addition to waning morale, exhaustion, and concern for their families' well-being, the Ottoman state's diminished capacity of control played a significant role in encouraging men to take the risk of desertion. As the state gradually lost its ability to enforce its many laws, it became significantly easier for soldiers to get away from the army. According to Liman von Sanders, every one of the divisions sent to the Caucasus front and south of the Taurus Mountains had lost thousands of soldiers.[119] Mustafa Kemal Pasha, the commander of the Seventh Army, also complained in 1917 that, of units departing Istanbul with a thousand men, even the best reached Aleppo with only five hundred.[120] In a report dated October 1917, Friedrich Kress von Kressenstein, the commander of the Eighth Army, gave a more accurate picture of the extent to which units were losing men at this later stage of the war: The 24th Division left the Haydarpaşa train station in Istanbul with 10,057 soldiers, yet only 4,635 of them eventually made it to the front. Of the initial troop strength, 19 percent fell ill and were hospitalized, 24 percent deserted, and 8 percent failed to return from temporary leave.[121] The ever-growing number of deserters and the decreasing chances of being caught led more and more soldiers to take their fate into their own hands. Hundreds of thousands of Ottoman soldiers joined those who had already deserted.[122] In the last two years of the war, desertion resembled a rapidly spreading, infectious disease, which the Ottoman state could not contain.

Even the harshest penalties imposed by the army for desertion had become ineffective—there were cases in which members of a firing squad who had executed a deserter deserted themselves the very next day.[123] As time passed, too, dramatic increases in the number of deserters made the death penalty impractical. In most cases, if they were caught, deserters were put back into the ranks again after a few days' imprisonment or a beating. This was a dilemma for the army's high command. On the one hand, the army's desperate need for able-bodied men made it practically impossible to execute or severely punish every single deserter. On the other, however, soldiers who heard that deserters were going unpunished became more likely to make their own attempts at escape. Capital punishment was therefore reserved for those who had deserted multiple times. In Kayseri, for instance, Vehip Pasha, then commander of the Third Army, first ordered the branding of the right hands of the deserters with an "F" (for *firari*, or deserter). If a soldier with a marked hand was caught deserting again, he was to be summarily executed. Yet even this method became ineffective due to the enormous number of repeat offenders, and Vehip issued a new order that lists be prepared and every tenth one of them be executed.[124]

As the manpower supply approached its limits, the decline in the quality of the new recruits became increasingly obvious. Older men in poorer health and with less experience took the place of the younger, healthier, better-trained conscripts of the war's first years. "The army is now much weaker than it was at the beginning of the war," Mustafa Kemal complained bitterly in a report dated September 1917. "The human resources of the empire are insufficient to meet this deficit. . . . Half of the 59th Division, which was sent to me with thousand-men-strong regiments to perform the most difficult duties in the world, consists of invalids who do not even have the strength to stand up. After they are separated out, seventeen- to twenty-year-old underdeveloped boys and forty-five- to fifty-five-year-old useless men make up the remaining soldiers."[125] On his way back from a hunting excursion, the Spanish consul in Jerusalem, Antonio de la Cierva Lewita, conde de Ballobar, came across recruits similar to those mentioned by Mustafa Kemal Pasha: "On the road back we met two battalions of Turkish infantry, and, frankly, the military spirit and physical resistance of the troops were noticeable just for their absence. Behind each battalion we found many, very many straggling, sick soldiers, leaning on a cane to walk or sitting at the side of the road. It was pitiful to see them."[126] These two high-ranking figures were not the only contemporaries who saw the army's situation as undeniably bleak. İlhan Bey, a noncommissioned officer during the war, recalled the new recruits entrusted to him in June 1917 to be trained for war. His regiment included a good number of soldiers who were blind, crippled, old, and "whose disabilities were obvious even without medical examination."[127] Moving them back to the local headquarters proved nearly impossible, since many of these soldiers did not even have enough strength to walk. This enormous pressure on the empire's human resources left an indelible mark on the Ottoman collective memory which is poignantly illustrated by a song heard by an officer on the streets of Birecik (Urfa):

Binbaşı geliyor eli sopalı	The major is coming, stick in hand.
Arkasına takmış körü, topalı	Behind him come the blind and the crippled.
Halimiz çok yaman oldu	We have been in such a disastrous state
Seferberlik çıkalı[128]	Since the order of the mobilization.

As early as the first months of 1917, the Ottoman Empire seemed to have reached the limits of its manpower supply. Reporting to the German Army Headquarters in March 1917, Bronsart von Schellendorff wrote that while Ottoman army headquarters had managed to replace the losses among its officers, it would no longer be possible to do so among the rank-and-file, "despite the fact that the bolt is screwed as tight as possible in this country."[129] According to an official estimate, 60,000 men were needed each month to make up for losses.[130] Having tapped into all other sources of manpower and having failed to keep desertion in check, however, the Unionists had few ways left to fill in the gaps. Reducing the age limit yet again seemed to be the easiest of these options. The government, despite objections, therefore revised the law of conscription once again in May 1917 and added seventeen-year-olds to the list of subjects who could be drafted.[131]

Despite the official wartime rhetoric encouraging women to sacrifice their husbands and sons for the greater good of the empire and religion, the reduction of the age limit met with a torrent of grief and resistance. Folklore repeatedly recounts the recruitment of these young boys, testifying to the deep wounds it inflicted on the Ottoman people's collective memory. The hundreds of songs and laments describing young boys' conscription and death are virtually a genre of their own according to Yaşar Kemal, one of the early collectors of them. Since these boys were so young when they were called to arms, they departed their villages crying, "Woe, my mother" (*vay anam*), villagers told Kemal. Hence the common term "'woe, my mother' conscription laments" (*vay anam kur'asının ağıtları*). In some villages, women expressed their grief even in the rugs they wove, called "'woe, my mother' conscription kilims" (*vay anam kur'asının kilimleri*).[132]

For the mothers who composed these laments, the recruits were mere children, poor vulnerable "rosebuds," too young to be sent to the front to die:[133]

Davul zurna çalınıyor	Drums are beaten, pipes are played
Onbeşliler gelsin deyi.	To call fifteeners to arms.
Onbeşliden asker m'olur?	Can a fifteener be a soldier?
Topluyorlar ölsün deyi.[134]	They're gathered up to die.

Countless songs like this "lament for the fifteeners"—*onbeşliler* ("fifteeners") were boys born in 1315 (1899-1900) and drafted when they were seventeen— tell a story of disaster very different from the official narrative of the war.

Conclusions

In March 1914, General Helmuth von Moltke, the German chief of staff, wrote gloomily to an Austrian colleague to the effect that

> Turkey militarily is of no value. The reports from our military mission are frankly hopeless. The army is in a state that defies all description. Whereas one used to speak of Turkey as the "sick man [of Europe]," now one has to speak of him as the dead [one]. He does not have power to live anymore and is irretrievably in a state of [mortal] agony. Our military mission resembles a group of doctors standing at the deathbed of a terminally ill patient.[135]

Both its allies and enemies underestimated the Ottoman Empire's war-making capacity. Disproving von Moltke's opinion, the Ottoman army performed remarkably well in World War I. Despite the serious problems discussed in this chapter, the empire succeeded in rejuvenating its army, devastated in the Balkan Wars, and mobilizing hundreds of thousands of civilians at short notice. Against considerable odds, the imperial army fought battles on several fronts and inflicted serious losses on its enemies.

The Ottoman policies of soldiering during the war were shaped by the relentless need to bring men onto the battlefields. To meet the ever-growing manpower needs of the army, the military and civilian authorities changed the age limits for conscription, abolished many of the existing exemptions, resorted to recruiting volunteers,[136] and fought, albeit ineffectively, against the evasion of military service. The link between the battlefront and the home front, which became even stronger as the war dragged on, influenced Ottoman policies. For many soldiers, their responsibilities to their families trumped their loyalty to the empire and their dedication to the war effort. As the war rolled on, soldiers became increasingly concerned about their families' helplessness to deal with deteriorating conditions, and hundreds of thousands of them evaded service or deserted their ranks. Soldiering, as a result, became a contested field of interaction between the state and its subjects, a field which played a significant role in determining the disastrous outcome of the war for the Ottoman Empire.

4 FEEDING THE ARMY, STARVING THE PEOPLE

On their way to the Caucasus Front, two young reserve officers, Şevket Süreyya and a friend, stopped at Kayseri. Because they lacked a vehicle or animals and the Ottoman railroad network did not extend to eastern Anatolia, they had no idea how to get to the front. A logistics officer who found them in distress promised to attach these two young officers to a military convoy. When the convoy failed to arrive, the logistics officer suggested a camel convoy, and, finally, that they use the pack animals of passing troops. When neither of these alternatives materialized, he finally decided to raid a marketplace and commandeer villagers' donkeys for reserve officers. The owner of the donkey given to Şevket and his friend was an exhausted old peasant whose animal was his only source of subsistence. For days, he followed them around and slept in front of the inns where they stayed in hopes of getting his animal back. He was relatively fortunate: Şevket and his friend eventually felt pity and gave the donkey back to him.[1] Many throughout the empire would not be so lucky.

Similar concerns overwhelmed members of the Ottoman elite with varying positions and responsibilities. At one point in the second half of the war, two high-ranking officers, Ali Fuad Bey (Erden) and İsmet Bey (İnönü), chiefs of staff of the Fourth and Second Armies, respectively, discussed transporting supplies between the two army zones. Camels bought in southern Arabia at the beginning of the war and previously employed in the Suez Canal campaign would be used for this purpose. Ten thousand of them would be transported to Resulayn in northeastern Syria by train, and from there they would carry supplies hundreds of kilometers in freezing weather to the Second Army, which was suffering debilitating shortages. Since they were hot climate breeds, Ali Fuad Bey was concerned about the fate of these animals:

> It was winter. They would certainly die even before reaching the front. I ex-
> pressed my concern to İsmet Bey. He said: "They'll carry supplies from the train
> station to the front once, only once, and [then] die. We'll make rawhide sandals
> [çarık] out of their hides." . . . The camels left. They all died and became rawhide
> sandals for [soldiers'] bare feet. The misery of these ten thousand camels, which
> had begun in the sand desert of Sinai, finally ended in the icy mountains of
> Çapakçur.[2]

These very different anecdotes shed light on a crucial dimension of the Ottoman war experience: the mobilization of material resources. They illustrate three key aspects of this process. First, both accounts demonstrate how the empire's structural limitations necessitated a heavy reliance on its readily available resources. Second, they offer a rare glimpse into how intrusively and recklessly the army acquired and employed these resources. Finally, they give an idea of how disastrously this process impacted the home front. From a broader perspective, all this points to the much bigger question of how to maintain an enormous battlefront army without jeopardizing the livelihood of civilians or depleting the empire's resources. This critical question vexed the CUP government right from the start of the war.

In all the belligerent nations, making war and civilian daily life became linked in World War I to a degree not seen in earlier conflicts. Nowhere was this intertwining more evident in the Ottoman Empire than in the tremendous task of provisioning hundreds of thousands of soldiers. The exigencies of the war required the allocation of vast human and material resources for military purposes. The effective extraction of these resources from society and their timely delivery to combat zones greatly affected the course of the war. This process, in turn, essentially obliterated the boundaries between *the military* and *the civilian*.

The Entente blockade of Ottoman ports and the underdeveloped and inefficient transportation network made this already daunting task even more difficult. The government and the army experimented with several provisioning systems and devised a number of policies to address the problem. These policies dramatically increased the presence of the state, its regulations, and its representatives in people's everyday lives, thereby imposing new burdens on them. By focusing on the provisioning policies during the war, this chapter aims to analyze these policies' impact on the home-front population, as well as people's reactions to them.

"Official Brigandage": The Policy of War Taxes

The mobilization order in August 1914 faced the Ottoman state with the enormous task of feeding, clothing, equipping, and sheltering hundreds of thousands of recently recruited men. As the army expanded to its wartime strength, its needs grew rapidly. The mobilizing army, as an Ottoman officer aptly noted, was like an "insatiable giant."[3] Daunting for all belligerents, the task of "satiating" this giant proved to be particularly formidable for the Ottoman Empire, given its predominantly agricultural economy, underdeveloped manufacturing base, unsound financial foundation, and inefficient transportation network. Without sufficient resources at hand and lacking the capacity to produce them at short notice, the Ottoman authorities resolved to meet the army's pressing needs in the most expedient yet most intrusive way: by requisitioning. The tumultuous months of *seferberlik* thus saw not only the mobilization of men but also the mobilization of resources on an unprecedented scale.

Military requisitioning, although employed in an utterly exploitative manner and thus raised considerable ire, was not an unlawful practice, at least on paper. Two main legal instruments resorted by state authorities, the Law on the Method of the Imposition of War Taxes (Tekalif-i Harbiye'nin Suret-i Tarhı Hakkında Kanun) and the Law on the Acquisition of Military Transport Vehicles (Tedarik-i Vesait-i Nakliye-i Askeriye Kanunnamesi), constituted its legitimate basis. These two laws remained in effect throughout the war, but were also supplemented by several others, especially during the latter half of the conflict, as they proved inadequate to meet the new challenges the government and the army faced. Furthermore, although these laws were two separate legal instruments, both the officials who employed them and the Ottomans who were subjected to their provisions perceived them as two means to the same end, namely, the appropriation of civilian property for military purposes.

The first of these laws, the Law on War Taxes, was a slightly modified version of a provisional law first implemented during the Balkan Wars.[4] It authorized the military to determine the regions of the empire in which war taxes (*tekalif-i harbiye*) would be imposed. The law charged the war taxes commissions, composed of the highest-ranking civilian and financial officials of the locality, a military representative, a member of the local administrative council, and a representative from the municipality, with commandeering all kinds of goods and supplies required by the army. The commission would leave an amount sufficient to meet the needs of the people and confiscate the rest, issuing official receipts to the owners of these confiscated goods and supplies. Another commission, composed of members of the local administrative council, municipality, and local chamber of commerce, would prepare a comprehensive list that would include local prices for all sorts of confiscated goods. These lists would be used in calculating the total value of impressed goods and supplies. The receipts distributed to people would bear this amount, which would be reimbursed from the annual budget of the year following the end of the mobilization.

To supplement the Law on War Taxes and to meet the army's needs for draft animals and vehicles, the state authorities resorted to a second legal instrument, the Law on Transport Vehicles.[5] This law required the delivery of privately owned animals and vehicles to the army during the mobilization period. It authorized the army general staff to determine the type and quantity of these vehicles and the breeds of the animals as well as the regions from which they would be collected. The law exempted two broad categories of animals and vehicles from the obligation: animals and vehicles that were required by civilian and military officials to execute their duties and animals that were either pregnant or used for breeding. Commissions established specifically for this purpose in town and city centers would conduct the collection of animals and vehicles upon the declaration of the mobilization. The law also imposed strict penalties for noncompliance. As the lawmakers anticipated open or disguised resistance to its implementation, the law prescribed the use of force when necessary to reach its goals.

The Ottoman state had resorted to both laws during the previous conflicts. The Law on Transport Vehicles, enacted in 1889, had been enforced during both the Greek-Ottoman War of 1897 and the Balkan Wars of 1912–13 while the Law on War Taxes had been implemented during the Balkan Wars. When put in practice, these laws attracted resentment from people and fierce criticism from politicians due mainly to the enormous burden they imposed upon society. The Law on War Taxes met with particularly strong opposition from deputies who had witnessed the abuses committed by local war taxes commissions during the Balkan Wars. In a parliamentary debate, Matyos Nalbandyan Efendi, the representative of Kozan, Kazım Bey of Biga, and Fazıl Berki Bey of Kengırı (Çankırı) all pointed to the fact that while the commissions had not hesitated to commandeer the only means of subsistence of the poor, the wealthy had managed to get around the impressments and protect their goods from confiscation. "We should not forget that these people fight against the enemy on the borders," Matyos Nalbandyan Efendi claimed. "They go to the war and leave their animals as a means of subsistence for their families. Then, we proceed to commandeer these animals on which these families are dependent."[6] Deputies rightfully drew attention to the law's vague language, as well as the extraordinary authority it allowed the commissions, which could (and did) lead to the arbitrary implementation of the policy by military officials, as had happened during the Balkan Wars. Notwithstanding all these complaints and concerns, it should be noted that the implementation of the laws in previous conflicts had remained limited in scope and confined to certain regions of the empire. During World War I, however, the CUP government put them into practice on an empirewide scale, for a much longer time period, and with significantly increased vigor.

In August 1914, the process of requisitioning started, almost simultaneously with the mobilization, in a swift and ambitious way. With the strong motivation to meet the immediate needs of an ever-growing army, the war taxes commissions laid their hands on as many sorts and quantities of goods and supplies as they could. Almost everything that might conceivably be needed for military purposes were added by local authorities to the list of items to be confiscated. The lists thus came to include everything from dried vegetables to coal, from kerosene to all kind of cereals. Everywhere war taxes commissions seized 25 percent of all livestock and foodstuffs in the hands of merchants, including items such as potatoes, beans, chickpeas, onions, and butter.[7] The impressments were not, however, limited to comestibles. In Beirut, for instance, the governor, who himself supervised the requisitioning process, ordered the tailors of the city to deliver a large quantity of clothing and underclothing for conscripts; as a result, many of the tailors closed their shops and fled the city.[8] In Harput, with the requisitioning of leather and cloth, all the tailors and shoemakers were gathered up to make clothes and footwear for the recruits.[9] Especially in urban centers the military authorities brutally used the law to confiscate not only items that were required by the war effort but also luxury consumer goods. Silk women's garments, stockings and petticoats, corsets, children's shoes and clothes, caviar, champagne, tableware, babies' slippers, and face powder were among the goods that were impressed by military authorities.[10]

The belief, at least in official circles, in the priority of the army's requirements vested the war taxes commissions and the requisitioning officers with extraordinary authority. Official rhetoric that the empire was fighting for its very existence equipped them with the shield of virtual unaccountability. In his postwar novel *Hakka Sığındık* (We Trusted in God), Hüseyin Rahmi compared the requisitioning officer's authority with the magician's wand:

> [W]hen he [the requisitioning officer] enters a place of business or a warehouse with the whip of war taxes in his hand, as if it were the magic wand of a magician, hundreds of barrels of olive oil, canisters of gas, sacks of sugar, baskets of rice, bales of wool, cotton, cloth vanish in the direction he points. . . . This officer had the power to confiscate all of the goods in the market just by scrawling a couple of numbers on a piece of paper. How did Istanbul, with all its movable and immovable properties, not pass into their own possession? And how did not we, all the inhabitants of the city, end up as their chained slaves? Quite a surprise![11]

Although grotesque and exaggerated, it is no coincidence that this well-known name of Ottoman literature reserved a special place for requisitioning in his 1919 novel, which forcefully criticized the Unionists' wartime policies. Other contemporary observers seem to have concurred with Hüseyin Rahmi. In the words of the U.S. vice consul in Izmir, for instance, the whole process of requisitioning turned into "official brigandage."[12] Even some Unionists were in the same opinion. "What has been done has reached the point of banditry," the minister of finance, Cavid Bey, noted in his diary.[13] For this leading Unionist, the army's confiscation of completely unnecessary luxury goods, the military authorities' indifference to the civilians' needs, and their ignorance of the danger of urban starvation were too much to turn a blind eye to.

Apart from the arbitrary use of authority and widespread corruption, the regular implementation of the law on the ground was immensely flawed. In many cases, the official receipts that should have been issued in exchange for goods delivered were not issued at all.[14] Even when they were, the official record did not mean much, for the recipients knew that the likelihood of reimbursement was extremely low.[15] When receipts were given, as one consular official wrote, they were merely "chance bits of paper scrawled on by a chaoush [*çavuş*, sergeant] or gendarme, bearing no seal or official character whatever."[16] It was also not uncommon for the military authorities to confiscate goods and supplies and only afterwards apply to the war taxes commissions for the assignment of a price, if they did so at all. On a number of occasions, officers bypassed the war taxes commissions and confiscated the needed goods and supplies, an act that generated tension between the military and civilian authorities who were supposed to collaborate in provisioning troops.[17] The deputy governor of Istanbul, for instance, who headed the war taxes commission of the city, wrote to the Ministry of Interior about numerous impressments carried out by army officials without informing the commission. According to the deputy governor, these acts could only be described as extortion [*gasp*], and the perpetrators should be prosecuted and punished.[18] The Ministry of Interior officials, themselves aware of the situation on the ground and concerned about the destabilizing impact of requisitioning, continually warned governors and district administrators about such cases and reminded them that no one, including military officers, was above the law. The minister asked them to prevent direct confiscation by military officers and to conduct the impressments through the war taxes commissions.[19] More often than not these warnings fell on deaf ears.

This sort of excessive and reckless requisitioning was not limited to the capital. In the provinces, too, military authorities resorted to it to meet the needs of their troops, also appropriating "everything that was pleasing and had value." Jakob Künzler, a Swiss missionary doctor in Urfa, described the requisitioning in the first days of the mobilization as "unbelievable": "There was nothing in storage that was not vital for the war and, which therefore, could not be requisitioned by the officers."[20] Reverend Henry Riggs, an American missionary in Harput, similarly writes in his memoirs that he saw soldiers making off with loads of easy chairs, "almost the entire stock in trade of a struggling young cabinetmaker."[21] Requisitioning officers justified such acts by stating that the sale of these items would generate income for the army to purchase necessary provisions.[22] In regions where ethno-religious relations were tense, war taxes were often implemented unequally between Muslims and non-Muslim citizens. In conjunction with the war taxes commissions, local big shots seized the opportunity to strip their non-Muslim rivals of their goods, possessions, and means of production.[23]

Cases of harsh and abusive requisitioning were far from being sporadic, isolated incidents. Eyewitness accounts of them can be found from all around the empire. These draconian measures attest to both the Unionists' fear of being caught unprepared for the impending conflict and their expectation of a short war and a speedy victory. Anticipating territorial and material gains after a few months' fighting, they focused on meeting the army's needs as quickly as possible, disregarding the needs of the civilian population and the soundness and stability of the imperial economy. In the eyes of the common people, however, such brutal requisitioning amounted to plunder, and they greatly resented those responsible for its implementation. Together with the harsh conscription process, widespread requisitioning thus damaged military-civilian relations from the very beginning of the conflict. Four long years of war would only make things worse.

Logistical Nightmares

In many Ottoman towns and cities, the first act of the military authorities in August 1914 was "to seize all the best horses in the streets."[24] The town criers who summoned men to the recruitment offices to enlist also instructed people to bring in all draft animals for official inspection,[25] which was rightly perceived by many as the first step towards their impressment for army service. The prospect of losing their only farm animals, which they desperately needed to cultivate their fields, led many owners to hide them instead of delivering to the commissions. The U.S. consul general in Beirut noted, for instance, that an exodus of animals from the city to Mount Lebanon had started in spite of "the cordon of gendarmes, which has been thrown tightly about the city."[26]

The government adopted harsh measures in an attempt to prevent evasion of this demand. A codicil was appended to the Military Penal Law making those who concealed their animals and vehicles subject to imprisonment.[27] Frequently, when people attempted to hide their animals or hesitated to deliver them to authorities, their houses were entered and the animals were forcibly impressed.[28] In short, animals and vehicles were collected in an excessively brutal and shortsighted manner despite the explicit call in the law for moderation in its implementation and concern for the maintenance of agricultural production.[29]

In the eyes of many people, what exacerbated the situation even further was the fact that the burden of war taxes was not imposed equally. It was common for local officials and military officers to agree not to confiscate goods, supplies, animals, and vehicles from wealthy people in exchange for bribes or other favors, while implementing the law to the fullest extent for the rest of the population.[30] Especially the veterinary boards that inspected animals for military impressment exercised enormous authority over the process. They often took bribes to reject strong horses as "unsound," while commandeering old, feeble ones.[31] Therefore, although the impressment process placed an unprecedented burden on the Ottoman population as a whole, it was particularly onerous for those of modest means. Most of the time, officers did not take into consideration the critical importance of confiscated goods, animals, or vehicles in these people's lives. Even the transport animals that had been distributed to refugees who had arrived during the Balkan Wars and were living in deplorable conditions could not escape commandeering.[32] The story of a poor peasant from Maraş (today's Kahramanmaraş) who found himself responsible for twelve members of his extended family after his four sons were conscripted into the army tells of how the commission of war taxes commandeered his horse, his family's only means of livelihood, when he brought firewood to sell in the town center. A song attributed to this old woodcutter probably reflects the agony of thousands who were similarly robbed of their animals in the name of war taxes:

Alman benim abaşımı [habeşimi]	Do not take my dark horse
Merhamet eylen efendim	Please pity me, sir.
Bundan başka malım yoktur	It is all I have.
Merhamet eylen efendim	Please pity me, sir.
Bununla tabur dolmaz	This won't meet the needs of the battalion.
Ben ağlarım yüzüm gülmez	I weep, unsmiling,
Dedi oğlum, halim bilmez	Says my son, ignorant of my fate.
Merhamet eylen efendim	Please pity me, sir.
Beş sene askerde durdum	I was in the army for five years.
Latif [redif] dediğin gördüm	I experienced reserve duty.
Paşalara boru çaldım	I sounded the bugle for commanders.
Merhamet eylen efendim[33]	Please pity me, sir

Apart from a deepened sense of urgency among the Unionists and fear of being caught unprepared, the aggressive impressment of vehicles and animals stemmed also from the structural problems of the Ottoman transportation network and the army's inadequate logistics. Large armies meant that their needs for food, fodder, weapons, ammunition, and other supplies and equipment would also be large. Furthermore, World War I armies, including the Ottoman army, were equipped with machine guns and modern artillery, and large amounts of ammunition for these were essential.[34] More than in any other wars of the past, the armies' performance on the battlefield came to depend on the effective transportation of supplies and ammunition across great distances and their timely delivery to troops.

For the Ottomans, these new features of the war posed particularly formidable challenges. In peacetime, the empire's major cities were connected to one another primarily by steamship. Regular maritime lines not only connected the port cities of Trabzon, Samsun, Istanbul, Izmir, Mersin, Alexandretta, Haifa, Jaffa, and Beirut with one another, but also with other major Mediterranean ports, the Black Sea, and beyond.[35] Following the outbreak of the war, however, maritime transport gradually ceased to be an option for the Ottoman Empire. The Entente blockade of the eastern Mediterranean cut off its port cities from the rest of the world and significantly curtailed coastal communications within the empire itself. On all the empire's coasts, enemy ships frequently torpedoed and sank civilian and military vessels alike, rendering even the small-scale shipping increasingly dangerous. Land travel, under these circumstances, was the only viable option.

By the time the war broke out, however, Ottoman roads and railroads were woefully inadequate to handle the heavy traffic resulting from the mobilization and frequent troop movements. The Ottoman railroad system was severely limited in capacity when compared with the extensive railroad networks of other belligerent nations. Germany had 64,000 kilometers of railroads for 540,000 square kilometers of territory, and France had 51,000 for 536,000, but there were only 5,759 kilometers of Ottoman railroads to cover an empire of 1,760,000 square kilometers.[36] Moreover, these railroad lines were not an integrated system but "a series of often fragmented single track lines of several different gauges."[37] The major single-track line that connected Istanbul to the empire's Arab provinces, which was thus the principal supply line for the armies in the region, was interrupted in the Taurus and Amanus Mountains in southern Anatolia. Despite the backbreaking work of labor battalions and prisoners of war, tunnels through the Amanus range were not completed until January 1917, and construction of the Taurus tunnels concluded only a month prior to the signing of the armistice in October 1918. Military supplies transported on the line therefore had to be unloaded at these points, carried on horseback over mountain roads, and reloaded again at the railhead on the other side.[38]

The fact that Ottoman railroads did not cover many parts of the empire compounded the logistical nightmare. Eastern Anatolia, which became a major zone of conflict between Ottoman and Russian forces, for instance, was a case in point. The Russians had built a new railroad connecting Tbilisi and Alexandropol to Kars and later to Sarıkamış in the 1890s, but Russian political pressure prevented any significant improvement of the transportation infrastructure on the other side of the frontier.[39] Ankara, the last station on the central Anatolian branch of the major railroad line, was approximately seven hundred kilometers from Erzurum, the headquarters of the Ottoman Third Army. The road more commonly used by military units deployed to the eastern front extended between the Ulukışla station of the Anatolian railroad and Sivas, and was approximately four hundred kilometers long. Draft animals, camels, donkeys, oxcarts and often porters drawn from the home-front population itself became the only means of transportation in these and other "railless" parts of the empire.

The army high command was obviously aware of the situation, nonetheless persisted in launching large-scale military campaigns in regions of the empire not reachable by rail. Before the Sarıkamış campaign, for instance, Enver Pasha urged the commander of the Third Army, Hasan İzzet Pasha, to make the entire local population carry provisions for the army on their backs if the available means of transport did not suffice.[40] Even the resignation of Hasan İzzet Pasha from his post, citing the almost impossible conditions for such a campaign, did not have a sobering effect on the high command. As planned, the duty of transportation was meted out to the civilian population, including women and children.[41] One day a week, they had to carry the army's supplies between designated stations. A "transport campaign," organized by the Erzurum local government, CUP clubs, and patriotic civil society organizations, occasioned heartrending scenes of schoolchildren carrying sacks of grain on their backs.[42] The campaign perfectly illustrates how the empire's underdeveloped transportation network not only hampered the Ottoman war effort but also aggravated the war's already heavy strain on the home-front population. To maintain the continuity of transportation, people had to be forced to labor and their animals had to be commandeered on a constant basis, while inadequate feeding, overloading, poor road conditions, and contagious diseases decimated them by the thousands.

From Abundance to Scarcity

With the empire facing major challenges, it did not take long for the first economic problems to manifest themselves on the Ottoman home front. As soon as the mobilization was declared, the price of almost all products rose rapidly in urban centers. Painful memories of recent wars and fear of impending shortages drove people to stockpile anything for sale. Alarmed by the panic, the government stepped in swiftly: a cap was imposed on the price of bread, the main staple item of the Ottoman diet, and a number of profiteering grocers, bakers, and shopkeepers were court-martialed and punished.[43] Newspapers, no doubt encouraged by the government, reported on these cases extensively, both to intimidate other merchants with similar intentions and to boost people's confidence in the authorities.[44] From mid-August 1914 on, the price of staples fell to (and occasionally below) their prewar levels, owing to the government's ban on exporting foodstuffs, which kept that year's bountiful harvest within the country. The Ottoman public's initial excitement gradually died down as normal prices for basic domestic items returned and reigned until the summer of 1915.

The government, meanwhile, proved incapable of regulating the price of imported products. The outbreak of the war had caused a dramatic increase in the prices of sugar, rice, coffee, kerosene, and matches, all of which the Ottoman Empire imported in large quantities. A decline in supply, exorbitant freight and insurance rates, and greater popular demand prompted merchants throughout the empire to charge high prices for all imported commodities.[45] Although they were sparsely available and expensive, however, these items could still be obtained in urban centers, even after the empire entered the war. Existing stocks were not yet exhausted, and they even continued to be replenished to a degree. The Dardanelles, the main artery that connected Istanbul and the Black Sea ports to the rest of the world, had been closed to traffic by late September 1914, but ships flying neutral flags continued to supply commodities to the capital through the Aegean port of Dedeağaç (now Alexandropolis), which was connected to Istanbul by rail. Izmir was similarly supplied through the small nearby port of Urla after the city's main port was closed in October.[46] Greek and Italian vessels were active in transporting high-value, low-bulk merchandise to all Ottoman Mediterranean ports, although in much decreased numbers as compared to peacetime. During these first months of the war, the Entente navies did not draw up a blockade policy in the Mediterranean and were reluctant to divert warships to blockading.[47]

Nevertheless, given the Ottoman Empire's declaration of war on its principal international trading partners and closure of the main waterways and vital ports, the prewar volume of trade through all Ottoman ports shrank dramatically. Before the war, most of the empire's rice, another staple of the Ottoman diet, had come from Egypt, India, Italy, and the Dutch East Indies. For cotton goods, the empire was mostly dependent on imports from Great Britain, from which it also imported significant amounts of coal. Moreover, considerable quantities of foreign flour reached Ottoman ports from Russia, France, Bulgaria, Romania, the United States, and Canada. War against the Entente thus meant cutting the empire off from its major overseas suppliers, ensuring shortages in many items of critical importance. The empire's wartime allies were far from capable of replacing these losses.

The dislocations created by war taxes further exacerbated the problems caused by the dwindling volume of imports. The widespread imposition of such taxes had a catastrophic impact on the Ottoman economy due mostly to the anxiety they provoked among producers and merchants. This climate of fear had a particularly unsettling effect on agricultural production. In addition to the loss of men and animals to the army, the requisitioning of grain and other products gradually reduced peasants' incentive to plant for the market.[48] Since they knew the army would impress their surplus product, peasants did not want to spend any money and labor to cultivate beyond what they needed. When they did, they increasingly avoided bringing their products to market for fear of confiscation. "With commandeering in full swing," a longtime resident of Baghdad wrote, farmers would, "naturally, not risk bringing their goods into the city. They dare not even winnow the grain lest the authorities should seize it, and if it were winnowed they could not get anyone to convey it into the market."[49] Baghdadi farmers' reaction was but an early example of how the state's aggressive intervention in local economies disrupted prewar trade networks. Together with the virtual cessation of seaborne trade and the military's takeover of railroad traffic, these disruptions would sever the ties that bound the empire's centers of consumption to its agricultural regions.

A few months into the war, the war taxes' impact began to be felt at a much deeper level. In February 1915, in a report voicing concerns shared by many, the governor of Aleppo identified several problems that the war taxes had created on the ground. According to the governor, the unequal and remorseless implementation of the war taxes policy had brought the region's once vibrant economy to a halt.[50] For example, administrators of soap-manufacturing towns had informed the governor that because of fear of confiscation by the military, soap was not being produced in their regions that year. In previous years, livestock traders from Aleppo had traveled to the provinces of Mosul, Van, Diyarbekir, and Erzurum to purchase large numbers of sheep. In 1914, however, the drovers had not attempted to bring even a single animal. Similarly, even though the season was passing, traders did not set out to tour villages and tribes to collect the wool that peasants and tribe members had produced. This would further depress the economy in the region, according to the governor, since the owners of livestock would not be able to pay their cattle taxes, which they normally did from the annual sale of wool. Expecting the war taxes commission to assign lower prices for their goods and supplies, merchants ceased importing from abroad and tried to sell off their goods below regular market prices. The governor described the situation as an economic crisis (*buhran-ı iktisadi*) and singled out the war taxes as the major cause of it. On the other hand, this system defeated its own purpose of assuring the provisioning of the army, since confiscations led to a sharp decline in production and the concealment of existing goods and supplies from governmental authorities. The governor proposed the abrogation of the war taxes and the adoption a new method of direct purchasing to feed and equip the army.[51]

Indeed, as early as October 1914, even before entering the war, the Ottoman government had realized the "impact that the current method of collecting war taxes inflicted on the economy" and established a commission to revise it.[52] A couple of months later, farmers' increasingly visible reluctance to cultivate for the market and deliver their products to the army compelled the government to take more concrete steps and adopt a new policy. Accordingly, the council of ministers set upper limits on the amount of goods and supplies that could be subjected to requisitioning. For instance, only 15 percent of all sheep and goats could be taken in the form of war taxes. The rest of the meat that the army needed would be purchased at the market. More important, the council decided that the army's need for grain would be met through the annual tithe. Again, if the tithe did not satisfy the army's needs, the missing amount would be purchased at the market. The decision strictly prohibited the confiscation of agricultural products from merchants and the general population.[53] In certain parts of the empire, most notably in eastern Anatolia and Mesopotamia, army units were already buying grain from producers to mitigate their immediate shortages.[54] But this practice remained mostly sporadic and did not constitute a consistent, empirewide policy. The realization that the war would not be over soon and the fear that declining imports and agricultural productivity would threaten the subsistence of the army and the civilian population led to the introduction of a more formal, standardized policy by the CUP government.[55]

Despite this radical policy change, however, urban areas had begun to be affected by the shortages before the first year of the war was over. In addition to imported products, basic items in the Ottoman diet could only be obtained with great difficulty. In the summer of 1915, the first queues were being formed in front of bakeries in major cities. Because unexhausted grain stocks from 1914 were still abundant in the interior, notwithstanding extensive requisitioning, these early shortages were mostly unforeseen, if not totally unexpected, by the authorities. Rev. Henry K. Wingate, a missionary in Talas, in central Anatolia, for instance, wrote in early 1915, "Owing to lack of transportation, flour is cheaper than it has been at any time during the past ten years, but [the prices of] all imported articles are out of sight."[56] In April 1915, a missionary from Antep reported along the same lines that "wheat was the cheapest ever known."[57] Yet a resident of the capital noted in his diary in May 1915 that he saw "many people crowded before bakers shops."[58]

The underlying cause of these first major shortages in urban areas was the Ottoman Empire's forced transition to reliance on its own resources, most notably grain and coal. Before the war, the empire's population centers met their needs for the ingredients of bread from both internal and external sources in varying degrees. Over the past decades, the construction of railroads, connecting port cities to their agricultural hinterlands, had generally increased the importance of domestic resources in provisioning. Yet some cities, including Istanbul, continued to be dependent on outside sources. The opening of the Anatolian Railway in 1896, for instance, facilitated the transport of Anatolian grain to the huge Istanbul market and lessened the capital's dependence on its traditional suppliers of grain, Russia, Romania, and Bulgaria.[59] This development was not, however, accompanied by a significant decline in the volume of imported flour to the city. As did other urban centers, the capital lacked enough flour mills to grind the amount of grain now reaching it from Anatolia. More important, foreign flour superior in quality to Anatolian flour continued to be easily obtainable from abroad. Even fifteen years after the completion of the Anatolian Railway, "foreign sources still satisfied half of Istanbul's bread ingredient needs."[60]

Beirut, the empire's third-busiest port city after Istanbul and Izmir, was no different. Despite its geographical proximity to the region's grain-growing areas, Beirut (and Mount Lebanon) imported flour, wheat, and barley in significant quantities either from other Ottoman ports or from Cyprus, Russia, and France due to the lower cost of maritime transportation.[61] Similarly, Jerusalem, another major population center, was dependent both on grain supplies from its hinterland of Karak and al-Salt and on imports by sea.[62] With the onset of war, however, importing flour from abroad ceased to be an option. The intermittent trade run by neutral ships in the first months of the war gradually came to a halt owing to stricter enforcement of the blockade by the Entente.[63] Italy's entry into the war on the Entente side further intensified the blockade's impact. In the Black Sea, the blockade also restricted the empire's access to foodstuffs from Bulgarian and Romanian ports. Now, only the grain produced by the empire was available to meet the needs of both the civilian population and a huge army.

Managing the transition to self-reliance turned out to be a major challenge. To begin with, the Ottoman railroad network was hardly conducive to tapping the empire's agricultural potential in its entirety. Many fertile regions remained beyond the reach of railroads due to the lack of extensive branch lines.[64] Farmers in those areas generally limited their cultivation to local need, since the transport of surplus grain to railroad stations, ports, or urban centers was prohibitively expensive. On the other hand, in the regions surrounding the railroads, this new form of transportation almost always coexisted with older forms of transport. From their fields and villages, farmers brought their products to railroad stations with their own animals and carts. Alternatively, camel and cart drivers, who embraced the role of the middlemen and bought grain directly from peasants, transported it to railroad stations and sold it to the agents of big merchant houses.[65] In either case, draft animals and wheeled carts played a critical role in connecting producers with urban consumers. "On busy days," wrote an observer of the Anatolian Railway in 1905, "over one thousand camels waited near the Ankara station to unload their cargoes."[66]

The mobilization crippled this delicate system of trade and transport. The conscription of men and extensive commandeering of carts and draft animals hampered the ability of farmers and middlemen to transport their products to railroad stations. Moreover, peasants became increasingly reluctant to bring their products to the stations, fearing that officials would confiscate them or seize their animals. As the war wore on and shortages began to threaten the war effort, the authorities frequently resorted to coercion to overcome these problems. Peasants were compelled to carry the grain the state bought (or requisitioned) from them with their own vehicles and animals.

The Ottoman Empire could have coped with the cessation of flour imports and the mobilization's paralyzing impact had it not been suffering from a concurrent coal shortage. Like its need for bread ingredients, the empire's ever-growing need for coal had been met by both domestic and external sources before the war. Coal was being extracted in increasingly larger amounts on the Black Sea coal coast, mostly at Zonguldak and Ereğli. This domestic production was supplemented by high-calorific coal imported mostly from Great Britain. While the domestic output was 764,000 tons in 1910 and 904,000 tons in 1911, total coal imports amounted to 347,000 tons in 1910 and 422,000 tons in 1911. British coal made up as much as 94 and 88 percent of these amounts, respectively. Around half of these annual import volumes were destined for Istanbul, while other port cities shared the rest.[67] In the empire, coal was used on the railroad network and in various industries to operate water pumps, flour mills, electrical stations, and other urban utilities, run steamships, and heat houses. By 1914, the empire's transportation system, economy, and urban life had thus become susceptible to the stoppage of coal supplies.

As in the case of flour, the war between the Ottoman Empire and its major foreign supplier of coal, Great Britain, compelled the empire to rely on its own fuel resources. Ottoman coal now had to meet the demands created not only by regular urban consumption but by military production, the navy, and dramatically heightened military activity on the railroads. Expecting a fuel crisis, the army had amassed large quantities of coal and oil during the mobilization, mostly by confiscation from private depots. Resources from the Black Sea coal coast also continued to reach the capital on a regular basis. After an initial, and mostly ineffective, bombardment of Zonguldak in early November, the Russian Black Sea Fleet gave priority to the defense of the Russian coastline and the interruption of Ottoman shipments to eastern Anatolia, leaving the Ottoman coalfields and transports mostly unmolested. Therefore, between the fall of 1914 and spring of 1915, the empire did not suffer from severe shortages of coal.

With the spring of 1915, however, the situation changed for the worse. In conjunction with the Entente's Dardanelles campaign, the Russian fleet intensified its activities in the Black Sea, especially around the Bosporus and the coal coast. The frequent shelling of coal mines, loading stages, powerhouses, and other facilities hampered mining operations in the coalfields. Together with labor and material shortages, the damage wrought by continuous bombardments led to a dramatic decline in coal production. From its 1911 peak of 904,000 tons, total output fell by more than half to 420,000 tons in 1915. In 1916, it declined another 50 percent to 208,000 tons and again to 158,000 tons in 1917. With a slight improvement, production reached 186,000 tons in 1918. In the war's last two years, the total amounts extracted from these best-developed coalfields of the empire fell even below that of their annual production levels two decades earlier.[68]

From the spring 1915 on, Russian squadrons also intercepted and sank unescorted Ottoman steamers, sailing vessels, and boats with increasing frequency, greatly disrupting the shipment of coal to the capital—and from there to the rest of the empire.[69] By the end of May, Russian efforts to halt coal traffic had become more systematic, coordinated, and effective. Especially after two Russian dreadnoughts became operational in the Black Sea in October and December of 1915, the Russian fleet seized the initiative for good. By the end of 1915, the Ottoman Empire had lost most of its large steamships, leaving small sailing vessels, tugs, and ferries as the primary carriers of coal.[70]

The new Russian strategy left the empire's capital, major cities, and railroad network short of fuel. With every passing month, the amount of coal shipped from the Black Sea coal coast to Istanbul decreased, causing much consternation in official circles and among the civilian population. What little coal could be obtained was reserved for operating military factories, running military trains, and fueling the navy. The lack of coal even forced battleships to economize on fuel. As early as May 1915, Admiral Wilhelm Souchon reported to Enver Pasha that the fleet "might run out of coal in six weeks' time."[71] Steamboat services on the Bosporus and the Golden Horn were reduced to a minimum. The waterworks in Istanbul ran only three days a week because there was not enough coal to keep the pumps operating.[72] Cities went dark. Civilian railroad services were curtailed.[73] The Bulgarians' entry into the war on the side of the Central Powers and the establishment of direct communications with Germany did not provide the much-anticipated relief. Although Germans began to send coal to the Ottoman Empire, the amount fell far short of what was needed to alleviate empirewide shortages.

Under these circumstances, wood came to serve as substitute fuel for the railroad network and domestic heating. As a Russian agent in Istanbul reported in June 1915, some three to four thousand workers chopped wood in Çerkez-köy area for the production of charcoal.[74] In 1917, all the useable trees in the city and its environs were cut down.[75] The almost exclusive use of wood diminished the locomotives' performance by some 40 percent,[76] as well as leading to the extensive depletion of forests, especially along the railroads. As the conflict progressed and all nearby forests were exhausted, however, the army let contractors supply wood from distant regions as well. Towards the end of the war, even olive trees and vines served "to feed the locomotives."[77] In April 1917, a local observer from Damascus aptly described the damage caused by the reliance on wood: "Deforestation has continued on a ruthless scale. Fruit trees of all sorts, the very life of these regions, have not been spared and as Damascus is the center of the military railway traffic, the hungry locomotives had to be fed, even if the country will bleed for years to come."[78]

Aside from its debilitating impact on the war effort and the devastation it wrought upon Ottoman forests, the shortage of coal deeply affected urban life and the provisioning of cities. The curtailment of railroad services made it difficult to bring grain to the population centers from their agricultural hinterlands. Now grain transportation on the railroads had to compete with military transportation for the available fuel.[79] According to some reports, the number of trains reserved for civilian transport on the Anatolian Railway was reduced to as few as one per week.[80] The lack of coal also hindered the operation of flour mills in urban centers. Izmir, for instance, had imported most of its coal before the war from Great Britain. Cessation of this trade with the outbreak of the war and the army's requisitioning of available stocks forced eight of the city's thirteen flour mills to suspend their operations.[81] Even when grain did reach major cities, it could only be ground to flour with significant difficulty.

Coal shortages also affected life in the cities of the Levantine coast and Mount Lebanon. Before the war, coal had either been imported to Greater Syria directly from Great Britain or shipped from other Ottoman ports. The outbreak of the war, however, brought this to a halt. According to the U.S. consul, Beirut's coal stock had already been depleted by May 1914, and not replenished since then.[82] The interruption of the empire's railroad network at the Taurus and Amanus Mountains hindered easy overland transport of coal from Anatolia to Syria. As in other parts of the empire, available fuel sources were reserved for the movement of troops and military supplies, reducing the numbers of freight trains connecting coastal cities to their agricultural hinterlands. Grain transport was further crippled by the commandeering of many animals for army use, which had played a critical role in connecting peasants' fields to railroad stations and nearby markets or smuggling products to grain-deficient areas. This resulted in serious shortages of grain in coastal cities and Mount Lebanon, although grain was plentiful in the Syrian interior well until the second half of 1915.[83] In this regard, the dynamics that led to the first serious scarcities in the coastal cities of Greater Syria resembled the ones that had created shortages in Istanbul and Izmir around the same time.

From late 1915 on, much earlier than in other parts of the empire, however, the Levantine coast and Mount Lebanon were plunged into famine. A rare convergence of political, military, and environmental factors in the region led to one of the most catastrophic civilian experiences of the Great War. The ground for famine was prepared by the coincidence of transportation difficulties and a historic locust attack in 1915 in a region struggling through wartime conditions.[84] In March 1915, locust swarms from the Sinai desert began arriving in Syria, descending upon anything green they could possibly devour. Contemporary accounts unequivocally testified to the unprecedentedness of the attack. A diary from a monastery in Mount Lebanon, for instance, recorded that, "our elders tell us that they have never seen in their mountains a locust attack anywhere near as intense as this one."[85] Between April and October 1915, the locusts devoured fruits, vegetables, and legumes, and destroyed a considerable portion of cereals in the region, amounting to at least half a million tons of foodstuffs.[86] The attack thus dealt a devastating blow to a population already suffering from shortages caused by wartime measures and transportation difficulties. Towards the end of the year, scenes of deep impoverishment and starvation became prevalent in the region.

In the meantime, the Entente blockade of the Levantine coast stifled the region's access to external sources of provisioning,[87] preventing the shipment of grain from other ports of the empire or neutral countries. Within the region itself, fuel shortages prevented effective and regular transportation of relief grain to suffering areas. From early 1916 on, the situation deteriorated dramatically: famine and accompanying epidemics caused thousands of deaths each month. Caught between the overall decline of agricultural production and the burning need to supply troops, efforts to stave off scarcities failed.[88] Nor could the Ottoman authorities effectively combat rampant profiteering and speculation. Their ineptitude in relieving the famine greatly contributed to the erosion of the empire's legitimacy in the region. In the second half of the war, famine assumed unprecedented proportions, affecting even the region's breadbasket areas.[89] By the end of the conflict, famine and epidemics had claimed a staggering proportion of the population. Of about 4 million people in Ottoman Syria, 350,000 to 500,000 fell victim to one of the greatest tragedies of the Great War. Unlike in other parts of the former empire, the war has thus been remembered in this region as "the war of famine" (*harb al-maja'a*).[90]

Centralization of the Provisioning System

The visibly worsening situation obliged the CUP government to adopt a new, more centralized provisioning policy in July 1916. By the first half of that year, it had already become obvious that while some provinces of the empire enjoyed relatively bountiful harvests, other regions suffered from severe shortages. Untended fields lay fallow, and agricultural production shrank everywhere in the empire. The area under cultivation gradually declined from sixty million *dönüm* in 1914, to thirty million in 1915, and finally to twenty-four million in 1916.[91] In addition to the ever-increasing withdrawal of able-bodied men and draft animals from farms and fields, two other factors exacerbated the agricultural downturn. First, starting in the summer of 1915, the CUP government implemented its large-scale policy of deportation and extermination of Ottoman Armenians, which eventually led to their wholesale destruction. Second, in eastern Anatolia, large swathes of land became a war zone in 1915 and was later occupied by Russian forces during the first half of 1916, creating hundreds of thousands of new refugees. M. Philips Price, a journalist for the *Manchester Guardian*, who accompanied the advancing Russian army, paints a grim picture of the region: "The villages of the plain were deserted and in ruins; not a living soul was to be seen except a few black spots, that indicated a patrol of Cossacks. What was recently a paradise of richness and beauty was now a desert."[92] Local agricultural economies, as a result, came to the brink of collapse. Notwithstanding this general trend of deterioration, however, some grain-producing regions continued to harvest more grain than was needed by their own populations,[93] but the surplus did not always reach the army or places where people faced food shortages or famine. When it did, the prices were usually too high for the poorer segments of the population. This empirewide imbalance was further accentuated by the inadequate, overburdened transportation network.

The new policy was a response to the problems that plagued the provisioning of the army and the penurious regions of the empire.[94] In the face of the prolonged conflict and the inadequacy of previous strategies, the Ottoman authorities decided to centralize the system of provisioning through a new government agency (İaşe-i Umumiye Heyeti) headed by the interior minister, which was given extraordinary authority over grain production, trade, and distribution.[95] Local branches of the agency (*tali heyetler*) functioned as its executive organs. The new policy divided the empire into three zones of provisioning and outlawed the transportation and trade of grain among these zones.[96] The law granted exclusive authority to the central agency and its representatives to purchase the remaining grain in the hands of the merchants and producers after deducting their own consumption and seed and fodder needs.[97] Not surprisingly, it was the agency's mandate to determine the "certain" amount of grain required for the daily subsistence of people and draft animals. The law also obliged producers and merchants to give information about the grain in their possession and, more important, to sell this grain to merchants and purchasers designated by the agency (*mübayaa vekilleri*) at officially determined prices. The agency then would deliver it to the army as well as to towns and villages whose production did not meet their needs.

The ultimate goal of the new organization was to extract the grain and other products from the countryside in a more efficient way and divert it to the portions of the army and the regions considered of critical importance. As the division of the empire into provisioning zones indicates, the government seemed to be particularly concerned about the provisioning of the two primary regions, along with meeting the needs of the army. First, by including the grain-producing regions of central Anatolia in the first zone and strictly regulating the grain trade there, the government attempted to secure the provisioning of the capital city, Istanbul, and thereby avoid potential unrest that might pose a threat to the regime. Second, the government authorized the highest-ranking official of the second zone to regulate the provisioning of most of the Arab provinces of the empire,[98] some of which had begun to suffer a terrible famine in 1915. In the regions that remained outside of these two zones, the government did not implement the law to control the grain trade, in effect leaving the army free to supply itself in the usual way.

The obligation of producers to deliver their products to the state at officially set prices was the backbone of the new system, as well as of the state's policy of provisioning for the remainder of the war. The aim was to protect the state from increasing market prices and to maintain a constant flow of grain to army troops and key urban centers, particularly the capital city.[99] To achieve this objective, the state's representatives consistently assessed prices for agricultural produce at well below the market level. However, even these low prices were not always paid to peasants.[100] In the face of skyrocketing prices for the draft animals, agricultural equipment, and manufactured goods that were commonly used by peasant households, this low-price policy led to widespread suffering in the Ottoman countryside. In Madaba, Transjordan, for example, officials offered eight piasters in paper money or four piasters in silver per *sa* (equal to 5.2–6.0 kilograms) of wheat, whereas the current market rate was eighteen piasters in gold.[101] In Kırkkilise, a small town in Thrace, peasants criticized officials who assigned less than half of the market value to their products while everything needed by cultivators increased in price eight to ten times over. Furthermore, the amount of grain allocated by the officials for peasants' sustenance, fodder, and seed was so low that it was insufficient to meet their needs for an entire year. Since bread was the main source of their nourishment, peasants pointed out, under these conditions, that they lacked the energy to move, let alone work in their fields.[102]

As these two examples from two different corners of the empire suggest, the new policy brought about little improvement to producers, inasmuch as the prices offered for grain were usually well below market levels.[103] There was, however, a bigger problem. Under the new policy, the agency would now purchase grain in the name of the government rather than confiscate it. But producers and merchants would be paid in paper currency, which was put into circulation in ever-increasing volume. Being able to sell produce to the state for cash in this form scarcely constituted relief for most people, however, especially after 1916, because the unprecedented proliferation of paper money led to consequent depreciation in its value and contributed to widespread economic dislocation.

By 1914, the Ottoman Empire did not have the means to finance a major conflict by itself. Handicapped by the underdeveloped nature of its capital markets, meager available reserves, and an inefficient taxation system, the empire was regularly dependent on foreign credits even during the peacetime. The Balkan Wars, as mentioned before, had saddled the imperial economy with a heavy cost, and the massive mobilization of August 1914 only exacerbated the empire's financial strains. On the other hand, the war with Great Britain and France severely curtailed the Porte's access to European financial markets, leaving Germany and Austria-Hungary as its sole potential creditors. From the beginning of the mobilization, the government secured loans and advances from its wartime allies, particularly from Germany. Once the available funds were exhausted, the Porte recurrently called upon Germans for new loans and negotiated with them over the terms. Unlike other belligerents, the CUP government rarely resorted to internal borrowing as a way to fund the costs of the war. Only in 1918 and under German pressure, did it decide to pursue this path, eventually raising the modest sum of eighteen million lira, which accounted for about less than 5 percent of the Ottoman Empire's total wartime budget.[104]

Ever-increasing war costs and government's inability to raise sufficient revenue through other means obliged the Porte simply to print money. In July 1915, after hesitating for several months, the government released 6.5 million lira in paper currency. As the war dragged on and swallowed up all resources the government generated, the Unionists resorted to printing money in ever-greater quantities. By the end of the war, there had been seven printings of paper lira, backed initially by gold deposited at German banks and later by German treasury bonds. From 3 million at the outbreak of the war, paper money in circulation reached 7.9 million by the end of 1915. Over the next two years, however, monetary expansion was particularly dramatic, and the paper lira in circulation reached 45.8 million by the end of 1916 and 124.1 million by the end of 1917. By the time the government signed the armistice in October 1918, a total of 161 million Ottoman paper lira was in circulation.[105]

Soon after they issued paper money in July 1915, the Unionists confronted with the grim fact that printing money and maintaining people's trust in it were two different things, especially under difficult wartime conditions. Even before World War I, people's confidence in paper money was already very low in the Ottoman Empire. In two previous military crises, the Crimean War of 1856 and the Russo-Ottoman War of 1877–78, the Porte had relied on paper money to finance its wartime expenses. In both cases, however, its value depreciated significantly, provoking high inflation, undermining social stability, and eroding confidence in paper currency almost completely. Elderly people still bitterly remembered the Russo-Ottoman War, when the value of Ottoman paper money fell by more than 90 percent.[106] As a result of these painful experiences, even after almost four decades, people did not regard paper money as a reliable and legitimate means of tender in daily transactions. The fact that 90 percent of the 53 million lira in circulation at the outset of the war consisted of gold, silver, or nickel coins was a reflection of this distrust.[107] By 1914, the five lira note was the smallest in circulation, and most paper money took the form of fifty or one hundred lira bills, used mostly in big business transactions.

The initial impact of the paper currency was the disproportionate rise in value of coins and their gradual disappearance from circulation. The value of gold and silver coins over paper money rose as each new issue of paper currency entered circulation. The rate and velocity of depreciation of paper money, however, varied throughout the empire. As a general rule, in the provinces where the government's authority was weaker, paper money suffered a bigger and faster depreciation. In provinces closer to the capital, it retained its value longer. Regardless of the depreciation of its value, however, the government continued to make its payments in paper currency most of the time. It almost invariably used paper lira to pay the salaries of state officials, dispense aid to soldiers' families, and purchase agricultural products.

Depending on local conditions, people's reaction to paper money ranged from reluctant acceptance to outright rejection. Anticipating people's unwillingness to accept paper currency, the government had already passed laws in order to make the notes legal tender for all commercial transactions "in the same manner as coin." At least on paper, these laws stipulated that no one could refuse the banknotes as payment and demand some other currency instead. Those who did not obey the law would be punished and imprisoned.[108] The laws, however, fell short of getting people to accept paper money. As the war dragged on, unpersuaded by the threat of imprisonment, merchants and farmers increasingly demanded payment in gold or silver and refused to sell their products for paper lira.[109] Local authorities increasingly resorted to employing compulsion to maintain the legitimacy of paper currency and make people accept paper lira. Cemal Pasha exiled a number of Arab merchants, including notable families, to Anatolia, for instance, on the grounds of their not accepting paper money. The governor of Mosul, Haydar Bey, ordered that the ears of those who refused to accept paper money be nailed to the wall.[110] While failing to provide necessary incentive for the producers, printing paper money and maintaining its legitimacy thus became another interface between the Ottoman state and its citizens during the war.

The Ottoman state's aggressive intervention in local agricultural economies, its low-price policy, and its insistence on making payments in paper money met with anger and resistance. Wherever they could, peasants withheld their products from the agency and its representatives.[111] They hid their grain from its men, bribed them to make them look the other way, or resisted them by force. Depending on the local conditions, the agency either responded in kind and forced peasants to release their products at official prices paid in depreciated paper currency or offered them much higher prices, not unusually in gold or silver, to reveal their products. The level of local resistance, political and strategic sensitivity of the region, and the availability of military units and gendarmes determined the cash/compulsion ratio in the agency's dealings with producers. In certain regions of the empire, most notably in the Arab provinces, however, this process set off an inflationary spiral.

Alternatively, peasants sought ways to transport their products to urban centers where grain was scarce and prices were accordingly high.[112] Grain smuggling became especially widespread in the border regions of the third provisioning zone, where the grain trade was not regulated by the new law. Producers in the first and second zones continually attempted to bring their products to the third zone to benefit from the relatively high prices the army paid there. In turn, this movement of grain put the subsistence of border provinces at risk, provinces whose populations had already increased due to immigrants fleeing the war on the Caucasus Front.[113] In April 1917, presumably as a response to widespread smuggling, the government revised the law's stipulations and divided the empire into five zones of provisioning, in each of which newly established central zone councils (*mıntıka merkez heyetleri*) would procure, transport, and distribute grain under the supervision of the central agency.[114] With this revision, the government attempted to bring the entire empire under the scope of the law, while taking account of local circumstances.[115]

Before long, however, it became apparent that the new policy of centralization and increasing bureaucratization did not yield the desired results. In several important regions, the system failed mostly because of the producers' resistance. In Syria, for instance, the local syndicate established by the agency had to be abolished because "the government was unable to compel all the cereal owners in the interior regions to submit to the orders of the syndicate and to accept the paper currency."[116] Moreover, the agency failed to overcome the imbalance among the provinces and provision the army at the same time. As a result, the tension between military and civilian authorities over provisioning became increasingly apparent during this period. Gradually declining production (and thus a decrease in the percentage that was allocated to the army), the perceived inefficiency of grain collection by the agency's civilian officials and designated merchants, and, finally, a heightening sense of urgency forced the army to intervene. In October 1916, the Ministry of War first ordered the army corps enlistment offices to supervise the process and provide necessary support in the collection of grain and its transportation to train stations. In a separate circular sent to the army corps, however, the ministry ordered the dispatch of military officials to towns and villages to obtain grain directly from peasants. The ministry ordered the officials to take this process as seriously as conscription and to disregard any opposition from civilian officials and local people. Local civilian authorities reacted to these orders by trying to resist the army's increasing intervention on the grounds that taking grain that had been stored for local consumption would upset the local populations and pit the civilian and military authorities against each other.[117]

Towards the End: An Empirewide Crisis

Increasing interference on the part of the army foreshadowed the military takeover of the entire system of provisioning less than a year later. In the summer of 1917, a government decree established a new agency (İaşe Müdüriyet-i Umumiyesi) under the Ministry of War.[118] The head of the army provisioning office, İsmail Hakkı Pasha (nicknamed "the Lame," *Topal*), was charged with administering the new agency. Similar to the previous organization, the agency enjoyed an absolute monopoly on purchasing and distributing grain and other supplies with the purpose of "provisioning of the imperial army, all institutions, and the regions whose population are in need."[119] The decree subordinated all governmental officials to orders and instructions given by the new agency and held them strictly responsible for the execution of those orders. Those who opposed the orders and instructions would be imprisoned and their goods would be confiscated.[120] Under the new structure, the empire was once again divided into provisioning zones. This time, however, each army zone was designated as a provisioning zone and army commanders became the heads of these new provisioning zones. At the lower levels of the new structure, military officials and gendarmerie commanders joined the commissions that administered procurement and regulated agriculture in their regions, with authority to employ all governmental officials in provisioning affairs. With all of these measures, the new system was a clear indication that the provisioning of the army had become the utmost concern of the state and that the *militarization of provisioning* had come to be perceived as the most effective way to address this concern.

The new legislation prohibited the transport of grain and other supplies from one town to another. It also entitled local provisioning commissions to determine the annual amount of grain needed by the cultivators for seed, fodder, and subsistence, as well as their annual need for rice, sugar, olive oil, and olives. Under this new structure, similar to the former civilian organization, the local commissions continued to maintain the exclusive authority to purchase excess grain and other supplies at the official prices they set. Unlike the previous regulations, however, the legislation provided a specific amount of grain to be purchased: 12.5 percent of annual production on top of the regular tithe, which itself amounted to 12.5 percent of the crops. Anticipating continued decline in production, it also left the door open to doubling this amount.[121] In short, the law equipped the army with the authority to acquire as much as three times the regular tithe (*aşar ve aşarın iki misli*) from producers right at the harvest. Given the significantly depreciated value of paper money, this policy came to mean an excessively heavy "tax-in-kind" burden for most peasants. Even on paper, the producers stood to lose 37.5 percent of their crops. In practice, however, they lost even more than that.

The radical transformation in 1917 came as a desperate response by the army and the government to an ever-deepening empirewide crisis of food production. As noted above, until mid-1917, the percentage of cultivated land shrank and agricultural production gradually declined throughout the empire. The centralization of the provisioning system in 1916 intensified the interactions between peasants and state representatives, but it did little to ameliorate growing scarcities. Local authorities tried to keep the prices of basic staple items under control by fixing prices, importing flour from neutral countries, and distributing bread through municipalities and associations. Severe shortages of staple items, however, remained mostly isolated incidents. The Syrian famine of 1915 and to a lesser extent the provisioning crisis in eastern Anatolia in 1916–17 were two major exceptions to this rule. As discussed above, they were precipitated by a unique combination of several political, military, and environmental factors.

Beginning in mid-1917, however, the food crisis transformed into an empirewide phenomenon, engulfing even the major grain-producing regions. In Syria, extreme shortages extended beyond the coastal regions to the cities of the interior, such as Aleppo and Damascus.[122] In addition to the intrusive state policies, this new situation was created by four distinct yet interrelated factors: the exhaustion of the empire's manpower; the depletion of its animal stock; population movements; and, finally, the exceptionally difficult environmental conditions in this period. The loss of some of the richest grain-producing regions of the empire compounded the impact of these factors. In addition to wide swathes of eastern Anatolia, the empire had also lost the control of the mid-Euphrates valley by mid-1917. As the new British oriental secretary in Baghdad, Gertrude Bell, observed, "the fact that the Turks have lost this rich food-producing area is to them one of the most disastrous consequences of the fall of Baghdad."[123]

It was no coincidence that the provisioning crisis overlapped with the army's manpower crisis. By 1917, the empire had reached the limits of its manpower supply. Continuous fighting on several fronts, epidemic diseases, malnutrition, and desperate conditions decimated a significant portion of its men of military age. As discussed in the previous chapter, the authorities attempted to fill the depleted ranks by conscripting ever younger and older draftees, which in effect turned these remaining menfolk from agricultural producers into consumers. The prolonged war not only reduced the agricultural work force, however, but also substantially altered its composition. In the absence of so many men, farmwork had increasingly to be done by women, children, and the elderly. Although these people strove to tend the fields as best as they could, agricultural production suffered dramatically. A young noncommissioned officer was told of the plight of elderly villagers in western Anatolia: "Sir, they [state officials] left two old oxen for the village, which till peasants' fields in turn. But, as they are weak and exhausted, we help them by pushing the plow. [But] we are old. How much work could women [*eksik etekler*] do? Young men could have performed this job, but they went to the frontiers. This is why our crops are not good. They would have been plentiful, had one or two young men remained in the village."[124] The grievances voiced by these old men were shared by thousands throughout the empire. The labor-intensive nature of Ottoman agriculture amplified the impact of the manpower shortage to the extent that the remaining home-front population was never able to compensate for the young men's absence. The situation was much worse in the sparsely populated regions of the empire.

The manpower crisis affected the provisioning crisis in other ways as well. In the last two years of the war, the imperial army lost more men to desertion than to battle. Even though these hundreds of thousands of men left their ranks in the army, they did not dare to return to their homes and villages, since the chances of getting caught still ran high. Instead, many of them joined brigand bands that had been formed by deserters like themselves.[125] Roaming in the mountains and preying on nearby villages, the presence of so many deserters kept the countryside in a perpetual state of insecurity. Peasants who feared for their lives could work in their fields only with considerable difficulty. Due to the insecurity of village roads, they did not want to make long trips to the town centers where they usually sold their produce at marketplaces. Producers thus gradually withdrew from local economies and cultivated exclusively for their own subsistence. Along with draining the army's fighting power, the overall impact of mass desertion in the countryside was the virtual isolation of local economies from one another.

The year of 1917 was also the breaking point for the empire's livestock, on which the prolonged war had a devastating impact. Very low levels of mechanization and the generally underdeveloped nature of Ottoman agriculture had made animal and human labor prime movers of production. A well-known literary figure, Ahmet Haşim, who traveled in Anatolia as a military inspector in 1917, noted the extraordinary role draught animals played in peasants' lives: "Anatolian people, rather than ancient Egyptians, should have held [the deity] Apis ox in the highest esteem. Here the ox is the pillar of life."[126] The war years, however, saw the widespread utilization of draught animals in military transportation, as well as their decimation during the service, which aggravated the labor crisis in agriculture and contributed to the sharp decline in production. Even at the beginning of the mobilization, local officials were writing alarming reports about the withdrawal of draught animals from agriculture and asking for moderation in the impressment process, usually to no avail. As the war dragged on, the situation worsened. Contemporary observers in the countryside noticed the disastrous impact of army service on peasants and their animals, witnessing the gradual disappearance of Ottoman livestock. George E. White, president of Anatolia College at Merzifon (Marsovan), a high school established and directed by American missionaries, was among those observers. The military transportation in the region started with horse-drawn wagons and continued until the horses were decimated by the strain. Two-wheeled ox-carts were then employed in transportation. Finally, camels and donkeys were called on for army service: "[A]nd then our neighbors in Marsovan shed tears, not that they were unwilling to do their bit, but they knew that poor Jack and Jenny from their little stalls under the house could not carry food enough to feed themselves all the way to the distant battle front, let alone reaching there with loads of military supplies."[127] According to some estimates, the empire's overall ox and buffalo population declined by 86.5 percent during the war.[128] The authorities usually left a few draught animals in villages to be used in turn by villagers. Overworked and weakened, these became susceptible to epidemics. Even if they survived the dramatically increased demands on them, the impressment of so many others shattered the established rhythms of local agricultural economies.

War-related problems were not, however, the only troubles that Ottoman peasants encountered. The summer drought of 1917 in northern Mesopotamia and northern Syria and the extraordinarily cold winter of 1917–18 in almost all provinces of the empire crippled farming activity even further. A German doctor passing through northern Syria in 1917 noticed the impact of the war and harsh weather on agriculture: "The train passed southward through a region which at other times yields abundantly wheat and oats, but this year looked almost barren. Many fields had not been ploughed at all and were covered by thistles of all colors."[129] His observations are confirmed by another eyewitness account, from Salahiye, further east, in November 1917: "Everywhere shortages and cost have reached their utmost levels. All of the fields are empty and uncultivated. Not even a single peasant is farming. There is no seed left, neither oxen nor [other] animals. Every source is dried up. The future looks scarily bleak."[130]

The army's takeover of the provisioning system came at such a critical moment. In the face of declining production, military control was aimed at increasing the system's efficiency by intervening in local economies more directly and forcefully. Especially in regions where troops confronted immediate shortages, military units themselves were employed in collecting grain from the peasants. This process, much to the outrage of producers, was usually far from peaceful. Soldiers intruded into homes and storehouses to conduct searches and seizures, beat peasants who hid their grain, and threatened to burn their houses and villages. In other provinces, the provisioning agency subordinated state officials to its orders and conducted the collection of tithes and quotas (*iaşe hissesi*) through them. This new mode of interaction and, worse, the two- and threefold increases in the tax burden had a deeply alienating effect on peasants. Mehmet Zekâi Bey (Konrapa), a teacher in Bolu during the war, was among those employed in this process. Struck by the general misery in villages, he personally observed the peasants' longing for the times when they submitted only their regular tithe and were subjected to tax farmers, about whom they used to complain bitterly before the war.[131] In a different part of the empire, Said Jawmar, a young man from the village of Deir Atiya in the Qalamoun mountains in Syria, described tax collectors in similarly harsh terms: "The state takes half of the wheat, oats, maize, raisins and all other crops. Those who do not pay are visited by the tax collectors—uninvited guests who are a heavy burden because they won't leave until all taxes have been paid; at times they practically rob the houses."[132]

The impact of the new system on cultivators varied considerably. Big farmers actually benefited from it, since they continued to sell their excess produce to the agency at elevated prices.[133] Rumors circulated that large farmers could not find enough room to store banknotes and were stashing them in large baskets in hay barns.[134] To poor peasants whose production barely exceeded their subsistence needs, however, the forced purchase of more than a third of their grain at fixed prices and with depreciated paper money was an intolerable burden. Coupled with the overall decline in production, intensified extortion of their already meager crops rendered their subsistence precarious. Hasan Fehmi Efendi, deputy of Sinop, vividly portrayed the suffering of peasants he had met:

> Whomever I talked to said that for the sake of the country's salvation and as
> a sign of sacrifice that was imposed on us by the nation, I had sent my father,
> brother, son, in brief, ten or fifteen people from my family and relatives, to the
> war. The news about the martyrdom of five, six, or seven of them reached us.

Three or four of them are living with us after having been maimed in the war. Two of them have been taken prisoner. A couple are still at the fronts. Although I was deprived of all manpower, I managed to produce ten kilos of wheat, which was taken from me, disregarding my need for seed to plant three months from now, fodder for the draught animals that I employ in my field, and, finally, my need for the wheat for sustenance. I was not paid for any of this.[135]

Peasants themselves were continually disgruntled that state agents were claiming too much of their produce and thus forcing them into starvation. Families who had lost their working hands were hit especially hard. Güllü, the wife of a soldier, wrote in the name of all women in the village of Telo of Pötürge (Mamûretülaziz) in eastern Anatolia, compellingly stating that their harvests did not reach five hundred or even two hundred kilos of grain. They could grow only seventy to eighty kilos, a quarter of which the provisioning officials purchased in addition to the regular tithe. The villagers would eagerly submit any grain in excess of their need for sustenance to the government for free. However, she wrote, even a single seed would not remain for them after the government's purchase.[136] In a similar vein, women from Keskin (Ankara) pleaded for the help of the minister of the interior and asked for exemption from the second round of purchases (ikinci misil mübayaa): "If we hand in this grain, we will surely be devastated, as will our children."[137] Farmers from Kırkkilise wrote that if the local provisioning commission insisted on purchasing their surplus grain, they would have no other option than to sell their possessions to feed their families and then quit farming.[138]

The impact of the new system was also observed by several members of the parliament, including the Unionists.[139] "Rather than serving the agriculture of the country, the agency devastated it," Nazım Bey, the deputy for Kirkuk, lamented.[140] He and other deputies rightfully argued that the extraordinary amount of grain that the state was forcibly purchasing from producers threatened to bring agricultural production to a complete halt. If the law was not revised, the deputies argued, it would condemn the majority of the peasantry to starvation and eventually deplete the resources needed to provision the army. They asked for at least the peasants' seed, fodder, and subsistence grain to be exempt from the regulations.[141] Against these observations and fiery criticisms, the government and the representatives of the army defended the law on the grounds that acquiring three times the normal tithe was the only way to provision the imperial army. Furthermore, the exemption of small producers from this regulation was unthinkable, since they constituted the majority of the farming population. Ali Cenani Bey, speaking for the subcommittee of the imperial budget, expressed the prevailing opinion among the Unionist ruling elite: "It is necessary that, under these [extraordinary] circumstances, peasants should be content with less bread. . . . It would not be appropriate to jeopardize the provisioning of the army on the grounds that this would slightly pressure the peasantry."[142]

Conclusions

World War I, as the historian Avner Offer aptly states, was "not only a war of steel and gold, but a war of bread and potatoes."[143] The issue of the food supply plagued all the belligerents of the Great War, especially during the second half of the conflict.[144] The Ottoman Empire was no exception. From early on, the Unionists realized that the food supply would play a critical role in determining the outcome of the war. Like the governments of other belligerent countries, the CUP government considered properly feeding the army and population in major cities, including the capital city, the most pressing problem to be addressed. To this end, the government and the army sought to regulate grain production and procurement, transportation, and distribution, applying generally inefficient and often conflicting measures. As the war dragged on, the government responded with increasingly expansive and intrusive systems and bureaucracies of agricultural production and food distribution. However, despite all these attempts, by the end of the war the government still had not solved the food production and distribution problems. Shortcomings in government policies led to increasingly dire shortages, and hunger appeared in many regions of the empire.

As discussed in this chapter, these policies constituted a significant component of Ottoman home-front life during the war. For the purposes of feeding, clothing, and equipping a huge army, the Ottoman state intervened forcefully and sometimes even destructively in the lives of people throughout the empire. This intervention often disrupted established patterns of activity in local economies and threatened people's lives, especially in regions where the margin of subsistence was narrow. Perhaps more than any other set of policies, the demands of military provisioning obliterated the distinction between the battlefront and the home front, imposing enormous physical and psychological burdens on ordinary people, damaging the legitimacy of the Ottoman state, and undermining the war effort.

5 IN THE HOME:
WIVES AND MOTHERS

On 31 December 1917, Grand Vizier and Interior Minister Talat Pasha received a telegram signed by ten peasant women from a small, relatively isolated village on the Black Sea coast. They were all the wives and mothers of soldiers who had been called off to military duty. In their telegram, these women complained bitterly about the harsh wartime policies of the Ottoman state and the pervasive poverty and hunger. Due to the lack of seed grain, their fields remained unsown. Their mules, horses, sheep, and cattle had been requisitioned by the military. The elderly and children of the village had been forced to work on the construction of roads and fortifications. Given the high prices of both staple items and consumer goods, these women bemoaned their inability to subsist under these conditions. Since the military had commandeered their houses for various purposes, moreover, people now had to resort to sleeping under trees. To make matters worse, deserters and refugees who were roaming the area had plundered their entire stock of hazelnuts and most of the maize. The remaining grain, the peasants protested, would only be sufficient to feed their children for two months. Despite these harsh conditions, state officials were still pressuring them to provide grain for the army at extremely low prices and even to sell the grain they had set aside to eat themselves. If the gendarmes could not find the grain the peasants had stashed away, they confiscated things like pots, pans, and cauldrons. Emphasizing that this was their third telegram, they demanded that the grand vizier intervene on their behalf. Their tone conveyed the hopelessness and anguish

as well as the determination and anger they felt: "Either deport us all to another place or cast us into the sea. We do not accept the law."[1]

The misery and destitution these peasant women described in their telegram was clearly not limited to their village. Their experience reflects the empirewide wartime crisis that engulfed Ottoman society as well as the state's
ever-increasing encroachment on women's lives. But their telegram also sug-
gests a new mode of interaction between women and state authorities based on
a perceived understanding of mutual obligations and expectations.

The Ottoman Empire's involvement in World War I resulted in the emergence of a new, wartime relationship between the state and its citizens. For millions of men, this relationship took the form of conscription and long-term
military service. For women, it primarily entailed the withdrawal of men from
their households and an increasing intrusion by the state into their daily lives.
During the war, women came into much more frequent and closer contact with
state officials. Focusing on their perceptions of and reactions to the war and the
dramatic changes it brought to Ottoman society, this chapter examines how the
war shaped women's relationships with the state and influenced their understanding of gender roles.

The War and Ottoman Women

Although World War I touched the life of nearly every Ottoman woman, it is
almost impossible to produce a coherent story of their war experiences. The
war's impact was not identical from class to class, ethnic group to ethnic group,
or region to region. Yet it would be safe to argue that the majority of Ottoman
women felt the disastrous impact of the conflict in both their personal and
social lives. Except for a relatively small, well-to-do segment of them, women
bore enormous material and emotional burdens during the war. Virtually everywhere throughout the empire, they had to work much longer and harder,
doing conscripted men's work on top of domestic chores such as cooking,
cleaning, and taking care of children and the elderly, which they already "naturally" had to deal with.

The withdrawal of hundreds of thousands of men from communal life and
the mobilizational demands of total war altered the circumstances of Ottoman
women beyond all recognition. The unforgiving wartime conditions, and the
ensuing economic difficulties often forced them to eke out a living on their
own. Many women found themselves in a difficult situation of taking over the
duty of providing for their families. Urban centers throughout the empire thus

saw an expansion in the number of women in the workforce during the war.[2] Even for middle-class families whose male members were conscripted into the army, privations became an everyday feature of life.[3] War, the disappearance of male members of the household, and the accompanying economic impoverishment brought on a decline in their social status, which, in turn, compelled women to work in various sectors of the urban economy for long hours and very low wages.[4] For those who had never worked before outside their homes, this meant a radical change in their lives.

Although the wartime experiences of peasant women were considerably different from those of urban women, they too had to cope with the problems created by large-scale conscription. With every call for enlistment, thousands of households joined the needy soldiers' families who could barely maintain their subsistence. Contemporary observers report on numerous villages throughout the empire whose entire young male populations had been drafted into military service. The Hungarian ethnographer Istvan Györff was not allowed to visit certain villages in Anatolia, since they were populated only by women and children.[5] Mehmet Zekâi Bey (Konrapa), the young teacher we met in the previous chapter, says of the villages he visited in the district of Bolu while conducting examinations of village schools: "No matter what village we visited, we did not come across a man. The war emptied all villages [of their men]."[6]

The war and the mass conscription of men made women the focal point of rural life, since most of the remaining males were either young boys or elderly men. Although older male members of the village community still occupied prominent roles, women usually had to do most of the farmwork themselves. Everyday life, as a result, became unbearably difficult for many. These women, many of whom were illiterate, poignantly expressed their feelings in folk songs. One of them conveys the despair of the war that pervaded the home front in the following lines:

Adam' olan hergediyor	Those [families] with males prepare their lands to sow
Onyedili harbediyor	Boys born in '17 (1317/1901) are fighting
Her nereye vardıysam	Wherever I go
Kız, gelin çifte gidiyor[7]	[I see] girls and brides go out to plow

Not only did women throughout the Ottoman countryside have to cultivate their own crops, but they also had to bring them to the market to sell or locate buyers elsewhere. An article published in *Vakit*, for instance, mentions a new stratum of traders (*esnaf tabakası*) composed entirely of women. These women brought their products from nearby towns and villages to Istanbul and established a new marketplace for themselves.[8] The capital, with its huge population, was the most important market for these women, but this also happened in other cities and towns throughout the empire. Falih Rıfkı (Atay) says of peasant women trying to sell fruit to passengers at train stations: "It is obvious that these clumsy, shy women had never left their villages and their hearths [before]."[9] Numerous such accounts attest to the increasingly ubiquitous presence of women in public life and the frequent transgression of established socioeconomic and cultural norms as a result.

From the start of the war, women throughout the empire were also employed, either willingly or forcibly, in various forms of military labor.[10] The empire's infrastructural deficiencies frequently required the authorities to rely on women's labor. Particularly in the provinces and in places lacking proper roads, officers short of men and means of transportation often demanded corvée of the local women, forcing them to haul military matériel and provisions to distant locations.[11] The army had already commandeered the stronger draft animals and better vehicles, so hauling such loads was a long and painful nightmare. Their weak animals perished on the way, their carts broke down, and convoys of women, children, and the elderly suffered, not only from hunger, cold, and the brutality of their overseers, but sometimes from the attacks of deserters who had turned to banditry.

As with other aspects of life on the home front, official narratives about civilians in the military labor force differ considerably from those of civilians who actually experienced it. Reporting on the war service of women from Erzurum, for instance, the Unionist daily *Tanin* applauded their sacrifice and altruism and likened them to the heroic women of the 1877–78 Russo-Ottoman war, saying: "Sending their men to the defense of borders and carrying boxes of ammunition on their shoulders along with their children, the women of Erzurum proved that they are daughters of the women of '93."[12] Similarly, according to Fevzi Çakmak, a high-ranking commander on the eastern front, women demonstrated a great willingness to transport military matériel, since they were fed along the way and received some money and food in exchange for their service. The duty assigned to these women (and their children) was that of carrying equipment and foodstuffs from the Black Sea shore up into the snowy mountains, from which they were sent on to army depots.[13] From this high commander's perspective, these women, described as a merely technical detail in his long narrative, were nothing but small cogs in the giant machine of the Ottoman Third Army.

Many women, however, clearly resented this forcible expropriation of their labor. In a telegram to the Ministry of Interior, Hatice and her fellow towns-women from Uşak in western Anatolia, who were all wives and mothers of sol-diers, bitterly complained that they were being forced to carry provisions to a district center that was ten hours away. Despite the cold weather and the lack of draft animals (they were plowing the fields of three or four households with a single yoke of oxen), local administrators used violence and compulsion (*şiddet ve cebr*) on these women to extract corvée from them in the form of trans-portation.[14] Soldiers' wives and mothers from Espiye similarly cried out that for eighteen months, they, together with the children and elderly women, had been employed in the transportation of matériel from Tirebolu on the Black Sea coast to military locations that were anywhere from five to twelve hours away without receiving any compensation.[15] Abdülkadir Kemali Bey, a reserve officer during the war, recalled women, children, and elderly villagers waiting for hours in front of the army supply office to transport grain with their own carts.[16] Women bitterly complained that they were forcibly employed in grain transportation without pay and that some of them were not even allowed to take their newborn babies with them.[17]

Women's interaction with the army was not, however, limited to their im-pressment into the military labor force. Close contact with military person-nel became a constant feature of everyday life on the home front. Soldiers of all ranks who were passing by towns and villages on their way to and from the war fronts encountered populations composed mostly or exclusively of women, children, and the elderly. Throughout the empire, newly recruited sol-diers marched on foot in columns to the nearest railroad station, army camp, or major depot. They had to cover hundreds of miles on foot or with animals be-cause of the limited extent of the Ottoman railroad network. Most of the time, these soldiers were obliged to live off the land and overnighted in whatever village they happened to be nearest to when the sun set.

In these desperate circumstances, soldiers on the move often summarily forced local people out of their houses and did not hesitate to resort to violence against villagers who did not comply with their demands. One very cold De-cember night, en route back from Palestine, "[W]e forced a young bride from her place [in a village called Kolsuz near Niğde in central Anatolia] and stayed there," Master Sergeant Sami noted in his diary.[18] As they passed through vil-lages and small towns, units simply took from the local population whatever goods, supplies, and animals they needed. Ragıb Efendi, a reserve officer on the eastern front, recalled his battalion's aggressive search for draft animals in vil-lages. Soldiers forced open the doors of houses whose male occupants had been drafted and impressed the few animals that had not already been requisitioned. Despite the begging and pleading of the peasant women, the soldiers did not pity them: "We beat up those who did not want to surrender their animals, knocked them down with kicks and slaps. May God forgive us! What injustice, cruelty, brutality, and torture[!]"[19] George E. White, president of Anatolia Col-lege in Merzifon closely observed the interaction between soldiers and local women during the war. His notes are worth quoting at length:

> A convoy of recruits would reach a village toward evening and the officer in charge would requisition lodging and supplies for the night. Most of the men were away doing their own soldier service, and the village women with their children and others would neither dare to refuse their uninvited guests nor re-main in their homes over night when soldiers were camping in their village. So the village families would go out to the fields or forests to pass the night and return cold and miserable in the morning to find that their hungry visitors had eaten what there was to eat; had burned what there was to burn; had carried away what there was to wear; and had left behind them a half-wrecked village. A few days later, the experience would be repeated, and this time one or more of the soldiers would be left behind sick with smallpox when the rest marched away, and soon the village cemetery would be crowded with fresh graves. Some villages were almost or entirely wiped out by such experiences. The atmosphere around us and around everybody in the country was quivering with excitement. This was war.[20]

The scenes described by Dr. White undoubtedly recurred in many other locali-ties throughout the empire.

Soldiers' families were one of the most vulnerable groups on the Ottoman home front. They carried the heaviest burden of the war and suffered most of its traumatic effects. More than any other group of women, their poverty and the absence of the male members rendered young female members of these households increasingly exposed to sexual exploitation. Prostitution as a result grew both in urban centers and in the countryside on an unprecedented scale during the war years. The public health director in Ankara, Muslihiddin Safvet, underscored the fact that extreme poverty led to a general deterioration of mo-rality, which had been sound until the beginning of the war. The increasing rate of prostitution arose from the seduction with promises of marriage of women whose husbands or fiancés had been killed in the war. Women who had lost male relatives and were compelled by poverty to become servants were also often seduced and then subsequently caught up in the increasingly wider net of prostitution, Safvet observed.[21] A diary writer in Jerusalem similarly noted that the conscription of their menfolk left women in a particularly precarious situation, and for many of them prostitution was the only means of survival.[22]

In some cases, desperate conditions coerced women, and particularly soldiers' family members, to submit to the sexual advances of state officials. As a local teacher in central Anatolia reported, pressure from tax collectors, gendarmes, police officers, and provisioning officials played the major role in forcing women into prostitution: "Young brides who lost all male members of their families had to fawn over these officials in order to be assigned family stipends, to receive their monthly payments, to obtain grain, and to hide husbands who had deserted."[23] Writing about the misery of soldiers' families in Giresun and governmental officials' exploitation of their despair, the local head of the CUP organization described the terrible situation vividly: "Honor was trampled to satisfy their sensual appetite[s]."[24] These observations were also confirmed by one of the highest-ranking authorities of the city of Kayseri, the mayor, Ahmed Bey, who witnessed women acceding to officials' sexual demands to get their thirty piaster monthly allowance.[25]

The CUP government actively, albeit ineffectively, sought to control prostitution, especially in urban centers, by regulating prostitutes[26] and establishing employment organizations.[27] The fight against prostitution was not limited to the capital city. Other parts of the empire also saw intense activity to save girls who had fallen into prostitution. In Jerusalem, for example, a women's employment society (Committee for Women's Employment) was established during the war with the goal of providing women with a livelihood without compromising them.[28] In Beirut, Ottoman authorities supported the activities of the Syrian Women's Association, which, in addition to other philanthropic activities, opened workshops for women and young girls where "they would be taught various crafts, given food, and paid [a] symbolic wage for their work."[29] However, these activities remained mostly an urban phenomenon, which had a very limited impact, if any, on the countryside, where prostitution proliferated dramatically.

The weakening of state authority throughout the countryside towards the end of the war only aggravated the vulnerability of Ottoman women. The thousands of deserters roaming the mountains became a real threat for families whose male members did not return from the war. *Ses*, a newspaper published in Balıkesir, in the Marmara region, reported that bandits there regularly pillaged villages, killing the elderly, ransacking peasants' goods, and stealing animals. They were also forcing young girls and even married women (after divorcing their husbands) to marry members of their band.[30] As a reaction, locals throughout the empire, aware of the inefficiency of governmental forces in preventing these gangs from pestering soldiers' families, were banding together on their own to "save the honor of their villages."[31]

The War, the State, and Soldiers' Families

What made World War I exceptionally onerous for Ottoman women was not only its length and destructiveness, but also the unprecedented transformation of the empire's conscription policies. Along with several other previously exempted social groups, the war saw the enlistment of tens of thousands of families' sole breadwinners (*muins*) for the first time. According to previous regulations on conscription, young men had the right to claim exemption from active military service if they could prove that their close relatives were entirely dependent upon them.[32] However, through the new Law of Military Obligation of 1914 the CUP government had completely abolished exemptions for sole breadwinners and required them to fulfill their military obligations like all other conscripts.[33]

As noted earlier, the Unionists regarded exemptions as a major cause of the Ottoman defeat in the Balkan Wars, and an enduring problem that had eroded the strength of the once-mighty Ottoman army. In their criticism, however, they reserved a special place for exemptions granted to sole breadwinners, the single largest group among the exempted. "It is mostly because of such leniencies that seven million people of the Balkans could defeat twenty-five million Ottomans," Hafız Hakkı Bey, a leading Unionist officer and the future commander in chief of the Ottoman Third Army, wrote. With a significant portion of the male population exempt from military service, these privileges were now starting to pose a serious threat to the very survival of the empire. "It is painful to separate a family, an old woman from her only support," Hafız Hakkı Bey asserted. But, since the empire needed to conscript all of its men in order to survive, people should endure this pain.[34] Lieutenant Colonel Behiç Bey similarly argued that the unnecessary leniency shown to the sole breadwinners had resulted in the Balkan Muslims' loss of their foremost protector, the Ottoman state: "Their properties were extorted, their chastity and honor were trampled,

their mosques were destroyed or converted into churches. The blood of inno-
cent women and elders was shed. Why? Because the army was incapable of
defending and protecting its nation."[35] Such exemptions, the Unionist leaders
believed, severely impaired the army's ability to fight. More than perhaps any
other factor, they constituted a major obstacle to the army's execution of its
most fundamental duty.

The new Law of Military Obligation was meant to address this problem
by completely abolishing exemptions granted to sole breadwinners. The shock
these men experienced in August 1914, when they learned that they too were
being called to the colors, was dreadful. Many folkloric accounts mention the
destabilizing experience that resulted from this policy change, reflecting deep
scars it left on the collective memory of the populace. An epic poem by Murad
Ali, a young conscript from Elbistan, in southern Anatolia, captures the anguish and distress engulfing the Ottoman home front:

Bin üçyüz otuzda bir emir çıktı.	An ordinance came out in 1330 [1914].
Nicesinin evin' başına yıktı.	It brought many [families'] homes down upon their heads.
Muinli muinsiz aradan kalktı.	The difference between *muinli* and *muinsiz* was abolished.
Herkes harmanını koyup gidiyor.[36]	Everybody abandons the harvests and goes.

In extending the reach of conscription, the Law of Military Obligation also
recast the relationship between the state and soldiers' families. In particular,
direct financial aid in the form of a monthly "separation allowance" was introduced for families whose male breadwinners had been drafted. In this way, the
state attempted to mitigate the negative effects of the loss of one (or more) male
members of the household to the army and compensate for the material losses
they endured. Thereby, it also sought to give the new recruits confidence that
their families would not suffer any material hardships in their absence, thus
encouraging them to join the army, stay in the ranks, and continue fighting.

During the Balkan Wars, the Ottoman state had briefly experimented with
a separation allowance scheme on a limited basis,[37] but it was not until World
War I that it was put into practice on a large scale. Relief for soldiers' families
under the new Law of Military Obligation differed in two ways from previous
forms of poor relief in the Ottoman Empire.[38] First, it was given to everyone
who qualified, regardless of the wishes of the benefactor. Second, it was generally regarded by the recipients, not as a handout, but as compensation for sol-

diers' sacrifices. Many people took it for granted that their sons, husbands, and fathers had earned this right for them through their military service.

The Ottoman Empire was indeed not alone in devising policies to diminish domestic hardships experienced by soldiers' relatives. During the war, almost every combatant nation developed financial support programs for families grappling with privation arising from the recruitment of family breadwinners. These programs varied considerably in terms of the amount of the allowance, the number of family members entitled to it, and the institution responsible for overseeing the program. In some countries, including the Ottoman Empire, state aid was extended based on "means testing." In others, like Great Britain and Russia, the coverage of the scheme was universal.[39] Some belligerent governments increased separation allowances periodically to keep pace with the rising cost of living. The Ottoman Empire, however, was among the countries where the monthly allowance amount remained flat throughout the conflict despite worsening wartime conditions.

In the hands of the governments, separation allowances also served to monitor and regulate recipients' behavior. Women's payments were cut off when the authorities thought they had behaved "immorally" or "improperly." Sexual misconduct, unfaithfulness to their absent husbands, or other similar acts usually provided the necessary excuse to take women out of the allowance scheme. The state, in the words of the historian Susan Pedersen, became "a surrogate husband" for soldiers' wives.[40]

Reactions towards the allowance recipients also varied dramatically among the belligerent nations. In Austria-Hungary and particularly Germany, for instance, soldiers' wives receiving state aid met with resentment and even hostility from other segments of the home-front population.[41] They were accused of squandering government payments, capitalizing on their husbands' sacrifice, and profiteering from the war. In other countries, such antagonism towards soldiers' wives was generally nonexistent. Likely due to steep wartime inflation, which significantly reduced the purchasing power of the monthly allowances, Ottoman soldiers' wives generally did not experience feelings of popular resentment directed against them.

The implementation of the financial aid program in the Ottoman Empire required the participation of various ranks of the imperial bureaucracy. At the local level, administrative councils (*meclis-i idare*) were charged with administering the program in collaboration with enlistment offices (*ahz-ı asker daireleri*) and revenue offices (*mal sandıkları*). Enlistment offices provided the records of families whose breadwinners had joined the army, and local revenue offices dispensed money to the members of these families by sending revenue officers to their villages and neighborhoods. In order to qualify for this allowance, the family members had to be entirely dependent on the conscript's earnings and have no income from any other source or any relatives who could be regarded as a substitute breadwinner.[42] The law provided for a monthly allowance of "a minimum of 30 piaster [*kuruş*] per person" and required disbursement without delay directly to the members of the soldier's family in the presence of the council of elders of a village or neighborhood. The first monthly allowance would be paid out after the conscript appeared in person at the enlistment center and began his military service.[43] If the soldier deserted his battalion or if he did not return from leave, his family would be taken out of the allowance scheme.[44] Termination of the military service of the conscript for any reason would automatically end the state's obligation to his family.

The implementation of the policy was far from flawless. With less than three months separating the enactment of the new law and the declaration of general mobilization, the administration was caught utterly unprepared. The new system of conscription and separation allowance distribution required a new infrastructure, and this was still incomplete when the government ordered the mobilization in August 1914. When put into practice, the system also suffered severely from the injustices and corruption of governmental employees.[45]

While the family allowance scheme was fraught with problems at the micro level, it did not function smoothly at the macro level either. Expecting a short war, Ottoman policy-makers did not foresee the enormity of the task of aiding hundreds of thousands of soldiers' dependents. The financial burden and administrative complexity of the scheme soon exceeded the policy-makers' projections. In December 1917, it was estimated that there were 1.5 million dependents who received such state aid.[46] The incessant demand of the army for new conscripts, of course, was the main reason behind the ever-expanding number of families seeking state help. But the increasingly unbearable economic conditions also compelled many families who had initially managed to endure the absence of their breadwinners to apply for monthly allowances.[47]

More often than not, however, the government failed to pay soldiers' families, along with other groups who depended on payments from the state.[48] In March 1916, for instance, the governor of Syria asked the Ministry of Finance to send the province twenty thousand lira because families without a supporter, widows, orphans, and other needy groups had become so disgruntled over unpaid pensions and consequent privations that "they could not be silenced anymore."[49] Similarly, MPs from various provinces who were unwilling to acquiesce often raised complaints about the state's failure to live up to its promises to these families.[50] Talat Pasha himself confessed before parliament that the government could not pay family allowances regularly. In some cities, during his trips throughout the country, the minister of the interior ordered the postponement of payment of governmental officials' salaries to disburse stipends to soldiers' families.[51]

Once the payments were made families realized that the depreciated Ottoman paper currency was worth hardly anything in many Ottoman provinces.[52] With increasing inflation, paper currency had completely lost its already low value as a medium of exchange. Despite this erosion, the monthly stipends were almost always disbursed in paper money. A group of women from Tarsus who described themselves as mothers and wives of "veteran or martyred Islamic soldiers" wrote to the minister of the interior that vendors did not honor paper currency and that they could not buy the items they needed. "[With] paper [money] in our hands, we'll die of hunger" ("Elimizde kağıt acımızdan öleceğiz"), they declared. They urged the minister to intervene in local provisioning by ordering the export of grain from neighboring regions and by preventing profiteering.[53]

Even though the family allowance scheme was fraught with problems, however, it nonetheless introduced a new understanding of mutual obligations between the state and its citizens. By codifying the principle of aiding soldiers' families from the state treasury, the Ottoman state pledged to support them in the absence of their sons, husbands, brothers, and fathers. In this respect, the law initiated a new relationship between the state and soldiers' families that had not previously existed in the Ottoman Empire. The wartime developments elevated the significance of this relationship and invested it with a new meaning.

Soldiers' families in general and soldiers' wives and mothers in particular frequently figured in official wartime discourse and propaganda as a symbol of Ottoman altruism and sacrifice. Politicians and intellectuals continually underlined the importance of providing for soldiers' families. As the soldiers were fighting on the fronts to defend the empire, they asserted, soldiers' families should be safeguarded by the Ottoman state and people. "The first thing to fulfill this duty [is] the maintenance of the welfare and livelihood [terfih ve ikdarı] of the families of our brave soldiers," Talat Pasha declared.[54] Calling on the army and the navy in the first days of the war to continue fighting bravely and avenge the "extinguished hearths, chafed wounds, and trampled martyrs [of the Balkan Wars]," the Ottoman parliament assured the troops: "Do not ever be concerned about your families, your hearths. They are entrusted to us for safekeeping by God's will [*onlar bize vediatullahtır*]."[55]

Civil society organizations, which generally acted in cooperation with the CUP government, also made a considerable effort to mobilize popular opinion in favor of soldiers' families.[56] Several philanthropic organizations were formed (or revitalized) during the war for the purpose of providing material support for soldiers' families in distress. The Ladies' Aid Society for Soldiers' Families (Asker Ailelerine Yardımcı Hanımlar Cemiyeti), founded by the wives and daughters of high-ranking Ottoman and German officials in early 1915, was arguably the most vocal and active among the new associations spawned by the war.[57] Echoing Talat Pasha, İrfan Bedri Hanım, the organization's accountant and the wife of Bedri Bey, the mayor of Istanbul, stated in a press release that it was the society's most important duty to "to support the soldiers' families in any way."[58] The activities of these organizations included organizing theatrical performances and concerts as fund-raisers, collecting donations to contribute to the welfare of these families, conducting campaigns to gather clothing, dried food, and sanitary materials, and running day nurseries.[59] The Ladies' Aid Society also took the lead to place a wooden cannon, the Souvenir of Bravery (Hatıra-i Celâdet Topu), in Istanbul's Beyazıt Square, symbolizing the bravery of Ottoman soldiers at Gallipoli. People could hammer a nail into the canon in exchange for a monetary donation, which would go to the soldiers' families.[60]

Major patriotic civil society organizations also broadened their scope of activities to extend aid to soldiers' families who were living in indigent circumstances. The Society of National Defense (Müdafaa-i Milliye Cemiyeti) was apparently the most active of these charity organizations that stepped in to support governmental and municipal welfare activities.[61] The wartime activities of the Society were not limited to Istanbul alone. In Izmir, for instance, charity organizations ran soup kitchens and opened sewing workshops that employed soldiers' female family members.[62]

In addition to conducting such activities, Ottoman civil society organizations and the press also sought to mobilize the patriotic and religious sentiments of the urban population to raise support for soldiers' families. The Women's Branch of the Ottoman Red Crescent (Osmanlı Hilal-i Ahmer Cemiyeti Hanımlar Merkezi), for instance, called upon Ottoman women to join their ranks: "Do not leave your hands and arms idle. . . . The nation is not defended merely with weapons. Defense also has a moral side. The first duty that falls upon women is to treat well and support the families of men who have gone to war in order to make them feel comfortable."[63] In a public declaration addressing the Ottoman people, the Müdafaa-i Milliye Society stated that the government, despite its hard work in attempting to meet the needs of the family members of soldiers, also depended upon the willingness of the Ottoman nation to embrace and support these families. Soldiers who rushed to the borders to defend the religion, chastity, honor, life, and property of the nation, the declaration read, should not be concerned with the needs of their families. If *jihad* was a duty that fell upon every Muslim, "nourishing deprived families that the soldiers left behind in their villages was an equally religious and humanitarian duty."[64] In a similar vein, the major religious journal of the era, *Sebilürreşad*, invoked Ottoman Muslims' sense of solidarity. Hacı Abdülhamid Hamid El-Berzenci and Aksekili Ahmet Hamdi Bey, prominent religious authorities of the period, reiterated that it was Muslims' obligation to help soldiers' families and called upon them to give alms to these families.[65]

By establishing and leading semi-official civil society organizations, organizing campaigns and fund-raisers, mobilizing public opinion through declarations, writings, speeches, and sermons, continually underscoring the state's and nation's responsibilities to soldiers' families, and, perhaps most important, assigning them a monthly allowance, the Ottoman state signified the special status of soldiers' relatives and increased their visibility on the home front. For soldiers' families, these policies, activities, and discourses must have strengthened their expectations and created an impression that their sacrifices would be acknowledged and their problems would be addressed.

"Engaging with the State": Soldiers' Wives and Mothers and the Politics of Sacrifice on the Ottoman Home Front

Soldiers' family members, especially soldiers' wives and mothers, were not passive observers of these developments. As they became the object of several wartime policies and discourses, they simultaneously entered into negotiations with government officials over their rights and privileges. By drawing attention to their husbands' and sons' service on behalf of the empire and increasing their calls for reciprocity in their sacrifice and service to the motherland, soldiers' wives and mothers established a more demanding relationship with the state. In this new relationship, the sons and husbands serving in the army came to represent the link between the state and women in wartime Ottoman society.

As in other belligerent countries, World War I upset the established patterns of women's personal, familial, and public presence in the Ottoman Empire.[66] Wartime conditions forced women to deal with issues beyond their immediate households as they struggled to survive. As a result, they came increasingly into contact with officials, a process that served to challenge entrenched assumptions about women's role in public life. Before the war, women's direct communication with officialdom had been quite limited.[67] The absence of men and the necessities of war, however, compelled them to interact with officials with increasing frequency. In order to collect their monthly pensions, receive their daily ration of bread from the municipal or military bakeries, register a complaint about a local official's misbehavior, apply for state aid to support themselves and their children, or resist a requisitioning officer, women repeatedly interacted with representatives of the Ottoman state and gradually entered the public arena as never before. Both for the women themselves and for functionaries who had previously had access to them only through their husbands or fathers, this spelled a dramatic change.

Women's petitions, letters, and telegrams to the minister of the interior bear witness to this wartime phenomenon. Frustrated by deteriorating local conditions and increasingly harsh state policies, Ottoman women from all parts of the empire sent petitions and letters to various ministries as well as to local authorities during the war years. The inadequacy of relief aid, the government's policies of impressment and forced employment, poverty, destitution, and poor treatment at the hands of state officials were the subjects that loomed large in their petitions.[68] In the hands of women, these petitions and telegrams became a major vehicle with which to urge the leaders of the Unionist regime to intervene in the local politics of subsistence on their side. The petitions that survive likely represent only a fraction of all the petitions and letters submitted by women during the war. They nevertheless constitute a major source of information about Ottoman women's wartime experiences and their engagement with state authorities.

The number of signatures on the petitions submitted to the interior minister indicates collective action among women. Although there were also documents signed or sealed by only one petitioner, sometimes officials received petitions signed by dozens of women. Occasionally, this cooperation also crossed ethnoreligious boundaries. For instance, a group of soldiers' wives who wrote from

Sındırgı (Kütahya) in western Anatolia to ask for the repeal of a decision to discontinue their pensions included Muslim women as well as their non-Muslim Greek neighbors.[69] It is also notable that the petitioners often went to great lengths to send their telegrams to state officials. Many of them had to travel long distances from their villages to get to a district center with a telegraph office. Women from Ordu on the Black Sea coast, for instance, walked twenty hours to the district center to wire a telegram about the horrors of the government's requisitioning policies. They also wrote, with an apologetic tone, that only nine of them could make the journey to the district center, because the others had to stay in the village to care for the children.[70]

The underlying, albeit implicit, message of many of these petitions and telegrams was that their husbands' and sons' military service was at odds with these women's welfare. Over and over again, women wrote of their own struggle with wartime hardships. A large group of women in Kırkkilise, who now did all of the agricultural work previously performed by menfolk, wrote: "We sent our sons and husbands to the army. They [governmental officials] don't leave anything [any grain] for our subsistence. They want to seize everything we produce. They don't take into account what we've given so far. We will starve!"[71] A telegram from women in Yozgat, in central Anatolia, likewise revealed the burden on soldiers' families. "Since our children are sacrificing their lives for the nation, performing their military service and even dying as martyrs, we remain without breadwinners," they complained. "We have no source of income. We sold our household items to meet our needs for sustenance." Clearly basing their claims on the state on their husbands' and sons' military service, they pleaded for the government to relieve their suffering.[72]

These petitions, letters, and telegrams both vividly illustrate the enormous difficulties with which the war confronted Ottoman women and shed light on the new social and political identity women embraced as soldiers' wives and mothers.[73] In almost all of the petitions they wrote, women unfailingly specified their identities in terms of their relations to family members in the military service. They signed the petitions "mother of" or "wife of," often underlining their sacrifice and contribution to the Ottoman war effort by mentioning how many relatives they had sent to the front. The rhetoric they employed clearly displayed their sense of the moral obligation that the state had towards soldiers' families, whom it had promised to shield in the absence of their protectors. "While our husbands are toiling on the borders to protect the glory and honor of the nation, the compassion of our exalted government will [surely] not permit their families to die of starvation," women wrote from İskilip (Çorum), in central Anatolia.[74] "At a time when our husbands and fathers entrusted us to your high protection and hastened to the frontiers, thinking nothing of their own lives and baring their chests to the enemy's bullets," Hatice, a soldier's wife, and her friends wrote in the name of all soldiers' wives in Beypazarı, in central Anatolia, "we often go hungry." They saw the drought and unprecedentedly high prices of grain as the two principal causes of their hunger. However, they essentially blamed the local government, which was sending the grain collected in their district to Istanbul in dereliction of its duty to distribute it to indigent families. To make the matters worse, local officials forced these women to transport this grain with their own animals, regardless of their incapacity to do so. The petitioners asked the interior minister to save them from hunger and drudgery.[75]

Women consciously underlined the contradiction between the horrendous conditions they were enduring and the benevolence and protection they expected from the representatives of the Ottoman state. Women in Konya, for instance, expressed keen awareness of the discrepancy between their sacrifices and the state's (or more accurately, local officials') treatment of them. They were in need of seed grain to cultivate and produce for "our husbands who are sacrificing their lives for the nation's cause," but the district governor had dismissed their appeal, saying that they were "not the people of this state."[76] Women from Malatya had a similar experience with governmental officials. They presented themselves to officials as "lonely and destitute families of Ottoman heroes who face the rifle and cannon of the enemy to defend the nation and religion and to protect our chastity." When they visited the town's accountant to complain about the inadequate payment of their allowances (they had received only one or two payments in the past eight to nine months), they were sworn at and driven away from the "government's door of mercy" (*hükümetin bab-ı merhameti*). While their husbands were shedding their blood, and their children were suffering "in an unendurable fire of hunger," these women asserted, functionaries were enjoying regular salaries.[77] Soldiers' wives contrasted their treatment with that of state officials and implied that they deserved better (or at least be treated as well as the officials) in exchange for the sacrifices they had made.[78]

Disheartened wives and mothers reminded the interior minister in petitions and telegrams of the "tacit contract" that soldiers and their families had with the state. "For years, our husbands and sons have sacrificed their lives and blood and performed their duties bravely," fourteen women in Boğazlıyan began their appeal. They, however, were deprived of food and were forced to resort to begging. The local government's policy of exporting existing grain to another town and its disregard for their needs rendered them helpless. This, the women implied, was a violation of the contract.[79] Similarly, thirty-four women from Ermenek in central Anatolia, again, mostly soldiers' wives and mothers, reported the hunger and poverty they experienced and singled out the army's requisitioning and harsh weather conditions as the main reasons for their suffering and pleaded with the interior minister not to "ignore the starvation of lonely women like us while our sons sacrifice their lives against the enemy."[80]

Women sometimes skillfully played state institutions against one another in their petitions. In Geyve and Akhisar, for instance, women who applied to the district governor to collect their [unpaid] pensions had been kicked out of the governor's office. Embittered by this brutal and humiliating treatment, they brought their complaint to the head of the enlistment office, presumably aware of the army's higher sensitivity concerning these issues. Correspondence among the recruitment office, the Ministry of War, and the Ministry of Interior regarding the case resulted in a stern warning to district governors that "these nasty situations would have a deleterious impact on the soldiers of the imperial army."[81] Similarly in Boğazlıyan, Armenian women petitioned the military inspector Hulusi Pasha, who was visiting the town in the summer of 1916, protesting against their unlawful treatment at the hands of local officials, who did not assign monthly payments to servicemen's wives who had converted from Christianity to Islam (*muhtediyes*).[82] Following the military inspector's report, the Ministry of War reminded the Ministry of the Interior and its personnel that the Law of Military Obligation applied to all Ottoman subjects, regardless of ethnicity and confessional community (*kavmiyet ve milliyet tefrik etmeksizin*), and that it ordered equal state support to all families in need.[83]

Conclusions

The overwhelming majority of Ottoman women suffered privation, hard work, and abuse or were otherwise adversely affected by World War I. Many of them also lost male members of their households. However, their suffering on the home front and their contribution to the war effort was generally downplayed in national memory, and their wartime experiences were excluded from official historiography. In both contemporary publications and later scholarly works, the war was depicted as a predominantly masculine enterprise. While valorizing the dedication, bravery, and altruism of soldiers, both contemporary observers and later historians relegated Ottoman women's experiences of the war to the margins of the official histories. This chapter, in contrast, has emphasized the importance of studying wartime gender relations to expand and complicate our understanding of the Ottoman experience of the Great War. By highlighting women's wartime actions and experiences, it aims to challenge the historical and cultural construction of war as exclusively male-centered.

War and its burdens singled out a certain group of women on the Ottoman home front: soldiers' wives and mothers. The Ottoman state devised several policies to alleviate their misery and to fill the gap that was created by the military service of their sons and husbands. These policies proved to be inadequate, however, and women directed their frustration at local, provincial, and imperial officials. Embracing a new and powerful identity as "soldiers' wives and mothers," they appealed to governmental officials for solutions to their problems. They did not ask for equal rights with men or the rights of citizenship. But they demanded that the government honor the implicit contract between the state and soldiers' families. In doing so, they developed an uneasy relationship with the representatives of the state. Their story remains an instructive part of the story of the empire's final years.

6 ON THE ROAD: DEPORTEES AND REFUGEES

Throughout the war, the Ottoman Empire was the scene of large-scale deportations and refugee movements. Millions were either forcibly deported by the state or fled their homes to escape the enemy. Over the course of the war, at least one in every ten Ottoman citizens became a deportee or refugee. Beginning in the spring of 1915, hundreds of thousands of Ottoman Armenians were uprooted from their homes and deported to the empire's southern provinces of Der Zor and Mosul. Smaller-scale deportations targeting other ethno-religious groups, most notably Greeks, Assyrians, Arabs, and Jews also took place during the war. These people, however, were not the only Ottomans on the move during the war. The Russian army's advance in eastern Anatolia in 1915 and 1916 precipitated massive waves of immigration. Close to a million Muslim refugees set off for provinces they thought would provide a safe haven for themselves and their families.

Being forced to leave one's home and travel in wartime to unfamiliar places was a harrowing experience for deportees and refugees, but the forced deportation of Armenians and the flight of Muslim refugees from the enemy were two categorically different forms of population displacement. The CUP government itself commanded the deportation of the Armenians, but in the case of the Muslim refugees, the government was coping with a movement imposed on it. In both cases, the population movements were orchestrated to reshape the empire's demographic structure. There would seem to have been a deliberate intention on the part of elements of the Unionist leadership to get rid of the Armenians permanently. With the Muslim refugees, however, the ultimate goal of the government's policy was to neutralize certain "undesirable" elements among them, most notably the Kurds, rather than eliminate them. The government tried to break them up into small groups and direct them into designated settlement areas.

The nature of the violence to which Armenian deportees and Muslim refugees were subjected therefore differed fundamentally. During their flight from the enemy, Muslim refugees undoubtedly suffered violent attacks, including abuse, assaults, robbery, rape, and murder. But these violent acts remained mostly sporadic and uncoordinated. Armenians, however, had to face sustained and systematic atrocities committed by various actors along their deportation routes or at their settlement camps. The state authorities usually turned a blind eye to these atrocities. In terms of their designated final destinations, the two mass migrations also differed dramatically. The Armenians' final destinations were generally remote and inhospitable regions. These areas lacked sufficient natural resources to accommodate the hundreds of thousands of Armenians who would survive the deportation marches. Conversely, Muslim refugees were usually settled in regions where they could, potentially at least, establish new lives. Finally, these two mass migrations also had very different outcomes. The process that began with the deportation of the Armenians gradually became radicalized over time, assuming genocidal proportions. Except for small enclaves, it brought a practical end to the Armenian presence in the Ottoman Empire. In contrast, many Muslim refugees managed to return to their homes when the war was over. Although they suffered from traumatic experiences during their flight, those sufferings did not amount to collective annihilation. Focusing on the individual and collective experiences of the Ottoman people as deportees and refugees, this chapter turns the spotlight on the cruel world of mass migration in the wartime Ottoman Empire.

Deportation and Destruction

The CUP government's policies of demographic engineering were shaped under wartime conditions, which encouraged the adoption of radical solutions. On the one hand, fighting a difficult war against formidable enemies made the Unionists exceedingly sensitive about any development that could possibly harm their war effort. In that sense, the war deepened the Unionists' sense of urgency and, once again, raised the specter of conflating the empire's minorities with its external enemies. On the other hand, the war offered the Unionists suitable conditions for implementing those policies once they were formulated.

It removed any possibility of European powers intervening to protect the empire's minorities and insisting on administrative and political reforms on their behalf. Equally important, the wartime policies allowed the army and the government to exercise unprecedented control over the empire's human and material resources. In particular, mass conscription of the young male members of these communities—those most capable of resistance—rendered them vulnerable to the government's attempts to deport, relocate, and/or eliminate them.

The Unionists entered World War I with two solidified perceptions about the interconnectedness of demography and warfare. First, demographic realities on the ground could determine outcomes on the battlefield. Second, the empire's non-Muslim minorities could hardly be counted on during military conflicts, especially if one or more foreign powers supported their noncompliance. As discussed in the first chapter, the possibility of war with Greece in 1914 had made the Unionists enact a systematic policy of "unmixing," which culminated in the expulsion of tens of thousands of Ottoman Greeks from their homelands in western Anatolia. During World War I, Greeks continued to be regarded with great suspicion by the authorities, and their loyalty to the empire and its war effort was routinely questioned. From the first weeks of the mobilization onward, a noticeable anti-Greek sentiment prevailed in the Ottoman press. Greek profiteers and deserters to Greek islands received particular scrutiny.[1] Slightly before the war, a popular humor magazine did not hesitate to depict Karagöz, the main character of the Ottoman shadow theater, with rat traps on his donkey's back, going to Izmir to catch Greek deserters.[2]

During the war, this entrenched suspicion of Ottoman Greeks led to their displacement from militarily sensitive regions to the interior.[3] In his response to Simonaki Simonoğlu Efendi, a deputy from Izmir, who had pled for the Anatolian Greeks to be permitted to return to their homes after the battle of Gallipoli, minister of the interior Talat Bey openly stated that "some people who lived under the title of citizen in this country have betrayed it and brought provisions to enemy submarines, and that is why this measure is deemed necessary."[4] By late 1916, the number of Ottoman Greeks displaced by the wartime measures had reached 93,088,[5] and by the end of the war this number had increased to 300,000.[6] Many of these were forcibly driven from their homes into the Anatolian interior to places that were substantially different from where they had been living. Despite its strong prejudices against the Ottoman Greeks, however, the CUP government refrained from a more destructive wartime campaign against them since obviously anti-Greek measures might well lead

Greece to join the Entente powers.[7] According to a prominent journalist writing in the postwar era, Ahmed Emin (Yalman), the deportations of the Greeks were "more or less a matter of military necessity," and, in terms of the level of suffering, they "certainly were not comparable with the treatment received by the Armenians."[8]

As for the other major non-Muslim community of the empire, the Armenians, the Unionists pursued a much more cautious approach at the beginning. As opposed to news coverage about the Greeks, the press regularly emphasized the Ottoman Armenians' contribution to the war effort and underlined their willingness to defend the fatherland. Armenians were commended for expressing their loyalty to the empire, praying for Ottoman victory, collecting donations, and engaging in similar patriotic acts.[9] These news reports were accurate. In many localities, the leading Armenian political party, the ARF, encouraged Armenians to enlist and perform their duty. In Bardizag/Bahçecik, for instance, the village's ARF trumpet band accompanied the five hundred Armenian recruits on their march to the nearby town center.[10]

The press's unusually favorable portrayal of the Armenians reflected the Unionists' deep anxiety about them. As discussed in the first chapter, the Unionists had unequivocally perceived the Armenian recalcitrance in the reform process as a sign of their collusion with Russia. During the mobilization, news reached the army's headquarters about the formation of voluntary battalions by Caucasian Armenians on the Russian side. The defection of a few famous Armenian revolutionaries to the Russian side, most notably Armen Garo, who was personally known by many leading Unionists, only fed the Unionists' suspicions.[11] The fact that the vast majority of Ottoman Armenians remained loyal to the empire and that the ARF actively supported the Ottoman mobilization in the provinces fell short of assuaging their concerns. These concerns were further compounded by the Unionists' exaggerated perception of the Armenian revolutionaries' commitment, boldness, and capacity for mobilization. The Unionists knew well that what distinguished Armenians from other ethno-religious communities was the presence of well-organized Armenian revolutionary organizations, which could potentially pose a deadly threat to the CUP government. From their own experiences, the Unionists were aware of what a small yet highly motivated and organized group could achieve. Later in the war, when U.S. Ambassador Morgenthau expressed his dismay at the arrest of Armenians, Talat Bey replied that he himself had "been at the head of revolutionaries and knows what can be done."[12] Together with heightened wartime anxiety, this perception of the Armenians led the Unionists to interpret isolated incidents of Armenian disobedience as parts of a larger, coordinated, empirewide uprising.

During the early months of the war, the CUP government approached the "Armenian question" strictly from a military perspective. The measures implemented aimed to change the demographic facts on the ground in militarily-sensitive, strategic areas to eliminate perceived imminent threats to the empire's war effort. Just as in the Balkan Wars, military officers frequently complained about the difficulties they faced in the regions inhabited by non-Muslims. According to these complaints, Armenian villagers spread ominous news among soldiers about the army's defeat, Enver Pasha's imprisonment, and the like. They also facilitated desertion from the ranks by providing shelter and provisions to deserters.[13] The military authorities took some preventive measures to deal with these problems. Yet these measures remained limited in scope and confined to certain regions. Although sporadic massacres were occurring, especially in the border provinces, in the words of the historian Ronald Suny, "no particular direction or clear intention was apparent."[14] By 1914, the eastern Anatolian borderlands had already been destabilized by decades-long intercommunal tensions and intermittent violence. From August 1914 on, frequent disturbances caused by conscription and requisitioning, constant troop movements, and, more important, a heightened sense of uncertainty about the future wreaked further havoc on the region. The disastrous Sarıkamış campaign took place in this volatile environment, further deepening suspicions among the Ottoman authorities about the Armenians' loyalty. The army's decision to disarm Armenian soldiers in late February 1915 and later to send them to labor battalions can be seen as a result of these deepened suspicions.

Soon afterwards, the policy towards Armenians evolved gradually from a relatively narrow security issue into large-scale ethnic cleansing. The specter of an Allied breakthrough at the Dardanelles in March combined with the well-organized Armenian resistance in the eastern Anatolian city of Van in April played a major role in the radicalization of the Unionist policy.[15] In the minds of the Unionists, the Van incident left no doubts about the Armenians' active collaboration with the Russians. Fearful of an empirewide Armenian uprising, on 24 April 1915, the government ordered the arrest and deportation of Armenian politicians, intellectuals, journalists, lawyers, and clerics at the capital, leaving the Armenian community virtually without leadership. Diran Kelekian, who was the editor of the daily *Sabah* and had given a fiercely patriotic speech at a Balkan War rally, was among them. Like many of his fellow deportees, he was soon to be killed. That same day, the government also ordered the closing of all branches of Armenian political parties throughout the empire. This order was soon followed by deportation orders for the Armenians living in the eastern Anatolian provinces of Erzurum, Bitlis, Van, and much of Cilicia.[16] From late May 1915 on, the government's policy towards Armenians assumed an increasingly expansive and destructive character. On 27 May 1915, it passed a provisional law authorizing army commanders to deport anyone in their army zones. This was an attempt on the part of the CUP to frame the deportations as a military necessity and to provide legal cover for the entire process. The scope of the deportations was soon extended to include provinces far from the border regions.[17]

Depending on where they lived, Armenians experienced the deportation process differently. Those from western Anatolia were usually sent by railroad in overcrowded cattle cars and thus had to cover relatively shorter distances on foot. For the Armenians uprooted from their homes in the eastern Anatolian provinces, however, the deportation marches entailed enormous suffering. The empire's infrastructure problems, which were hampering the Ottoman war effort, dramatically worsened their plight. The lack of railroads, widespread military requisitioning of other means of transportation and draft animals, and inhospitable terrain and climate led to the deaths of tens of thousands of Armenians from exhaustion, exposure, starvation, and disease. Deportees from the eastern provinces were also subjected to extreme violence. During the earlier phases of the marches, Armenian men who had remained out of the conscription net were usually gathered together and killed. Deportation convoys were frequently attacked by Turkish and Kurdish irregulars, "special organization" (*teşkilat-ı mahsusa*) units,[18] or local tribal groups. The few gendarmes who escorted the convoys could not or did not provide protection to the deportees.[19] Out of religious or material motivations or a combination of both, local people along the deportation routes attacked Armenians and plundered whatever they carried with them. Many took the opportunity offered by "state-permitted lawlessness."[20]

Under these conditions, the deportation process became an ordeal for the Armenians. Families broke apart on the marches. Elderly people who could not keep up with the strain were left behind. Desperation and the fear of death obliged mothers to abandon their children on the roadside or hand them over to Muslims. Yervant Odian, himself a deportee, witnessed such scenes between Osmaniye and Islahiye:

> Thousands of women, girls and children, bent under heavy loads, broken and racked with pain, walked along undulating, stony and muddy roads, crying and lamenting. Bodies could be seen here and there, ravaged by birds of prey, dogs, and hyenas. Sick people were groaning without help under trees. Newborn children abandoned, crying with hunger. Bodies so badly buried that arms and legs stuck out of the ground . . . scenes from hell that no Dante could have imagined.[21]

A nationalist military officer, Abidin Ege, similarly noted in his diary: "What is most frequently encountered on the roads are Armenian corpses."[22]

In the absence of menfolk and government protection, Armenian women and girls suffered horrific abuses on their deportation marches. They were sexually assaulted by marauders, gendarmes, and others.[23] Many of them were raped, and many others were abducted by Turks, Kurds, and Arabs. The motives of abduction varied greatly. As Reverend Henry Riggs recounted, "some of the girls who thus entered Turkish families were treated fairly kindly and seemed to adapt themselves to the unnatural life. But others suffered indescribably, and some lost their minds."[24] This extremely traumatic experience was described in a Turkish-language lament recorded in the 1950s by the ethnographer Verjine Svazlian:

Giden giden Ermeni kızlar!	Armenian girls who go and go!
Bir gün ölüm bize düşer.	One day death will come upon us.
Düşmana avrat olmamaya	Before I become the wife of the enemy,
Yeprat'ın içinde ölüm bulayım.[25]	Let me find death in the Euphrates.

Many Armenian children similarly ended up in Muslim homes or orphanages where most of them would forget their Armenian background. One of those children, Hampartzoum Chitjian, was amazed at "how quickly and unconsciously we completely forgot how to speak Armenian." The Ottomanist anthem they learned in school stood in stark contrast to what they were going through: "Freedom, justice, fraternity—long live the people / We are Ottomans, brotherhood is our ancient custom."[26] The aftermath of the war would thus see an extensive effort to locate and rescue those women and children who had been absorbed by Muslim families.[27]

Those who survived the marches and reached their destinations were forced to live in makeshift camps established in the Syrian desert and along the Euphrates under desperate circumstances. The authorities did not bother to provide food, clean water, or fuel to the Armenians on a regular basis when the army itself was struggling to secure these resources. Epidemic diseases dealt a devastating blow to this physically weakened group of people. Tens of thousands of Armenian survivors of deportation marches would perish in these camps. Many others were killed by irregulars and tribal units.

Lacking coherent and careful planning ahead of time, the process of deportation and settlement was chaotic from the very beginning, but this chaotic implementation did not mean that the deportation process was not under the control of the Ottoman central authorities. Once it became an official policy, the central government was directly involved in monitoring, regulating, and executing the deportations. The Ministry of the Interior and the CUP strove to ensure the compliance of local officials with the general policy and keep them under strict control by sending executive secretaries (*katib-i mesuls*) to the provinces. Local administrators who were perceived as too lenient towards Armenians were regularly replaced by others who would adopt sterner attitudes or, in some cases, were even assassinated.[28] The Interior Ministry officials regularly obtained detailed information from local authorities about the numbers and characteristics of the deported Armenians. They were therefore fully aware of the deportees' suffering during their marches and in the camps. This micromanagement also included data collection about abandoned Armenian properties, emptied villages, and their location and agricultural quality with the specific purpose of settling Muslim deportees into them.[29] Once the deportation phase ended, the CUP government proceeded to take radical measures to prevent the return of Armenians in the aftermath of the war. The government seized individual and communal properties that belonged to Armenians and auctioned off their perishable goods and livestock while passing regulations that made this seizure practically irreversible.[30]

According to Talat Pasha's own records, 924,158 out of approximately 1.5 million Ottoman Armenians were deported during the war. This, however, was an underestimate, as his calculations did not include deported Armenians from several localities, the adding of which, according to the historian Taner Akçam, would bring the total number close to 1.2 million.[31] According to Fuat Dündar's estimates, the CUP government did not deport around 281,000 Ottoman Armenians who were either inhabitants of certain cities (most notably, Istanbul, Izmir, and Edirne), were critical for the continuation of the war effort, were Catholics or Protestants, or were converts to Islam. Approximately 255,000 Armenians managed to flee abroad, primarily to Russia. Finally, about 300,000 deportees survived the deportation marches and resettlement process. Dündar calculates that of the empire's 1.5 million Armenians, 664,000 perished as a result of the Unionists' policy.[32] In terms of its scope, destructiveness, and long-term impact, the disaster that befell the Ottoman Armenians was shockingly gruesome. The Armenian Genocide destroyed the lives and well-being of hundreds of thousands of people, ravaged the established patterns of intercommunal life, and marked the end of the communal presence of Ottoman Armenians in eastern Anatolia, which they had inhabited for thousands of years. In the words of a leading Unionist, Ottoman history had never before witnessed "such a colossal slaughter and such extensive cruelty."[33]

The Refugee Crisis

Although the Armenian Genocide constituted the bloodiest episode of the Ottoman home front, it is virtually impossible to grasp the enormity of population displacements in the wartime Ottoman Empire without examining the refugee movements. The flight of the refugees in eastern Anatolia began immediately after the official declaration of war between Russia and the Ottoman Empire. Muslim villagers living in the border regions left their homes even before the first Russian troops had crossed the border.[34] The first clashes between the Ottoman and Russian forces around Köprüköy and Azap in northeastern Anatolia displaced many more Armenians and Muslim Ottomans.[35] Indeed, the Ottoman strategy of meeting a probable Russian offensive around Hasankale had resulted in the army's withdrawal of forces from the border zones. Thus, the villages between the border and Hasankale were left unprotected against enemy assaults. In the meantime, about 30,000 Armenian villagers living in the border areas sought refuge behind Russian lines to protect themselves and their families from the aggression of Ottoman troops and irregulars.[36] These first refugees, whether Muslim or Christian, ended up in villages and towns not very far from their homes.

Refugee movements continued into 1915. With the advance of the Russian army towards Van and Bitlis, people from this region poured into neighboring provinces. The capture of Van by Russian forces and Armenian bands in May 1915, its recapture by the Ottoman army in the following months, and the subsequent interethnic violence between Muslims and Armenians triggered the migration of a significant portion of the entire province's population. Similarly, the first deportations of Armenians in the aftermath of the fall of Van sparked a wave of panic among Ottoman Armenians who fled into Russian territory by the tens of thousands.[37]

The worst, however, was yet to come. This stream of refugees, which never completely stopped after the beginning of the war, swelled to a flood all across the front in the early months of 1916, when the Russian army began its advance into Ottoman territory and captured all the cities and towns on its way, including Erzurum in February 1916, Bitlis and Rize in March 1916, Trabzon in April 1916, and Bayburt and Erzincan in July 1916. The Ottoman army's retreat turned hundreds of thousands of villagers and townspeople from all over the eastern front into refugees, who followed the retreating troops and headed south or west in search of safety. Many of them must have feared Russian cruelty and especially Armenian retribution. Muslims from eastern Anatolia, who had witnessed and occasionally taken part in the deportation of the Armenian population a year earlier, anticipated a "wave of revenge" by bands of Armenian irregulars. Rather than enduring the enemy occupation, *muhacir çıkmak* (becoming a refugee) seemed to be the only rational choice for many.

As the exodus of refugees slowed towards the end of the year, Ottoman senior officials were beginning to learn the dimensions of the unfolding human disaster. In October 1916, the total number of refugees had reached about 702,000, according to a report presented by the Ministry of the Interior to the Prime Ministry.[38] This number was appraised at 800,000 in a statement made by the head of the Directorate of Tribes and Refugees (Aşair ve Muhacirin Müdüriyet-i Umumiyesi), Şükrü Bey, in the senate in early 1917.[39] At the end of the year, the official records of the Directorate stated that refugee population amounted to more than a million people.[40] Together with the approximately 1.2 million Armenian and Greek deportees, the total number of displaced persons was roughly more than 10 percent of the total prewar population of the Ottoman Empire.[41] These statistics, however, likely underestimated the actual figures. The real number of those who were displaced from their homes for one reason or another must certainly have been higher.

In response to the rapidly growing number of refugees, the Ottoman government in March 1916 created the Directorate of Tribes and Refugees to deal with "the refugee problem."[42] Based on a critique of previous ineffective, inadequate refugee policies, the new agency aimed to regulate the refugee flow, organize the transport and resettlement of incoming refugees, and keep track of the refugee population. Although the immediate goal of the agency was to get the refugee problem under control, its mission also included the task of "civilizing the tribes" by facilitating their assimilation into the sedentary way of life.[43] The establishment of this new agency marked the increasing institutionalization and bureaucratization of governmental responses to the refugee problem, which had so far been handled by temporary commissions set up during the consecutive refugee crises of the previous decades.[44]

Not surprisingly, the mass movements of refugees imposed enormous financial and material burdens on the Ottoman state. In 1914, the government was still dealing with the consequences of the disastrous refugee crisis of the Balkan Wars. When World War I broke out, tens of thousands of refugees from former Ottoman provinces were still dependent on state assistance for their provisioning, accommodation, and employment. Furthermore, full-scale mobilization, two years of fighting, and the deportation of the Armenians had already drained the financial power of the government and exhausted the Ottoman people. By the time the Russian advance began in the winter of 1916, the Ottoman authorities were utterly unprepared to deal with refugees arriving from the occupied provinces by the thousands within a matter of weeks.

Nevertheless, the refugees immediately became the main concern not only of the central government and the Directorate of Tribes and Refugees but also of the governorships of the provinces in the region. The Directorate attempted to regulate the "flood" of eastern Anatolian refugees by dividing it into four "streams" and directing each of these streams to different parts of the empire to avoid overcrowding in provinces adjoining the war zone and prevent refugees from perishing en route, a noticeable difference from the handling of Armenian deportations. Two factors, the physical condition of the roads and the availability of provisions at the refugees' final destinations, were critical in determining these four routes.[45] The Directorate also prepared a detailed set of instructions for the local administrations to handle the transportation, settlement, provisioning, and support of refugees.[46]

These regulations designated the provinces bordering the theater of war as "temporary regions of settlement."[47] After being kept in these temporary regions of settlement, refugees were to be sent to their final destinations. All of the provinces designated as temporary regions for settlement were actually provinces to which the refugees had fled and been resettled before the Russian advance in the winter of 1916. As it became clear that the flood of hundreds of thousands of new refugees would further deepen the already acute provisioning crisis in these regions and jeopardize the war effort, the government decided to send new refugees into provinces not directly adjacent to the war zone.[48] These provinces, the government hoped, could sustain significant increases in their populations resulting from the arrival of new refugees.

A fundamental goal of the Ottoman policy of refugee settlement was to keep the refugees in the places where they were settled, at least for the duration of the war. They were allowed to change their settlement locations only if they could prove that they had relatives in other places who could help them, that they had found jobs, or that they could not adapt to the climate in their settlement location.[49] After being settled, however, refugees continued to change their locations despite strict orders from the local and imperial authorities. Migration by many refugees therefore continued unabated until the end of the war.

A variety of factors, ranging from high local bread prices to frequent conflicts with host communities, dissatisfaction, and hope of finding a better place to settle, often encouraged refugees to take to the road again.[50] Refugees in eastern Anatolia, if they were not very far from the war zone, sought to return to their villages after every advance of the Ottoman army, only, as often as not, to be displaced again by Russian counterattacks. Despite these many frustrations, refugees almost always retained the hope of returning to their homes soon. Thus, many of them did not want to travel far from their homes and attempted to find temporary refuge as close to them as possible. Repeated attacks by enemy forces, however, would dash refugees' hopes and push them out of their temporary retreats over and over again. Regardless of why they decided to change their locations, the continuous movement of refugees increased the burden on the wartime government.[51]

At specific locations along the migration routes, the Directorate, in cooperation with the army and local administrations, opened soup kitchens and provisioning stations to provide refugees with daily food. At these stations, refugees were also vaccinated against contagious diseases, which had begun to exact increasingly heavy tolls on the refugee population. This policy again constituted one of the many differences in how refugees and deportees were treated by the government. At their final destinations, local administrations, civil society organizations, philanthropists, and missionaries continued to distribute food to refugees and attended to their needs to the extent their resources allowed.[52] The Directorate also opened orphanages in some locations and employed a relatively small number of the refugees in workshops. This was especially done in the case of women to save them from falling into the trap of prostitution.

The Ottoman state also assigned refugees a daily stipend of two kuruş for adults and one kuruş for children, which was later increased to three kuruş for adults and sixty para (one and a half kuruş) for children.[53] According to its director's statement, however, the Directorate's resources allowed it to assign salaries to only half of the total number of refugees.[54] As with other state allowances, payments to refugees were usually in arrears, sometimes by months. Furthermore, as the war dragged on, the ninety-kuruş monthly payment to refugee families eroded in the face of widespread shortages and high inflation. Especially in the Third Army region in eastern Anatolia, the state decided to distribute flour or wheat to refugees to prevent starvation instead of raising their stipends.[55]

The sheer number of refugees and the already depleted resources of the Ottoman state, however, precluded the Directorate from being able to ameliorate the refugees' sufferings and improve their living standards. Despite all the measures taken, thousands of refugees fell into despair and destitution. The immediate impact of the refugee crisis was felt in the provinces bordering the theater of war, but, gradually, even provinces far from the war zone suffered from the problems of increased population coupled with declining agricultural production. Thanks to the relentless stream of refugees coming from the occupied regions, provinces like Sivas and Mosul, but especially cities with relatively smaller prewar populations such as Urfa, Samsun, and Çorum, saw their populations grow rapidly. Similarly, the Russian advance along the Black Sea coast pushed the local population westward, a mass migration that, according to a contemporary observer, nearly tripled the population of every town and village not yet occupied by the Russian army. This unprecedented accumulation of refugees led to a combined crisis of provisioning, housing, and public health, something hitherto unknown.[56]

Despite the diligent work of the Ottoman relief organization, especially in major population centers, the size of the problem soon exceeded its capacity. In early 1918, Hamdi Bey, who succeeded Şükrü Bey as the director of the agency, admitted to the Ottoman senate that the organization was struggling just to keep the refugees from dying: "What a great success [it would be]," he said, "if we manage to keep these refugees and immigrants alive."[57]

By the time the director made this statement, however, death had become a routine occurrence within the refugee communities scattered throughout the empire. Northern Anatolian towns, for instance, saw hundreds of "half-naked, skeleton-like" refugee children (*muhacir çocukları*) wandering city squares like "living mummies and shadows." Municipal garbage carts collected the bodies of dead people from the streets every morning. Muzaffer Lermioğlu, a refugee who had heard rumors of this while in Samsun, followed these carts one morning and saw with his own eyes workers placing twenty-three bodies, most of them children, in mass graves.[58] In his memoirs, the Swiss doctor Jakob Künzler describes "a long line of beggars, walk[ing] the streets of the city, knocking on all doors" in Urfa, in southeastern Anatolia, from early in the morning until late at night. They repeated the same words: "Have mercy, we are victims; for God's sake, give us a piece of bread!" (Heyran, kurban, Allahın hatırı için bir parça ekmek verin!). Künzler observed the terrible toll that hunger exacted on these miserable refugee children, up to seventy of whom died every day.[59]

Refugees who moved from occupied territories to southern Anatolia received even less assistance from the state and the army, and thus suffered more when compared with refugees who moved in other directions.[60] Refugees from Erzurum and Bitlis who were settled in Urfa, for instance, sent Rıza Paşa, a prominent member of the Ottoman senate, a telegram describing the wretched conditions in which they lived and the numerous deaths from hunger among refugees despite the availability of grain in the storehouses held by the state and the army. Sordid conditions forced many refugees to consume the discarded blood and inner organs of animals they collected from slaughterhouses.[61]

The Refugee Crisis and Demographic Engineering

Based on the official documents and correspondence between the central government and provincial administrators, it is clear that the Ottoman state perceived the war and subsequent refugee crisis as an opportunity to demographically redesign Ottoman society. The transportation and settlement of refugees were thereby turned into effective instruments of "population politics" in the hands of state authorities.[62] War and the consequent expansion of the state apparatus, as discussed in previous chapters, equipped the Ottoman government with the necessary infrastructural power and legal tools to transform prevailing social hierarchies and loyalties, deemed archaic but nonetheless powerful and persistent. Against this background, the Unionists eagerly sought to eliminate the challenges that threatened their authority, especially in the countryside, by regulating the movement of hundreds of thousands of people already displaced by the war.

Eastern Anatolia and upper Mesopotamia became the main theater of this process of demographic redesign. After uprooting hundreds of thousands of Armenians concentrated mostly in these regions, relocating and annihilating them constituted the major, most well-known aspect of this process. The Unionist government, however, also attempted to undermine the feudal social structure of the Kurds and integrate them into the predominantly Turkish regions of central Anatolia.[63] In his telegram to the province of Diyarbekir, Talat Pasha explicitly opposed the idea of transporting Kurdish refugees who had fled the war zone to Arab provinces of the empire. "They would remain a useless and harmful element," Talat Pasha declared, "as they would either be Arabized there or preserve their nationality [*milliyet*]."[64] To prevent this from happening, Turkish refugees were to be settled in localities such as Urfa, Maraş, and Ayntep, where the majority of the local population was composed of non-Turks. Kurdish refugees, on the other hand, were to be transported to predominantly Turkish provinces and settled in a scattered way. Settled Kurdish refugees were never to exceed 5 percent of the local population. In order to put an end to their tribal life and eliminate their previous affiliations, tribal and religious leaders were to be separated from the refugees and settled in different provinces, preferably in town and city centers.[65]

The correspondence between the Directorate and the provinces clearly indicates that the CUP leadership considered the settlement of Kurdish refugees in central Anatolia as a long-term demographic engineering project, not a temporary wartime measure. When some Kurdish refugees began to leave the Anatolian provinces in which they had been settled after receiving news of the recapture of Muş and Bitlis by the Ottoman Second Army in August 1916, the government fiercely resisted this development.[66] The Unionists strongly believed that the time had come to "make [the Kurds] abandon their tribal lives and turn them from an unreliable element into a useful one," and thus had no intention of allowing Kurdish refugees to return to their homelands after the war.[67] In their new homes, the Unionist leadership hoped, they would gradually be assimilated into the local population and develop new identities.

Despite the determination of the central government, however, the project of integrating Kurdish refugees into the central Anatolian population did not yield the desired results. Due mostly to the primitive state of the transportation network, many refugees simply could not be sent to their intended final destinations. On several occasions, attempts to transport them farther into Anatolia encountered resistance from the refugees themselves, who insisted on settling in areas more familiar to them.[68] On some other occasions, civilian and military officials opposed the directives of the government on the grounds that such movements would certainly lead to the deaths of many refugees en route.[69]

As part of its wartime population politics, the Ottoman government also directed the settlement of refugees from occupied provinces in the villages emptied by the deported Armenians.[70] Indeed, given its depleted financial resources, the Ottoman government saw financing the settlement of the refugees with the Armenian communities' seized assets as the most feasible policy option. The Ministry of the Interior ordered local administrations to satisfy the needs of the refugees for shelter, clothing, grain, and other goods by distributing property left behind by the Armenians when they were driven out (*emval-i metruke*).[71] When they arrived in towns and cities, refugees were given Armenian houses, where these existed, according to their social status and occupation. The wealthy and the governmental officials frequently abused their authority in this process of distribution. Upon moving to new towns, they immediately allocated for their personal use the most spacious and beautiful buildings, which could otherwise have easily sheltered multiple destitute refugee families.[72] Most of the time, however, refugees would be confronted with the harsh reality that the Armenian properties had already been occupied by the local people before their arrival. Despite numerous orders from the Ministry of the Interior, local people, sometimes in collaboration with local officials, actively refused to vacate these buildings for the use of the refugees.[73]

The government spent considerable time and effort trying to settle Muslim refugees in villages abandoned by the deported Armenians, and redistribute the lands and houses in these villages.[74] Even before the massive wave of migration began in the winter of 1916, the government had tried to ascertain the feasibility of resettling refugees in abandoned Armenian villages and continually demanded information from local authorities about these villages' locations, agricultural potential, and housing capacity.[75] Through this policy, the government sought to achieve two major objectives: offset the decline in agricultural production caused by the deportation of Armenians, troop movements, and mass mobilization, and bring the constant movement of refugees to an end. In these villages, the commissions sent by the central government dispensed arable land and seed grain to the refugees and also furnished them with farm animals and tools for agriculture. Rev. Henry H. Riggs of Harput, who provides an invaluable eyewitness account of this process of distribution, states that the government provided refugees with seed grain "very generously, as it was quite important that the land should be properly tilled and cared for that winter and spring."[76] Helping the refugees to establish themselves in the former Armenian villages and thus turning them from consumers into producers was critical for the Ottoman state, not only in terms of alleviating the government's burden of provisioning for them, but also in meeting the sustenance need of the armies in the region. In the absence of Armenian peasants, these refugees constituted the only available labor force that could bring the untilled land under cultivation again.

Although settling in villages vacated by Armenians provided refugees with shelter, they experienced enormous problems in adapting to their new lives, which would be fashioned under significantly different circumstances from the ones they had been used to. A variety of factors, ranging from climate to location, availability of natural resources, fear of imminent Russian attacks, tensions with the local population, and discontent with the new and different lifestyle, made their adaptation extremely difficult, if not impossible. Rev. Henry Riggs, for instance, reported that "far from being pleased with the action which the government had taken, they were without exception quite discontented, and said that it would be impossible for them to stay there." When the weather and road conditions allowed, refugees such as the ones observed by Rev. Riggs would take to the roads again and move to a different place. Before leaving, refugees either sold the farm equipment and animals given to them by the state in the market[77] or left the villages "absolutely empty, having slaughtered and eaten the cattle, eaten the seed grain which was left to them, and burned up the implements for firewood."[78]

Not surprisingly, the failure to get the refugees permanently settled in abandoned Armenian villages had disastrous consequences. It increased the number of people on the move, thus multiplying the burden on the central government and local administrations. The failure to bring stability to the lives of refugees or turn them into agricultural producers also led to a serious shortage of provisions and the neglect of thousands of acres of land on which the government had been counting to feed the military, town dwellers, and incoming refugees.

On the Road

Rev. Lyndon S. Crawford, an American missionary stationed in Trabzon, described the plight of refugees fleeing the Russian army thus:

> The road over the bluff and winding along the seashore for miles, as we see it from our home, was black with frightened people hurrying along, the women, old and young, with their kneading-troughs, beds, and babies bound to their backs; other little barefooted tots were running along beside them. Older boys and girls were driving sheep or pulling along the unwilling, weary cattle and horses. Some of those of the older ones died in our city; more of them and of the little ones must have died further on their way. So little proportion will ever reach the coveted lands vacated by Armenians to the west and southwest from here.[79]

Studies of mass migration tend to ignore the individual dimension of the refugee experience illustrated by Crawford's observations. Displacements and massive refugee movements often cause tremendous societal upheavals and they almost universally bring uncertainty, apprehension, and, usually, profound destitution and misery to the individuals who experience them. The Ottoman refugee experience was no exception.

Refugee convoys, as Crawford saw, consisted mostly of women, young children, and old men but, young and middle-aged men who had paid the military exemption tax, secured exemption from the military service in some other way, or received furloughs also sometimes led these migrating groups. The government's decision as the war dragged on to conscript refugee men, however, separated most of them from their families. Retreating soldiers occasionally deserted their ranks to help their families migrate, especially if their units were stationed close to their hometowns or villages.[80] Most of the time, however, women found themselves with little choice but to take matters into their own hands and negotiate the enormous difficulties of migration. It was not unusual that in the absence the household's male members, the oldest woman would first lead the family in their migration; then, after her death, younger women would take the lead.[81] Having spent most of their lives in their villages subject to patriarchal social structures, and knowing little of the world outside their immediate environments, these women found the refugee experience highly disorienting.

In addition to physical suffering, a deep sense of uncertainty about the future and the accompanying psychological strain also overwhelmed the refugees. The suffering of the previous mass migrations in eastern Anatolia, especially the one caused by the 1877–78 Russo-Ottoman War, were deeply ingrained in the collective memory, which also added to the refugees' distress. Especially during the early months of the war, refugees usually lacked any clear idea of where to go and where to obtain food and shelter. They sometimes did not even know which direction they should take. They often simply wanted to take refuge behind Ottoman lines as quickly as possible to avoid any potential harassment from the enemy. Aziz Samih, an Ottoman officer who served in eastern Anatolia during the war, described the movement of the refugees as being "towards an unknown horizon" (*meçhul bir ufka doğru*): "Every retreat of the army repeats these scenes of migration. . . . Men who shouldered their infirm, old mothers, women who wrapped their children with blankets, shouldered, and embraced them, children who strove to walk behind oxcarts. If you ask them where they are going, they don't know either." A year later, he observed a similar lack of guidance: "I asked them their destination. All of them, senseless and oblivious, [are] lost travelers in a scary nightmare. . . . What guides them is a natural drift [*sevk-i tabii*]."[82]

The underdeveloped and already overburdened transportation infrastructure of the empire added significantly to the misery of the refugees. As mentioned before, the railroad network did not extend into eastern Anatolia. Despite the intense activity of hundreds of labor battalions, overland routes were still torn up and in primitive condition. They could not handle hundreds of thousands of refugees and deportees without interrupting military transportation to and from the war zone. The turmoil on the roads and at meeting points astonished many contemporary observers. A young reserve officer, Şevket Süreyya (Aydemir), who was on his way to the eastern front, remembered that they found the small town of Suşehri in Sivas province in the "turmoil of doomsday" (*mahşer karışıklığı*) caused by the refugee flow and the personnel and equipment of the retreating army.[83] Ali Oğlu Reşid, a refugee who had left Van in the aftermath of the Russian occupation, described the situation in a different region with similar words: "People from towns and districts were swarming like ants as if doomsday or the Great Flood had come."[84] *Mahşer* or *mahşer günü* (doomsday or judgment day) became the most common metaphor through which the refugees articulated at least the initial parts of the migration experience.

Heavy military and civilian traffic accelerated the deterioration of roads, especially in the winter and the spring. Mud was, therefore, a recurrent theme in the refugees' narratives of migration. Muddy and snowy roads damaged dilapidated carts, injured undernourished animals, and exhausted people traveling by foot. The inadequacy of the supply stations on the roads, which were supposed to provide food, medical assistance, and shelter to refugees, made the journeys even more unbearable. According to German consular reports, even wealthy refugees froze to death on their migration routes from Erzurum to Erzincan.[85] Halil Ataman, a reserve officer in the retreating Ottoman army, recalls awful scenes of suffering refugees trying to march onward in extremely cold weather:

> At night, the temperature was forty degrees centigrade below zero; oxcarts, donkeys, women, men, the elderly, and children, everybody on the road was in a miserable state. I even saw a heart-wrenching mother [with two children]; one [was] bound on her back and the other walked. Grasping that child with one hand, her other hand was on the headgear of the oxen pulling the cart on which she had loaded all of her belongings. What suffering had this woman who guided the oxen endured. . . . We stopped again. A call, "The road is closed," was heard. Another oxcart broke down, its oxen frozen. Wrapped in quilts, the woman who owned the cart and her children just stood there.[86]

In order to avoid congestion on the roads and prevent the refugees from perishing, the civilian authorities in some cases tried to persuade people not to leave their localities. In Erzurum, for instance, the governor, Tahsin (Uzer) Bey, spent considerable energy trying on orders from the army to stop the residents from evacuating the city. Third Army headquarters was clearly convinced that people would not suffer more under Russian occupation than they would as refugees: "If the poor, the infirm, and children do not migrate and instead remain where they are, their attrition rate would by no means exceed the losses that migration would cause. This is the reason we write to the governorship, to prevent migration."[87] Despite these measures, preventing the majority of people from leaving their hometowns proved to be impossible. In his letter to the Minister of the Interior, the governor expressed his deep regret that, although he had done everything to prevent migration, those fearful of Armenian retribution could not be stopped.[88] The huge number of refugees as a result clogged the roads, making it nearly impossible for troops to move to and from the battle zones.

The transportation network was in no better shape in northern Anatolia along the Black Sea coast, where only small causeways linked towns to one another. Although some refugees, especially the wealthy and the influential, preferred to travel by sea, taking to the roads seemed to be the only viable alternative for many others who could not afford to purchase or rent any means of transportation.[89] Upon receiving news of the Russian advance and the Ottoman retreat, families of government officials and people with financial resources hastily sought to escape on small sailboats. Given the anxiety generated by the rumors of the advancing enemy, the scarcity of sailboats and the local government's requisitioning of boats for the transportation of official records, as well as officers' and officials' families, caused their prices to skyrocket.[90] Contemporary observers recalled astounding injustices and inequalities surrounding this process. Senior governmental officials' personal belongings, furniture, even their flowerpots took precedence over poor refugees with small children who desperately waited on the docks for a seat on one of these sailboats. One contemporary observer recounts the cry of poor soldiers' families, which fell on deaf ears: "Our men are in the army. We have neither money nor men to guide us; do not let the enemy trample us and our children; please save us by taking us into your sailboats; our honor and chastity are entrusted to the state; you know that, please take us along."[91]

In addition to the poor quality of the roads, the lack of bridges over overflowing rivers and streams, characteristic of the Black Sea coast, rendered the migration of thousands of refugees unendurable. Especially in the early days of the migration, thousands of people massed on the banks of these streams awaiting help from the state and the army. The Harşit River near Tirebolu proved to be particularly impassable. The huge crowd assembled on the eastern bank of Harşit, Muzaffer Lermioğlu notes in his memoirs, did not leave "any grass to eat nor any leaf to chew."[92] Some did not hesitate to turn the misery and desperation of these people into lucrative business opportunities. One local boatman, for instance, would ferry people across the Harşit in exchange for an Ottoman gold lira, a very significant amount of money at the time.[93]

Refugees usually left their villages in a group and made every effort to stick together wherever the current took them. Şevket Süreyya, a young reserve officer who had listened to his family's dramatic tales of migration during his childhood, during the Balkan Wars, had seen refugees from the Balkan provinces in his hometown, Edirne (Adrianople). Once again witnessing the behavior of displaced groups of people during World War I, he accurately observed that "the refugees strove to continue the life to which they were accustomed on the roads, with the same people, the same connections, the same hierarchy."[94] Due to losses and illnesses, however, refugee convoys would often have to leave some of their members behind, and would eventually fragment.[95] Once refugees lost contact with their relatives and fellow townspeople, life became much more miserable for them, both physically and emotionally.

The deaths of family members, relatives, and friends during the migration was a common experience for refugees. Harsh weather conditions, improper clothing, and inadequate nourishment made the journey extremely exhausting for everyone. The death toll on the road was exceedingly high, especially among the elderly, children, and the infirm. "A dead person under every bush," as a refugee remembered years later.[96] For want of implements, refugees usually could not bury their dead properly. The panic and anxiety caused by the advancing enemy, the sense of urgency to find a safe haven, and the group pressure from other refugees usually obliged them to leave bodies unburied, which would quickly decompose, creating unbearable scenes that were embedded in the refugees' memories.

One of the principles of the Directorate in handling the refugee problem was to keep refugees together as a group and prevent them from dispersing to places other than those determined by the state. Traveling together in unsanitary conditions, however, led to the outbreak of infectious diseases among the refugees, especially when the local governments and the army could not keep them properly vaccinated. Weakened by malnutrition and overall exhaustion, they were particularly vulnerable to the ravages of epidemic disease. Consequently, the mortality rate among them was very high. According to the Directorate records, at least 20 percent of the refugees who traveled towards Diyarbekir died en route.[97] With every move of these refugee groups, cholera, typhus, typhoid fever, dysentery, and other diseases spread to uninfected sections of the empire.

Migrations and deportations proved particularly traumatic for families with small children. Especially during the winter months, children who were improperly clothed and insufficiently fed suffered greatly, and their parents could do little to protect them from the deplorable conditions. Out of desperation, many handed over their little children to officers who they thought could provide a safer future for them. One officer who witnessed such a sorrowful scene on the eastern front recalls, "Those who had lost hope for themselves or were too weak to carry themselves, tried to hand their children off to the passers-by. 'Take them and save . . .' they say, but nobody stops to listen and [everyone] goes on."[98]

Some children got lost in the confusion of migration and were never found.[99] On more desperate occasions, families were forced by the dreadful conditions on the road to abandon their children when they were no longer able to provide for them.[100] Other refugees, suffering the same hardships, could not take these abandoned children into their own families, as having to clothe and feed an additional child would mean having one less piece of bread and scrap of cloth for their own children. Orphan refugee children were thus some of the most heart-rending figures to emerge out of the Ottoman refugee experience during World War I. Equipped with only their natural instincts for survival, these abandoned refugee children formed "gangs," the size of which could reach up to three to four hundred children. These starving child gangs launched "attacks" on villages, stripping them of everything edible they could find. Yaşar Kemal, who heard stories of these children from his own relatives and a beggar who actually had been a member of one of these gangs, likened them to "swarms of locusts": "The children had become herds, hungry, impoverished, stark naked. . . . They meandered as herds, attacking villages and towns. Hundreds of children would attack a village they had spotted, entering from one end and exiting from the other. No edibles would remain in the village. They were like a swarm of locusts."[101]

Just like the Armenian deportees a year earlier, refugees usually had little time to settle their affairs and pack up their belongings before they left. In towns and cities, fear of the approaching enemy led them to sell whatever they could at well below market prices and look for means of transportation, which had become extremely expensive and difficult to find.[102] The army's requisitioning policies had created a shortage of healthy, strong draft animals and sound carts. The mass retreat of Ottoman troops generated a sense of urgency and magnified the already pressing need for more animals and vehicles. Given the weaknesses of pack animals and the scarcity of transport, refugees usually could not take much with them and were forced to leave many of their belongings behind. Along the road, they would often have to abandon their last remaining possessions.

Refugees from the villages were often more fortunate in being able to find working carts. If they were lucky enough, they would also have managed to take a couple of cattle with them. Sooner or later, however, their cattle starved en route, since the refugees could not carry enough fodder, or they were stolen or slaughtered by other refugees, deserters, and brigands.[103] Before leaving their homes, women usually baked bread and prepared other foodstuffs. Refugees often had to spend their nights under trees, since the few available inns and other buildings on the road were already overcrowded by either retreating soldiers or refugee groups ahead of them. In towns and cities, they slept in mosque yards, school gardens, *medreses*, stables, haystacks, and graveyards. If they were lucky enough or had maintained good relations with governmental officials, they might be allowed to stay in properties abandoned by Armenian deportees.

In towns and villages where they took temporary refuge during their migration or were settled by the state authorities, refugees were met with a spectrum of reactions from the local population. Depending on a number of factors, people provided assistance to refugees, remained indifferent to their sufferings, or, in several cases, were openly hostile. In some Black Sea towns, refugees were looked down upon and called *kirli muhacir* (dirty refugee).[104] Some eastern Anatolian villagers did not let refugees stay in their villages. The Swiss missionary doctor Jakob Künzler, based in Urfa, reports that the inhabitants of a nearby Turkish village quickly shut their doors to Kurdish refugees out of fear. From the second half of 1916 on, when the Ottoman state's provisioning policies were exceptionally severe, the local populations in these villages "jealously guarded their dwindling supplies" from these refugees.[105] Another refugee who migrated from Kelkit (Gümüşhane) to the village of Alaca close to Çorum, where he stayed for a year, remembered the huge fight between refugees and the local people that was sparked by a rumor that the locals had stolen the refugees' money.[106] On the other hand, some women and men from Harput banded together to help refugees who had fled from the Russian advance. This effort was described by a contemporary observer as "remarkable" because it was "so unusual for a Moslem city."[107]

Refugees came from all ethno-religious groups and all socioeconomic classes. Refugee convoys even included a significant number of wealthy and once-influential individuals and families, but the trying experience of migration gradually leveled the social and economic distinctions between them and the refugees from poorer sections of Ottoman society. This dramatic upheaval in their lives and drastic change in their living standards, of which the wealthy refugees had perhaps never conceived the possibility, brought about both severe physical and emotional strains. Once-influential notables now had to seek refuge in villages near Erzurum and till the soil in the fields abandoned by Armenians.[108] Fevzi Güvemli, then an eleven-year-old boy from Trabzon who had migrated to Samsun with his family, remembered people from upper-class families queuing up in front of bakeries to get the daily bread ration, *vesika ekmeği*, distributed by the state to refugees: "Every day we gathered in front of the bakery where the bread was dispensed and waited for the opening of the shutters. The baker read our names one by one: Cennetkuşuzade Melek Hanım . . . Osmanefendizade Fevzi Efendi . . . Zade . . . Zade. . . . We were a group of refugees composed of elites [*zadegan*]."[109]

The lives of poorer refugees were nonetheless much more miserable than those of their relatively affluent counterparts. Many of them had no choice but to rely upon the inadequate assistance provided by the government and municipalities, as well as by charity organizations. Begging for food and money became common practice for these hard-pressed families in the towns where they were settled. The desolate conditions forced many refugee women to resort to prostitution as the only way to obtain a livelihood. Destitution rendered them especially vulnerable to officials and war profiteers.[110]

The entire process of migration, with all its miseries, was engraved in the collective memory of people as *muhacir çıkmak* (becoming a refugee). Women, once again, expressed the pain of leaving their homes and villages through laments:

Çocuklar dizi dizi,	Children all lined up,
Terk ettik köyümüzü.	We left our village.
Urus gözün körolsun,	Damn you, Russians!
Muhacir ettin bizi.[111]	You made us refugees.

Another song narrates how people perceived the entire experience of being a refugee:

Ah bu muhacirlik şimdi büktü belimi.	Oh, this refugee life has worn me down.
Zalim Urus yaktı, yıktı evimi.[112]	The cruel Russian burnt my home and destroyed it.

Indeed, the refugee experience devastated the lives of hundreds of thousands of people; it "wore them down." Even if they managed to return to their villages (many of them could not), however, they seldom found peace and tranquility. Many refugees who returned to their homes after the conflict had ended found their properties partially or completely destroyed, or occupied by other people who had also been displaced during the war. Having rushed back to their towns and villages in the hope of resuming their prewar lives, tens of thousands of people thus remained without shelter, food, fodder, draft animals, or any means of production.[113] Recognizing this as a socioeconomic crisis that now plagued eastern and northern Anatolia, the government prohibited refugees from returning to their homes. Only those who could afford their own seed and provisions were allowed to return.[114]

Many others who had been relocated to houses abandoned by deported Armenians and, to a smaller extent, Greeks were pushed out of these dwellings upon the return of the surviving deportees. The Directorate, which, during the war, had organized the settling of Muslim refugees in buildings and villages abandoned by non-Muslim Ottomans, was charged with resettling Armenians and Greeks in their homelands.[115] For thousands of refugees, returning their temporary dwellings to their original owners came to mean another dramatic upheaval in their lives. If they were fortunate enough, the Directorate and local governments would allow them to move in to other properties that had not yet been reclaimed by their previous owners.[116] Many, however, perceived the return of the deported Armenians and Greeks as bringing with it the same sufferings they had experienced in the migration only a couple of years previously. For this reason, in some provinces, Muslim refugees resisted the return of the Greeks and Armenians to their own villages.[117] These dramatic events, so ubiquitous in postwar Anatolia, must have significantly deepened the already existing interethnic tensions among different ethno-religious communities.

Conclusions

Millions of people throughout the world were displaced by the war between 1914 and 1918. Everywhere the movement of armies produced massive waves of refugees. The German occupation forced Belgian and French civilians to flee their homes and move to safer regions. Hundreds of thousands of civilians in Galicia in eastern Europe sought refuge in Austro-Hungarian cities before the advancing Russian army. The Italian army's disastrous defeat at Caporetto led to the displacement of one and a half million ethnic Italians. The joint campaign orchestrated by the Austro-Hungarian and Bulgarian armies turned most of the Serbian population into refugees.[118] None of the belligerents, except the United States and Great Britain, could escape the destabilizing impacts of these voluntary and forced displacements of people during the war.

A sustained comparison would reveal that the Ottoman experience of displacement during the war was among the most disruptive of all. The sheer size of the Ottoman refugee and deportee population, the underdeveloped transportation infrastructure, and the state's inadequate and ineffective measures to deal with this gigantic problem turned mass migration into a disaster for millions of families throughout the empire. Despite this unfolding human tragedy, the CUP government sought to make use of the crisis for its demographic engineering projects. Worse, unlike any other belligerent of the Great War, the Unionists engaged in a destructive policy towards one of the main ethno-religious communities of the empire. By the end of the war, this policy had uprooted Ottoman Armenians from their ancient homelands and led to their destruction.

The misery of the Ottoman population did not come to an end with the armistice in October 1918 and the collapse of Unionist single party rule. With the start of another war between the invading Greek army and the nationalist forces, hundreds of thousands of people again found themselves facing inter-ethnic violence and forced or voluntary dislocation. Their migration or dis-placement once again generated heart-wrenching scenes similar to the ones discussed above. The compulsory population exchange between Anatolian Greeks and Greek Muslims stipulated by the Treaty of Lausanne signed in 1923 closed this tragic chapter of Ottoman history, after which Anatolia acquired a religiously homogeneous demographic structure.

CONCLUSION

"Wars do not consist of a clash between two armies any more. Two countries, like two whole worlds, walk onto each other. . . . During the recent war, we learned these two terms: 'battlefront' and 'home front.' Armies did the fighting together with the people. Those who want to tell us about a battlefront, should first tell us about its home front," Falih Rıfkı (Atay) wrote in his first book, *Ateş ve Güneş* (Fire and the Sun), published only a few weeks after the armistice of October 1918.[1] Then a young officer who had served at the Ottoman Fourth Army headquarters in Damascus, Falih Rıfkı keenly observed the changing nature of warfare and its dramatic impact on noncombatants. I hope the present book serves to shed light on Ottoman civilians' wartime experiences and incorporate the Ottoman home front into the broader narrative of World War I.

The Ottoman people lived the ten long years between 1912 and 1922 in a "continuum of crisis" shaped by successive conflicts.[2] The Balkan Wars (1912–13), World War I (1914–18), and the War of Independence (1919–22) literally exhausted the human capital of the empire, leaving millions of people dead, wounded, and captive, and millions of others widowed, orphaned, and bereaved. World War I was fought on a much larger scale than the conflicts preceding and following it, however. By the time the guns fell silent in October 1918, Ottoman society had been deeply traumatized due to the high number of casualties, a devastated economic infrastructure, voluntary and involuntary displacement, ethnic cleansing, political instability, and cultural anxiety.

World War I was a watershed for all the belligerents; it was a significantly different experience from earlier conflicts. For almost four and a half years, the fighting nations mobilized their societies and subordinated their economies to the war effort in unprecedented ways. As this book has argued, what distinguished the Ottoman experience of World War I from those of other major combatants, and what makes its case truly unique, was its lack of the means necessary to fight a war on such a grand scale. Above all, the Unionists wrestled with enormous challenges posed by the empire's weak industrial base, low agricultural productivity, and underdeveloped transportation infrastructure. The Entente navies' blockade of the empire's coasts, frequent natural disasters, and the significant loss of manpower to conscription and ethnic cleansing, in particular, further increased the challenges that the empire confronted during the war. Against this backdrop, Ottoman civilian and military authorities constantly experimented with new policies to meet the endless needs of the war.

Each policy devised for this purpose brought about further intervention by the state in the daily lives of ordinary citizens. While earlier conflicts had similarly required the extraction of men and resources from across society, the degree of state intervention in World War I far surpassed anything that had occurred before. The magnitude and duration of the conflict, the sheer size of the army, the multitude of battlefronts, the unrealistic war aims, and the large-scale destruction inflicted by modern warfare necessitated extensive mobilization and the continuous allocation of vast resources for military purposes. As Falih Rıfkı observed, victory in the war became increasingly dependent on the successful integration of the military with the civilian population, a process that inescapably led to the erosion of the distinctions between them. Without access to external sources, the intensified exploitation of material and human resources of the empire appeared to the Ottoman authorities to be their only effective policy.

This process had profound implications for Ottoman society. Virtually every Ottoman citizen, regardless of age, gender, or ethno-religious affiliation, had to cope with deprivation, bereavement, and hardships of all kinds. Except for a small, fortunate segment of society, the Ottoman people had to shoulder the enormous physical and emotional burdens created by the war. The unprecedented expansion of the state apparatus, however, inevitably created new sites of interaction between the state and society, transforming existing modes of interaction. Conscription, requisitioning, provisioning, forced employment in agriculture and transportation, deportation, resettlement, and other wartime policies of the CUP government gave rise to new fields of contestation.

Women emerged as important actors in this period. Throughout the empire, women bore the brunt of the war on the home front and the wartime domestic policies of the Ottoman state. In the absence of men, they tilled the soil, tended the animals, brought products to market, and took care of their families. At the same time, they were employed in military transportation, obligated to work in agriculture, subjected to a variety of state policies and regulations, and mistreated and abused by state officials and other men on the home front. During the war, women came into direct contact with the Ottoman state more frequently than ever before. For most Ottoman women, the war did not bring about economic empowerment and social liberation. Yet they developed a powerful collective identity as "soldiers' wives and mothers," through which they negotiated with local and imperial officials, often demanding that the latter extend welfare and protection to soldiers' families.

The enormity of the problems that plagued the Ottoman war effort did not stop the Unionist leadership from engaging in ambitious demographic engineering projects. On the contrary, the Unionists gradually realized that the war offered a convenient opportunity to eliminate certain ethno-religious communities, whether by assimilation or annihilation. The war enabled the regime to act freely without foreign interference, giving it total control over policy-making, jurisdiction, and law enforcement, and an almost absolute monopoly on the use of violence. While all the belligerents of World War I practiced "population politics" through internment, deportation, and resettlement, none of these reached the degree of destructiveness the Unionist policies had on the Ottoman Empire's long-established Armenian community. These policies reflected the same aggressiveness, shortsightedness, and disproportionality that characterized the Unionists' other wartime policies, but had much more destructive consequences. While the CUP government and the army strove to maximize the human and material resources that would be allocated for the war effort, they did not hesitate to uproot more than a million people and exterminate a significant portion of them.

Developments on the Ottoman home front during World War I also had far-reaching consequences for the future of the empire. By the end of the war, the legitimacy of the Ottoman state, the Ottoman army, the Committee of Union and Progress, and, above all, the idea of the empire had significantly diminished in the eyes of the majority. Many rightfully saw the state as nothing but an oppressive force that constantly demanded that their sons, fathers, and husbands enlist in the army, ruthlessly impressed their properties and products, compelled them to work in military transportation and agriculture, and forcibly settled them in far-off, unfamiliar provinces. Meanwhile, this same force could not protect them from marauders and assailants, greedy war profiteers, or advancing enemy forces. Nor could it maintain the welfare of the destitute and the needy, many of whom were victims of the war, or help them to piece their lives back together. Innumerable deaths, mounting social problems, and economic hardships, all combined with the conviction that government officials were involved in widespread injustices, turned many citizens away from the war effort and the Unionist regime, which had been its champion. The depth of this resentment is perhaps best illustrated by a conversation that an officer had with angry peasants in a small village near Konya during the process of demobilization. When his company demanded to be quartered and fed, the villagers told him angrily:

> All the healthy men were taken by the army. We've been told that 80 percent of them were martyred. No news about the rest. We've given up hope about their fate. We, the elderly, widows, and orphans, are devastated, and we are spending our days in destitution. The government did not do anything but exploit, suppress, and torment us. Now, when you are leaving us to the enemy, you still want to be quartered and fed. We have no place for you. The enemy would do us no greater harm.[3]

The Great War's destruction and the widespread resentment it created on the ground was also observable during the nationalist remobilization following the Greek army's occupation of western Anatolia in 1919. Although official Turkish historiography attempts to lump together all local revolts that broke out in Anatolia in the post–World War I period as reactionary movements organized by fanatics, foreign intelligence agencies, and ethnic separatist organizations, hatred of the Ottoman state's previous wartime policies contributed to all of them. Highlighting the enormous difficulties that they faced in the process of remobilization, Rahmi Apak, a senior officer who participated in both World War I and the Turkish War of Independence, noted that peasants did not want to embark on another adventure that would jeopardize their existence. They would have rather acquiesced to the foreign invasion: "Peasants who constituted 80 percent of the population bore the brunt of the war. Each household lost several youths. People suffered not only from the enemy's bullets but also from a series of diseases caused by misadministration. This situation provoked the hostility of everyone, especially that of the peasants."[4] Hüsrev Bey (Gerede), who was sent by the Grand National Assembly to the Bolu-Düzce region in April 1920 as the head of the "counseling committee" (*heyet-i nasiha*), similarly recalled that rebellious peasants shouted at them "no more mobilization, no more war."[5] It is thus not an exaggeration to argue that the possibility of renewed mobilization and war was one of the major reasons that local revolts plagued post–World War I Anatolia.

Under these conditions of intense hostility to everything associated with war, the remobilization for the nationalist struggle could only be made possible through extensive use of coercion imposed by the Independence Courts (*İstiklal Mahkemeleri*) and an intensive propaganda effort based on familiar themes of Islamic-oriented patriotism. At the same time, the leaders of the nationalist movement spent considerable energy distancing themselves from the Unionist regime, despite the movement drawing much of its strength from the Unionist organization in Anatolia and its inclusion of numerous former Unionists.[6] During the War of Independence, nationalists reimplemented many of the wartime policies that had been experimented with during World War I, some to an even more destructive degree. Unlike in the previous conflict, however, this time the policies significantly contributed to the defeat of the enemy.

People living in provinces far from the imperial center were similarly, if not more, disenchanted with the war, as well as with the Ottoman administration. The tyrannical rule of Cemal Pasha in Syria and his merciless treatment of Arab notables and intellectuals, as well as the Ottoman wartime policies of conscription and confiscation and widespread shortages and famine, alienated Arabs from the Ottoman state. The utterly devastating wartime experiences of the Arab subjects of the empire, both on the battlefront and on the home front, played a considerable role in the upsurge of antagonistic feelings towards Ottoman rule in the Arab provinces of the empire. "Four miserable years of tyranny," as the historian Salim Tamari has observed, erased "four centuries of a rich and complex Ottoman patrimony."[7] Ottoman Greeks, Kurds, and others, who had been subjected to intrusive measures by the government and forcibly resettled in distant provinces were similarly alienated from the state. Even before the empire officially ceased to be the unifying political framework for all Ottoman citizens, the cataclysm of the war and the destructiveness of wartime policies had eroded its legitimacy. For Ottoman Armenians, however, that cataclysm had a much different meaning: it marked the irrevocable devastation of a people.

Falih Rıfkı was well aware of how deeply this long war scarred the empire and its people. "I have traveled across a huge country," he noted in his book, "but nowhere have I heard a cheerful word, nowhere have I seen a happy face."[8] Until recently, historians have rarely discussed the Great War's impact on Ottoman people. In this book, I offer an alternative glimpse into the war by focusing on what it meant for the Ottoman people on the home front. War, in this study, is approached, not as the domain of politicians and military men, but as an experience shared by all members of society. It is my hope that this examination of the Ottoman people's interaction with the state's ruinous wartime policies will enhance our understanding of the late Ottoman period, provide a new perspective on the disintegration of the empire, and contribute to the growing body of comparative analyses of the belligerents in World War I.

NOTES

Introduction

1. Yaşar Kemal, *Ağıtlar*, 26, 153.

2. For early examples of Turkish songs and laments, see Yalgın, "Cihan Harbi ve Halk Türküleri"; Akça, "Seferberlik Destanı." Zürcher, "Between Death and Desertion," 254–56, calls attention to soldiers' songs.

3. Aslanoğlu, "Seferberlik Destanları," 5.

4. Kabacalı, *Gül Yaprağın' Döktü Bugün*, 303.

5. Kennan, *Decline of Bismarck's European Order*, 3.

6. For the Ottoman Empire's search for an alliance, see Aksakal, *Ottoman Road to War*.

7. For recent surveys of the Great War in the Middle East, see Rogan, *Fall of the Ottomans*; McMeekin, *Ottoman Endgame*; Gingeras, *Fall of the Sultanate*; and Ulrichsen, *First World War*. For a detailed history of the Ottoman army in the war, see Erickson, *Ordered to Die*.

8. Beşikçi, *Ottoman Mobilization*, 112–15; Erickson, *Ordered to Die*, 207–211; Özdemir, *Ottoman Army*, 52, 121, 124; Larcher, *Guerre turque*, 86–87. For the estimate of the number of the prisoners of war, see Yanıkdağ, *Healing the Nation*, 20.

9. McCarthy, *Muslims and Minorities*, 120. Webster, *Turkey of Atatürk*, 59, cites an even higher percentage of widows. For Greater Syria, see Thompson, *Colonial Citizens*.

10. Imlay, "Total War," 553; Purseigle, "Home Fronts," 257–84.

11. The literature on "total war" is voluminous. For some major reflections, see Horne, "War and Conflict"; Chickering, "Total War"; Geyer, "Militarization of Europe."

12. Beckett, *Great War, 1914–1918*; Chickering and Förster, eds., *Great War, Total War*; Sondhaus, *World War One*.

13. Schilcher, "Famine of 1915–1918"; Tanielian, "War of Famine," 19–48; Fawaz, *Land of Aching Hearts*, 88–110.

14. For a general discussion, see Purseigle, "Transformations of the State." Ulrichsen observes the same phenomenon for the British campaigns in the Middle East in his *Logistics and Politics*.

15. Here I use the term "infrastructure" in the sense that has been developed by Michael Mann in his "Autonomous Power of the State."

16. Strachan, "Total War and Modern War," 351, observes that "[a] total war need not be modern: a modern war need not be total."

17. Strachan, "First World War as a Global War"; Miller, *Europe and the Maritime World*, 213–44.

18. Das, ed., *Race, Empire*, 1–32; Rogan, *Fall of the Ottomans*, 60–67, 71; Fawaz, *Land of Aching Hearts*, 205–32.

19. Trumpener, *Germany and the Ottoman Empire*; Mühlmann, *Deutsch-türkische Waffenbündnis*.

20. For a detailed account of this last phase of the Ottoman Empire's war, see Reynolds, *Shattering Empires*, 219–51; Arslan, *1918 Kafkas Harekâtı*.

21. On Germany's extraction of food and other resources from occupied Poland, in comparison, see Kauffman, *Elusive Alliance*.

22. For a recent work on the impact of the Balkan wars, see Ginio, *Ottoman Culture of Defeat*.

23. Hall, *Balkan Wars*, 130.

24. There is an extensive literature on the Armenian Genocide. For representative works, see Kevorkian, *Armenian Genocide*; Suny, *They Can Live*; Akçam, *Young Turks' Crime*; Üngör, *Making of Modern Turkey*.

25. Kramer, "Combatants and Noncombatants," 193. For a similar discussion, see Von Hagen, "Mobilization of Ethnicity."

26. Zürcher, "What Was Different," 9–11.

27. For the most detailed treatment of desertion during the war, see Beşikçi, *Ottoman Mobilization*, 247–309. See also Zürcher, "Between Death and Desertion."

28. Der Matossian, *Shattered Dreams*; Campos, *Ottoman Brothers*.

29. Khalidi, "Arab Experience," 643; Aksakal, "Ottoman Empire," 462; Fawaz, *Land of Aching Hearts*, 238–39.

30. On the postwar international order, see Manela, *Wilsonian Moment*; Patrick, *King-Crane Commission*.

31. Kazmaz, *Sarıkamış'ta Köy Gezileri*, 26.

Chapter 1

1. Cavid Bey, *Meşrutiyet Ruznamesi*, 1: 521.

2. See, e.g., Clark, *Sleepwalkers*; Kramer, *Dynamic of Destruction*; Mulligan, *Great War for Peace*, 11–47.

3. For an extensive discussion of this process of soul-searching, see Ginio, *Ottoman Culture of Defeat*; Kerimoğlu, *Osmanlı Kamuoyunda*; Aksakal, *Ottoman Road to War*, 19–41; Akyaz, "Legacy and Impacts." The fact that many Unionists hailed from the empire's Balkan provinces deepened their trauma. Zürcher, "Children of the Borderlands?"

4. Erickson, *Defeat in Detail*; Hall, *Balkan Wars*, 22–68; Uyar and Erickson, *Military History of the Ottomans*, 225–35.

5. Facey and Safwat, eds., *Soldier's Story*, 40.

6. Mahmud Muhtar Paşa, *Üçüncü Kolordu'nun*, 45–46.

7. Babanzade İsmail Hakkı, "İnikad-ı Sulh," *Tanin* 1617 (31 May 1913): 1.

8. Erickson, *Defeat in Detail*, 329.

9. Bardakçı, ed., *İttihadçı'nın Sandığı*, 61.

10. "Niçin Uzuyor," *Tanin* 1460 (4 October 1912): 1.

11. See, e.g., D[iran] K[elekyan], "Artık Yeter," *Sabah* 8287 (15 October 1912): 1; Türk Cebe, "Artık Yeter: Ya Namus ve İstiklal Ya Ölüm!," *Tercüman-ı Hakikat* 11311 (3 October 1912): 1–2.

12. "Dünkü Büyük Nümayişler: Harp! Harp!" *Tanin* 1461 (5 October 1912): 3; Aktar, "Harp Mitingleri," 114–39.

13. Peker, *Tüfek Omza*, 58.

14. *Cem* 41 (5 October 1912): 8 reproduced in Heinzelmann, *Die Balkankrise*, 221.

15. Hüseyin Cahid, "Muharebe," *Cenin* [Tanin] 1474 (18 October 1912): 1. *Cenin* was the replacement of *Tanin*, which was shut down by the government in the first days of the war.

16. Feldmann, *İstanbul'da Savaş Günleri*, 38. See also Pırnar and Pırnar, *Baba Oğul Anıları*, 1: 22.

17. Abdullah Paşa, *1328 Balkan Harbi'nde*, 86–92; Hallı, *Balkan Harbi*, 1: 280.

18. Feldmann, *İstanbul'da Savaş Günleri*, 52; Ağanoğlu, *Balkanlar'ın Makus Talihi*, 60.

19. Kerimi, *İstanbul Mektupları*, 210–11; Andonyan, *Balkan Savaşı*, 263.

20. For the observations of a journalist who traveled through Istanbul's hinterland during the war's aftermath, see Ahmet Şerif, *Anadolu'da Tanin*, 1: 352. On the war's empirewide impact, see also Swanson, "Note."

21. Kayalı, *Arabs and Young Turks*, 131.

22. Kerimi, *İstanbul Mektupları*, 210–11.

23. NARA, RG 59, 867.142/29, 31 January 1913.

24. Ibid.

25. İpek, "Balkans, War, Migration," 649–52.

26. "Refugees in Syria," *The Near East* 162 (12 June 1914): 177. See also Gingeras, *Fall of the Sultanate*, 95–96.

27. See, e.g., Hanioğlu, ed., *Kendi Mektuplarında*, 216–17, 224; "Hakk-ı İhtilal," *Tercüman-ı Hakikat* 11421 (24 January 1913): 1.

28. "11 Receb 1327 Tarihli Matbuat Kanunu'nun 23. Maddesini Muaddel Kanun-ı Muvakkat," *Düstur*, İkinci Tertip, vol. 6, 22 Zilhicce 1331 (22 November 1913): 49. See also earlier measures along the same lines "Matbuat Kanunu'nun Bazı Maddelerini Muaddel Kanun-ı Muvakkat," *Düstur*, İkinci Tertip, vol. 5, 13 Rebiülahir 1331 (22 March 1913): 181–85.

29. *British Documents on Foreign Affairs*, 20: 420.

30. Karay, *Minelbab İlelmihrab*, 51.

31. TNA, FO 195/2459/1465, Fontana to Mallet, 3 April 1914. For more details on the 1914 elections, see Demir, *Meclis-i Mebusan Seçimleri*, 300–329.

32. For more on these changes, see "İttihat ve Terakki'nin Teşkilat-ı Cedidesi," *Tanin* 1729 (15 October 1913): 2; Emmanuilidis, *Osmanlı İmparatorluğu'nun Son Yılları*, 32–34.

33. For Talat Bey's remarks on the need of raising a minister of war "of their own," see Cavid Bey, *Meşrutiyet Ruznamesi*, 1: 770.

34. See, e.g., "Ordu ve Gençlik-I," *Tanin* 1720 (14 September 1913): 1. This anonymous article attracted the ire of Ahmet İzzet Pasha, then minister of war, and *Tanin* was forced to suspend its publication for about two weeks. Cavid Bey, *Meşrutiyet Ruznamesi*, 2: 94.

35. For more on the purge, see Turfan, *Rise of the Young Turks*, 355–60; Akmeşe, *Birth of Modern Turkey*, 155–63.

36. "Harbiye Nazırı Enver Paşa ile Mülakat," *Tanin* 1812 (10 January 1914): 1; Hüseyin Cahid, "Genç Ordu," *Tanin* 1812 (10 January 1914): 1.

37. Schreiner, *From Berlin to Bagdad*, 331.

38. Polat, *Müdafaa-i Milliye Cemiyeti*, 23–24. Ahmad, "War and Society," 270, notes the similar ways in which the Ottoman Unionists and the French revolutionary Jacobins mobilized their societies for war. See also Özbek, "Defining the Public Sphere."

39. "Osmanlılara Hitap," *Tanin* 1666 (18 July 1913): 2.

40. Trabzon Müftüsü Mahir, "Vatan Bütün Evladlarını İmdadına Çağırıyor," *İkdam* 5734 (8 February 1913): 4.

41. "Beyanname-i Meşihatpenahi," *İkdam* 5733 (7 February 1913): 3.

42. For a similar observation, see Ginio, "Paving the Way," 287–88.

43. "Harp Mitingi," *Tanin* 1460 (4 October 1912): 1; Kevorkian, *Armenian Genocide*, 135–36.

44. "Hitabe-i Harb: Devlet-i Osmaniye'nin Hudut-ı Tabiisi Tuna Boyudur," *Sabah* 8277 (5 October 1912): 1.

45. "Muharebe Başlıyor," *Cenin* [Tanin] 1471 (15 October 1912): 1.

46. D[iran] K[elekyan], "Vatan Muharebesi: Muharebe-i Hazıra Osmanlılık Muharebesidir," *Sabah* 8290 (18 October 1912): 1. See also "Hilal ve Salib Kavgası İmiş," *Alemdar* 138 (20 October 1912): 1–2.

47. "İttihat ve Terakki'nin Düşüncesi," *Renin* [Tanin] 1493 (6 November 1912): 1–2.

48. For more on this subject, see Van Os, "Feminism, Philanthropy," 297–99, 408–12, 442–50; Atamaz, "Fighting on Two Fronts."

49. Tüccarzade İbrahim Hilmi, *Neden Münhezim Olduk?* 6. For a detailed discussion of the Ottoman "military renaissance" in the Balkan Wars' aftermath, see Uyar, "Osmanlı Askeri Rönesansı."

50. Beşikçi, *Ottoman Mobilization*, 95–102; Hacısalihoğlu, "Inclusion and Exclusion," 277–84; Gülsoy, *Osmanlı Gayrimüslimlerinin*, 127–71; Bein, "Politics, Military Conscription," 294–98.

51. Bilgin, "Öğretmen Halim Gençoğlu-I," 48.

52. A series of unsigned articles published in *Tanin* under the title of "Problems and Remedies" (Derdler ve Devalar) in May 1913 offers perhaps the most succinct statement of this position. The author of these articles was most probably Hafız Hakkı Bey, a leading Unionist officer, close companion of Enver, and future member of the General Staff. The unorthodox views expressed in these articles not only shed light on the Unionists' perception of the defeat but also foreshadow how they would proceed to reform the army.

53. "Derdler ve Devalar: Devlet-i Aliyye ve Balkan Orduları," *Tanin* 1596 (10 May 1913): 3.

54. Hallı, *Balkan Harbi*, 1: 121–22; Uyar and Erickson, *Military History*, 232–33. For a more detailed discussion of the reserve system's failure, see Beşikçi, "Redif Teşkilatının İflası."

55. Mahmud Muhtar Paşa, *Üçüncü Kolordu'nun*, 173; Yüzbaşı Selanikli Bahri, *Balkan Savaşı'nda*, 108; Karabekir, *Edirne Hatıraları*, 27; Facey and Safwat, eds., *Soldier's Story*, 40.

56. Yüzbaşı Selanikli Bahri, *Balkan Savaşı'nda*, 35.

57. Hüseyin Cemal, *Yeni Harb*, 231.

58. "Enver Paşa'nın Beyanatı," *Tanin* 1821 (19 January 1914): 2.

59. Beşikçi, *Ottoman Mobilization*, 102–07; Erickson, *Ottoman Army Effectiveness*, 6–13.

60. "Mükellefiyet-i Askeriye Kanun-ı Muvakkatı," *Düstur*, İkinci Tertip, vol. 6, 16 Cemaziyelahir 1332 (12 May 1914): 662–704.

61. Abdullah Cevdet, "Harbiye Nazırımız Enver Paşa Hazretleriyle Mülakat," *İçtihad* 103 (6 May 1914): 45–50.

62. The new law of conscription was never ratified by the Ottoman parliament and remained in effect provisionally throughout the war and its aftermath. In republican Turkey, it was replaced with a new law enacted in 1927.

63. "Millet-i Müsellahaya Doğru: Ordu Nasıl Teşkil Edilir?" *Tanin* 1980 (27 June 1914): 3. The term "armed nation" was famously coined by Colmar von der Goltz (later as Goltz Pasha, the reformer of the Ottoman army and the commander of the Ottoman Sixth Army in Iraq during World War I) in his extremely influential *Das Volk in Waffen* (1883).

64. Ibid. See also "Millet-i Müsellahaya Doğru: Yeni Ahz-ı Asker Kanunu Etrafında," *Tanin* 1976 (23 June 1914): 3.

65. Salibi, "Beirut under the Young Turks," 211. Egyptian newspapers *al-Ahram* and *al-Muqattam* also published passionate articles reflecting the Arabs' opposition to the law. Fawaz, *Land of Aching Hearts*, 166.

66. Kaligian, *Armenian Organization*, 220.

67. "Ermeni Patrikhanesi Meclis-i Umumisi'nin İçtimaı: Patrik Zaven Efendi'nin Nutku," *İkdam* 6198 (24 May 1914): 4.

68. Cavid Bey wrote in his diary about Talat Bey, who had just returned from the front, deploring the soldiers' attitude. Cavid Bey, *Meşrutiyet Ruznamesi*, 1: 493.

69. Ahmet İzzet Paşa, *Feryadım*, 1: 177; Mahmud Beliğ, *Mürettep 4. Kolordu'nun*, 517.

70. "İlan-ı Cihad," *Alemdar* 152 (8 November 1912): 4; "Ulemaya Hitaben Cihad Beyannamesi," *Sebilürreşad* 219 (25 October 1912): 212.

71. Cavid Bey, *Meşrutiyet Ruznamesi*, 1: 508–9; Babuş, ed., *Savaş Yıllarından Anılar*, 169; Mahmud Beliğ, *Mürettep 1. Kolordu'nun*, 69–70.

72. Elhac Ahmed Tahir and Mustafa Necati, "Esbab-ı Hezimet Hakkında Ulema-ı Dinin Mütalaatı," *İkdam* 5655 (30 November 1912): 1.

73. In *Ottoman Mobilization*, 72–75, Beşikçi similarly emphasizes the importance of religion as a motivating factor in the army.

74. "Ordu ve Din," *Tanin* 1822 (20 January 1914): 2.

75. Artuç, "Ahmed Cemal Paşa (1877–1922)," 128. For the full text of the statement, see "Havadis-i Askeriye: Bir Tamim," *Tasfir-i Efkar* 917 (21 November 1913): 3.

76. Mehmet Nihad, *Trakya Seferi*, 25; Mahmud Beliğ, *Mürettep 4. Kolordu'nun*, 517–18; Tüccarzade İbrahim Hilmi, *Neden Münhezim Olduk?* 66–67.

77. Adanır, "Non-Muslims in the Ottoman Army," 122–23; Aksakal, "Ottoman Empire," 21.

78. Hüseyin Cahid, "Gayrimüslimlerin Askerliği," *Tanin* 1799 (27 December 1913): 1

79. For a discussion, see Beşikçi, *Ottoman Mobilization*, 95–98; Zürcher, "Ottoman Conscription System"; Aktar, "Ermeni Askerler."

80. Helmreich, *Diplomacy of the Balkan Wars*, 130–31.

81. Among many examples, see Hüseyin Cahid, "Istatüko," *Renin* [Tanin] 1489 (2 November 1912): 1.

82. "Tehlikeli Devre," *İkdam* 5720 (21 January 1913): 1.

83. "Devletlerin Teşebbüs-i Müştereki," *Tanin* 1685 (8 August 1913): 1.

84. *İkdam* 5926 (20 August 1913): 1. Unionist leaders shared the same opinion. See, e.g., Hanioğlu, ed., *Kendi Mektuplarında*, 240. For the atrocity propaganda in the Ottoman press, see Çetinkaya, "Illustrated Atrocity."

85. The atrocities did, however, arouse concern in Europe and America, and an international commission to investigate them was funded by the Carnegie Endowment for International Peace.

86. Hüseyin Cahid, "1914 Hediyesi," *Tanin* 1822 (20 January 1914): 1.

87. "Nota Verildi," *İkdam* 6100 (15 February 1914): 1.

88. "1330 Senesine Mahsus Tekalif-i Fevkalade Kanun-ı Muvakkatı," *Düstur*, İkinci Tertip, vol. 6, 18 Rebiülevvel 1332 (14 February 1914): 186–87.

89. Cavid Bey, *Meşrutiyet Ruznamesi*, 1: 759.

90. For skepticism among the Arabs, see Kayalı, *Arabs and the Young Turks*, 126–28; among the Kurds, see Klein, *Margins of Empire*, 125–27.

91. Hüseyin Cahid, "İş Başına," *Tanin* 1757 (15 November 1913): 1.

92. For a detailed treatment of the decentralist/reformist movement among the Arabs, see Tauber, *Arab Movements*; Haddad, "Rise of Arab Nationalism"; Fawaz, *Land of Aching Hearts*, 22–25, 35. The First Arab Congress in Paris in June 1913 was the venue where decentralist demands were voiced most vocally.

93. Kayalı, *Arabs and the Young Turks*, 138, 140; Gingeras, *Fall of the Sultanate*, 206; Tauber, *Arab Movements*, 277–78; Thomas, "First Arab Congress," 320–22.

94. "Memalik-i Osmaniye'de Mevki-i Tatbik ve İcraya Konulacak Bazı Tedabir-i Esasiye-i Islahiye Hakkında İrade-i Seniyye," *Düstur*, İkinci Tertip, vol. 5, 4 Ramazan 1331 (7 August 1913): 618–19. For earlier measures on the use of Arabic in education, judiciary, and administration in Arab provinces, see "Arabistan Vilayetlerinde Lisan-ı Arabın Suret-i İstimali ve Teferruatı Hakkında İrade-i Seniyye," *Düstur*, İkinci Tertip, vol. 5, 12 Cemaziyyülevvel 1331 (19 April 1913): 318–19; Mahmut Şevket Paşa, ed., *Sadaret Günlüğü*, 163.

95. "Arab-Türk Muhadeneti," *Tanin* 1683 (6 August 1913): 1–2.

96. Ahmed Agayef, "Arab-Türk Muhadeneti," *Tercüman-ı Hakikat* 11615 (7 August 1913): 1.

97. *British Documents on Foreign Affairs*, 20: 430.

98. Ozil, *Orthodox Christians*; Ilıcak, "Osmanlı Rumlarının."

99. See, e.g., Mahmud Beliğ, *Mürettep 4. Kolordu'nun*, 517; Karabekir, *Edirne Hatıraları*, 57, 77; Durukan, *Günlüklerde Bir Ömür*, 1: 97–98, 458–59.

100. Ladas, *Exchange of Minorities*, 20; Dündar, *Türkiye'nin Şifresi*, 188–91.

101. *Tanin* 1760 (18 October 1913): 1. For the islands crisis, see Aksakal, *Ottoman Road to War*, 42–56.

102. "Türkiye ve Adalar," *Tanin* 1831 (29 January 1914): 1.

103. Hüseyin Cahid, "Yeni Bir Suret-i Hal," *Tanin* 1827 (25 January 1914): 1.

104. Söylemezoğlu, *Atina Sefareti*, 146.

105. Talat contemplated "retrieving the islands from the Greeks by the use of force," Cavid Bey noted in his diary on 24 September 1913 (*Meşrutiyet Ruznamesi*, 2: 107). "Talat thinks war [with Greece] is inevitable," U.S. Ambassador Morgenthau similarly noted on 19 June 1914 (*Diaries*, 70).

106. For the most detailed treatment of the boycott movement, see Çetinkaya, *Young Turks and the Boycott Movement*.

107. "The Fleet Subscriptions," *The Near East* 143 (30 January 1914): 407.

108. "The Fleet Subscriptions," *The Near East* 145 (13 February 1914): 467.

109. Erol, "Organised Chaos"; Akçam, *Young Turks' Crime*, 63–96; Bjørnlund, "1914 Cleansing"; Gingeras, *Sorrowful Shores*, 12–54; Dündar, *Türkiye'nin Şifresi*, 194–203.

110. For the complexity of ARF–CUP relations, see Moumdjian, "Eastern Vilayets"; Türkyılmaz, "Devrim İçinde Devrim."

111. Quoted in Koptaş, "Zohrab, Papazyan," 163.

112. Ibid., 165.

113. For the most detailed treatment of this process, see Reynolds, *Shattering Empires*. See also Somakian, *Empires in Conflict*, 50–57.

114. Bloxham, "Development of the Armenian Genocide," 261.

115. Hovannisian, *Armenia on the Road*, 33.

116. For the international dimension of the reform process, see Davison, "Armenian Crisis"; Bloxham, *Great Game*.

117. Hüseyin Cahid, "Şarki Anadolu ve Devletler," *Tanin* 1765 (27 November 1913): 1.

118. Cavid Bey, *Meşrutiyet Ruznamesi*, 2: 250–51, 280–81.

119. Quoted in Van der Dussen, "Question of Armenian Reforms," 21.

120. Kaligian, *Armenian Organization*, 179.

121. Quoted in Koptaş, "Zohrab, Papazyan," 174.

122. Hovannisian, *Armenia on the Road*, 38; Somakian, *Empires in Conflict*, 61–62.

123. "Anadolu Islahatı," *Tanin* 1845 (12 February 1914): 1.

124. Gingeras, *Fall of the Sultanate*, 157.

125. Pasdermadjian, "My Last Interview with Talaat Pasha," 122.

126. Odian, *Accursed Years*, 8.

Chapter 2

This chapter partly draws on research previously published in "Seferberlik: Building Up the Ottoman Home Front," in *World War I and the End of the Ottomans,* ed. Hans-Lukas Kieser, Kerem Öktem, and Maurus Reinkowski (London: I. B. Tauris, 2015), pp. 54–73.

1. "heyecan içinde, meyus ve mükedder," Sunguroğlu, *Harput Yollarında*, 4: 79.

2. I borrow the term "mobilization of the imagination" from Domansky, "Transformation of State and Society," 49.

3. Horne, *State, Society, and Mobilization*, 1.

4. For the most detailed treatment of this process, see Aksakal, *Ottoman Road to War*. See also McMeekin, *Ottoman Endgame*, 83–91, 97–100.

5. Cavid Bey, *Meşrutiyet Ruznamesi*, 2: 631.

6. Cited from his diaries in Jeffrey, *Sir Henry Wilson*, 104–5. Original emphasis.

7. M. N. Girs, Russia's ambassador to the Porte, report dated 23 March 1914 to Foreign Minister Sergei Sazonov, cited in Reynolds, *Shattering Empires*, 107.

8. Sabis, *Harb Hatıralarım*, 1: 111; Kaymakam Şerif Bey, *Sarıkamış İhata Manevrası*, 60–61. See also the statements of Bronsart von Schellendorff on the lack of reliable data about the people who would and could be drafted. Kurat, ed., *Birinci Dünya Savaşı Sırasında*, 27.

9. In some districts, sealed envelopes containing mobilization posters had been distributed to village leaders beforehand, with strict instructions not to open them until ordered to do so. Following the mobilization, gendarmes brought orders to open the envelopes. Rogan, *Frontiers of the State*, 220; Çöl, *Çanakkale-Sina Savaşları*, 21–22; Newton, *Fifty Years in Palestine*, 105.

10. Beşikçi mentions specific army regulations for the use of drummers, *Ottoman Mobilization*, 86.

11. Odian, *Accursed Years*, 2.

12. *Türk Silahlı Kuvvetleri Tarihi*, 3: 288; Akbay, *Birinci Dünya Harbi'nde*, 1: 127. Larcher, *Guerre turque*, 590, places the number at 150,000, saying that the active Ottoman army was made up of two classes.

13. "Seferberlik," *Tasvir-i Efkar* 1158 (4 August 1914): 3.

14. "45 Yaşına Kadar Olanların Hizmet-i Askeriye ile Mükellefiyetleri Hakkında Kanun-ı Muvakkat," *Düstur*, İkinci Tertip, vol. 6, 11 Ramazan 1332 (3 August 1914): 912–13; "Seferberlik: Yirmiden Kırk Beş Yaşına Kadar Herkes Asker," *Tasvir-i Efkar* 1160 (6 August 1914): 1. These groups had been liable for service since 1909, but the law once again underlined their obligation.

15. Erickson, *Ordered to Die*, 7; Akbay, *Birinci Dünya Harbi'nde*, 1: 127; Sabis, *Harb Hatıralarım*, 1: 195–96. For an informed discussion of these numbers in a comparative perspective, see Beşikçi, *Ottoman Mobilization*, 112–15.

16. Engin, ed., *Seferden Sefere*, 87.

17. TNA, FO 371/2143/56867, Irvin and Sellers to Grey, 17 September 1914; "Conditions in the Holy Land," *The Near East* 177 (25 September 1914): 681.

18. "Harb-i Umumi-Seferberlik," *Tanin* 2016 (3 August 1914): 1.

19. See, e.g., Yunus Nadi, "Hükümetimizin Bitaraflığı," *Tasvir-i Efkar* 1157 (3 August 1914): 1; D[iran] K[elekyan], "Vazifemiz," *Sabah* 8936 (4 August 1914): 1; "Sevişelim ve Çalışalım," *Tanin* 2034 (21 August 1914): 1.

20. "Seferberlik," *Tanin* 2016 (3 August 1914): 1. See also "Türkiye'de Seferberlik," *Tanin* 2040 (27 August 1914): 3.

21. "İstanbul'da Seferberlik: Askerler Şen ve Şakrak Giderken," *İkdam* 6276 (11 August 1914): 1; "Şehrimizde Seferberlik Tezahüratı," *İkdam* 6271 (6 August 1914): 1; "Asker Olanlar Silah Başına: Seferberlik İçin Talik Olunan Levhalar," *Donanma* 56 (17 August 1914): 125.

22. *İkdam* 6268 (3 August 1914): 1.

23. TNA, FO 195/2457/215, Major Samson to Mallet, 6 August 1914. For a German view along the same lines, see Kress von Kressenstein, *Türklerle Beraber*, 6.

24. "The Mobilization of Adana Vilayet," *The Near East* 176 (18 September 1914): 651.

25. Eti, *Doğu Cephesi Günlüğü*, 8.

26. Haigaz, *The Fall of the Aerie*, 30.

27. Işık, *Malatya*, 763.

28. See, e.g., the observations of the Rev. John E. Merrill, president of the Central Turkey College in Antep (Aintab): Merrill, "Seen and Heard in Aintab," *Missionary Herald* 110, no. 11 (November 1914): 509.

29. Caferoğlu, *Anadolu Ağızlarından Toplamalar*, 157.

30. Işık, *Malatya*, 762. The author heard this song from his mother in 1943 and recorded it in his school notebook.

31. See, e.g., Ahmed Agayef, "Ordu ve Millet İçin Ölüm Geride, Selamet ve Saadet İleridedir," *Tercüman-ı Hakikat* 11975 (13 August 1914): 1.

32. BOA, DH.HMŞ 23/102, 6 August 1914; "Askeri Ceza Kanunu'na Müzeyyel Kanun-ı Muvakkat," *Düstur*, İkinci Tertip, vol. 6, 14 Ramazan 1332 (6 August 1914): 981–82. For the circular issued by the Ministry of War on the implementation of this law, see Yarbay Selahattin, *Kafkas Cephesi'nde*, 5.

33. Morgenthau, *Diaries*, 86.

34. Yarbay Selahattin, *Kafkas Cephesi'nde*, 6.

35. Rado, ed., "Bir Emekli Subayın Not Defteri," 5; Hartunian, *Neither to Laugh*, 52; Sunata, *Gelibolu'dan Kafkaslara*, 20; Riggs, *Days of Tragedy*, 3; Tergeman, *Daughter of Damascus*, 176; "Mobilization in Palestine," *The Near East* 175 (11 September 1914): 624; "The Troubles of Diarbekir," *The Near East* 177 (25 September 1914): 676.

36. Ajay, "Mount Lebanon," 157.

37. NARA, RG 59, 867.00/735, 8 August 1914. See also "Mükellefiyet-i Askeriye," *Tanin* 2151 (17 December 1914): 4.

38. Sürmenyan, *Harbiyeli Bir Osmanlı Ermenisi*, 45.

39. Baki, *Büyük Harpte*, 1: 36

40. Kuntman, *Bir Doktorun Harp*, 71; Alpat, *Bir Osmanlı Askerinin*, 67.

41. Derveze, *Osmanlı Filistininde*, 316.

42. "Seferberlik İlanı," *İkdam* 6268 (3 August 1914): 1; Çakır, *Elli Yıl Önce Şark Cephesi*, 9; Erginsoy, ed., *Dedem Hüseyin Atıf Beşe*, 135; Ussher, *American Physician*, 216.

43. Önal, ed., *Tuğgeneral Ziya Yergök'ün Anıları*, 23–24; Riggs, *Days of Tragedy*, 6. For similar observations in Syria, see Cummings, "Economic Warfare," 25, 27–28.

44. Karabekir, *Birinci Cihan Harbine*, 2: 163–64.

45. Simon, "View from Baghdad," 40–41; Derveze, *Osmanlı Filistininde*, 315–16; Arıkoğlu, *Hatıralarım*, 63; Abramson, ed., *Soldiers' Tales*, 75.

46. Zaken, *Jewish Subjects*, 272.

47. In Beirut, e.g., people fled to Mount Lebanon, as this region enjoyed a special status that provided its residents exemption from several taxes and military service. NARA, RG 59, 867.00/638, 3 August 1914; ibid., 867.00/659, 22 August 1914. On the special status of Mount Lebanon in this period, see Akarlı, *Long Peace*.

48. Fawaz, *Land of Aching Hearts*, 85–86; Mays, "Transplanting Cosmopolitans," 105–78.

49. Tunaya, *Türkiye'de Siyasal Partiler*, 1: 109. See also "Millet-i Müsellahaya Doğru: Ordu Nasıl Teşkil Edilir?" *Tanin* 1980 (27 June 1914): 3.

50. Revenues yielded through the military exemption fee constituted 14.5, 18.2, and 22.2 percent of the imperial budget in 1330 [1914], 1331 [1915], and 1332 [1916], respectively. Öztel, *II. Meşrutiyet Dönemi Osmanlı Maliyesi*, 91.

51. Beşikçi, *Ottoman Mobilization*, 140–42.

52. The government extended this period of payment three times, first for a week (13 August 1914), then for ten days (21 August 1914), and finally for a month (7 October 1914).

53. "Taht-ı Silaha Celb Olunan Milel-i Gayri Müslime Efrad-ı İhtiyatiyesinden Bedel-i Nakdi Kabulü Hakkında Kanun-ı Muvakkat," *Düstur*, İkinci Tertip, vol. 6, 11 Ramazan 1332 (3 August 1914): 913.

54. "Taht-ı Silaha Celb Olunan Milel-i Gayri Müslime Efrad-ı Müstahfazasından Bedel-i Nakdi Kabulü Hakkında Kanun-ı Muvakkat," *Düstur*, İkinci Tertip, vol. 6, 14 Ramazan 1332 (6 August 1914): 926; "Müslim Efrad-ı İhtiyatiye ve Müstahfazasının Gayri Muallem Kısmından da Bedel-i Nakdi Kabulü Hakkında Kanun-ı Muvakkat," vol. 6, 16 Ramazan 1332 (8 August 1914): 931. The state defined the "trained" (*muallem*) as individuals who had received three months of rudimentary military training.

55. Morgenthau, *Diaries*, 83.

56. Yet he also added that "practically every Christian able to secure 43 lira pays for his exemption." NARA, RG 84, Damascus, vol. 24 (15 August 1914). Beşikçi, *Ottoman Mobilization*, 142, relates a very similar incident in Aleppo.

57. Cavid Bey, *Meşrutiyet Ruznamesi*, 2: 630.

58. Riggs, *Days of Tragedy*, 10.

59. Eldem, *Osmanlı İmparatorluğu'nun İktisadi Şartları*, 214–15.

60. Sazak, *Emin Bey'in Defteri*, 94. For similar reports, see "Baghdad and the War," *The Near East* 180 (16 October 1914): 763, and "Near East Markets-Angora," ibid., 182 (30 October 1914): 836.

61. Traboulsi, *History of Modern Lebanon*, 72. See also the report by the U.S. consul in Aleppo, NARA, RG 59, 867.00/677, 3 August 1914.

62. Cited in Kieser, *Der verpasste Friede*, 336.

63. W. Stanley Hollis, "Olive Crop Reports: Low Prices in Syria," *Daily Consular and Trade Reports* no. 235 (7 October 1914): 127.

64. Arıkoğlu, *Hatıralarım*, 63; Sazak, *Emin Bey'in Defteri*, 94; McGilvary, *Dawn of a New Era*, 58.

65. "30'uncu Tümenin Harp Ceridesi," 313–14.

66. Özdemir, *Öyküleriyle Ağıtlar I*, 32.

67. Kemal, "Yayımlanmamış On Ağıt," 174.

68. McGilvary, *Dawn of a New Era*, 58.

69. Musil, *Middle Euphrates*, 128–29; "Baghdad and the War," *The Near East* 180 (16 October 1914): 763. Trade was at a standstill and half of the shops in the bazaar were closed, according to a missionary in Maraş, E. C. Woodley, "The State of Things in Marash," *Missionary Herald* 110, no. 11 (November 1914): 510. For similar observations in Beirut, see "Syrian Notes," *The Near East* 175 (11 September 1914): 625; for Adana, Tarsus, and Mersin, "The Mobilization of Adana Vilayet," ibid., 176 (18 September 1914): 651; and for Diyarbekir, "The Troubles of Diarbekir," ibid., 177 (25 September 1914): 676.

70. Odian, *Accursed Years*, 2–3. For the panic in Jerusalem, see Jacobson, *From Empire to Empire*, 23–24.

71. This first moratorium was effective for a month. The Ministry of Finance subsequently prolonged the moratorium, first for shorter periods and then for longer ones, until the end of the war, ten times altogether. Its conditions, however, did not apply to debts owed to the government.

72. This was a particularly burning problem for the province of Adana where the labor required for cotton picking was scarce and expensive. Nicham V. Zelveyan, "Notes from Mersina, Turkey," *Levant Trade Review* 4, no. 2 (September 1914): 146. For a detailed discussion of the mobilization's impact on Çukurova, see Gratien, "Mountains Are Ours," 360–66.

73. BOA, HR.MA, 1104/81, 3 August 1914, reproduced in *Osmanlı Belgelerinde Birinci Dünya Harbi*, 1: 26–27.

74. BOA, HR.MA, 1105/18, 6 August 1914, reproduced ibid., 31–32.

75. On the imposition of censorship on the press, see Karabekir, *Birinci Cihan Harbine*, 2: 166; Ahmed Emin, *Turkey in the World War*, 104–5, 265–66. For detailed regulations about the implementation of censorship, see *Sansür Talimatnamesi*. Censorship of the press lasted approximately four years, until June 1918.

76. "Tebliğ: Başkumandanlık Vekalet-i Celilesinden," *Tanin* 2109 (5 November 1914): 2.

77. "Mektuplar Açık Yazılacak," *Tanin* 2109 (5 November 1914): 3.

78. "Constantinople Letter," *The Near East* 173 (28 August 1914): 563.

79. "Boğazlar Niçin Kapandı," *Tanin* 2073 (30 September 1914): 1; Besbelli, *Deniz Harekatı*, 105.

80. Pamuk, "Ottoman Economy," 113; Fawaz, *Land of Aching Hearts*, 10–14; Harlaftis and Kardasis, "International Shipping," 233–65.

81. This was especially a serious blow to Mount Lebanon where as much as 40 percent of the region's income came from Syrian émigrés abroad. Fawaz, *Land of Aching Hearts*, 28–29; Pitts, "Fallow Fields," 40.

82. Ballobar, *Jerusalem in World War I*, 66.

83. For the Ministry of Interior's general warning to regularly inform all the administrative units down to townships (*nahiye*), see BOA, DH.KMS 32/30, 18 May 1915.

84. Very few copies of the Osmanlı Milli Telgraf Ajansı bulletins have survived. The translation of this rare example dated 19/20 January 1915 is by Ruth A. Parmelee, an American missionary in Harput during the war, who described the bulletins as "our only daily newspaper during the war between Turkey and the Allies." Hoover Institution Archives, Ruth A. Parmelee Papers, box 1.

85. Güvemli, *Bir Zamanlar Ordu*, 11. See also Kayra, *Hoşça Kal Trabzon*, 37.

86. A young sergeant, Ali Rıza Eti, noted in his diary that he read the Osmanlı Milli Telgraf Ajansı news posted on a wall in the remote eastern Anatolian town of Mamahatun. Eti, *Doğu Cephesi Günlüğü*, 19. For reading aloud in marketplaces in Antep, see Çitçi and Yener, *Gaziantep'te Sanat ve Ticaret Dalları*, 40–41.

87. TNA, FO 371/2140/56937, Monck-Mason to Beaumont, 11 August 1914.

88. Konrapa, *Bolu Tarihi*, 615.

89. "The Situation in Smyrna," *The Near East* 177 (25 September 1914): 675. For a similar situation in Edirne, see TNA, FO 371/2146/70603, Major Samson to Mallet, 20 October 1914.

90. Ussher, *American Physician*, 213–14.

91. Cited in Kieser, *Nearest East*, 85.

92. Yalman, *Yakın Tarihte*, 1: 270; "The Finances of Turkey," *The Near East* 177 (25 September 1914): 693; "Turkey: From Varied Fields," *Missionary Herald* 110, no. 12 (December 1914): 571; TNA, FO 371/2146/70602, Monahan to Mallet, 14 October 1914.

93. Önal, ed., *Tuğgeneral Ziya Yergök'ün Anıları*, 32; Gratien, "Mountains Are Ours," 365–66.

94. Akbay, *Birinci Dünya Harbi'nde*, 1: 138.

95. Gilbert, *Winston S. Churchill*, 44.

96. Güvenç, *Osmanlıların Drednot Düşleri*, 37–38.

97. Ibid., 61; Rooney, "British Naval Missions," 12–13.

98. Beşikçi, "İktidarın Çelik Sembolleri."

99. Cunliffe-Owen, "Entry of Turkey into the War," 614.

100. For examples, see Beşikçi, *Ottoman Mobilization*, 49–50.

101. Ryan, *Last of the Dragomans*, 95–96.

102. TNA, FO 371/2138/42346, Mallet to Grey, 23 August 1914.

103. Ibid., 371/2140/56937, Monck-Mason to Beaumont, 11 August 1914.

104. Ibid., 371/2143/52738, Fiani to Kelly, 28 August 1914. See also "Notes from Jaffa," *The Near East* 177 (25 September 1914): 676.

105. "The Situation in Smyrna," *The Near East* 177 (25 September 1914): 675.

106. Beşikçi, *Ottoman Mobilization*, 47, argues that the incident also had an "accelerating effect on the Ottoman decision to enter the First World War."

107. Emphasizing the defensive nature of their war effort was not a strategy unique to the Ottomans. Especially during the first half of the war, all the major belligerent nations based their propaganda campaigns on the narrative of victimization, and pre-

sented their war efforts as self-defense against external aggression. Marquis, "Words as Weapons"; Winter, "Propaganda and the Mobilization of Consent," 217–18.

108. "Şayan-ı Teessüf Bir Muamele," *Sabah* 8941 (9 August 1914): 1 (*Osmanlı milletinin ve İslam ümmetinin*).

109. Yunus Nadi, "Hezar Lanet," *Tasfir-i Efkar* 1161 (7 August 1914): 1. See also "Hiç Bir Vakit Unutamayacağımız İki Gemimiz," *Tasfir-i Efkar* 1223 (9 October 1914): 1.

110. For the escape of *Goeben* and *Breslau*, see Sondhaus, *Great War at Sea*, 94–107.

111. "Osmanlılar Müjde!" *İkdam* 6276 (11 August 1914): 1; "Yavuz Drednotu ve Midilli Zırhlı Kruvazörü," *İkdam* 6277 (12 August 1914): 1.

112. TNA, FO 195/2459/6035, Dewey to Mallet, 15 October 1914.

113. "Türkiye'nin Bitaraflığı," *Tanin* 2049 (5 September 1914): 1.

114. Resentment of the capitulations did not begin with the Unionists; see Ahmad, "Ottoman Perceptions of the Capitulations." For the Unionists' earlier negotiations with the Great Powers, see Ahmad, "Ottoman Armed Neutrality," 44–50.

115. Tunaya, *Türkiye'de Siyasal Partiler*, 1: 106.

116. Heller, *British Policy*, 138.

117. Ambassador Ahmed Rüstem to the secretary of state, 10 September 1914, cited in Ahmad, "War and Society," 285.

118. "Tangier to Teheran," *The Near East* 176 (18 September 1914): 654. For the decision of abrogation and reactions to it, see Elmacı, *İttihat Terakki ve Kapitülasyonlar*, 84–94; Ahmad, "Ottoman Armed Neutrality," 51–53.

119. "Hayat-ı Siyasiye-i Devletin ve Ümmetin En Mühim Günü," *Tasfir-i Efkar* 1195 (10 September 1914): 1.

120. "Şehrimizde Tezahürat-ı Milliye," *İkdam* 6307 (12 September 1914): 1; "Her Tarafta İstiklal-i Milli Şenlikleri," *Tanin* 2025 (12 September 1914): 1; Elmacı, *İttihat Terakki ve Kapitülasyonlar*, 74–84; Ahmad, "Ottoman Armed Neutrality," 53–54.

121. Beşikçi, *Ottoman Mobilization*, 59–63.

122. TNA, FO 195/2460/4852, Heathcote-Smith to Mallet, 17 September 1914.

123. Hoover Institute Archives, Ruth A. Parmelee Papers, box 1.

124. TNA, FO 195/2460/679, Cumberbatch to Mallet, 14 September 1914.

125. "Hayat-ı Siyasiye-i Devletin ve Ümmetin En Mühim Günü," *Tasfir-i Efkar* 1195 (10 September 1914): 1.

126. "Donanma Cemiyeti'nin," 17.

127. Mombauer, ed., *Origins of the First World War*, 542 (emphasis in original).

128. Kress von Kressenstein, *Türklerle Beraber*, 7 (*şark diplomasisinin şaheseri*). For the German impatience with the Ottomans and their delaying tactics, see Aksakal, *Ottoman Road to War*, 137–52; McMeekin, *Ottoman Endgame*, 113–33.

129. Hafız Hakkı Paşa, *Sarıkamış Günlüğü*, 42–43, 162; Ahmad, "Ottoman Armed Neutrality," 66.

130. Bobroff, *Roads to Glory*, 96–111.

131. Besbelli, *Deniz Harekatı*, 477. See also Cavid Bey, *Meşrutiyet Ruznamesi*, 2: 673.

132. For the official communiqué, see "Karadeniz'de Mühim Hadisat," *Tercüman-ı Hakikat* 12052 (30 October 1914): 1. For newspaper reports, see "Karadeniz'deki Vakıa-i

Ahire," *İkdam* 6356 (31 October 1914): 1; "Beklenmeyen Vak'a," *Tanin* 2104 (31 October 1914): 1.

133. "Hal-i Harbin İlanı," *İkdam* 6368 (12 November 1914): 1; "Beyanname-i Hümayun Suretidir," *Tanin* 2117 (13 November 1914): 1.

134. *Meclis-i Mebusan Zabıt Cerideleri* (Minutes of the Sessions/Proceedings of the Ottoman Parliament, cited below as *MMZC*), Term 3 [the parliamentary period between 1914 and 1918], Year of Session 2, vol. 1, 12 Teşrinisani 1331 (25 November 1915), 26 (*tecavüzat-ı namerdaneleri*).

135. "İnkıta-i Münasebat," *Tanin* 2106 (2 November 1914): 1.

136. For an eloquent discussion of the Ottoman jihad, see Beşikçi, *Ottoman Mobilization*, 63–80; Aksakal, "Ottoman Empire," 25; Zürcher, ed., *Jihad and Islam*. For the historic background of the 1914 jihad, see Aksakal, "'Holy War Made in Germany?'"

137. Among numerous articles in the press, see Yunus Nadi, "Umumi Harb ve İslam Alemi," *Tasfir-i Efkar* 1179 (25 August 1914): 1; S. M. Tevfik, "Harb-i Umumi ve İslam Alemi," *Sebilürreşad* 309 (2 September 1914): 393; "Müslümanlar ve Harb-i Umumi," *İkdam* 6302 (6 September 1914): 1; "Hakk-ı Hayatımızı İspat Edelim," *Tercüman-ı Hakikat* 12056 (3 November 1914): 1; "Gaza-yı Ekber: Silah Başına," *İkdam* 6359 (3 November 1914): 1; "Şeytanlara Karşı Melaike-i Gazab," *İkdam* 6360 (4 November 1914): 1.

138. A.Y., "Cihan Harbi ve Türkler," *Türk Yurdu* 73 (24 December 1914): 21–22.

139. Ahmet Ağaoğlu, "Türkiye'nin ve İslam Aleminin Kurtuluşu," *Harb Mecmuası* 1 (November 1915): 7–9.

140. Sunguroğlu, *Harput Yollarında*, 1: 164.

141. Al-Qattan, "Safarbarlik."

142. "The sense of the tragic" is a phrase famously coined by Henry Kissinger in his *A World Restored*, 6.

143. Zürcher underlines this point as one of the main differences between the European and Ottoman war experiences. Zürcher, "What Was Different," 5.

Chapter 3

1. Babuş, ed., *Savaş Yıllarından Anılar*, 156–61.

2. For Haim's wartime memoirs, see Abramson, ed., *Soldiers' Tales*, 189–270.

3. See further Beşikçi's brilliant *Ottoman Mobilization*, as well as Zürcher's pioneering articles "Between Death and Desertion" and "Little Mehmet in the Desert."

4. Ussher, *American Physician*, 227; Riggs, *Days of Tragedy*, 3–4, 38–44.

5. Gingeras, *Fall of the Sultanate*, 208.

6. Çanlı, ed., *Hüseyin Avni Gençoğlu'nun Hatıraları*, 34–37; Eti, *Doğu Cephesi Günlüğü*, 14; Aaronsohn, *With the Turks in Palestine*, 7–17.

7. Beşikçi, *Ottoman Mobilization*, 111–12, 261.

8. Zürcher, "Between Death and Desertion," 247–48; Guse, *Kaukasusfront*, 17; Akbay, *Birinci Dünya Harbi'nde*, 1: 123, 138; Yeğinatı, *Büyük Harbin Başında*, 8, 10, 42.

9. Ussher, *American Physician*, 216.

10. "Aintab Anecdotes," *The Orient* 5 (9 September 1914): 356.

11. Guhr, *Anadolu'dan Filistin'e*, 43, 72; Aziz Samih, *Büyük Harpte*, 3–4, 43, 77; Salim, "Sıhhi Harb Tarihi Tetkikleri," 492, 496–97; Baytın, *İlk Dünya Harbi'nde*, 31, 165; Riggs, *Days of Tragedy*, 11–12.

12. Önal, ed., *Tuğgeneral Ziya Yergök'ün Anıları*, 33.

13. In order to accelerate the marches, army commanders occasionally removed stops that had normally been scheduled. Yarbay Selahattin, *Kafkas Cephesi'nde*, 34.

14. Şerif Bey, *Sarıkamış İhata Manevrası*, 67, 80.

15. Guhr, *Anadolu'dan Filistin'e*, 107.

16. NARA, RG 59, 867.00/719, 17 October 1914. See also Çiçek, *War and State Formation*, 170–71.

17. Baykoç, *Büyük Harpte*, 12.

18. Ataman, *Esaret Yılları*, 38.

19. Guse, *Kaukasusfront*, 65; Avcı, *Irak'ta Türk Ordusu*, 130.

20. Süleyman Nuri, *Uyanan Esirler*, 80; Çanlı, ed., *Hüseyin Avni Gençoğlu'nun Hatıraları*, 72; Apak, *Yetmişlik Bir Subayın Hatıraları*, 129.

21. For his statement about the impossibility of such an action to the CUP's Central Committee, see Cavid Bey, *Meşrutiyet Ruznamesi*, 2: 678. See also Karabekir, *Günlükler*, 1: 404–5.

22. Uyar, "Ottoman Strategy," 174.

23. In *Caucasian Battlefields*, 284, Allen and Muratoff put Ottoman Third Army casualties as high as 75,000.

24. Kurat, ed., *Alman Generallerinin Raporları*, 28. See also Kaymakam Şerif Bey, *Sarıkamış İhata Manevrası*, 16, 252; Aziz Samih, *Büyük Harpte*, 1, 47.

25. The literature on the Gallipoli campaign is voluminous. For examples, see Erickson, *Ordered to Die*, 76–95; Rogan, *Fall of the Ottomans*, 129–58, 185–215; McMeekin, *Ottoman Endgame*, 163–97, 199–221, 247–61; Prior, *Gallipoli*.

26. Between fall 1914 and summer 1915, the Ottoman forces engaged in two other significant military campaigns, both against the British: in the Sinai peninsula to capture the Suez Canal, and in lower Mesopotamia to regain Basra. The casualty rates in these campaigns paled, however, in comparison with the winter offensive in the Caucasus. Rogan, *Fall of the Ottomans*, 115–28; McMeekin, *Ottoman Endgame*, 138–45, 154–61, 263–70.

27. "Gayri Muallem Efradın Mezuniyeti," *İkdam* 6278 (13 August 1914): 1; "Yaşlı Efrad," *İkdam* 6279 (14 August 1914): 1.

28. Guse, *Kaukasusfront*, 16; Uyar, "Ottoman Strategy," 171. See also Erickson, "Armenians and Ottoman Military Policy."

29. Aziz Samih, *Büyük Harpte*, 24–25. The governor of Diyarbekir criticized the policy along the same lines; see Eken, ed., *Kapancızade Hamit Bey*, 466.

30. Beşikçi, *Ottoman Mobilization*, 297. For a detailed discussion of the gendarmerie and its reorganization during World War I, see Beşikçi, "Devlet İktidarı ve İç Güvenlik."

31. "Hizmet-i Askeriye Haricinde Bulunan Efraddan Silah İstimaline Kabiliyetli Olanların Suret-i Celb ve İstihdamı Hakkında Kanun-ı Muvakkat," *Düstur*, İkinci Tertip, vol. 7, 20 Cemaziyelevvel 1333 (5 April 1915): 545–46.

32. *MMZC*, Term 3, Year of Session 2, vol. 1, 7 Kanunuevvel 1331 (20 December 1915), 186–93.

33. "16 Cemaziyelahir 1332 tarihli Mükellefiyet-i Askeriye Kanun-ı Muvakkatı'nın 2, 3, 4, 5. Maddelerini Muaddel Kanun-ı Muvakkat," *Düstur*, İkinci Tertip, vol. 7, 14 Cemaziyelahir 1333 (29 April 1915): 589–91.

34. Refugees who came in the wake of Crimean War (1856) and Russo-Ottoman War of 1877–78 were exempted from the service for twenty-five years. In 1888, the state reduced this period of exemption to six years. Eren, *Göç ve Göçmen Meseleleri*, 41, 42; Dündar, *İttihat ve Terakki'nin Müslümanları*, 197–98; Beşikçi, *Ottoman Mobilization*, 149.

35. BOA, MV 196/36, 5 March 1915; BOA, DH.SN.M, 36/4, 15 April 1915; "16 Cemaziyelahir 1332 Tarihli Mükellefiyet-i Askeriye Kanun-ı Muvakkatına Müzeyyel Kanun-ı Muvakkat," *Düstur*, İkinci Tertip, vol. 7, 20 Cemaziyelevvel 1333 (5 April 1915): 546. See also Öğün, *Unutulmuş Bir Göç Trajedisi*, 51–53.

36. "Mükellefiyet-i Askeriye Haricinde Bulunan Efrad," *Tanin* 2263 (8 April 1915): 3.

37. BOA, DH.I.UM 14/18, 29 December 1915; ibid., 14/21, 9 January 1916. Despite these orders, however, in many regions military units continued to draft refugees fleeing from the Russian advance. Ibid., 14/28, 17 February 1916; ibid., 14/26, 3 April 1916.

38. *Meclis-i Ayan Zabıt Cerideleri* (cited below as *MAZC*), Term 3, Year of Session 2, vol. 2, 8 Şubat 1331 (21 February 1916), 119.

39. BOA, DH.SN.M 36/64, 15 April 1915; BOA, DH.UMVM 123/89, 18 August 1915.

40. BOA, DH.HMŞ 23/123, 24 October 1916; "Muhacirinin Mükellefiyetine Müt-edair 25 Rebiülahir 1334 Tarihli Kanuna Müzeyyel Kanun-ı Muvakkat," *Düstur*, İkinci Tertip, vol. 8, 26 Zilhicce 1334 (24 October 1916): 1353; *Meclis-i Umuminin Mün'akid Olmadığı*, 1332, 95.

41. BOA, DH.IUM E26/59, 7 January 1917; İpek, "Birinci Dünya Savaşı Esnasında," 204.

42. Cited in Popplewell, "British Intelligence," 150–51.

43. "Anasır-ı Gayrimüslimenin Kuraları Hakkında Kanun," *Düstur*, İkinci Tertip, vol. 1, 20 Recep 1327 (7 August 1909): 420; Kuneralp, "Gayrimüslimlerin Askerlik Meselesi"; Beşikçi, *Ottoman Mobilization*, 95–102.

44. Zürcher, "Ottoman Conscription System," 87–90; Gülsoy, *Osmanlı Gayrimüslim-lerinin*; Hacısalihoğlu, "Inclusion and Exclusion."

45. BOA, DH.ŞFR 43/214, 10 August 1914.

46. TNO, FO 371/2146/70602, Monahan to Mallet, 14 October 1914; Beşikçi, *Ottoman Mobilization*, 130–31.

47. Beşikçi, *Ottoman Mobilization*, 132–33.

48. Aaronsohn, *With the Turks in Palestine*, 24.

49. Khalil Sakakini, *Yawmiyat*, vol. 2, 28 March 1915, 158–59. Cited in Tamari, ed., *Year of the Locust*, 45. See also Çiçek, *War and State Formation*, 173–74.

50. Beşikçi, *Ottoman Mobilization*, 134; Ussher, *American Physician*, 217.

51. Zürcher, "Ottoman Labour Battalions," 191; Shaw, *Ottoman Empire in World War I*, 1: 339–52.

52. Tamari, "Erasure of Palestine's Ottoman Past," 108. See also Erden, *Suriye Hatıraları*, 94; Çiçek, *War and State Formation*, 191–96.

53. Zürcher, "Ottoman Labour Battalions," 192; Kévorkian, "Soldats-ouvriers arméniens."

54. Showalter, "Mastering the Western Front," 51.

55. Morgenthau, *Diaries*, 236.

56. Selçuk, *Çanakkale Seferberliği*, 108–13.

57. Van Os, "Feminism, Philanthropy," 450–68.

58. Selçuk, *Çanakkale Seferberliği*, 11–18.

59. Sürgevil, *II. Meşrutiyet Döneminde İzmir*, 79–80.

60. Mehmed Emin, "Orduya Selam," 196. "Orduya Selam" was originally published in the second edition of *Ordunun Destanı* (1918). Köroğlu, *Propagandadan Milli Kimlik İnşasına*, 284–98.

61. Doğan and Tığlı, "Çanakkale Gazeli," 44.

62. Faik Ali, *Payitahtın Kapısında*, 76.

63. Ali Ekrem, *Ordunun Defteri*, 70.

64. Celal Sahir, "Köyde Kalanın Türküsü," *Türk Yurdu* 75 (21 January 1915): 35.

65. Mehmed Rifat, "Galiçya Mefahirinden," *Harb Mecmuası* 15 (December 1916): 227–33.

66. Mehmed Emin, *Ordunun Destanı*, 14, 16.

67. Cenab Şehabeddin, "Makale-i Mahsusa: Hatırat-ı Harbiye," *Harb Mecmuası* 21 (August 1917): 322–26.

68. "Türk Anası Ne Düşünüyor," *Harb Mecmuası* 17 (March 1917): 267–69.

69. Mehmed Emin, "Orduya Selam," 198.

70. Winter and Robert, eds., *Capital Cities at War*, 1: 10.

71. Aslanoğlu, "Bir Demette Beş Çiçek," 12. In the first verse of the poem, "*möyünlü möyünsüz*" is the folk pronunciation of "*muinli muinsiz*," and it refers to the abandonment of the exemption of sole breadwinners and their consequent conscription, a process, which is discussed in detail in the fifth chapter of this book.

72. Zürcher, "Between Death and Desertion," 246; Beşikçi, *Ottoman Mobilization*, 267–68.

73. Sandes, *Tales of Turkey*, 149.

74. Sabis, *Harp Hatıralarım*, 5: 174. See also Beşikçi's detailed discussion of many causes of desertion during the war in his *Ottoman Mobilization*, 247–309.

75. Jernazian, *Judgment unto Truth*, 44.

76. BOA, DH.IUM 88/3–4/33, 23 February 1916; Beşikçi, *Ottoman Mobilization*, 286.

77. BOA, DH.IUM E/23–51, 24 October 1916; ibid., E/46–34, 29 October 1917.

78. Avşar, "Birinci Dünya Savaşı'nda Propaganda Faaliyetleri," 297–99, citing ATASE, Birinci Dünya Harbi Koleksiyonu, K.3471 D.150 F.8–13. For more on Entente propaganda targeted at Ottoman soldiers, see Sarısaman, *Beyannamelerle Psikolojik Harp*.

79. Avşar, "Rus Propaganda Faaliyetleri," 83.

80. Avşar, "Birinci Dünya Savaşı'nda Propaganda Faaliyetleri," 304, citing ATASE, Birinci Dünya Harbi Koleksiyonu, K.3471 D.150 F.8–19.

81. Ibid., 311, citing ATASE, Birinci Dünya Harbi Kolleksiyonu, K.368 D.1467 F.7–1.

82. Guhr, Anadolu'dan Filistin'e, 106.

83. Manastırlı M. Hasib, "Hasan Çavuş'un Anasından Name-i Teşci," Harb Mecmuası 16 (February 1917): 250.

84. Kalkan, Kayseri ve Yöresi, 23.

85. BOA, DH.HMŞ 23/113, 3 January 1915.

86. BOA, DH.SN.M 36/49, 27 March 1915.

87. "Seferberlikte Erkan ve Ümera ve Zabitan ve Efrad ve Mensubin-i Askeriyenin Zevcat ve Meharimine Taarruz Edenlerin Merci-i Takip ve Muhakemesi Hakkında Kanun-ı Muvakkat," Düstur, İkinci Tertip, vol. 7, 28 Şevval 1333 (8 September 1915): 716–17. For more on the military tribunals during the war, see Köksal, "Divan-ı Harb-i Örfiler."

88. "Kanun-ı Ceza'nın 206. Maddesine Müzeyyel Fıkra Hakkında Kanun-ı Muvakkat," Düstur, İkinci Tertip, vol. 7, 7 Zilkade 1333 (16 September 1915): 725.

89. Özdemir and Mutaf, eds., Çanakkale Muharebatı, 63; Liman von Sanders, Five Years in Turkey, 104; Erickson, Ordered to Die, 94–95.

90. Allen and Muratoff, Caucasian Battlefields, 384. "The victory over first the British fleet and then the Allied armies was a tremendous morale booster for the Ottomans, but in the long run it broke the back of the army" (Zürcher, "Little Mehmet in the Desert," 233).

91. Robinson, "Decision at Erzerum," 478. For the 1916 campaign, see also McMeekin, Ottoman Endgame, 271–86.

92. Cebesoy, 1916–1917 Yılındaki Vaziyeti, 10.

93. Mühlmann, Deutsch-türkische Waffenbündnis, 106–8, 120–24, 184; Uyar, "Ottoman Strategy," 180.

94. Liman von Sanders, Five Years in Turkey, 120–23; Ahmet İzzet Paşa, Feryadım, 1: 246; Trumpener, Germany and the Ottoman Empire, 131–32.

95. "Mükellefiyet-i Askeriyenin 50 Yaşına Kadar Temdidi ve Teferruatı Hakkında Kanun," Düstur, İkinci Tertip, vol. 8, 15 Cemaziyelevvel 1334 (20 March 1916): 730.

96. 1331 (1915) Senesi Meclis-i Mebusan Encümen Mazbataları, 364–65.

97. "Sinn-i Mukayyetlerine Göre Vasıl-ı Mükellefiyet Olmadıkları Halde Hizmet-i Askeriyeye Elverişli Bulunanların Celbi Hakkında Kanun-ı Muvakkat," Düstur, İkinci Tertip, vol. 8, 26 Zilhicce 1334 (24 October 1916): 1353–54.

98. For the government's reasoning, see Meclis-i Umuminin Mün'akid Olmadığı, 1332, 96.

99. Erkin, Hatırat, 153.

100. Sadri Sema, Eski İstanbul Hatıraları, 458.

101. Elkus, Memoirs, 86.

102. Under the CUP rule, "provisional laws" (kavanin-i muvakkata) became a pow-

erful policy instrument. During the war, the Unionists issued hundreds of these pro-visional laws that went into effect upon the sultan's decree (*irade*), pending later par-liamentary approval. With this mechanism, the government aimed to act swiftly when faced with a problem and bypass any obstacle that might be created by members of parliament. Tunaya, *Türkiye'de Siyasal Partiler*, 3: 385–88. The Ministry of War had a "bureau of laws," which was charged with preparing drafts of laws in line with the army's demands. Erden, *İsmet İnönü*, 77.

103. *MMZC*, Term 3, Year of Session 3, vol. 2, 23 Kanunusani 1332 (5 February 1917), 111. For the discussion, see 111–12, 319–27, 392–96.

104. *MMZC*, Term 3, Year of Session 3, vol. 2, 23 Kanunusani 1332 (5 February 1917), 322.

105. "Sinn-i Mukayyetlerine Göre Vasıl-ı Mükellefiyet Olmadıkları Halde Hizmet-i Askeriyeye Elverişli Bulunanların Celbine Dair 26 Zilhicce 1334 Tarihli Kanun-ı Muvakkatın Reddi Hakkında Meclis-i Mebusan Kararnamesi," *Düstur*, İkinci Tertip, vol. 9, 12 Rebiülahir 1335 (5 February 1917): 142–43. See also *1332–1333 Meclis-i Mebusan Encümen Mazbataları*, 379–80.

106. Cebesoy, *1916–1917 Yılındaki Vaziyeti*, 18.

107. *Meclis-i Umuminin Mün'akid Olmadığı, 1332*, 84.

108. "Efrad-ı İhtiyatiye ve Müstahfazadan Bedel-i Nakdi Vermiş Olanların İhtiyac-ı Mübrem Halinde Taht-ı Silaha Alınması Hakkında Kanun-ı Muvakkat," *Düstur*, İkinci Tertip, vol. 8, 21 Zilhicce 1334 (19 October 1916): 1334.

109. This, however, never happened according to contemporary observers. Pomi-ankowski, *Zusammenbruch*, 243.

110. For the discussions in the parliament, see *MMZC*, Term 3, Year of Session 3, vol. 2, 19 Kanunusani 1332 (1 February 1917), 69–79, 163.

111. *MAZC*, Term 3, Year of Session 3, vol. 2, 10 Mart 1333 (10 March 1917), 182. See also "İkinci Kolordu Ahz-ı Asker Heyeti Riyasetinden," *Tanin* 2853 (22 November 1916): 4.

112. U.S. Ambassador Abram I. Elkus noted this slowdown in the Ottoman econ-omy in autumn 1916 (Elkus, *Memoirs*, 65).

113. BOA, DH.I.UM E/25–86, 23 December 1916; ibid., E/27–58, 8 February 1917; ibid., E/29–125, 1 April 1917; *1332–1333 Meclis-i Mebusan Encümen Mazbataları*, 304, 426–27, 763, 848, 851, 862.

114. For this last phase of the war in Palestine and Mesopotamia, see Gingeras, *Fall of the Sultanate*, 218–27; Ulrichsen, *First World War*, 106–18, 137–46; McMeekin, *Ottoman Endgame*, 341–63.

115. Larcher, *Guerre turque*, 601; Mühlmann, *Deutschland und die Türkei*, 81.

116. For the most detailed treatment of desertion, see Beşikçi, *Ottoman Mobiliza-tion*, 247–309.

117. Liman von Sanders, "Türk Ordusunun Bugünkü Durumu," in Kurat, ed., *Birinci Dünya Savaşı Sırasında*, 21.

118. Hans von Seeckt, "Türkiye'nin Yıkılmasının Sebepleri," in ibid., 64. For a com-parison with other belligerents, see Beşikçi, *Ottoman Mobilization*, 249–52.

119. Liman von Sanders, "Türk Ordusunun Bugünkü Durumu" (cited n. 117 above), 24.

120. Cebesoy, *1916–1917 Yılındaki Vaziyeti*, 28.

121. Kress von Kressenstein, *Türklerle Beraber*, 173.

122. For a deserter's "lifestyle," see Beşikçi, *Ottoman Mobilization*, 268–78.

123. Erkin, *Hatırat*, 143

124. Çalıka, ed., *Kurtuluş Savaşında Adalet Bakanı*, 22. For a similar treatment of deserters, see Koraltan, *Bir Politikacının Anıları*, 61.

125. Cebesoy, *1916–1917 Yılındaki Vaziyeti*, 28.

126. Ballobar, *Jerusalem in World War I*, 88.

127. Pırnar and Pırnar, *Baba Oğul Anıları*, 1: 55.

128. Apak, *Yetmişlik Bir Subayın*, 154.

129. Mühlmann, *Deutsch-türkische Waffenbündnis*, 184. For the process of recruitment of reserve officers, see Beşikçi, *Ottoman Mobilization*, 150–54.

130. Cebesoy, *1916–1917 Yılındaki Vaziyeti*, 23–24.

131. "Mükellefiyet-i Askeriye Kanun-ı Muvakkatının 14 Cemaziyelahir 1333 Tarihli 2. Madde-i Muaddelesini Muaddel Kanun-ı Muvakkat," *Düstur*, İkinci Tertip, vol. 9, 15 Receb 1335 (7 May 1917): 666.

132. Yaşar Kemal, *Ağıtlar*, 26.

133. Kabacalı, *Gül Yaprağın' Döktü Bugün*, 280.

134. Kalkan, *Kayseri ve Yöresi Ağıtları*, 19. For another version of the same lament, see Sevinçli, "Bir Seferberlik Ağıtı." For a very similar version of the same lament sung for *onaltılılar*, or "sixteeners," see Elçin, *Türkiye Türkçesinde Ağıtlar*, 14–16; for *onyedililer*, or "seventeeners," see Özdemir, *Öyküleriyle Ağıtlar I*, 31.

135. Quoted in Wallach, *Anatomie einer Militärhilfe*, 150.

136. Mehmet Beşikçi discusses the role played by the volunteers during the war and the Ottoman state's policies towards them in significant detail in *Ottoman Mobilization*, 157–202.

Chapter 4

1. Aydemir, *Suyu Arayan Adam*, 79–80.

2. Erden, *İsmet İnönü*, 106.

3. Aziz Samih, *Büyük Harpte*, 32.

4. "Tekalif-i Harbiye'nin Suret-i Tarhı Hakkında Kanun-ı Muvakkat," *Düstur*, İkinci Tertip, vol. 5, 21 Safer 1331 (30 January 1913): 48–49.

5. "Tedarik-i Vesait-i Nakliye-i Askeriye Kanunnamesi," *Düstur*, Birinci Tertip, vol. 6, 12 Muharrem 1307 (8 September 1889): 430–44.

6. *MMZC*, Term 3, Year of Session 1, vol. 1 (İçtima-ı Fevkalade), 2 Haziran 1330 (15 June 1914), 311. See also ibid., vol. 2, 24 Haziran 1330 (7 July 1914), 17, 546.

7. Toprak, *İttihat-Terakki ve Cihan Harbi*, 128.

8. NARA, RG 59, 867.00/659, 22 August 1914; Ricks, *Diaries of Khalil Totah*, 152.

9. "Some Events at Harpoot during the Great War of 1914–1915," Hoover Institution Archives, Ernest Wilson Riggs Papers, box 1.

10. Pomiankowski, *Zusammenbruch*, 92; Ahmet İzzet Paşa, *Feryadım*, 1: 190; Rado,

ed., "Bir Emekli Subayın Not Defteri," 6; Birgen, *İttihat ve Terakki'de On Sene*, 1: 305; McGilvary, *Dawn of a New Era*, 59; Karabekir, *Birinci Cihan Harbine*, 2: 163–64.

11. Hüseyin Rahmi, *Hakka Sığındık*, 9–10.

12. NARA, RG 59, 867.00/651.

13. Cavid Bey, *Meşrutiyet Ruznamesi*, 2: 621. See also Eken, ed., *Kapancızade Hamit Bey*, 468–69.

14. Observations of the U.S. vice-consul-general in Izmir, NARA, RG 59, 867.00/643, and of the U.S. consular agent in Haifa, ibid., 867.00/653, 867.00/657; McGilvary, *Dawn of a New Era*, 59.

15. Jakob Künzler witnessed the requisitioning process on his way to Baghdad. "[E]very salesman knew that the slip of paper left behind as a receipt could be torn up because the goods would never be paid for," he writes (Künzler, *In the Land of Blood and Tears*, 10).

16. NARA, RG 59, 867.00/651.

17. *Memurin-i Mülkiye ve Maliyenin Seferberlik Esnasındaki Vezaifini Mübeyyin Talimat*, 5–6, 8.

18. BOA, DH.IUM 93/4–1/16, 9 February 1916.

19. Ibid., E/27–18, 31 January 1917.

20. Künzler, *In the Land of Blood and Tears*, 9. The observations of the U.S. consul-general in Beirut confirm this (NARA, RG 59, 867.00/639).

21. Riggs, *Days of Tragedy*, 12.

22. Seikaly, "Unequal Fortunes," 400. Officers proudly displayed these goods, Seikaly says.

23. See numerous telegrams sent to the Armenian patriarch from the provinces. Der Yeghiayan, *My Patriarchal Memoirs*, 32–50. See also Jernazian, *Judgment unto Truth*, 46–47. Jernazian observed that "Armenian shopkeepers were almost stripped in the process, whereas Turkish shopkeepers were required to give very little." For similar observations, see Aktar and Kırmızı, "Diyarbekir, 1915," 299-301; Sürmenyan, *Harbiyeli Bir Osmanlı Ermenisi*, 50; Novichev, *Ekonomika Turtsii*, 83. I am grateful to my student Sophia Horowitz for the translations from Novichev's book. Feroz Ahmad first drew attention to this important work in his "War and Society."

24. NARA, RG 84, Damascus, vol. 24 (15 August 1914); TNA, FO 371/2146/70602, Monahan to Mallet, 14 October 1914; "Beyrout Letter," *The Near East* 174 (4 September 1914): 595; "Mobilization in Palestine," *The Near East* 175 (11 September 1914): 624. See also Çiçek, *War and State Formation*, 234.

25. Sürgevil, *II. Meşrutiyet Döneminde İzmir*, 126; "Vesait-i Nakliye," *Tanin* 2070 (27 September 1914): 3. According to some eyewitness accounts, the threat of hanging accompanied these announcements. Rado, ed., "Bir Emekli Subayın Not Defteri," 5.

26. NARA, RG 59, 867.00/639; "Beyrout Letter," *The Near East* 181 (23 October 1914): 796.

27. "Askeri Ceza Kanunnamesine Müzeyyel Kanun-ı Muvakkat," *Düstur*, İkinci Tertip, vol. 6, 16 Şevval 1332 (25 Ağustos 1914): 1258.

28. Baki, *Büyük Harpte*, 37–38, 42; Riggs, *Days of Tragedy*, 13.

29. "Tedarik-i Vesait-i Nakliye-i Askeriye Kanunnamesi," 433.

30. Baki, *Büyük Harpte*, 41; Yarbay Selahattin, *Kafkas Cephesi'nde*, 7.

31. Günday, *Hayat ve Hatıralarım*, 109; NARA, RG 59, 867.00/639.

32. TNA, FO 371/2146/70603, Major Samson to Mallet, 20 October 1914.

33. Besim Atalay, *Maraş Tarihi*, 85–86.

34. From the perspective of logistics, World War I marked a revolutionary turning point for all belligerents. Van Creveld, "Revolution in Logistics."

35. Pamuk, "Ottoman Economy," 115.

36. Ahmed Emin, *Turkey in the World War*, 85. A different source gives this number as 5,411 kilometers. Onur, *Türk Demir Yolları Tarihi*, 29.

37. Stanley, "Turkish Asiatic Railways," 189; D[ominian], "Railroads in Turkey," 934–40.

38. Zürcher, "Between Death and Desertion," 250–51.

39. Allen and Muratoff, *Caucasian Battlefields*, 224.

40. Hafız Hakkı Paşa, *Sarıkamış Günlüğü*, 57.

41. Ibid., 85; Tugay, *İbret*, 2: 180.

42. Aziz Samih, *Büyük Harpte*, 11.

43. BOA, HR.MA, 1105/38_1–3, 8 August 1914, reproduced in *Osmanlı Belgelerinde Birinci Dünya Harbi*, 1: 34–36; "Havayic-i Zaruriye Meselesi Hakkında Hükümet Tedbirleri," *İkdam* 6269 (4 August 1914): 1; "Ekmek Meselesi," *Tanin* 2039 (26 August 1914): 3.

44. Among many similar news reports, see, e.g., "Muhtekirler Divan-ı Harbe," *İkdam* 6271 (6 August 1914): 4; "Divan-ı Harb-i Örfide," *Tanin* 2047 (3 September 1914): 4.

45. This was a universal practice throughout the empire. For Beirut, see Tanielian, "Feeding the City," 744–45.

46. Sürgevil, *II. Meşrutiyet Döneminde İzmir*, 128.

47. Bell, *History of the Blockade*, 374–75.

48. Eldem, *Harp ve Mütareke Yıllarında*, 39; Chalabi, *Shi'is of Jabal 'Amil*, 46.

49. "Baghdad and the War," *The Near East* 180 (16 October 1914): 763.

50. For the prosperity of the region in the prewar period, see Sluglett, "Aleppo in Transition."

51. BOA, DH.SYS 123–2/2–5, 20 February 1915.

52. The commission would be composed of the undersecretaries of the Ministry of the Interior and Ministry of Finance and the head of the army provisioning office: BOA, MV.193/42, 7 October 1914; TNA, FO 371/2145/77254, Crawford to Tyrell, 26 November 1914.

53. BOA, DH.IUM E/14–49, 4 May 1915.

54. Öğün, *Kafkas Cephesinin*, 48.

55. BOA, DH.IUM 93/4–1/31, 7 March 1916.

56. "Turkey: Letters from Varied Scenes," *Missionary Herald* 111, no. 4 (April 1915): 191. Writing from Samsun in early 1915, William Peter reported that there was "considerable grain in stock as the crops were abundant." "Situation at Samsun," *Levant Trade Review* 4, no. 4 (March 1915): 349. See also Novichev, *Ekonomika Turtsii*, 18–19.

57. "Turkey: Light and Shade at Aintab," *Missionary Herald* 111, no. 8 (August 1915): 378.

58. Morgenthau, *Diaries*, 238.

59. Quataert, "Limited Revolution," 139–60.

60. Ibid., 159.

61. Gratien, "Mountains Are Ours," 367–68; Gratien and Pitts, "Human and Natural Disasters," 240; Pitts, "Fallow Fields," 46-47.

62. Jacobson, "Jerusalem during World War I," 90.

63. Cummings, "Economic Warfare," 59–65.

64. For this problem along the Hijaz railroad, see Ochsenwald, *Hijaz Railroad*, 134.

65. Quataert, "Age of Reforms," 821.

66. Cited from *The Times* (London), Quataert, "Agricultural Trends," 77.

67. "The Opening of the Dardanelles: Turkey's Coal Supplies," *The Near East* 220 (23 July 1915): 337. For 1910 and 1911 figures, see Quataert, *Miners and the State*, 28.

68. For production rates, see ibid., 28, 218; for labor and material shortages, 218–23.

69. For a detailed discussion of the Russian Fleet's 1915 and 1916 operations on the coal coast, see Pavlovich, *The Fleet in the First World War*, 1: 315–43, 393–417.

70. Langensiepen and Güleryüz, *Ottoman Steam Navy*, 49.

71. Cited in Halpern, *Naval War*, 114.

72. "Food Condition in the Central Powers, March–April 1917," Hoover Institution Archives, Henry Garfield Alsberg typescript.

73. "Anadolu Şimendifer Hututunda Nakliyat," *Tanin* 2148 (14 December 1914): 4.

74. Novichev, *Ekonomika Turtsii*, 72.

75. Ibid., 103.

76. Stanley, "Turkish Asiatic Railways," 194.

77. Liman von Sanders, *Five Years in Turkey*, 258. See also Beyoğlu, ed., *İki Devir Bir İnsan*, 318; McMurray, *Distant Ties*, 123–24; Range, *Vier Jahre Kampf*, 31–32.

78. NARA, RG 84, Damascus, vol. 34 (3 April 1917). For Lebanon, see Pitts, "Fallow Fields," 51-53.

79. "Muvasalat Hakkında," *Tanin* 2562 (1 February 1916): 3.

80. "News from Turkey," *The Near East* 240 (10 December 1915): 148.

81. "Smyrna and the War: Commercial and Financial Stagnation," *The Near East* 218 (9 July 1915): 280.

82. Stanley Hollis, *Supplement to Commerce Reports: Turkey, Beirut*, no. 18c (30 September 1915), 1.

83. Williams, "Economy, Environment, and Famine," 153; Çiçek, *War and State Formation*, 235.

84. Along with these wartime factors, Gratien and Pitts also emphasize the critical importance of longer-term "commercialization of agricultural production amidst substantial population growth." Gratien and Pitts, "Human and Natural Disasters," 239. On this subject, see also Pitt's recent dissertation "Fallow Fields," 38-45.

85. Cited in Foster, "1915 Locust Attack," 374. For similar descriptions, see Fawaz, *Land of Aching Hearts*, 93–96.

86. Foster, "1915 Locust Attack," 376–80. See also Gratien, "Mountains Are Ours," 372–74.

87. Thompson, *Colonial Citizens*, 21–22; Tanielian, "War of Famine," 29–30; Aksakal, "Ottoman Empire," 31.

88. Tanielian, "Feeding the City."

89. Williams, "Economy, Environment, and Famine," 156. Fawaz and Al-Qattan provide heartbreaking accounts of famine in Greater Syria. Fawaz, *Land of Aching Hearts*, 101–10; Al-Qattan, "When Mothers Ate Their Children"; Pitts, "Fallow Fields."

90. Tanielian, "Feeding the City," 738.

91. *MMZC*, Term 3, Year of Session 3, vol. 2, 13 Şubat 1332 (26 February 1917), 312. See also C.S., "Ticaret ve Ziraat Nazırıyla Mülakat," *İktisadiyat Mecmuası* 1 (21 February 1916): 6–10. For the same statistics, see Novichev, *Ekonomika Turtsii*, 19–20.

92. Price, *War & Revolution*, 135. Mahmud Kamil Pasha, the commander of the Third Army, feared that this situation would possibly have catastrophic consequences for his army. Aksakal, "Ottoman Empire," 476.

93. BOA, DH.IUM 98/2–1/36, 23 March 1916; ibid., 98/2–1/55, 13 May 1916; ibid., 98/2–1/58, 15 May 1916; Zürcher, "Little Mehmet in the Desert," 234.

94. For the government's reasoning, see *Meclis-i Umuminin Münakid Olmadığı, 1332*, 40–41.

95. "İaşe Kanun-ı Muvakkatı," *Düstur*, İkinci Tertip, vol. 8, 22 Ramazan 1334 (23 July 1916): 1230–32; Toprak, *İttihat-Terakki ve Cihan Harbi*, 138–43.

96. The first zone of provisioning would include the provinces of Istanbul, Edirne, Hüdavendigar, Konya, Ankara, Aydın, and Kastamonu and the districts (*liva*) of Bolu, Çatalca, Kale-i Sultaniye, Karesi, İzmit, Eskişehir, Kütahya, Karahisar-ı Sahib, Niğde, Menteşe, and Antalya. The second zone of provisioning would be composed of the provinces of Syria, Beirut, Adana and the districts of Aleppo (center), Jerusalem, Mount Lebanon, and İçel. The districts and provinces that remained outside of these two zones would comprise the third zone.

97. "22 Ramazan 1334 Tarihli İaşe Kanun-ı Muvakkatının Suver-i Tatbikiyesi Hakkında Nizamname," *Düstur*, İkinci Tertip, vol. 8, 13 Zilkade 1334 (11 September 1916): 1275–81.

98. Grobba, *Getreidewirtschaft*, 24–25.

99. "İaşe Meselesi," *Tanin* 2815 (15 October 1916): 1; "[T]he whole empire is being denuded of cattle and grain to feed Constantinople and the army," U.S. Ambassador Elkus reported (U.S. Department of State, *Lansing Papers*, 1: 782).

100. Beyoğlu, ed., *İki Devir Bir İnsan*, 320–21. For the confession of Ali Cenani Bey, deputy of Ayntep and a member of financial subcommittee, see *MMZC*, Term 3, Year of Session 4, vol. 3, 9 Mart 1334 (9 March 1918), 65. For the observations of Mehmet Ömer Vehbi Bey, deputy of Karesi, see *MMZC*, Term 3, Year of Session 4, vol. 3, 10 Mart 1334 (10 March 1918), 85.

101. Rogan, *Frontiers of the State*, 222.

102. BOA, DH.IUM E/20–99, 27 September 1916.

103. Ahmad, *Kurdistan during the First World War*, 135.

104. Toprak, *İttihat-Terakki ve Cihan Harbi*, 117–24; Georgeon, "1918 Osmanlı İç İstikrazı."

105. Toprak, "Osmanlı Devleti'nin Birinci Dünya Savaşı Finansmanı," 212.

106. Hasan Ferid, *Nakid ve İtibar-ı Milli*, 2: 78, 153. Bitter memories about the *kaime* (paper money) were kept alive by retelling over successive generations in families. See, e.g., Bali, ed., *Hikmet Tuna'nın*, 17.

107. Köklü, *Türkiye'de Para Meseleleri*, 19.

108. Akyıldız, *Kağıt Para*, 182. Among many newspaper articles on the issue, see "Evrak-ı Nakdiye Kabul Etmeyenler," *Tanin* 2779 (7 September 1916): 3; "Polis Müdüriyet-i Umumiyesinden," *Tanin* 2809 (7 November 1916): 3.

109. Novichev, *Ekonomika Turtsii*, 117.

110. Günday, *Hayat ve Hatıralarım*, 177.

111. For Syria, see Çiçek, *War and State Formation*, 237; Williams, "Economy, Environment, and Famine," 157.

112. For the observations of Ziya Bey, deputy from Izmit, see *MMZC*, Term 3, Year of Session 3, vol. 3, 10 Mart 1333 (10 March 1917), 149; Schilcher, "Famine of 1915–1918," 237.

113. See, e.g., the case of Çorum, which was on the border of the first and third zones of provisioning, BOA, DH.IUM E/32–46, 15 April 1917. For attempts at smuggling grain to the capital, see BOA, DH.IUM E/20–81, 24 September 1916. For the observations of a number of governors and district administrators, see BOA, DH.IUM 98/2–1/51, 3 May 1916.

114. In the revised version, the first zone of provisioning would include the provinces of Istanbul, Edirne, Hüdavendigar, Konya, Ankara, Aydın, Kastamonu (excluding the district of Sinop) and the districts (*liva*) of Bolu, Çatalca, Kale-i Sultaniye, Karesi, İzmit, Eskişehir, Kütahya, Karahisar-ı Sahib, Niğde, Menteşe, and Teke. The second zone of provisioning would be composed of the provinces of Diyarbekir and Mamuretülaziz and the districts of Maraş, Urfa, and Ayntab. The third zone would include the provinces of Sivas and Trabzon and the districts of Kayseri, Samsun, and Sinop. The provinces of Syria, Beirut, Adana, and Aleppo and the districts of Jerusalem, Mount Lebanon, and İçel would comprise the Fourth Zone. The Fifth Zone would include the province of Mosul and the district of Zor.

115. The government's proposed amendment mentions only that the previous regulations did not serve the purpose sufficiently ("maksada kafi gelmediği"): BOA, MV 247/23, 9 April 1917; BOA, DH.IUM E/32–9, 19 April 1917. For the new regulations, see "Ordu-yu Hümayun ile Ahalinin İaşesini Temin Zımnında Neşr Edilen 10 Temmuz 1332 Tarihli Kanun-ı Muvakkatın Suver-i Tatbikiyesi Hakkında 29 Ağustos 1332 Tarihli Nizamname Makamına Kaim Olmak Üzere Tanzim Olunan Nizamname," *Düstur*, İkinci Tertip, vol. 9, 20 Cemaziyelahir 1335 (12 April 1917): 646–48.

116. NARA, RG 84, Damascus, vol. 34 (3 April 1917).

117. BOA, DH.IUM E/23–87, 9 November 1916.

118. This transition has commonly been interpreted as the military prevailing over the civilian administration: Bayur, *Türk İnkılabı Tarihi*, 3: 537–38.

119. "İaşe-i Umumiye Kararnamesi," *Düstur*, İkinci Tertip, vol. 9, 29 Şevval 1335 (18 August 1917): 708–10; BOA, MV 247/87 (15 August 1917).

120. For İsmail Hakkı Pasha's dispatch on the confiscation of these goods and the role of police officers in this process, see BOA, DH.IUM E/38–95, 3 September 1917.

121. Once again, fixed prices were set for these purchases. For the additional 12.5 percent, six times the average of local prices for three years preceding the mobilization would be paid to producers, and double this price for an additional 12.5 percent.

122. Schilcher, "Famine of 1915–1918," 230, 249; Williams, "Economy, Environment, and Famine," 158–61.

123. Quoted in Ulrichsen, *Logistics and Politics*, 68.

124. Münim Mustafa, *Cepheden Cepheye*, 112–13.

125. Beşikçi, *Ottoman Mobilization*, 268–78; Gratien, "Mountains Are Ours," 397–99.

126. Enginün and Kerman, eds., *Ahmet Haşim*, 4: 69. Ahmet Haşim uses the word *zemberek*, literally, "hairspring."

127. White, *Adventuring with Anatolia College*, 88.

128. Mears, *Modern Turkey*, 289.

129. His, *German Doctor*, 174; Williams, "Economy, Environment, and Famine," 158–59.

130. Ege, *Harp Günlükleri*, 556–57.

131. Konrapa, *Bolu Tarihi*, 640.

132. Hanna, "First World War," 305.

133. Ahmad points out the emergence of a small class of "prosperous middle class" during the war years. Ahmad, "Agrarian Policy," 284; Ahmad, "War and Society," 281–82. For Syria, see Hanna, "First World War," 309.

134. Konrapa, *Bolu Tarihi*, 646.

135. *MMZC*, Term 3, Year of Session 4, vol. 3, 9 Mart 1334 (9 March 1918), 70.

136. BOA, DH.IUM E/38–74, 16 September 1917.

137. Ibid., E/39–46, 1 October 1917.

138. Ibid., E/43–37, 10 November 1917.

139. The decree was put into practice provisionally in August 1917 without the approval of parliament, which only discussed the decree in March 1918, eight months after its enactment.

140. *MMZC*, Term 3, Year of Session 4, vol. 3, 10 Mart 1334 (10 March 1918), 83.

141. See discussions in *MMZC*, Term 3, Year of Session 4, vol. 3, 10–14 Mart 1334 (10–14 March 1918), 56–74, 82–92, 129–59, 168–93, 198–222, 444–72.

142. *MMZC*, Term 3, Year of Session 4, vol. 3, 14 Mart 1334 (14 March 1918), 177. Vehip Pasha, then commander of the Third Army, thought along the same lines, saying: "It is necessary for those on the front to eat their fill and that the ones on the home front live abstemiously [*kanaatkarane*]" (Çalıka, ed., *Kurtuluş Savaşında*, 18).

143. Offer, *An Agrarian Interpretation*, 1.

144. For similar experiences in the European context, see Bonzon and Davis, "Feeding the Cities."

Chapter 5

Parts of this chapter draws on research previously published in "War, Women, and the State: The Politics of Sacrifice in the Ottoman Empire during the First World War," copyright © 2014 The Johns Hopkins University Press. It first appeared as an article in the *Journal of Women's History* 26, no. 3 (Fall 2014): 12–35.

1. The original text reads "*Umumen bir tarafa ihrac olunmamızı [isteriz] yahud denize ilka ediniz. Kanuna razı değiliz.*" BOA, DH.IUM 20/2–2/3, 31 December 1917.

2. "Kadınların Muharebeden İstifadeleri," *Sabah* 10025 (13 October 1917): 3; Karakışla, *Women, War and Work*; Lorenz, "Frauenfrage." For a recent, detailed treatment, see Van Os, "Feminism, Philanthropy," 337–78.

3. For examples, see Orga, *Portrait of a Turkish Family*; Torossian, *From Dardanelles to Palestine*, 98; Bekiroğlu, *Şair Nigar Hanım*, 110–18.

4. For the wartime struggles of a young mother and wife who lost her husband during the war and had to work in an army workshop sewing uniforms for soldiers, see Orga, *Portrait of a Turkish Family*.

5. Çolak, "Macar Etnograf Istvan Györff," 946.

6. Konrapa, *Bolu Tarihi*, 619, 641.

7. Özdemir, *Öyküleriyle Ağıtlar I*, 32.

8. M., "Kadın Tüccarlar Pazarında," *Vakit* 82 (11 January 1918): 2.

9. Falih Rıfkı, *Ateş ve Güneş*, 20. On the same subject, see also the reminiscences of Bahri Savcı, who was a child during the war. Quoted in Özdemir, *Adramyttion'dan Efeler Toprağı Edremit'e*, 348. Böcüzade Süleyman Sami recounts that conservatives in Isparta reacted against women's increasing presence in trade. *Isparta Tarihi*, 325.

10. Van Os, "Feminism, Philanthropy," 337–78; Toprak, "Osmanlı Kadınları Çalıştırma Cemiyeti"; Sarısaman, "Kadın İşçi Taburu."

11. See, e.g., Gökçe and Üster, eds., *Tevfik Sağlam*, 264.

12. "Erzurum'da Osmanlı Kadınları," *Tanin* 2172 (7 January 1915): 4. The year 1293 in the Islamic religious calendar corresponds to 1877–78. See also "Cihad ve Kadınlarımız," *Tanin* 2173 (8 January 1915): 1.

13. Çakmak, *Birinci Dünya Savaşı'nda Doğu Cephesi*, 312.

14. BOA, DH.IUM 20/1–1/14, 17 March 1918.

15. Ibid., 20/11–3/1, 1 January 1918.

16. Öğütçü, ed., *Abdülkadir Kemali'nin Anıları*, 213–15.

17. Later, during and after the War of Independence, the nationalist government in Ankara appropriated this image of the "woman with the oxcart" and turned it into a symbol of national unity and sacrifice to save the motherland. It was inscribed on the Medal of Independence (*İstiklal Madalyası*) awarded to those who fought in the War of Independence.

18. Yengin, *Drama'dan Sina-Filistin'e*, 124. See also Guhr, *Anadolu'dan Filistin'e*, 92, 95–96.

19. Güven, ed., *Yaşam Öyküm*, 78–79. For similar instances, see Eti, *Bir Onbaşının Doğu Cephesi Günlüğü*, 43, 46, 47, 49; M. Emin Zeki, *Kürdistan Tarihi*, 140.

20. White, *Adventuring with Anatolia College*, 88.

21. Dr. Muslihiddin Safvet, *Ankara Vilayeti*, 55–56. See also Mehmed Hayri, *Niğde Sancağı*, 167–68.

22. The writer of the diary, Ihsan Tourjman, mentions Jewish, Christian, and Muslim prostitutes. Tamari, ed., *Year of the Locust*, 114. See also Jacobson, "Negotiating Ottomanism," 76–78; Fawaz, *Land of Aching Hearts*, 117–19. For prostitution among the survivors of the Armenian Genocide, see Üngör, "Orphans, Converts," 186–89. The unprecedented expansion of prostitution led to an equally unprecedented spread of venereal diseases, most notably syphilis. Yılmaz, "Love in the Time of Syphilis," 237–81.

23. Sapancalı H. Hüseyin, *Karaman Ahval-i İctimaiyye*, 77.

24. BOA, DH.IUM E/36-3, 13 June 1917.

25. Çalıka, ed., *Kurtuluş Savaşında*, 18. Sergeant Berkli Muhittin witnessed similar incidents of sexual exploitation in exchange of daily bread. Sabuncuoğlu, *Çorum Tarihine Ait*, 103.

26. See, e.g., Yılmaz, "Love in the Time of Syphilis," 263–67; Özbek, "Regulation of Prostitution"; Toprak, "İstanbul'da Fuhuş." See also Bali, ed., *Jews and Prostitution*.

27. Van Os, "Feminism, Philanthropy," 352–60; Karakışla, *Women, War and Work*; Toprak, "Osmanlı Kadınları Çalıştırma Cemiyeti." The second article of the Society for the Employment of Ottoman Muslim Women states that its aim was to "safeguard women by accustoming them to moral maintenance of livelihood through finding them employment." *Kadınları Çalıştırma Cemiyet-i İslamiyesi, Nizamname*, 2.

28. Shilo, *Princess or Prisoner?* 123. Much of this work was done by women themselves. See also idem., "Women as Victims of War."

29. Tanielian, "Politics of Wartime Relief," 76.

30. "Zavallı Köylülerimiz," *Ses* (5 December 1918), quoted in Çantay, *Kara Günler*, 53. For the postwar turmoil in the region, see Gingeras, *Sorrowful Shores*, 55–104. For similar incidences from central Anatolia, see Peker, *Tüfek Omza*, 275, 296.

31. For examples, see Çamurdan, *Doğu Kilikya*, 83; Güvemli, *Bir Zamanlar Ordu*, 51.

32. Moreau, *L'Empire ottoman à l'âge des réformes*, 52–65; Zürcher, "Ottoman Conscription System," 86–87.

33. Erkin, *Hatırat*, 121; Van Os, "Taking Care of Soldiers' Families," 97; Beşikçi, *Ottoman Mobilization*, 142–43.

34. Hafız Hakkı, *Bozgun*, 145–46.

35. Kaymakam Behiç [Erkin], *Mükellefiyet-i Askeriye*, 9. For a similar emphasis, see also his memoirs, Erkin, *Hatırat*, 121.

36. Koz, "Bir Ozan, Bir Destan," 7584. The terms *muinli* and *muinsiz* refer to the families with and without breadwinners, respectively.

37. Van Os, "Taking Care of Soldiers' Families," 96–97.

38. For poor relief in the late Ottoman Empire, see Özbek, *Osmanlı İmparatorluğu'nda Sosyal Devlet*.

39. For Britain and France, see Pedersen, *Family Dependence*, 79–133. For Russia, see Pyle, "Village Social Relations."

40. Pedersen, "Gender, Welfare, and Citizenship," 985.

41. Healy, *Vienna and the Fall of the Habsburg Empire*, 193–97; Davis, *Home Fires Burning*, 32–45; Daniel, *War from Within*, 182–84.

42. For the details of the law, see Van Os, "Taking Care of Soldiers' Families," 97–99; Van Os, "Feminism, Philanthropy," 307–17.

43. BOA, DH.IUM 4/3–9/57, 15 May 1916.

44. Ibid., E/8–58, 16 July 1915; BOA, DH.HMŞ 23/120, 16 July 1915.

45. In March 1917, Minister of Finance Cavid Bey confirmed to parliament the widespread rumors about the corruption involved in the assignment and distribution of women's pensions. *MMZC*, Term 3, Year of Session 3, vol. 3, 11 Mart 1333 (11 March 1917), 186. For a more detailed discussion of the implementation of the scheme on the ground, see Akın, "Ottoman Home Front," 147–53.

46. *1332–1333 Meclis-i Mebusan Encümen Mazbataları*, 279.

47. BOA, DH.IUM 88/3–4/39, 7 May 1916.

48. Gelvin, *Divided Loyalties*, 23. For examples from around the empire, see BOA, DH.IUM 88/3–4/30, 11 March 1916; ibid., 88/3–4/34, 29 March 1916; ibid., E/23–47, 11 May 1917.

49. BOA, DH.IUM 4/1–41, 2 May 1916.

50. See, e.g., Hamdullah Emin Pasha's (Antalya) complaints in *MMZC*, Term 3, Year of Session 3, vol. 1, 29 Kanunuevvel 1332 (11 January 1917), 321.

51. *MMZC*, Term 3, Year of Session 3, vol. 1, 8 Kanunuevvel 1332 (1 December 1916), 185.

52. The situation was particularly dire in Arab provinces. Gelvin, *Divided Loyalties*, 23; Hudson, *Transforming Damascus*, 127–30.

53. BOA, DH.IUM E/15–51, 10 January 1916.

54. *MMZC*, Term 3, Year of Session 2, vol. 1, 26 Kanunusani 1331 (8 February 1916), 511.

55. *MMZC*, Term 3, Year of Session 1, vol. 1, 8 Kanunuevvel 1330 (21 December 1914), 26. See also "Sevişelim ve Çalışalım," *Tanin* 2034 (21 August 1914): 1.

56. See, e.g., "Seferberlikde Ahalinin Vazifesi," *İkdam* 6318 (23 September 1914): 1; "Asker Aileleri Hakkında," *Tanin* 2100 (27 October 1914): 4.

57. "Bir Fazilet Dersi," *İctihad* 126 (28 January 1915): 462. For a detailed account on the activities of the society, see Van Os, "Aiding the Poor Soldiers' Families," 255–89.

58. İrfan Bedri, "Asker Ailelerine Elimizden Gelen Her Türlü Yardım En Büyük Vazifemiz," *Tanin* 2189 (24 January 1915): 3.

59. "Asker Ailelerine Yardımcı Hanımlar Heyeti Faaliyeti," *Tanin* 2186 (21 January 1915): 3; *Osmanlı Hilal-i Ahmer Cemiyeti*, 54–55.

60. Akın, "Hatıra-i Celadet Topu"; Van Os, "Aiding Poor Soldiers' Families," 268–71. See also "Hatıra-i Celadet: Resm-i Müşaşa Münasebetiyle," *Servet-i Fünun* 1295 (13 April 1916): 250.

61. Polat, *Müdafaa-i Milliye Cemiyeti*, 71, 85, 213.

62. Aksoy, *Bir Kent, Bir İnsan*, 134–38; Bayar, *Ben de Yazdım*, 5: 1545–46.

63. "Osmanlı Hanımlarına," *Tanin* 2227 (3 March 1915): 3.

64. "Müdafaa-i Milliye Cemiyeti," *İkdam* 6324 (29 September 1914): 2.

65. Ahmed Hamdi Aksekili, "Zekatınızı Asker Ailelerine Veriniz," *Sebilürreşad* 343 (June 1331 [1915]): 36–37; Hacı Abdülhamid Hamid El-Berzenci, *Fezail-i Cihad*, 24–25. See also Beşikçi, *Ottoman Mobilization*, 75, 145.

66. Ahmed Emin, *Turkey in the World War*, 231–38; Toprak, "Family, Feminism, and the State."

67. This is not to say that Ottoman women did not interact with governmental officials in the years preceding World War I. Before the war, women engaged with the representatives of the state on many occasions. See, e.g., Quataert, "Machine Breaking"; Kark and Fischel, "Palestinian Women in the Public Domain." Wartime conditions, however, dramatically increased the frequency of these interactions.

68. Metinsoy, "Osmanlı Kadınlarının"; idem, "Ordinary Ottoman Women," 26–30; Kutluata, "Ottoman Women and the State."

69. BOA, DH.IUM E/14–117, 3 April 1916.

70. BOA, DH.IUM 20/11–3/18, 20 February 1918.

71. BOA, DH.IUM E/80–35, 7 October 1916.

72. BOA, DH.IUM 20/4–2/72, 3 October 1918.

73. Here my use of the term "political" is inspired by Keith Michael Baker, who defines it as a general process of "making claims; as the activity through which individuals and groups in any society articulate, negotiate, implement, and enforce the competing claims they make upon one another and upon the whole." This conceptualization offers historians the advantage of rescuing politics from the monopoly of elite circles, parliamentary debates, and governmental decrees and providing a new analytical lens to the everyday experiences of broader segments of society. Baker, *Inventing the French Revolution*, 4.

74. BOA, DH.IUM 20/3–2/33, 11 May 1918.

75. BOA, DH.IUM E/24–35, 22 November 1916.

76. Instead of working for the provisioning of the nation and the army, the women claimed, they were now spending time idly [due to lack of seed grain]. Here, women successfully managed to relate their needs to those of the nation and its fighting forces. BOA, DH.IUM E/33–65, 8 April 1917.

77. BOA, DH.IUM E/8–83, 8 April 1915.

78. In several other petitions women highlighted the contrast between themselves and state officials, whom, they argued, were receiving their salaries in a timely manner. See, e.g., the petition of soldiers' families from Alaşehir in BOA, DH.IUM E/23–19, 31 October 1916; the petition of Nefise from Silifke in BOA, DH.IUM 88/2–4/38, 15 June 1915; the petition of Şükriye, Adile, Refike, Aişe from Yozgat in BOA, DH.IUM 20/4–2/72, 3 October 1918. In fact, state officials throughout the empire also suffered significantly from wartime inflation and the government's failure to pay their salaries regularly. See also Metinsoy, "Osmanlı Kadınlarının," 58–59.

79. BOA, DH.IUM 20/11–3/44, 10 April 1918.

80. BOA, DH.IUM E/23–2, 28 October 1916.

81. BOA, DH.IUM 88/3–4/31, 22 February 1916.

82. BOA, DH.IUM E/25–50, 17 December 1916. The district governor of Boğazlıyan,

Mehmed Kemal Bey, was found guilty and hanged in 1919 for his role in the deportation of Armenians. See Bilgi, *Ermeni Tehciri*. For more on the forced conversion process, see Akçam, *Ermenilerin Zorla Müslümanlaştırılması*, 77–243.

83. The archival material in the Prime Ministry Ottoman Archives does not enable us to determine the extent to which non-Muslims were denied allowances.

Chapter 6

1. See, e.g., "Asker Kaçakları," *Tanin* 2032 (19 August 1914): 4; "Asker Kaçakları," *Tanin* 2048 (4 September 1914): 1; "Divan-ı Harb-i Örfide," *Tanin* 2059 (16 September 1914): 2; "Rum Firariler," *Tasvir-i Efkar* 1185 (31 August 1914): 3.

2. *Karagöz* 633 (4 July 1914): 4.

3. Akçam, *Young Turks' Crime*, 97–123; Dündar, *Türkiye'nin Şifresi*, 230–46; Morack, "Ottoman Greeks," 222–23; Berber, *Sancılı Yıllar*, 57–72.

4. MMZC, Term 3, Year of Session 3, vol. 1, 10 Kanunuevvel 1332 (23 December 1916), 212.

5. Bardakçı, ed., *Talat Paşa'nın Evrak-ı Metrukesi*, 79.

6. Kieser and Bloxham, "Genocide," 600. Dündar, *Türkiye'nin Şifresi*, 246, estimates 150,000–250,000.

7. Akçam, *Young Turks' Crime*, 99–105.

8. Ahmed Emin, *Turkey in the World War*, 210.

9. "Mersin'de Ermeniler," *Tanin* 2120 (16 November 1914): 1; "Teyid-i Sadakat," *Tanin* 2130 (26 November 1914): 2; "Ermeni Etibba Cemiyeti'nin Hamiyeti," *Tanin* 2139 (5 December 1914): 3; "İzmir Ermenilerinin Vatanperverliği," *Tanin* 2139 (5 December 1914): 3; "Ermeni Patrikhanesinin Teşebbüsat-ı Vatanperveranesi," *Tasvir-i Efkar* 1251 (6 November 1914): 3; "Harput ve Sivas Ermenilerinin Hamiyeti," *Tanin* 2213 (17 February 1915): 2.

10. Mkhalian, *Bardizag*, 335.

11. Suny, *They Can Live*, 231.

12. Morgenthau, *Diaries*, 217.

13. Baykoç, *Büyük Harpte*, 12; Aziz Samih, *Büyük Harpte*, 33.

14. Suny, *They Can Live*, 251.

15. Üngör, *Making of Modern Turkey*, 61, 66–67. For a recent, most comprehensive treatment of the Van incident, see Türkyılmaz, "Rethinking Genocide."

16. Bloxham, "Development of the Armenian Genocide," 268; Dündar, *Crime of Numbers*, 80–83.

17. Dündar, *Crime of Numbers*, 90–93.

18. Özel, "Tehcir ve Teşkilat-ı Mahsusa."

19. See, e.g., Üngör, *Making of Modern Turkey*, 71–83.

20. Suny, *They Can Live*, 362. There were also many Ottomans who resisted the government's orders and helped Armenians. Gerçek, *Akıntıya Karşı*.

21. Odian, *Accursed Years*, 88.

22. Ege, *Harp Günlükleri*, 233.

23. Bjørnlund, "'A Fate Worse Than Dying'"; Derderian, "Common Fate."

24. Riggs, *Days of Tragedy*, 98–99; Sarafian, "Absorption of Armenian Women."

25. Svazlian, *Armenian Genocide*, 83.

26. Chitjian, *Hair's Breadth*, 100–101. For Armenian orphans, see Üngör, "Orphans, Converts," 175–81.

27. Watenpaugh, *Bread from Stones*, 124–56; Ekmekçioğlu, "Climate for Abduction."

28. Akçam, *Young Turks' Crime*, 196; Göçek, *Denial of Violence*, 227.

29. Dündar, *Crime of Numbers*, 94–103.

30. For detailed discussion of this process, see Üngör and Polatel, *Confiscation and Destruction*; Akçam and Kurt, *Kanunların Ruhu*, 31–48; Kaiser, "Armenian Property."

31. Akçam, *Young Turks' Crime*, 258.

32. Dündar, *Crime of Numbers*, 150–51.

33. Cavid Bey, *Meşrutiyet Ruznamesi*, 3: 135.

34. Yeğinatı, *Büyük Harbin Başında*, 21.

35. Akkılıç, ed., *Askerin Romanı*, 116–17. Akkılıç states that his unit was assigned the duty to "attack these [non-Muslim] groups who tried to flee towards Kars."

36. Leverkuehn, *German Officer*, xxxvi.

37. Sanborn, "Unsettling the Russian Empire," 313.

38. Refugees who did not apply for state assistance but migrated and settled with their own resources were not included in this number. ATASE, no. 1/2, kls.361, dos.1445, fih.15–22, 23 reproduced in *Askeri Tarih Belgeleri Dergisi* 81 (1982): 219–22.

39. *MAZC*, Term 3, Year of Session 3, vol. 1, 22 Kanunuevvel 1332 (4 January 1917), 225–26. Şükrü (Kaya) Bey was later the early Turkish Republic's interior minister.

40. *MMZC*, Term 3, Year of Session 4, vol. 1, 22 Kanunuevvel 1333 (22 December 1917), 361.

41. Citing the population statistics of the Ottoman state in the year 1914, Karpat, *Ottoman Population*, 189, puts the total at 18,520,016.

42. BOA, DUIT 27/1–1, 2 March 1916; "Aşair ve Muhacirin Müdüriyet-i Umumiyesi Teşkilatı Hakkında Kanun," *Düstur*, İkinci Tertip, vol. 8, 7 Cemaziyelevvel 1334 (12 March 1916): 661–62. The Directorate of Tribes and Refugees (Aşair ve Muhacirin Müdüriyet-i Umumiyesi) replaced the Directorate for the Settlement of Tribes and Refugees (İskan-ı Aşair ve Muhacirin Müdüriyeti), which was founded primarily for the purpose of dealing with the refugee crisis created by the Balkan Wars.

43. For the long history of the Ottoman state's attempts to settle and "civilize" the tribes, see Kasaba, *Moveable Empire*; Dündar, *İttihat ve Terakki'nin Müslümanları*, 52–56.

44. For a summary of the institutional history of the refugee problem, see Dündar, *İttihat ve Terakki'nin Müslümanları*, 57–62; İpek, "Birinci Dünya Savaşı Esnasında," 179–81; Kaya, *Vilayat-ı Şarkiyye*, 1–6; Ağanoğlu, *Osmanlı'dan Cumhuriyet'e*, 149–55; Blumi, *Ottoman Refugees*, 43-65.

45. First route: Black Sea coast; second route: Sivas–Tokat–Amasya–Çorum–Yozgat–Ankara; third route: Kemah–Harput–Malatya–Besni; fourth route: Diyarbekir–Urfa–Maraş–Adana. *MAZC*, Term 3, Year of Session 3, vol. 1, 22 Kanunuevvel 1332 (4 January 1917), 227.

46. *Menatık-ı Harbiyeden Vürud Eden.*

47. Ibid., 1. These provinces were Adana, Diyarbekir, Aleppo, Mamuretülaziz, Mosul, Sivas, and Van, as well as the *sancak*s of Canik, Maraş, Urfa, and Zor.

48. For instance, due to the concern that two hundred thousand refugees massed in Diyarbekir would put the provisioning of the Second Army at risk, the army head command ordered the dispersal of these refugees to other provinces. BOA, DH.ŞFR 73/99, 13 July 1917.

49. *Menatık-ı Harbiyeden Vürud Eden,* 2.

50. BOA, DH.IUM E/32–46, 13 May 1917.

51. BOA, DH.HMŞ 27/72, 14 December 1916.

52. In Samsun, e.g., the U.S. vice-consul organized a soup kitchen that distributed food to a thousand refugees on a daily basis. Kieser, *Verpasste Friede,* 349–50. In Urfa, the Swiss missionary doctor Jakob Künzler organized a relief effort to distribute grain to arriving refugees. Künzler, *In the Land of Blood and Tears,* 68–69.

53. BOA, DH.IUM E/16–44, 4 August 1916; BOA, DH.ŞFR 70/18, 15 November 1916.

54. *MAZC,* Term 3, Year of Session 3, vol. 2, 12 Mart 1333 (12 March 1917), 214.

55. *MMZC,* Term 3, Year of Session 4, vol. 1, 17 Teşrinisani 1333 (17 November 1917), 60; BOA, DH.IUM 98–4/1–48, 28 October 1917; BOA, DH.IUM 20–2/2–7, 26 December 1917. An adult refugee would be given 400 grams of flour (or 600 grams of bread) daily; a child was entitled to 300 grams of flour (or 450 grams of bread).

56. Lermioğlu, *Akçaabat Tarihi,* 225, 260, 262.

57. *MAZC,* Term 3, Year of Session 4, vol. 1, 3 Kanunusani 1334 (3 January 1918), 208.

58. Lermioğlu, *Akçaabat Tarihi,* 264.

59. Künzler, *In the Land of Blood and Tears,* 76–77. For similar observations on the misery of refugee children, see Erginsoy, ed., *Dedem Hüseyin Atıf Beşe,* 193.

60. McCarthy, *Death and Exile,* 222.

61. *MAZC,* Term 3, Year of Session 4, vol. 1, 23 Şubat 1334 (23 February 1918), 425. Other members of the senate mentioned that they had received similar telegrams.

62. The Ottoman state authorities' attempts to change the demographic structure of certain regions to which they assigned strategic importance started well before World War I. For the settlement of 1877–78 refugees from the Caucasus and Rumelia in Thrace and Gallipoli, see İpek, *Rumeli'den Anadolu'ya;* Deringil, "Göç Olgusu Üzerine."

63. Üngör, *Making of Modern Turkey,* 110; Dündar, *İttihat ve Terakki'nin Müslümanları,* 137–55.

64. BOA, DH.ŞFR 63/172, 2 May 1916, reproduced in Dündar, *İttihat ve Terakki'nin Müslümanları,* 141.

65. *Menatık-ı Harbiyeden Vürud Eden,* 4.

66. BOA, DH.ŞFR 66/206, 17 July 1916.

67. BOA, DH.ŞFR 63/188, 4 May 1916, reproduced in Dündar, *İttihat ve Terakki'nin Müslümanları,* 144.

68. BOA, DH.ŞFR 63/283, 11 May 1916.

69. Ahmet İzzet Paşa, *Feryadım,* 1: 256–57.

70. Adanır and Kaiser, "Migration, Deportation," 283.

71. BOA, DH.ŞFR 63/67, 10 May 1916; ibid., 61/122, 21 June 1916; ibid., 61/124, 30 September 1916; Üngör, *Making of Modern Turkey*, 119–20.

72. Lermioğlu, *Akçaabat Tarihi*, 261.

73. Kieser, *Verpasste Friede*, 484.

74. BOA, MV 198/163, 30 May 1915; BOA, DH.ŞFR 54/189, 27 June 1915.

75. BOA, DH.ŞFR 54/15, 14 June 1915; ibid., 54/136, 24 June 1915.

76. Riggs, *Days of Tragedy*, 180.

77. BOA, DH.SN.M 35/99, 2 March 1915.

78. Riggs, *Days of Tragedy*, 180. See also Cebeciyan, *Bir Ermeni Subayın*, 134.

79. "Current News," *New Armenia* 8 (1 August 1916): 265.

80. Altınbilek and Kır, *Kafkas Cephesi, 3. Ordu Harekatı*, 39–40, 44.

81. See, e.g., Koloğlu Safiye Duman's memories of her family's migration. İlker, *Artvin Zeytinlik Bucağı*, 45–46.

82. Aziz Samih, *Büyük Harpte*, 17, 19, 98. Heart-rending sights such as these are recounted in many other eyewitness accounts. For examples, see Guhr, *Anadolu'dan Filistin'e*, 35; Çanlı, ed., *Hüseyin Avni Gençoğlu'nun Hatıraları*, 70.

83. Aydemir, *Suyu Arayan Adam*, 85. For similar observations, see Süleyman Nuri, *Uyanan Esirler*, 90.

84. *Ermeniler Tarafından Yapılan*, 1: 13.

85. Leverkuehn, *German Officer*, lxxii.

86. Ataman, *Esaret Yılları*, 73. For similar observations, see Akkılıç, ed., *Askerin Romanı*, 166.

87. Aziz Samih, *Büyük Harpte*, 95. The government announced through street criers that Erzurum was strong enough to hold out for two years even if it was surrounded [by the enemy]: "Do not be afraid, do not flee. There is no need to be miserable on the roads." Önal, ed., *Tuğgeneral Ziya Yergök'ün Anıları*, 259.

88. Uzer, *Makedonya Eşkiyalık Tarihi*, 337.

89. Lermioğlu, *Akçaabat Tarihi*, 225, 260; Aksoy, ed., *Bir Ömür Bir Şehir*, 209.

90. Kayra, *Hoşça Kal Trabzon*, 44.

91. Öksüz and Usta, *Mustafa Reşit Tarakçıoğlu*, 128.

92. Lermioğlu, *Akçaabat Tarihi*, 260; Öksüz and Usta, *Mustafa Reşit Tarakçıoğlu*, 131.

93. Kocal, *Ömrümün 90 Yılından*, 43; Gedikoğlu, *Trabzon Efsaneleri*, 97.

94. Aydemir, *Suyu Arayan Adam*, 84.

95. Yaşar Kemal's family, located originally in the village of Ernis on Lake Van, departed along with the entire village population in the spring of 1915. After a year and a half of migration, his family was the only remnant of this group that was able to reach Çukurova. Yaşar Kemal, *Yaşar Kemal Kendini Anlatıyor*, 21.

96. San, *Rusların Gümüşhane İlini İşgali*, 80.

97. *MAZC*, Term 3, Year of Session 3, vol. 2, 12 Mart 1333 (12 March 1917), 213. This number dropped to 5 percent as a result of an intensive vaccination campaign. No similar measure was taken for the Armenian deportees.

98. Aziz Samih, *Büyük Harpte*, 73. Some officers, however, tried to save at least some of these children from misery. Mustafa Kemal Pasha (later Atatürk) took a twelve-year-

old refugee orphan child, Ömer, with him. Three more orphans were brought to him, but he only gave money to them. Tezer, ed., *Atatürk'ün Hatıra Defteri*, 71.

99. See, e.g., Güvemli, *Bir Zamanlar Ordu*, 23.

100. Muzaffer Lermioğlu narrates the story of a young soldier's wife who committed suicide after losing three children to starvation. Lermioğlu, *Akçaabat Tarihi*, 260–61.

101. Yaşar Kemal, *Yaşar Kemal Kendini Anlatıyor*, 23.

102. Riggs, *Days of Tragedy*, 181. For the increased prices in Trabzon, see Kayra, *Hoşça Kal Trabzon*, 47–48.

103. İlker, *Artvin Zeytinlik Bucağı*, 46; Aydemir, *Suyu Arayan Adam*, 84.

104. Öksüz and Usta, *Mustafa Reşit Tarakçıoğlu*, 134.

105. Künzler, *In the Land of Blood and Tears*, 68.

106. San, *Rusların Gümüşhane İlini İşgali*, 91.

107. Riggs, *Days of Tragedy*, 178.

108. Sezen, ed., *İki Kardeşten Seferberlik*, 112.

109. Güvemli, *Bir Zamanlar Ordu*, 22. The suffix *-zade*, Persian for "son of," was usually an indicator of a family's elite status.

110. Without providing much detail, Lermioğlu mentions in his memoirs that every day they witnessed many of these tragedies. Lermioğlu, *Akçaabat Tarihi*, 264. In his diary, Hüseyin Atıf Bey complains about officers fornicating with refugee women, who could be had for a slice of bread. Erginsoy, ed., *Dedem Hüseyin Atıf Beşe*, 225.

111. Albayrak, *Doğu Karadeniz Muharebesi*, 188. See also Öztürkmen, "Remembering Conflicts in a Black Sea Town."

112. Gedikoğlu, *Trabzon Efsaneleri*, 97.

113. *MMZC*, Term 3, Year of Session 5, vol. 1, 23 Teşrinisani 1334 (23 November 1918), 188–90, 253–54, 276–80. Ahmed Refik, *Kafkas Yollarında*.

114. BOA, DH.ŞFR 84/186, 20 February 1918; *Ahval ve Zaruret-i Harbiye Neticesiyle*. For details of refugees' return, see İpek, "Birinci Dünya Savaşı Esnasında," 206–15.

115. Dündar, *İttihat ve Terakki'nin Müslümanları*, 88–92.

116. Shaw, "Resettlement of Refugees in Anatolia."

117. BOA, DH.ŞFR 96/7, 1 February 1919, reproduced in *Osmanlı Belgelerinde Ermeniler*, 211.

118. Gatrell, "Refugees and Forced Migrants"; Proctor, *Civilians in a World at War*, 113–24; Kuschner and Knox, *Refugees in an Age of Genocide*, 43–63.

Conclusion

1. Falih Rıfkı, *Ateş ve Güneş*, 15.

2. I borrow the term "continuum of crisis" from Holquist's *Making War, Forging Revolution*.

3. Pırnar and Pırnar, *Baba Oğul Anıları*, 1: 64. See also Atay, *Zeytindağı*, 139.

4. Apak, *Garp Cephesi Nasıl Kuruldu?* 43.

5. Çağlar, *Hüsrev Bey Heyet-i Nasihası*, 66.

6. Zürcher, *Unionist Factor*.

7. Tamari, ed., *Year of the Locust*, 5. See also Khalidi, "Arab Experience," 648; Fawaz, *Land of Aching Hearts*, 238–48.

8. Falih Rıfkı, *Ateş ve Güneş*, 27.

BIBLIOGRAPHY

Archival Sources

Başbakanlık Osmanlı Arşivi (BOA, Prime Ministry Ottoman Archives), Istanbul

Dahiliye Nezareti
Emniyet-i Umumiye (DH.EUM)
Hukuk Müşavirliği (DH.HMŞ)
İdari Kısım (DH.İD)
İdare-i Umumiye (DH.İUM)
Kalem-i Mahsus Müdüriyeti (DH.KMS)
Mebani-i Emiriye ve Hapishaneler Müdüriyeti (DH.MB.HPS)
Şifre Kalemi (DH.ŞFR)
Siyasi Kısım (DH.SYS)
Dosya Usulü İradeler (İ.DUİT)
Meclis-i Vükela Mazbataları (MV)

The U.S. National Archives and Records Administration (NARA), College Park, Maryland

Record Group 59, Records of the Department of State
Records of the Department of State Relating to Internal Affairs of Turkey, 1910–1929 (microfilm)
Record Group 84, U.S. Consular Archives
Baghdad; Beirut; Damascus; Istanbul; Trebizond (Trabzon)

The National Archives (TNA; formerly Public Record Office), London

FO 195, Foreign Office, Embassy and Consulates, Turkey (formerly Ottoman Empire), General Correspondence
FO 371, Foreign Office, Political Departments, General Correspondence, 1906–1966

Hoover Institution Library & Archives, Palo Alto, California

Ernest Wilson Riggs Papers
Henry Garfield Alsperg Typescript
Ruth A. Parmelee Papers

Newspapers and Periodicals

Daily Consular and Trade Reports
Harb Mecmuası
İkdam
İktisadiyat Mecmuası
Levant Trade Review
Missionary Herald
The Near East
The Orient
Sabah
Sebilürreşad
Servet-i Fünun
Tasvir-i Efkar (Tasfir-i Efkar)
Tanin (Cenin, Renin, Senin)
Tercüman-ı Hakikat
Türk Yurdu

Official Publications

Ahval ve Zaruret-i Harbiye Neticesiyle Bir Müddet İşgal Altında Kalmış Olan Vilayat Ahalisinden Dahile Mecbur-ı İltica Olanların Suret-i Sevk ve İadesi Hakkında Talimatname. Istanbul: Matbaa-i Amire, 1334 [1918].

Akbay, Cemal. Birinci Dünya Harbi'nde Türk Harbi. Vol. 1, Osmanlı İmparatorluğu'nun Siyasi ve Askeri Hazırlıkları ve Harbe Girişi. Ankara: Genelkurmay Askeri Tarih ve Stratejik Etüt Başkanlığı Yayınları, 1991.

Altınbilek, Hakkı, and Naci Kır. Birinci Dünya Harbi'nde Türk Harbi. Vol. 2, pt. 1, Kafkas Cephesi, 3ncü Ordu Harekatı. Ankara: Genelkurmay Basımevi, 1993.

Bell, A. C. A History of the Blockade of Germany and the Countries Associated with Her in the Great War, Austria-Hungary, Bulgaria, and Turkey, 1914–1918. London: Her Majesty's Stationery Office, 1961 [1937].

Besbelli, Saim. Birinci Dünya Harbi'nde Türk Harbi. Vol. 8, Deniz Harekatı. Ankara: Genelkurmay Harp Tarihi Yayınları, 1976.

1331 (1915) Senesi Meclis-i Mebusan Encümen Mazbataları ve Levayih-i Kanuniyye. Vol. 1. Ankara: TBMM Basımevi, 1992.

1332–1333 Meclis-i Mebusan Encümen Mazbataları ve Levayih-i Kanuniyye. Vol. 1. Ankara: TBMM Basımevi, 1993.

British Documents on Foreign Affairs: Reports and Papers from the Foreign Office Confidential Print. Series B, The Near East and Middle East, 1856–1914. Vol. 20. Frederick, MD: University Publications of America, 1985.

Ermeniler Tarafından Yapılan Katliam Belgeleri. Vol. 1. Ankara: Devlet Arşivleri Genel Müdürlüğü Yayınları, 2001.

Hallı, Reşat. Balkan Harbi (1912–1913). Vol. 1, Harbin Sebepleri, Askeri Hazırlıklar ve Osmanlı Devletinin Harbe Girişi. Ankara: Genelkurmay Basımevi, 1970.

İskan-ı Muhacirin Nizamnamesi. Istanbul: Matbaa-i Amire, 1329 [1913].

Kadınları Çalıştırma Cemiyet-i İslamiyesi, Nizamname. Istanbul: Matbaa-i Askeriye, 1332 [1916].

Meclis-i Ayan Zabıt Cerideleri. Ankara: TBMM Basımevi, 1991. Cited as *MAZC.*

Meclis-i Mebusan Zabıt Cerideleri. Ankara: TBMM Basımevi, 1991. Cited as *MMZC.*

Meclis-i Umuminin Mün'akid Olmadığı Esnada Hey'et-i Vükelaca Ba-İrade-i Seniyye Mevki-i İcraya Konulan Levayih-i Kanuniyye, 1332. Ankara: n.p., n.d.

Memurin-i Mülkiye ve Maliyenin Seferberlik Esnasındaki Vezaifini Mübeyyin Talimat. Istanbul: Matbaa-i Askeriye, 1327 [1909].

Menatık-ı Harbiyeden Vürud Eden Mültecilerin Sevk, İskan, İaşe ve İkdarlarını Mübeyyin Talimatname. Istanbul: Matbaa-i Osmaniye, 1332 [1916].

Osmanlı Belgelerinde Birinci Dünya Harbi. 2 vols. Istanbul: Başbakanlık Devlet Arşivleri Genel Müdürlüğü, 2013.

Osmanlı Belgelerinde Ermeniler (1915–1920). Ankara: Devlet Arşivleri Genel Müdürlüğü Yayınları, 1995.

"30'uncu Tümenin Harp Ceridesi." *Askeri Tarih Belgeleri Dergisi* no. 122 (2009).

Özdemir, Bülent, and Abdülmecit Mutaf, eds. *Çanakkale Muharebatı: Cihan Harbinde Osmanlı Harekat-ı Tarihçesi.* Ankara: Türk Tarih Kurumu, 2012.

Sansür Talimatnamesi. Istanbul: Matbaa-i Askeriye, 1330 [1914].

Sene 1334 Meclis-i Mebusan Encümen Mazbataları ve Levayih-i Kanuniyye. Vol. 2. Ankara: TBMM Basımevi, 1993.

Türk Silahlı Kuvvetleri Tarihi. Vol. 3, pt. 6, *(1908–1920).* Ankara: Genelkurmay Basımevi, 1971.

United States. Department of State. *Papers Relating to the Foreign Relations of the United States: The Lansing Papers, 1914–1920.* Vol. 1. Washington, DC: Government Printing Office, 1939.

Published Memoirs, Diaries, Interviews, Letters, Literary Pieces, and Speeches

Aaronsohn, Alexander. *With the Turks in Palestine.* Boston: Houghton Mifflin, 1916.

Abdullah Cevdet. "Harbiye Nazırımız Enver Paşa Hazretleriyle Mülakat." *İçtihad* 103 (1330 [1914]): 45–50.

Abdullah Paşa. *1328 Balkan Harbi'nde Şark Ordusu Kumandanı Abdullah Paşa'nın Balkan Harbi Hatıratı.* Edited by Tahsin Yıldırım and İbrahim Öztürkçü. Istanbul: Dün Bugün Yarın Yayınları, 2012 [1920].

Abramson, Glenda, ed. *Soldiers' Tales: Two Palestinian Jewish Soldiers in the Ottoman Army during the First World War.* London: Vallentine Mitchell, 2013.

Ahmed Refik. *Kafkas Yollarında: Hatıralar ve Tahassüsler.* Istanbul: Kitabhane-i İslam ve Askeri, 1919.

Ahmet İzzet Paşa. *Feryadım.* Vol. 1. Istanbul: Nehir Yayınları, 1992.

Ahmet Şerif. *Anadolu'da Tanin.* 2 vols. Edited by Mehmed Çetin Börekçi. Ankara: Türk Tarih Kurumu, 1999.

Akkılıç, Yılmaz, ed. *Askerin Romanı: E. Sv. Alb. Abdülhalim Akkılıç'ın Savaş ve Barış Anıları*. Kocaeli: Körfez Ofset Yayınları, 1994.

Aksoy, Hikmet, ed. *Bir Ömür Bir Şehir: Trabzonlu Gazeteci Cevdet Alap'ın Anıları*. Trabzon: Trabzon Gazeteciler Cemiyeti Yayınları, 2008.

Aksoy, Yaşar. *Bir Kent, Bir İnsan: İzmir'in Son Yüzyılı, S. Ferit Eczacıbaşı'nın Yaşamı ve Anıları*. Istanbul: Dr. Nejat F. Eczacıbaşı Vakfı Yayınları, 1986.

Ali Ekrem. *Ordunun Defteri*. Istanbul: Ahmed İhsan ve Şürekası, 1336 [1920].

Alpat, Levent. *Bir Osmanlı Askerinin Anıları*. Edited by Ozan Arslan and Ahmet Mehmetefendioğlu. İzmir: Şenocak Yayınları, 2010.

Andonyan, Aram. *Balkan Savaşı*. 2nd ed. Translated by Zaven Biberyan. Istanbul: Aras Yayıncılık, 2002.

Apak, Rahmi. *İstiklal Savaşında Garp Cephesi Nasıl Kuruldu?* Ankara: Türk Tarih Kurumu, 1990.

———. *Yetmişlik Bir Subayın Hatıraları*. Ankara: Türk Tarih Kurumu, 1988.

Arıkoğlu, Damar. *Hatıralarım*. Istanbul: Tan Gazetesi ve Matbaası, 1961.

Ataman, Halil. *Esaret Yılları: Bir Yedek Subayın 1. Dünya Savaşı Şark Cephesi Hatıraları*. Edited by Ferhat Ecer. Istanbul: Kardeşler Matbaası, 1990.

[Atay], Falih Rıfkı. *Ateş ve Güneş*. Istanbul: Halk Kitabhanesi, 1334 [1918].

———. *Zeytindağı*. 3rd ed. Istanbul: Remzi Kitabevi, 1943 [1932].

Aydemir, Şevket Süreyya. *Suyu Arayan Adam*. Istanbul: Remzi Kitabevi, 1999 [1959].

Aziz Samih. *Büyük Harpte Kafkas Cephesi Hatıraları: Zivinden Peteriçe*. Ankara: Büyük Erkanıharbiye Matbaası, 1934.

Babuş, Fikret, ed. *Savaş Yıllarından Anılar: Balkan Savaşları, Birinci Dünya Savaşı, Kurtuluş Savaşı*. Istanbul: Ozan Yayıncılık, 2013.

Baki. *Büyük Harpte Kafkas Cephesi*. Vol. 1, *Methal: Teşkilat, Seferberolma, Tecemmü, Harp İlanına Kadar*. Istanbul: Askeri Matbaa, 1933.

Bali, Rıfat N., ed. *Hikmet Tuna'nın Hatıraları*. Istanbul: Libra, 2014.

Ballobar, Antonio De la Cierva Lewita, conde de. *Jerusalem in World War I: The Palestine Diary of a European Diplomat*. Edited by Eduardo Manzano Moreno and Roberto Mazza. London: I. B. Tauris, 2011.

Bardakçı, Murat, ed. *İttihadçı'nın Sandığı: İttihad ve Terakki Liderlerinin Özel Arşivlerindeki Yayınlanmamış Belgeler ile Atatürk ve İnönü Dönemlerinde Ermeni Gayrimenkulleri Konusunda Alınmış Bazı Kararlar*. Istanbul: Türkiye İş Bankası Kültür Yayınları, 2014.

———, ed. *Talat Paşa'nın Evrak-ı Metrukesi: Sadrazam Talat Paşa'nın Özel Arşivinde Bulunan Ermeni Tehciri Konusundaki Belgeler ve Bazı Hususi Yazışmalar*. Istanbul: Everest Yayınları, 2008.

Bayar, Celal. *Ben de Yazdım*. Vol. 5, *Milli Mücadeleye Giriş*. Istanbul: Baha Matbaası, 1967.

Baykoç, Hulusi. *Büyük Harpte Kafkas ve Irak Cephesinde Beşinci Kuvvei Seferiye (52. Tümen)*. Istanbul: Askeri Matbaa, 1938.

Baytın, Arif. *İlk Dünya Harbi'nde Kafkas Cephesi: Sessiz Ölüm, Sarıkamış Günlüğü*. Edited by İsmail Dervişoğlu. Istanbul: Yeditepe Yayınevi, 2007 [1946].

Besim Atalay. *Maraş Tarihi ve Coğrafyası*. Istanbul: Matbaa-i Amire, 1339 [1923].

Beyoğlu, Süleyman, ed. *İki Devir Bir İnsan: Ahmet Faik Günday ve Hatıraları*. Istanbul: Bengi Yayınları, 2011.

Bilgin, Mehmet. "Bir Cumhuriyet Neferi: Öğretmen Halim Gençoğlu-I." *Türk Dünyası Tarih Dergisi* 143 (1998): 47–50.

Birgen, Muhittin. *İttihat ve Terakki'de On Sene*. Vol. 1, *İttihat ve Terakki Neydi?* Edited by Zeki Arıkan. Istanbul: Kitap Yayınevi, 2006.

Böcüzade Süleyman Sami. *Kuruluşundan Bugüne Kadar Isparta Tarihi*. Edited by Suat Seren. Istanbul: Serenler Yayını, 1983.

Cebesoy, Ali Fuat. *Büyük Harpte Osmanlı İmparatorluğunun 1916–1917 Yılındaki Vaziyeti: Birüssebi-Gazze Meydan Muharebesi ve Yirminci Kolordu*. Istanbul: Askeri Matbaa, 1938.

Cemal Paşa. *Hatırat*. 5th ed. Edited by Metin Martı. Istanbul: Arma Yayınları, 1996 [1922].

Cavid Bey. *Meşrutiyet Ruznamesi*. 4 vols. Edited by Hasan Babacan and Servet Avşar. Ankara: Türk Tarih Kurumu, 2014.

Cebeciyan, Avedis. *Bir Ermeni Subayın Çanakkale ve Doğu Cephesi Günlüğü, 1914–1918*. Istanbul: Aras Yayıncılık, 2015.

Chitjian, Hampartzoum Mardiros. *A Hair's Breadth from Death: The Memoirs of Hampartzoum Mardiros Chitjian*. London: Taderon, 2004.

Cunliffe-Owen, F. "The Entry of Turkey into the War: The Action of H.M. Embassy." *The National Review* 96 (1931): 611–22.

Çakır, Fahri. *Elli Yıl Önce Şark Cephesi ve Anadolu Hatıraları*. Istanbul: Çınar Matbaası, 1967.

Çakmak, Mareşal Fevzi. *Birinci Dünya Savaşı'nda Doğu Cephesi: 1935 Yılında Harp Akademisi'nde Verilen Konferanslar*. Ankara: Genelkurmay ATASE ve Genelkurmay Denetleme Başkanlığı Yayınları, 2005 [1936].

Çalıka, Hurşit, ed. *Kurtuluş Savaşında Adalet Bakanı Ahmet Rifat Çalıka'nın Anıları*. Istanbul: n.p., 1992.

Çanlı, Mehmet, ed. *Çanakkale'den Doğu Cephesine Hüseyin Avni Gençoğlu'nun Hatıraları*. Ankara: Murat Kitabevi, 2007.

Çantay, Hasan Basri. *Kara Günler ve İbret Levhaları*. Istanbul: Ahmed Said Matbaası, 1964.

Çöl, Emin. *Çanakkale-Sina Savaşları: Bir Erin Anıları*. Istanbul: Nöbetçi Yayınevi, 2009 [1977].

Der Yeghiayan, Zaven. *My Patriarchal Memoirs*. Edited by Vatche Ghazarian. Barrington, RI: Mayreni Publishing, 2002.

Derveze, İzzet. *Osmanlı Filistininde Bir Posta Memuru*. Translated by Ali Benli. Istanbul: Klasik Yayınları, 2007.

"Donanma Cemiyeti'nin Kapitülasyonların Kaldırılmasıyla İlgili Bildirisi (1914)." *Toplumsal Tarih* 38 (1997): 17.

Durukan, Eyüp. *Günlüklerde Bir Ömür*. 3 vols. Edited by Murat Uluğtekin. Istanbul: Türkiye İş Bankası Kültür Yayınları, 2013.

Ege, Abidin. *Çanakkale, Irak ve İran Cephelerinden Harp Günlükleri.* Edited by Celali Yılmaz. Istanbul: Türkiye İş Bankası Kültür Yayınları, 2011.

Eken, Halit, ed. *Bir Milli Mücadele Valisi ve Anıları: Kapancızade Hamit Bey.* Istanbul: Yeditepe Yayınları, 2008.

Elkus, Abram I. *The Memoirs of Abram Elkus: Lawyer, Ambassador, Statesman.* Edited by Hilmar Kaiser. Princeton, NJ: Gomidas Institute, 2004.

Emmanuilidis, Emmanuil. *Osmanlı İmparatorluğu'nun Son Yılları.* Translated by Niko Çanakçıoğlu. Istanbul: Belge Yayınları, 2014 [1924].

Engin, Sebahattin, ed. *Seferden Sefere: Piyade Albay M. Hilmi Engin'in Balkan, 1. Dünya ve Kurtuluş Savaşı Anıları.* Konya: Kömen Yayınları, 2007.

Enginün, İnci, and Zeynep Kerman, eds. *Ahmet Haşim Bütün Eserleri.* Vol. 4, *Frankfurt Seyahatnamesi, Mektuplar, Mülakatlar.* Istanbul: Dergah Yayınları, 1991.

Erden, Ali Fuad. *Birinci Dünya Savaşı'nda Suriye Hatıraları.* Istanbul: Türkiye İş Bankası Kültür Yayınları, 2003.

———. *İsmet İnönü.* 2nd ed. Ankara: Bilgi Yayınları, 1999 [1952].

Erginsoy, Güliz Beşe, ed. *Dedem Hüseyin Atıf Beşe: Bir Cemiyet-i Osmaniye Askerinin Savaş Hatıratı ve Bir Türkiye Cumhuriyeti Vatandaşının Yaşam Öyküsü.* Istanbul: Varlık Yayınları, 2004.

Erkin, Behiç. *Hatırat, 1876–1958.* Edited by Ali Birinci. Ankara: Türk Tarih Kurumu, 2010.

———. See also under Kaymakam Behiç below.

Eti, Ali Rıza. *Bir Onbaşının Doğu Cephesi Günlüğü, 1914–1915.* Edited by Gönül Eti. Istanbul: Türkiye İş Bankası Kültür Yayınları, 2009.

Facey, William, and Najdat Fathi Safwat, eds. *A Soldier's Story from Ottoman Rule to Independent Iraq: The Memoirs of Jafar Pasha al-Askari (1885–1936).* London: Arabian Publishing, 2003.

Faik Ali. *Payitahtın Kapısında: İki Perdelik Manzum Temaşa.* Istanbul: Ahmed İhsan ve Şürekası Matbaacılık Osmanlı Şirketi, 1918.

Feldmann, Wilhelm. *İstanbul'da Savaş Günleri.* Translated by Necmettin Alkan. Istanbul: Selis, 2004 [1913].

Gilbert, Martin. *Winston S. Churchill.* Companion vol. 3, pt. 1, *July 1914–April 1915.* Boston: Houghton Mifflin, 1973.

Gökçe, Tevfik İsmail, and S. Neşati Üster, eds. *Tevfik Sağlam, 1882–1963.* 2 vols. Istanbul: İsmail Akgün Matbaası, 1968.

Grobba, Fritz. *Die Getreidewirtschaft Syriens und Palästinas seit Beginn des Weltkrieges.* Hannover: Orient-Buchhandlung Heinz Lafaire, 1923.

Guhr, Hans. *Anadolu'dan Filistin'e Türklerle Omuz Omuza.* Translated by Eşref Özbilgen. Istanbul: Türkiye İş Bankası Kültür Yayınları, 2007 [1937].

Guse, Felix. *Die Kaukasusfront im Weltkrieg: Bis zum Frieden von Brest.* Leipzig: Koehler & Amelang, 1940.

Günday, A. Faik Hurşit. *Hayat ve Hatıralarım.* Istanbul: Çelikcilt Matbaası, 1960.

Güvemli, Fevzi. *Bir Zamanlar Ordu-Anılar.* Edited by İbrahim Dizman. Ankara: Kültür Bakanlığı Yayınları, 1999.

Güven, Ahmet Emin, ed. *Yaşam Öyküm: Kayserili Başkatipzade Teğmen Ragıp Bey'in Eğitim, Savaş, Tutsaklık, Kurtuluş Anıları.* Ankara: Dizayn Ofset, 2003.

Hacı Abdülhamid Hamid El-Berzenci. *Fezail-i Cihad ve Ulu'l-Emre İtaatin Vücubu ve Gazavat-ı Müslimine İanatı Havi Dini, Vatani, Askeri Risale-i İrşadiye.* Istanbul: Karabet Matbaası, 1331 [1915].

Hafız Hakkı Paşa. *Bozgun.* Istanbul: Tercüman Yayınları, 1972 [1914].

———. *Hafız Hakkı Paşa'nın Sarıkamış Günlüğü.* Edited by Murat Bardakçı. Istanbul: Türkiye İş Bankası Kültür Yayınları, 2014.

Haigaz, Aram. *The Fall of the Aerie.* Translated by H. Baghdoian. Boston: Ararat, n.d. [1935].

Hanioğlu, M. Şükrü, ed. *Kendi Mektuplarında Enver Paşa.* Istanbul: Der Yayınları, 1989.

Hartunian, Abraham H. *Neither to Laugh nor to Weep: A Memoir of the Armenian Genocide by Abraham H. Hartunian.* Translated by Vartan Hartunian. Boston: Beacon Press, 1968.

Hasan Ferid. *Nakid ve İtibar-ı Mali.* Vol. 2, *Evrak-ı Nakdiye.* Edited by Mehmet Hakan Sağlam. Istanbul: Hazine Müsteşarlığı Darphane ve Damga Matbaası, 2008 [1918].

His, Wilhelm. *A German Doctor at the Front (Die Front der Arzte).* Translated by Gustavus M. Blech and Jefferson R. Kean. Washington, DC: National Service Publishing Co., 1933.

Hüseyin Cemal. *Yeni Harb, Başımıza Tekrar Gelenler: Edirne Harbi, Muhasarası, Esaret ve Esbab-ı Felaket.* Edited by Aziz Korkmaz. Ankara: Türk Tarih Kurumu, 2014 [1916].

Hüseyin Rahmi. *Hakka Sığındık: İşitilmedik Bir Vaka.* Istanbul: Matbaa-i Orhaniye, 1335 [1919].

Jernazian, Ephraim K. *Judgment unto Truth: Witnessing the Armenian Genocide.* Translated by Alice Haig. New Brunswick, NJ: Transaction Publishers, 1990.

Karabekir, Kazım. *Birinci Cihan Harbine Nasıl Girdik.* Vol. 2. Istanbul: Emre Yayınları, 1994 [1937].

———. *Edirne Hatıraları.* Edited by Ziver Öktem. Istanbul: Yapı Kredi Yayınları, 2009.

———. *Günlükler, 1906–1948.* Vol. 1. Edited by Yücel Demirel. Istanbul: Yapı Kredi Yayınları, 2009.

Karay, Refik Halid. *Minelbab İlelmihrab: 1918 Mütarekesi Devrinde Olan Biten İşlere ve Gelip Geçen İnsanlara Dair Bildiklerim.* 2nd ed. Istanbul: İnkılap Kitabevi, 1992 [1964].

Kaymakam Behiç. *Mükellefiyet-i Askeriye Kanun-ı Muvakkatının İzahı.* Istanbul: Kitabhane-i İslam ve Askeri, 1331 [1915].

———. See also under Erkin, Behiç, above.

Kaymakam Şerif Bey. *Sarıkamış İhata Manevrası.* Edited by Murat Çulcu. Istanbul: Arba Yayınları, 1998 [1922].

Kayra, Mediha. *Hoşça Kal Trabzon: Bir Kız Çocuğunun Günlüğünden Birinci Dünya Savaşı'nda Anadolu.* Edited by Cahit Kayra. Istanbul: Dünya Kitapları, 2005.

Kerimi, Fatih. *İstanbul Mektupları.* Edited by Fazıl Gökçek. Istanbul: Çağrı Yayınları, 2001.

Kocal, Celal Ferdi. *Ömrümün 90 Yılından Bazı Hatıralar*. Istanbul: Yaylacık Matbaası, 1983.

Konrapa, Mehmet Zekâi. *Bolu Tarihi*. Bolu: Bolu Vilayet Matbaası, 1960.

Koraltan, Refik. *Bir Politikacının Anıları: Her Şey Vatan İçin*. Edited by Coşkun Ertepınar. Ankara: Hacettepe-Taş Kitapçılık, 1999.

Kress von Kressenstein, Friedrich. *Türklerle Beraber Süveyş Kanalına*. Istanbul: Askeri Matbaa, 1943 [1938].

Kuntman, Mehmet Derviş. *Bir Doktorun Harp ve Memleket Anıları*. Edited by Metin Özata. 2nd ed. Ankara: Genelkurmay Askeri Tarih ve Stratejik Etüt Başkanlığı Yayınları, 2010 [1966].

Künzler, Jakob. *In the Land of Blood and Tears: Experiences in Mesopotamia during the World War (1914–1918)*. Edited by Ara Ghazarians. Arlington, MA: Armenian Cultural Foundation, 2007 [1921].

Lermioğlu, Muzaffer. *Akçaabat—Akçaabat Tarihi ve Birinci Genel Savaş—Hicret Hatıraları*. Istanbul: Kardeşler Basımevi, 1949.

Leverkuehn, Paul. *A German Officer during the Armenian Genocide: A Biography of Max von Scheubner-Richter*. Translated by Alasdair Lean. London: Gomidas Institute, 2008 [1938].

Liman von Sanders, Otto Viktor Karl. *Five Years in Turkey*. Annapolis, MD: The United States Naval Institute, 1927 [1920].

M. Emin Zeki. *Kürdistan Tarihi*. Ankara: Beybun Yayınları, 1992.

Mahmud Beliğ. *Balkan Harbi'nde Mürettep 1. Kolordu'nun Harekatı*. Istanbul: Askeri Matbaa, 1929.

———. *Balkan Harbi'nde Mürettep 4. Kolordu'nun Harekatı*. Istanbul: Askeri Matbaa, 1928.

Mahmud Muhtar Paşa. *Üçüncü Kolordu'nun ve İkinci Şark Ordusu'nun Muharebatı*. Dersaadet: Kanaat Matbaası, 1331 [1915].

Mahmut Şevket Paşa. *Mahmut Şevket Paşa'nın Sadaret Günlüğü*. Edited by Murat Bardakçı. Istanbul: İş Bankası Kültür Yayınları, 2014.

McGilvary, Margaret. *The Dawn of a New Era in Syria*. Reading, England: Garnet Publishing, 2001 [1920].

Mehmed Emin. *Ordunun Destanı*. Istanbul: Matbaa-i Ahmed İhsan ve Şürekası, 1331 [1915].

———. "Orduya Selam." Transcribed in *Mehmed Emin Yurdakul'un Eserleri*. Vol. 1, *Şiirler*, edited by Fevziye Abdullah Tansel, 196-98. Ankara: Türk Tarih Kurumu, 1969.

Mehmed Hayri. *Türkiye'nin Sıhhi ve İçtimai Coğrafyası: Niğde Sancağı*. Edited by İlhan Gedik. Niğde: n.p., 1994 [1922].

Mehmet Nihad, *1328–29 Balkan Harbi Trakya Seferi*. Vol. 1, *Harekat-ı Harbiyenin İbtidarına Kadar*. Istanbul: Matbaa-i Askeriye, 1340 [1925].

Mkhalian, Krikor. *Bardizag and Its People*. Translated by Ara Stepan Melkonian. London: Gomidas Institute, 2014.

Morgenthau, Henry. *United States Diplomacy on the Bosphorus: The Diaries of Ambas-*

sador Morgenthau, 1913–1916. Edited by Ara Sarafian. Princeton, NJ: Gomidas Institute, 2004.

Muslihiddin Safvet. *Türkiye'nin Sıhhi İctimai Coğrafyası: Ankara Vilayeti.* Istanbul: Hilal Matbaası, 1925.

Münim Mustafa. *Cepheden Cepheye: İhtiyat Zabiti Bulunduğum Sırada Cihan Harbinde Kanal ve Çanakkale Cephelerine Ait Hatıralarım.* Istanbul: Arma Yayınları, 1998 [1940].

Newton, Frances E. *Fifty Years in Palestine.* London: Coldharbour Press, 1948.

Odian, Yervant. *Accursed Years: My Exile and Return from Der Zor, 1914–1919.* Translated by Ara Stepan Melkonian. London: Gomidas Institute, 2009.

Orga, İrfan. *Portrait of a Turkish Family.* London: Gollancz, 1950.

Osmanlı Hilal-i Ahmer Cemiyeti Hanımlar Heyet-i Merkeziyesi Tarafından Tertib Edilen Takvim. Istanbul: n.p., 1332 [1916].

Öğütçü, Işık, ed. *Orhan Kemal'in Babası Abdülkadir Kemali'nin Anıları.* Istanbul: Epsilon Yayınları, 2005.

Önal, Sami, ed. *Tuğgeneral Ziya Yergök'ün Anıları: Sarıkamış'tan Esarete (1915–1920).* 6th ed. Istanbul: Remzi Kitabevi, 2006.

Pasdermadjian, Karekin. "My Last Interview with Talaat Pasha." *Armenian Review* 35 (1982): 115–27.

Peker, Nurettin. *Tüfek Omza: Balkan Savaşı'ndan Kurtuluş Savaşı'na Ateş Hattında Bir Ömür.* Edited by Orhan Peker and Hilal Akkartal. Istanbul: Doğan Kitap, 2009.

Pırnar, İhsan, and Tuğrul Pırnar. *Baba Oğul Anıları: Bir Cumhuriyet Ailesinin Yüz Yıllık Öyküsü.* Vol. 1, *Pravuşta 1894–Ankara 1967.* Izmir: Meta Basım, 2010.

Pomiankowski, Joseph. *Der Zusammenbruch des Ottomanischen Reiches: Erinnerungen an die Türkei aus der Zeit des Weltkrieges.* Zurich: Amalthea, 1928.

Price, M. Philips. *War & Revolution in Asiatic Russia.* New York: Macmillan, 1918.

Rado, Şevket, ed. "Türk İstiklal Savaşının Arifesinde Bir Emekli Subayın Not Defteri: Birinci Umumi Harpte ve Mütareke Günlerinde İstanbul-I." *Hayat Tarih Mecmuası* 1, no. 1 (1971): 5–10.

Range, Paul. *Vier Jahre Kampf ums Heilige Land.* Lübeck: Charles Coleman, 1939.

Ricks, Thomas M. *Turbulent Times in Palestine: The Diaries of Khalil Totah, 1886–1955.* Jerusalem: Institute of Palestine Studies & Passia, 2009.

Riggs, Henry H. *Days of Tragedy in Armenia: Personal Experiences in Harpoot, 1915–1917.* Ann Arbor, MI: Gomidas Institute, 1997.

Ryan, Andrew. *The Last of the Dragomans.* London: Geoffrey Bles, 1951.

Sabis, Ali İhsan. *Harb Hatıralarım.* Vol. 1, *Birinci Cihan Harbinden Evvelki Hadiseler, Harbin Zuhuru ve Seferberlik İlanı, Harbe Nasıl Sürüklendik?* Istanbul: İnkılap Kitabevi, 1943.

———. *Harp Hatıralarım.* Vol. 5, *İstiklâl Harbi ve Gizli Cihetleri.* Istanbul: Nehir Yayınları, 1990.

Sabuncuoğlu, M. İhsan. *Çorum Tarihine Ait Derlemelerim I-II-III & Maarif Hayatımız.* Edited by Abdulkadir Ozulu and İrfan Yiğit. Çorum: Çorum Belediyesi Kültür Yayınları, 2010.

Sadri Sema. *Eski İstanbul Hatıraları*. Edited by Ali Şükrü Çoruk. Istanbul: Kitabevi, 2002.

Salibi, Kamal S. "Beirut under the Young Turks: As Depicted in the Political Memoirs of Salim 'Ali Salam (1868–1938)." In *Les Arabes par leurs archives (XVIe–XXe siecles)*, edited by Jacques Berque and Dominique Chevallier, 193–215. Paris: Centre national de la recherche scientifique, 1976.

Salim, Tevfik. "Sıhhi Harb Tarihi Tetkikleri: Büyük Harbde Kafkas Cephesindeki Sıhhi Vaziyete Dair Bir Tetkik." *Askeri Mecmua* 97 (1935): 487–504.

Sandes, E. W. C. *Tales of Turkey*. London: John Murray, 1924.

Sapancalı H. Hüseyin. *Karaman Ahval-i İctimaiyye ve Coğrafiyye ve Tarihiyyesi*. Edited by İbrahim Güler. Ankara: Türk Tarih Kurumu, 1993 [1922].

Sazak, M. Emin. *Emin Bey'in Defteri: Hatıralar*. Edited by Himmet Kayıhan. Ankara: Tolkun Yayınları, 2007.

Schreiner, George Abel. *From Berlin to Bagdad: Behind the Scenes in the Near East*. New York: Harper & Brothers, 1918.

Sezen, Yıldırım, ed. *İki Kardeşten Seferberlik Anıları*. Ankara: T.C. Kültür Bakanlığı Yayınları, 1999.

Söylemezoğlu, Galip Kemali. *Hatıraları: Atina Sefareti (1913–1916)*. Istanbul: Türkiye Yayınevi, 1946.

Sunata, İ. Hakkı. *Gelibolu'dan Kafkaslara: Birinci Dünya Savaşı Anılarım*. Istanbul: Türkiye İş Bankası Kültür Yayınları, 2003.

Sunguroğlu, İshak. *Harput Yollarında*. 4 vols. Istanbul: Elazığ Kültür ve Tanıtma Vakfı Yayınları, 1959.

Süleyman Nuri. *Çanakkale Siperlerinden TKP Yönetimine: Uyanan Esirler*. Istanbul: TÜSTAV Yayınları, 2002.

Sürmenyan, Kalusd. *Harbiyeli Bir Osmanlı Ermenisi: Mülazım-ı Sani Sürmenyan'ın Savaş ve Tehcir Anıları*. Translated and edited by Yaşar Tolga Cora. Istanbul: Tarih Vakfı Yurt Yayınları, 2015.

Talat Paşa. *Hatıralarım ve Müdafaam*. 2nd ed. Istanbul: Kaynak Yayınları, 2006.

Tergeman, Siham. *Daughter of Damascus*. Translated by Andrea Rugh. Austin: Center for Middle Eastern Studies, University of Texas at Austin, 1994.

Tezer, Şükrü, ed. *Atatürk'ün Hatıra Defteri*. Ankara: Türk Tarih Kurumu, 1972.

Torossian, Sarkis. *From Dardanelles to Palestine: A True Story of Five Battle Fronts of Turkey and Her Allies and a Harem Romance*. Boston: Meador Publishing Co., 1947 [1929].

Tugay, Asaf. *İbret*. Vol. 2. Istanbul: Sucuoğlu Matbaası, 1962.

Tüccarzâde İbrahim Hilmi. *Neden Münhezim Olduk?* Istanbul: Kitabhane-i İntibâh, 1329 [1913].

Ussher, Clarence Douglas. *An American Physician in Turkey: A Narrative of Adventures in Peace and in War*. Boston: Houghton Mifflin, 1917.

Uzer, Tahsin. *Makedonya Eşkiyalık Tarihi ve Son Osmanlı Yönetimi*. Ankara: Türk Tarih Kurumu, 1979.

White, George E. *Adventuring with Anatolia College*. Grinnell, IA: Herald-Register, 1940.

Yalman, Ahmed Emin. *Yakın Tarihte Gördüklerim ve Geçirdiklerim*. Vol. 1, *1888–1918*. Istanbul: Yenilik Basımevi, 1970.

Yarbay Selahattin. *Kafkas Cephesi'nde 10 ncu Kolordunun Birinci Dünya Savaşı'nın Başlangıcından Sarıkamış Muharebelerinin Sonuna Kadar Olan Harekatı*. Edited by Zekeriya Türkmen, Alev Keskin, and Fatma İlhan. Ankara: Genelkurmay Askeri Tarih ve Stratejik Etüt Başkanlığı Yayınları, 2006 [1931].

Yeğinatı, Süleyman İzzet. *Büyük Harbin Başında 2. İhtiyat ve Nizamiye Süvari Tümenlerile* [sic] *Aras Cenup Müfrezesinin Muharebeleri*. Istanbul: Askeri Matbaa, 1939.

Yengin, Sami. *Drama'dan Sina-Filistin'e Savaş Günlüğü (1917–1918)*. Edited by Ahmet Tetik, Sema Demirtaş, and Ayşe Seven. Ankara: Genelkurmay Askeri Tarih ve Stratejik Etüt Başkanlığı Yayınları, 2007.

Yüzbaşı Selanikli Bahri. *Balkan Savaşı'nda Sırp Ordusu ve Batı Ordusu*. Edited by Mustafa Toker. Istanbul: Alfa Yayınları, 2012 [1915].

Secondary Sources

Adanır, Fikret. "Non-Muslims in the Ottoman Army and the Ottoman Defeat in the Balkan War of 1912–1913." In *A Question of Genocide: Armenians and Turks at the End of the Ottoman Empire*, edited by Ronald Grigor Suny, Fatma Müge Göçek, and Norman M. Naimark, 113–25. Oxford: Oxford University Press, 2011.

Adanır, Fikret, and Hilmar Kaiser. "Migration, Deportation, and Nation-Building: The Case of the Ottoman Empire." In *Migrations et migrants dans une perspective historique: Permanences et innovations / Migrations and Migrants in Historical Perspective: Permanencies and Innovations*, edited by René Leboutte, 273–92. New York: Peter Lang, 2000.

Ağanoğlu, H. Yıldırım. *Osmanlı'dan Cumhuriyet'e Balkanlar'ın Makus Talihi Göç*. Istanbul: Kum Saati Yayınları, 2001.

Ahmad, Feroz. "The Agrarian Policy of the Young Turks, 1908–1918." In *Économie et sociétés dans l'Empire ottoman (fin du XVIIIe–début du XXe siècle)*, edited by Jean-Louis Bacqué Grammont and Paul Dumont, 275–88. Paris: Éditions du C.N.R.S., 1983.

———. "Ottoman Armed Neutrality and Intervention, August–November 1914." In *Studies on Ottoman Diplomatic History IV*, edited by Sinan Kuneralp, 41–69. Istanbul: Isis Press, 1990.

———. "Ottoman Perceptions of the Capitulations, 1800–1914." *Journal of Islamic Studies* 11, no. 1 (2000): 1–20.

———. "War and Society under the Young Turks, 1908–1918." *Review* 11, no. 2 (1988): 265–86.

Ahmad, Kamal Madhar. *Kurdistan during the First World War*. Translated by Ali Maher Ibrahim. London: Saqi Books, 1994.

Ahmed Emin. *Turkey in the World War*. New Haven, CT: Yale University Press, 1930.

Ajay, Nicholas Z., Jr. "Mount Lebanon and the Wilayah of Beirut, 1914–1918: The War Years." PhD diss., Georgetown University, 1972.

Akarlı, Engin. *The Long Peace: Ottoman Lebanon, 1861–1920*. Berkeley: University of California Press, 1993.

Akça, Kemal. "Seferberlik Destanı." *Folklor Postası* 19 (1946): 11–14.

Akçam, Taner. *Ermenilerin Zorla Müslümanlaştırılması: Sessizlik, İnkar ve Asimilasyon.* Istanbul: İletişim Yayınları, 2014.

———. *The Young Turks' Crime against Humanity: The Armenian Genocide and Ethnic Cleansing in the Ottoman Empire.* Princeton, NJ: Princeton University Press, 2012.

Akçam, Taner, and Ümit Kurt. *Kanunların Ruhu: Emval-i Metruke Kanunlarında Soykırımın İzini Sürmek.* Istanbul: İletişim Yayınları, 2012.

Akın, Yiğit. "The Ottoman Home Front during World War I: Everyday Politics, Society, and Culture." PhD diss., Ohio State University, 2011.

———. "Savaş, Milliyetçilik, Sivil Toplum: Çivi Anıtların İstanbul'daki Örneği Hatıra-i Celadet Topu." *Toplumsal Tarih* 243 (2010): 22–27.

Akmeşe, Handan Nezir. *The Birth of Modern Turkey: The Ottoman Military and the March to World War I.* London: I. B. Tauris, 2005.

Aksakal, Mustafa. "'Holy War Made in Germany?': Ottoman Origins for the 1914 Jihad." *War in History* 18, no. 2 (2011): 184–99.

———. "Ottoman Empire." In *Empires at War, 1911–1923*, edited by Robert Gerwarth and Erez Manela, 17–33. Oxford: Oxford University Press, 2014.

———. "Ottoman Empire." In *The Cambridge History of the First World War.* Vol. 1, *Global War*, edited by Jay Winter, 459–78. Cambridge: Cambridge University Press, 2014.

———. *The Ottoman Road to War in 1914: The Ottoman Empire and the First World War.* Cambridge: Cambridge University Press, 2008.

Aktar, Ayhan. "1. Dünya Savaşı'nda Osmanlı Ordusunda Ermeni Askerler." *Toplumsal Tarih* 255 (2015): 30–38.

Aktar, Ayhan, and Abdülhamit Kırmızı. "Diyarbekir, 1915." In *Diyarbakır Tebliğleri: Diyarbakır ve Çevresi Toplumsal ve Ekonomik Tarihi Konferansı*, edited by Bülent Doğan, 289-323. Istanbul: Hrant Dink Vakfı, 2013.

Aktar, Yücel. "1912 Yılı 'Harp Mitingleri' ve Balkan Harbi'ne Etkileri." In *İkinci Askeri Tarih Semineri: Bildiriler*, 114–36. Ankara: Genelkurmay ATASE Yayınları, 1985.

Akyıldız, Ali. *Osmanlı Finans Sisteminde Dönüm Noktası: Kağıt Para ve Sosyo-Ekonomik Etkileri.* Istanbul: Eren Yayıncılık, 1996.

Akyaz, Doğan. "The Legacy and Impacts of the Defeat in the Balkan Wars of 1912–1913 on the Psychological Makeup of the Turkish Officer Corps." In *War and Nationalism: The Balkan Wars, 1912–1913, and Their Sociopolitical Implications*, edited by M. Hakan Yavuz and Isa Blumi, 739–68. Salt Lake City: University of Utah Press, 2013.

Albayrak, Haşim. *1. Dünya Savaşında Doğu Karadeniz Muharebesi ve Of Direnişi.* Istanbul: Yesevi Yayıncılık, 2004.

Al-Qattan, Najwa. "*Safarbarlik*: Ottoman Syria and the Great War." In *From the Syrian Land to the States of Syria and Lebanon*, edited by Thomas Philipp and Christoph Schumann, 163–73. Würzburg: Ergon, 2004.

———. "When Mothers Ate Their Children: Wartime Memory and the Language of

Food in Syria and Lebanon," *International Journal of Middle East Studies* 46, no. 2 (2014): 719–36.

Allen, W. E. D., and Paul Muratoff. *Caucasian Battlefields: A History of the Wars on the Turco-Caucasian Border, 1828–1921.* Cambridge: Cambridge University Press, 1953.

Arslan, Ozan. *Osmanlı'nın Son Zaferleri: 1918 Kafkas Harekâtı.* Istanbul: Doğan Kitap, 2010.

Artuç, Nevzat. "Ahmed Cemal Paşa (1877–1922): Askeri ve Siyasi Hayatı." PhD diss., Süleyman Demirel University, 2005.

Aslanoğlu, İbrahim. "Cönklerden Derlemeler: Bir Demette Beş Çiçek." *Sivas Folkloru* 6 (1973): 12–13.

———. "Cönklerden Derlemeler: Seferberlik Destanları." *Sivas Folkloru* 21 (1974): 4–5, 12.

Atamaz, Serpil. "Fighting on Two Fronts: The Balkan Wars and the Struggle for Women's Rights in Ottoman Turkey." In *War and Nationalism: The Balkan Wars, 1912–1913, and Their Sociopolitical Implications,* edited by M. Hakan Yavuz and Isa Blumi, 298–315. Salt Lake City: University of Utah Press, 2013.

Avcı, Orhan. *Irak'ta Türk Ordusu, 1914–1918.* Ankara: Vadi Yayınları, 2004.

Avşar, Servet. "Birinci Dünya Savaşı'nda Propaganda Faaliyetleri." MA thesis, Kırıkkale University, 2002.

———. "Birinci Dünya Savaşı'nda Rus Propaganda Faaliyetleri ve Osmanlı Devleti." *OTAM* 14 (2003): 65–127.

Baker, Keith Michael. *Inventing the French Revolution: Essays on French Political Culture in the Eighteenth Century.* Cambridge: Cambridge University Press, 1990.

Bali, Rıfat N. ed. *The Jews and Prostitution in Constantinople, 1854–1922.* Istanbul: Isis Press, 2008.

Bayur, Yusuf Hikmet. *Türk İnkılabı Tarihi.* Vol. 3, *1914–1918 Genel Savaşı,* pt. 4, *Savaşın Sonu.* Ankara: Türk Tarih Kurumu, 1967.

Bein, Amit. "Politics, Military Conscription, and Religious Education in the Late Ottoman Empire." *International Journal of Middle East Studies* 38, no. 2 (2006): 283–301.

Beckett, Ian F. W. *The Great War, 1914–1918.* 2nd ed. London: Routledge, 2014.

Bekiroğlu, Nazan. *Şair Nigar Hanım.* Istanbul: İletişim Yayınları, 1998.

Berber, Engin. *Sancılı Yıllar: İzmir, 1918–1922, Mütareke ve Yunan İşgali Döneminde İzmir Sancağı.* Ankara: Ayraç Yayınları, 1997.

Beşikçi, Mehmet. "Balkan Harbi'nde Osmanlı Seferberliği ve Redif Teşkilatının İflası." *Türkiye Günlüğü* 110 (2012): 27–43.

———. "Birinci Dünya Savaşı'nda Devlet İktidarı ve İç Güvenlik: Asker Kaçakları Sorunu ve Jandarmanın Yeniden Yapılandırılması." In *Türkiye'de Ordu, Devlet ve Güvenlik Siyaseti,* edited by Evren Balta Paker and İsmet Akça, 144–71. Istanbul: Istanbul Bilgi Üniversitesi Yayınları, 2010.

———. "İktidarın Çelik Sembolleri: I. Dünya Savaşı'nda Donanma Sembolizmi ve Milliyetçi Propaganda." *Toplumsal Tarih* 127 (2004): 92–95.

———. *The Ottoman Mobilization of Manpower in the First World War: Between Voluntarism and Resistance.* Leiden: Brill, 2012.

Bilgi, Nejdet. *Ermeni Tehciri ve Boğazlıyan Kaymakamı Mehmed Kemal Bey'in Yargılanması.* Ankara: KÖK Sosyal ve Stratejik Araştırmalar Vakfı, 1999.

Bjørnlund, Matthias. "'A Fate Worse Than Dying': Sexual Violence during the Armenian Genocide." In *Brutality and Desire: War and Sexuality in Europe's Twentieth Century*, edited by Dagmar Herzog, 16–58. London: Palgrave Macmillan, 2008.

———. "The 1914 Cleansing of Aegean Greeks as a Case of Violent Turkification." *Journal of Genocide Research* 10, no. 1 (2008): 41–57.

Bloxham, Donald. "The First World War and the Development of the Armenian Genocide." In *A Question of Genocide: Armenians and Turks at the End of the Ottoman Empire*, edited by Ronald Grigor Suny, Fatma Müge Göçek, and Norman M. Naimark, 260–75. Oxford: Oxford University Press, 2011.

———. *The Great Game of Genocide: Imperialism, Nationalism, and the Destruction of the Ottoman Armenians*. Oxford: Oxford University Press, 2005.

Blumi, Isa. *Ottoman Refugees, 1878-1939: Migration in a Post-Imperial World*. London: Bloomsbury, 2013.

Bobroff, Ronald P. *Roads to Glory: Late Imperial Russia and the Turkish Straits*. London: I. B. Tauris, 2006.

Bonzon, Thierry, and Belinda Davis. "Feeding the Cities." In *Capital Cities at War: Paris, London, Berlin, 1914-1919*. Vol. 1, edited by Jay Winter and Jean-Louis Roberts, 305–41. Cambridge: Cambridge University Press, 1997.

Caferoğlu, A. *Anadolu Ağızlarından Toplamalar: Kastamonu, Çankırı, Çorum, Amasya, Niğde İlbaylıkları Ağızları, Kalaycı Argosu ve Geygelli Yürüklerinin Gizli Dili*. Istanbul: Bürhaneddin Matbaası, 1943.

Campos, Michelle U. *Ottoman Brothers: Muslims, Christians, and Jews in Early Twentieth-Century Palestine*. Stanford: Stanford University Press, 2011.

Chalabi, Tamara. *The Shi'is of Jabal 'Amil and the New Lebanon: Community and Nation-State, 1918-1943*. New York: Palgrave Macmillan, 2006.

Chickering, Roger. "Total War: The Use and Abuse of a Concept." In *Anticipating Total War: The German and American Experiences, 1871-1914*, edited by Manfred F. Boemeke, 13–28. Cambridge: Cambridge University Press, 1999.

Chickering, Roger, and Stig Förster, eds. *Great War, Total War: Combat and Mobilization on the Western Front, 1914-1918*. Cambridge: Cambridge University Press, 2000.

Clark, Christopher. *Sleepwalkers: How Europe Went to War in 1914*. New York: Harper, 2013.

Cummings, Lindsey. "Economic Warfare and the Evolution of the Allied Blockade of the Eastern Mediterranean: August 1914–April 1917." MA Thesis, Georgetown University, 2015.

Çağlar, Günay. *Hüsrev Bey Heyet-i Nasihası (Nisan-Haziran 1920)*. Ankara: Atatürk Araştırma Merkezi Yayınları, 1997.

Çamurdan, Ahmet Cevdet. *Kurtuluş Savaşında Doğu Kilikya Olayları*. Adana: Toros Basımevi, 1969.

Çetinkaya, Y. Doğan. "Illustrated Atrocity: The Stigmatisation of Non-Muslims through Images in the Ottoman Empire during the Balkan Wars." *Journal of Modern European History* 2, no. 4 (2014): 460–78.

————. *The Young Turks and the Boycott Movement: Nationalism, Protest and the Working Classes in the Formation of Modern Turkey*. London: I. B. Tauris, 2014.

Çiçek, M. Talha. *War and State Formation in Syria: Cemal Pasha's Governorate during World War I, 1914–17*. London: Routledge, 2014.

Çitçi, Hasan Remzi, and Şakir Sabri Yener. *Osmanlı Devleti'nin Son Yıllarında Gaziantep'te Sanat ve Ticaret Dalları*. Gaziantep: Yeni Matbaa, 1971.

Çolak, Melek. "Macar Etnograf Istvan Györff ve Kuzey Marmara Bölgesi İnceleme Gezisi (1918)." *Belleten* 265 (2008): 943–51.

Daniel, Ute. *The War from Within: German Working-Class Women in the First World War*. Providence, RI: Berghahn Books, 1997.

Das, Santanu, ed. *Race, Empire, and First World War Writing*. Cambridge: Cambridge University Press, 2011.

Davis, Belinda. *Home Fires Burning: Food, Politics, and Everyday Life in World War I Berlin*. Chapel Hill: University of North Carolina Press, 2000.

Davison, Roderic H. "The Armenian Crisis, 1912–1914." *American Historical Review* 53, no. 3 (1948): 481–505.

Demir, Fevzi. *Osmanlı Devleti'nde II. Meşrutiyet Dönemi Meclis-i Mebusan Seçimleri, 1908–1914*. Ankara: İmge Kitabevi, 2007.

Der Matossian, Bedross. *Shattered Dreams of Revolution: From Liberty to Violence in the Late Ottoman Empire*. Stanford: Stanford University Press, 2014.

Derderian, Katharine. "Common Fate, Different Experience: Gender-Specific Aspects of the Armenian Genocide, 1915–1917." *Holocaust and Genocide Studies* 19, no. 1 (2005): 1–25.

Deringil, Selim. "19. Yüzyılda Osmanlı İmparatorluğunda Göç Olgusu Üzerine Bazı Düşünceler." In *Bekir Kütükoğlu'na Armağan*, 435–42. Istanbul: İstanbul Üniversitesi Edebiyat Fakültesi Basımevi, 1991.

Doğan, Enfal, and Fatih Tığlı. "Sultan V. Mehmed Reşad'ın Çanakkale Gazeli ve Bu Gazele Yazılan Tahmisler." *İstanbul Üniversitesi Edebiyat Fakültesi Türk Dili ve Edebiyatı Dergisi* 33 (2005): 41–96.

Domansky, Elizabeth. "The Transformation of State and Society in World War I Germany." In *Landscaping the Human Garden: Twentieth-Century Population Management in a Comparative Framework*, edited by Amir Weiner, 46–63. Stanford: Stanford University Press, 2003.

D[ominian], L[eon]. "Railroads in Turkey." *Bulletin of the American Geographical Society* 47, no. 12 (1915): 934–40.

Dündar, Fuat. *Crime of Numbers: The Role of Statistics in the Armenian Question, 1878–1918*. New Brunswick, NJ: Transaction Publishers, 2010.

————. *İttihat ve Terakki'nin Müslümanları İskân Politikası (1913–1918)*. Istanbul: İletişim Yayınları, 2001.

————. *Modern Türkiye'nin Şifresi: İttihat ve Terakki'nin Etnisite Mühendisliği, 1913–1918*. Istanbul: İletişim Yayınları, 2008.

Ekmekçioğlu, Lerna. "A Climate for Abduction, A Climate for Redemption: The Politics of Inclusion during and after the Armenian Genocide." *Comparative Studies in Society and History* 55, no. 3 (2013): 522–53.

Elçin, Şükrü. *Türkiye Türkçesinde Ağıtlar.* Ankara: T.C. Kültür Bakanlığı Yayınları, 1990.

Eldem, Vedat. *Harp ve Mütareke Yıllarında Osmanlı İmpartorluğu'nun Ekonomisi.* Ankara: Türk Tarih Kurumu, 1994.

———. *Osmanlı İmparatorluğu'nun İktisadi Şartları Hakkında Bir Tetkik.* Ankara: Türkiye İş Bankası Kültür Yayınları, 1970.

Elmacı, Mehmet Emin. *İttihat Terakki ve Kapitülasyonlar.* Istanbul: Homer Kitabevi, 2005.

Eren, Ahmet Cevat. *Türkiye'de Göç ve Göçmen Meseleleri: Tanzimat Devri, İlk Kurulan Göçmen Komisyonu, Çıkarılan Tüzükler.* Istanbul: Nurgök Matbaası, 1966.

Erickson, Edward J. "The Armenians and Ottoman Military Policy, 1915." *War in History* 15, no. 2 (2008): 141–67.

———. *Defeat in Detail: The Ottoman Army in the Balkans, 1912–1913.* Westport, CT: Praeger, 2003.

———. *Ordered to Die: A History of the Ottoman Army in the First World War.* Westport, CT: Greenwood Press, 2001.

———. *Ottoman Army Effectiveness in World War I: A Comparative Study.* London: Routledge, 2007.

Erol, Emre. "Organised Chaos as Diplomatic Ruse and Demographic Weapon: The Expulsion of the Ottoman Greeks (*Rum*) from Foça, 1914." *Tijdschrift voor Sociale en Economische Geschiedenis* 10, no. 4 (2013): 66–96.

———. *The Ottoman Crisis in Western Anatolia: Turkey's Belle Époque and the Transition to a Modern Nation State.* London: I. B. Tauris, 2016.

Fawaz, Leila Tarazi. *A Land of Aching Hearts: The Middle East in the Great War.* Cambridge, MA: Harvard University Press, 2014.

Foster, Zachary J. "The 1915 Locust Attack in Syria and Palestine and Its Role in the Famine during the First World War." *Middle Eastern Studies* 51, no. 3 (2015): 370–94.

Gatrell, Peter. "Refugees and Forced Migrants during the First World War." *Immigrants and Minorities* 26, nos. 1–2 (2008): 82–110.

Gedikoğlu, Haydar. *Trabzon Efsaneleri ve Halk Hikayeleri.* Trabzon: Trabzon Valiliği İl Kültür Müdürlüğü Yayınları, 1998.

Gelvin, James L. *Divided Loyalties: Nationalism and Mass Politics in Syria at the Close of the Empire.* Berkeley: University of California Press, 1998.

Georgeon, François. "Harp Maliyesi ve Milli İktisat: 1918 Osmanlı İç İstikrazı." In *Osmanlı-Türk Modernleşmesi, 1900–1930,* 159–78. Istanbul: Yapı Kredi Yayınları, 2006.

Gerçek, Burçin. *Akıntıya Karşı: Ermeni Soykırımında Emirlere Karşı Gelenler, Kurtaranlar, Direnenler.* Istanbul: İletişim Yayınları, 2016.

Geyer, Michael. "Militarization of Europe, 1914–1945." In *The Militarization of the Western World,* edited by John Gillis, 65–102. New Brunswick, NJ: Rutgers University Press, 1989.

Gingeras, Ryan. *Fall of the Sultanate: The Great War and the End of the Ottoman Empire, 1908–1922*. Oxford: Oxford University Press, 2016.

———. *Sorrowful Shores: Violence, Ethnicity, and the End of the Empire, 1912–1923*. Oxford: Oxford University Press, 2009.

Ginio, Eyal. *The Ottoman Culture of Defeat: The Balkan Wars and Their Aftermath*. Oxford: Oxford University Press, 2016.

———. "Paving the Way for Ethnic Cleansing: Eastern Thrace during the Balkan Wars (1912–1913) and Their Aftermath." In *Shatterzone of Empires: Coexistence and Violence in the German, Habsburg, Russian, and Ottoman Borderlands*, edited by Omer Bartov and Eric D. Weitz, 283–97. Bloomington: Indiana University Press, 2013.

Göçek, Fatma Müge. *Denial of Violence: Ottoman Past, Turkish Present, and Collective Violence against the Armenians, 1789–2009*. Oxford: Oxford University Press, 2015.

Gratien, Christopher. "The Mountains Are Ours: Ecology and Settlement in Late Ottoman and Early Republican Cilicia, 1856–1956." PhD diss., Georgetown University, 2015.

Gratien, Chris, and Graham Auman Pitts. "Towards an Environmental History of World War I: Human and Natural Disasters in the Ottoman Mediterranean." In *The World during the First World War*, edited by Helmut Bley and Anorthe Kremer, 237–50. Essen: Klartext, 2014.

Gülsoy, Ufuk. *Osmanlı Gayrimüslimlerinin Askerlik Serüveni*. Istanbul: Simurg Yayınları, 2000.

Güvenç, Serhat. *Birinci Dünya Savaşı'na Giden Yolda Osmanlıların Drednot Düşleri*. Istanbul: Türkiye İş Bankası Kültür Yayınları, 2009.

Hacısalihoğlu, Mehmet. "Inclusion and Exclusion: Conscription in the Ottoman Empire." *Journal of Modern European History* 5, no. 2 (2007): 264–86.

Haddad, Mahmoud. "The Rise of Arab Nationalism Reconsidered." *International Journal of Middle Eastern Studies* 26, no. 2 (1994): 201–22.

Hall, Richard C. *The Balkan Wars, 1912–1913: Prelude to the First World War*. London: Routledge, 2000.

Halpern, Paul G. *The Naval War in the Mediterranean, 1914–1918*. Annapolis, MD: Naval Institute Press, 1987.

Hanna, Abdallah. "The First World War According to the Memories of 'Commoners' in the Bilad al-Sham." In *The World in World Wars: Experiences, Perceptions, and Perspectives from Africa and Asia*, edited by Heike Liebau, Katrin Bromber, Katharina Lange, Dyala Hamzah, and Ravi Ahuja, 299–311. Leiden: Brill, 2010.

Harlaftis, Gelina, and Vassilis Kardasis. "International Shipping in the Eastern Mediterranean and the Black Sea: Istanbul as a Maritime Center, 1870–1910." In *The Mediterranean Response to Globalization before 1950*, edited by Şevket Pamuk and Jeffrey G. Williamson, 233–65. London: Routledge, 2000.

Healy, Maureen. *Vienna and the Fall of the Habsburg Empire: Total War and Everyday Life in World War I*. Cambridge: Cambridge University Press, 2004.

Heinzelmann, Tobias. *Die Balkankrise in der osmanischen Karikatur: Die Satirezeitschriften Karagöz, Kalem und Cem, 1908–1914*. Stuttgart: Steiner, 1999.

Heller, Joseph. *The British Policy Towards the Ottoman Empire, 1908–1914.* London: Frank Cass, 1983.

Helmreich, Ernst Christian. *The Diplomacy of the Balkan Wars, 1912–1913.* Cambridge, MA: Harvard University Press, 1938.

Holquist, Peter. *Making War, Forging Revolution: Russia's Continuum of Crisis, 1914–1921.* Cambridge, MA: Harvard University Press, 2002.

Horne, John. *State, Society, and Mobilization in Europe during the First World War.* Cambridge: Cambridge University Press, 1997.

———. "War and Conflict in Contemporary European History, 1914–2004." *Zeithistorische Forschungen / Studies in Contemporary History* 3, no. 1 (2004): 347–62.

Hovannisian, Richard G. *Armenia on the Road to Independence, 1918.* Berkeley: University of California Press, 1967.

Hudson, Leila. *Transforming Damascus: Space and Modernity in an Islamic City.* London: I. B. Tauris, 2008.

Ilıcak, H. Şükrü. "Osmanlı Rumlarının Bilinmeyen 'Hürriyet' Hikayeleri." In *İkinci Meşrutiyet'in İlanının 100üncü Yılı,* edited by Bahattin Öztuncay, 18–23. Istanbul: Sadberk Hanım Müzesi, 2008.

Imlay, Talbot. "Total War." *Journal of Strategic Studies* 30, no. 3 (2007): 547–70.

Işık, Adnan. *Malatya, 1830–1919.* Istanbul: n.p., 1998.

İpek, Nedim. "The Balkans, War, and Migration." In *War and Nationalism: The Balkan Wars, 1912–1913, and Their Sociopolitical Implications,* edited by M. Hakan Yavuz and Isa Blumi, 621–64. Salt Lake City: University of Utah Press, 2013.

———. "Birinci Dünya Savaşı Esnasında Karadeniz ve Doğu Anadolu'da Cereyan Eden Göçler." *Ondokuz Mayıs Üniversitesi Eğitim Fakültesi Dergisi* 12 (1999): 161–223.

———. *Rumeli'den Anadolu'ya Türk Göçleri, 1877–1890.* Ankara: Türk Tarih Kurumu, 1994.

Jacobson, Abigail. "A City Living through Crisis: Jerusalem during World War I." *British Journal of Middle Eastern Studies* 36, no. 1 (2007): 73–92.

———. *From Empire to Empire: Jerusalem between Ottoman and British Rule.* Syracuse, NY: Syracuse University Press, 2011.

———. "Negotiating Ottomanism in Times of War: Jerusalem during World War I through the Eyes of a Local Muslim Resident." *International Journal of Middle East Studies* 40, no. 1 (2008): 69–88.

Jeffrey, Keith. *Field Marshal Sir Henry Wilson: A Political Soldier.* Oxford: Oxford University Press, 2006.

Kabacalı, Alpay. *Gül Yaprağın' Döktü Bugün: Ağıtlar.* Istanbul: Yapı Kredi Yayınları, 1997.

Kaiser, Hilmar. "Armenian Property, Ottoman Law, and Nationality Policies during the Armenian Genocide, 1915–1916." In *The First World War as Remembered in the Countries of the Eastern Mediterranean,* edited by Olaf Farschid, Manfred Kropp, and Stephan Dähne, 49–71. Würzburg: Ergon, 2006.

———. "Genocide at the Twilight of the Ottoman Empire." In *The Oxford Handbook of Genocide Studies,* edited by Donald Bloxham and A. Dirk Moses, 365–85. Oxford: Oxford University Press, 2010.

Kaligian, Dikran Mesrob. *Armenian Organization and Ideology under Ottoman Rule, 1908–1914*. New Brunswick, NJ: Transaction Publishers, 2004.

Kalkan, Emir. *Kayseri ve Yöresi Ağıtları*. Kayseri: Kültür Müdürlüğü Yayınları, 1992.

Karakışla, Yavuz Selim. *Women, War and Work in the Ottoman Empire: Society for the Employment of Ottoman Muslim Women, 1916–1923*. Istanbul: Ottoman Bank Research Center, 2005.

Kark, Ruth, and Roy Fischel. "Palestinian Women in the Public Domain during the Late Ottoman and Mandate Periods, 1831–1948." *Hawwa* 10, nos. 1–2 (2012): 77–96.

Karpat, Kemal H. *Ottoman Population, 1830–1914: Demographic and Social Characteristics*. Madison: University of Wisconsin Press, 1985.

Kasaba, Reşat. *A Moveable Empire: Ottoman Nomads, Migrants, and Refugees*. Seattle: University of Washington Press, 2009.

Kauffman, Jesse. *Elusive Alliance: The German Occupation of Poland during World War I*. Cambridge, MA: Harvard University Press, 2015.

Kaya, Erol. *Birinci Dünya Savaşı ve Milli Mücadele'de Türk Mültecileri: Vilayat-ı Şarkiyye ve Aydın Vilayeti Mültecileri (1915–1923)*. Ankara: Ebabil Yayıncılık, 2007.

Kayalı, Hasan. *Arabs and Young Turks: Ottomanism, Arabism, and Islamism in the Ottoman Empire, 1908–1918*. Berkeley: University of California Press, 1997.

Kazmaz, Süleyman. *Sarıkamış'ta Köy Gezileri: Halk Kültürü Alanında Araştırma ve İncelemeler*. Ankara: Atatürk Kültür Merkezi Yayınları, 1995.

Kemal, Yaşar. *Ağıtlar*. Istanbul: Adam Yayınları, 1996.

———. *Yaşar Kemal Kendini Anlatıyor: Alain Bosquet ile Görüşmeler*. Istanbul: Yapı Kredi Yayınları, 2004.

———. "Yayımlanmamış On Ağıt." In *Folklor ve Etnografya Araştırmaları 1985*, edited by İ. Gündağ Kayaoğlu, 169–77. Istanbul: Anadolu Sanat Yayınları, 1985.

Kennan, George F. *The Decline of Bismarck's European Order: Franco-Russian Relations, 1875–1890*. Princeton, NJ: Princeton University Press, 1979.

Kerimoğlu, Hasan Taner. *Osmanlı Kamuoyunda Balkan Meselesi, 1908–1914*. Istanbul: Libra, 2015.

Kévorkian, Raymond H. *The Armenian Genocide: A Complete History*. London: I. B. Tauris, 2011.

———. "Recueil de témoignages sur l'extermination des amele tabouri ou battaillons de soldats-ouvriers arméniens de l'armée ottomane." *Revue d'histoire arménienne contemporaine* 1 (1995): 289–303.

Kieser, Hans-Lukas. *Nearest East: American Millennialism and Mission to the Middle East*. Philadelphia: Temple University Press, 2010.

———. *Der verpasste Friede: Mission, Ethnie und Staat in den Ostprovinzen der Türkei, 1839–1938*. Zurich: Chronos, 2000.

Kieser, Hans-Lukas, and Donald Bloxham. "Genocide." In *The Cambridge History of the First World War*, Vol. 1, *Global War*, edited by Jay Winter, 585–614. Cambridge: Cambridge University Press, 2014.

Kissinger, Henry A. *A World Restored: Metternich, Castlereagh and the Problems of Peace, 1812–22*. Boston: Houghton Mifflin, 1957.

Khalidi, Rashid. "The Arab Experience of the War." In *Facing Armageddon: The First World War Experienced*, edited by Hugh Cecil and Peter H. Little, 642–55. London: Leo Cooper, 1996.

Klein, Janet. *The Margins of Empire: Kurdish Militias in the Ottoman Tribal Zone*. Stanford: Stanford University Press, 2011.

Köklü, Aziz, *Türkiye'de Para Meseleleri: 1914–1946 Devresinde Para Siyasetimiz ve Paramızın Kıymeti*. Ankara: Milli Eğitim Basımevi, 1947.

Köksal, Osman. "Tarihsel Süreci İçinde Bir Özel Yargı Organı Olarak Divan-ı Harb-i Örfiler (1877–1922)." PhD diss., Ankara University, 1996.

Koptaş, Rober. "Zohrab, Papazyan ve Pastırmacıyan'ın Kalemlerinden 1914 Ermeni Reformu ve İttihatçı-Taşnak Müzakereleri." *Tarih ve Toplum Yeni Yaklaşımlar* 5 (2007): 159–78.

Köroğlu, Erol. *Türk Edebiyatı ve Birinci Dünya Savaşı (1914–1918): Propagandadan Milli Kimlik İnşasına*. Istanbul: İletişim Yayınları, 2004.

Koz, M. Sabri. "Bir Ozan, Bir Destan." *Türk Folklor Araştırmaları* 16 (1975): 7584.

Kramer, Alan. "Combatants and Noncombatants: Atrocities, Massacres, and War Crimes." In *A Companion to World War I*, edited by John Horne, 188–201. Chichester, England: Wiley-Blackwell, 2010.

——. *Dynamic of Destruction: Culture and Mass Killing in the First World War*. Oxford: Oxford University Press, 2007.

Kuneralp, Sinan. "İkinci Meşrutiyet Döneminde Gayrimüslimlerin Askerlik Meselesi, 1908–1912." *Toplumsal Tarih* 72 (1999): 11–15.

Kurat, Akdes Nimet, ed. *Birinci Dünya Savaşı Sırasında Türkiye'de Bulunan Alman Generallerinin Raporları*. Ankara: Türk Kültürünü Araştırma Enstitüsü Yayınları, 1966.

Kuschner, Tony, and Katharine Knox. *Refugees in an Age of Genocide: Global, National, and Local Perspectives during the Twentieth Century*. London: Frank Cass, 1999.

Kutluata, Zeynep. "Ottoman Women and the State during World War I." PhD diss., Sabancı University, 2014.

Ladas, Stephen. *The Exchange of Minorities: Bulgaria, Greece, and Turkey*. New York: Macmillan, 1932.

Langensiepen, Bernd, and Ahmet Güleryüz. *The Ottoman Steam Navy*. Translated and edited by James Cooper. Annapolis, MD: Naval Institute Press, 1995.

Larcher, Maurice. *La guerre turque dans la guerre mondiale*. Paris: Berger-Levrault, 1926.

Lorenz, Charlotte. "Die Frauenfrage im Osmanischen Reiche mit Besonderer Berücksichtigung der Arbeitenden Klasse." *Die Welt des Islams* 6 (1918): 72–214.

Manela, Erez. *The Wilsonian Moment: Self-Determination and the International Origins of Anticolonial Nationalism*. Oxford: Oxford University Press, 2007.

Mann, Michael. "The Autonomous Power of the State: Its Origins, Mechanisms and Results." *Archives européenes de sociologie* 25, no. 2 (1984): 185–213.

Marquis, A. G. "Words as Weapons: Propaganda in Britain and Germany during the First World War." *Journal of Contemporary History* 13, no. 3 (1978): 467–98.

Mays, Devi. "Transplanting Cosmopolitans: The Migrations of Sephardic Jews to Mexico, 1900–1934." PhD diss., Indiana University, 2013.

McCarthy, Justin. *Death and Exile: The Ethnic Cleansing of Ottoman Muslims, 1821–1922*. Princeton, NJ: Darwin Press, 1995.

———. *Muslims and Minorities: The Population of Ottoman Anatolia and the End of the Empire*. New York: New York University Press, 1983.

McMeekin, Sean. *The Ottoman Endgame: War, Revolution, and the Making of the Modern Middle East, 1908–1923*. New York: Penguin Press, 2015.

McMurray, Jonathan S. *Distant Ties: Germany, the Ottoman Empire, and the Construction of the Baghdad Railway*. Westport, CT: Praeger, 2001.

Mears, Eliot Grinnell. *Modern Turkey: A Politico-Economic Interpretation, 1908–1923*. New York: Macmillan, 1924.

Metinsoy, Elif Mahir. "I. Dünya Savaşı'nda Osmanlı Kadınlarının Gıda ve Erzak Savaşı." *Toplumsal Tarih* 243 (2014): 56–61.

———. "Writing the History of Ordinary Ottoman Women during World War I." *Aspasia* 10 (2016): 18–39.

Miller, Michael B. *Europe and the Maritime World: A Twentieth-Century History*. Cambridge: Cambridge University Press, 2012.

Mombauer, Annika, ed. *The Origins of the First World War: Diplomatic and Military Documents*. Manchester: Manchester University Press, 2013.

Morack, Ellinor. "The Ottoman Greeks and the Great War, 1912–1922." In *The World during the First World War*, edited by Helmut Bley and Anorthe Kremers, 215–30. Essen: Klartext, 2014.

Moreau, Odile. *L'Empire ottoman à l'âge des réformes: Les hommes et les idées du "Nouvel Ordre" militaire, 1826–1914*. Paris: Maisonneuve et Larose, 2007.

Moumdjian, Garabet K. "The Eastern Vilayets, 1909–1914: ARF–CUP Collusion, Russian Stratagems, and the Kurdish Menace." In *War and Collapse: World War I and the Ottoman State*, edited by M. Hakan Yavuz with Feroz Ahmad, 705–80. Salt Lake City: University of Utah Press, 2016.

Mulligan, William. *The Great War for Peace*. New Haven, CT: Yale University Press, 2014.

Musil, Alois. *The Middle Euphrates: A Topographical Itinerary*. New York: AMS Press, 1978 [1927].

Mühlmann, Carl. *Deutschland und die Türkei 1913–1914*. Berlin: Dr. Walther Rothschild, 1929.

———. *Das deutsch-türkische Waffenbündnis im Weltkriege*. Leipzig: Koehler & Amelang, 1940.

Novichev, A. D. *Ekonomika Turtsii v Period Mirovoi Voin*. Leningrad: Izd-vo Akademii nauk SSSR, 1935.

Ochsenwald, William. *The Hijaz Railroad*. Charlottesville: University Press of Virginia, 1980.

Offer, Avner. *The First World War: An Agrarian Interpretation*. Oxford: Oxford University Press, 1989.

Onur, Ahmet. *Türk Demir Yolları Tarihi*. Istanbul: K.K.K. İstanbul Askeri Basımevi, 1953.

Osman, İlker. *Artvin Zeytinlik Bucağı Aşağı Maden ve Aşağı Madenliler (A. Hod ve A. Hodlular)*. Vol. 1, *Köyün Doğal ve Toplumsal Yapısı*. Istanbul: Aşağı ve Yukarı Maden Köyleri Kültür ve Dayanışma Derneği Yayınları, 1992.

Overmans, Rüdiger. "Military Losses (Casualties)." In *Brill's Encyclopedia of the First World War*. Vol. 2, edited by Gerhard Hirschfeld, Gerd Krumeich, and Irina Renz, 731–34. Leiden: Brill, 2012.

Öğün, Tuncay. *Kafkas Cephesinin I. Dünya Savaşındaki Lojistik Desteği*. Ankara: Atatürk Araştırma Merkezi Yayınları, 1999.

———. *Unutulmuş Bir Göç Trajedisi: Vilayat-ı Şarkiye Mültecileri, 1915–1923*. Ankara: Babil Yayıncılık, 2004.

Öksüz, Hikmet, and Veysel Usta. *Mustafa Reşit Tarakçıoğlu: Hayatı, Hatıratı ve Trabzon'un Yakın Tarihi*. Trabzon: Serander Yayınları, 2008.

Özbek, Müge. "The Regulation of Prostitution in Beyoğlu, 1875–1915." *Middle Eastern Studies* 46, no. 4 (2010): 555–68.

Özbek, Nadir. "Defining the Public Sphere during the Late Ottoman Empire: War, Mass Mobilization and the Young Turk Regime (1908–18)." *Middle Eastern Studies* 43, no. 5 (2007): 795–809.

———. *Osmanlı İmparatorluğu'nda Sosyal Devlet: Siyaset, İktidar ve Meşrutiyet, 1876–1914*. Istanbul: İletişim Yayınları, 2002.

Özdemir, Ahmet Z. *Öyküleriyle Ağıtlar I*. Ankara: Kültür Bakanlığı Yayınları, 2002.

Özdemir, Hikmet. *The Ottoman Army: Disease and Death on the Battlefield*. Translated by Şaban Kardaş. Salt Lake City: University of Utah Press, 2008.

Özdemir, Zekeriya. *Adramyttion'dan Efeler Toprağı Edremit'e*. Ankara: n.p., 2000.

Özel, Oktay. "Tehcir ve Teşkilat-ı Mahsusa." In *1915: Siyaset, Tehcir, Soykırım*, edited by Fikret Adanır and Oktay Özel, 377–407. Istanbul: Tarih Vakfı Yurt Yayınları, 2015.

Ozil, Ayşe. *Orthodox Christians in the Late Ottoman Empire: A Study of Communal Relations in Anatolia*. London: Routledge, 2012.

Öztel, Muharrem. *II.Meşrutiyet Dönemi Osmanlı Maliyesi*. Istanbul: Kitabevi Yayınları, 2009.

Öztürkmen, Arzu. "Remembering Conflicts in a Black Sea Town: A Multi-sited Ethnography of Memory." *New Perspectives on Turkey* 34 (2006): 93–115.

Pamuk, Şevket. "The Ottoman Economy in World War I." In *The Economics of World War I*, edited by Stephen Broadberry and Mark Harrison, 112–36. Cambridge: Cambridge University Press, 2005.

Patrick, Andrew. *America's Forgotten Middle East Initiative: The King-Crane Commission of 1919*. London: I. B. Tauris, 2015.

Pavlovich, N. B. *The Fleet in the First World War*. Vol. 1, *Operations of the Russian Fleet*. New Delhi: Amerind Publishing, 1979.

Pedersen, Susan. *Family Dependence and the Origins of the Welfare State: Britain and France, 1914–1945*. Cambridge: Cambridge University Press, 1993.

———. "Gender, Welfare, and Citizenship in Britain during the Great War." *American Historical Review* 95, no. 4 (1990): 983–1006.

Pitts, Graham A. "Fallow Fields: Famine and the Making of Lebanon." PhD diss., Georgetown University, 2016.

Polat, Nazım H. *Müdafaa-i Milliye Cemiyeti*. Ankara: Kültür Bakanlığı Yayınları, 1991.

Popplewell, Richard. "British Intelligence in Mesopotamia, 1914–16." *Intelligence and National Security* 5, no. 2 (1990): 139–72.

Prior, Robin. *Gallipoli: The End of the Myth*. New Haven, CT: Yale University Press, 2009.

Proctor, Tammy M. *Civilians in a World at War, 1914–1918*. New York: New York University Press, 2010.

Purseigle, Pierre. "The First World War and the Transformations of the State." *International Affairs* 90, no. 2 (2014): 249–64.

——. "Home Fronts: The Mobilisation of Resources for Total War." In *The Cambridge History of War*, Vol. 4, *War and the Modern World*, edited by Roger Chickering, Dennis Showalter, and Hans van de Ven, 257–84. Cambridge: Cambridge University Press, 2012.

Pyle, Emily. "Village Social Relations and the Reception of Soldier's Family Aid Policies in Russia, 1912–1921." PhD diss., University of Chicago, 1997.

Quataert, Donald. "The Age of Reforms, 1812–1914." In *An Economic and Social History of the Ottoman Empire, 1300–1914*, edited by Halil İnalcık with Donald Quataert, 759–943. Cambridge: Cambridge University Press, 1994.

——. "Agricultural Trends and Government Policy in Ottoman Anatolia." *Asian and African Studies* 15 (1981): 69–84.

——. "Limited Revolution: The Impact of the Anatolian Railway on Turkish Transportation and the Provisioning of Istanbul, 1890–1908." *Business History Review* 51, no. 2 (1977): 139–60.

——. "Machine Breaking and the Changing Carpet Industry of Western Anatolia, 1860–1908." *Journal of Social History* 19, no. 3 (1986): 473–89.

——. *Miners and the State in the Ottoman Empire: The Zonguldak Coalfield, 1822–1920*. New York: Berghahn Books, 2006.

Reynolds, Michael A. *Shattering Empires: The Clash and Collapse of the Ottoman and Russian Empires, 1908–1918*. Cambridge: Cambridge University Press, 2011.

Robinson, Paul. "Decision at Erzerum." *The Historian* 76, no. 3 (2014): 461–78.

Rogan, Eugene. *The Fall of the Ottomans: The Great War in the Middle East*. New York: Basic Books, 2015.

——. *Frontiers of the State in the Late Ottoman Empire: Transjordan, 1850–1921*. Cambridge: Cambridge University Press, 1999.

Rooney, Chris B. "The International Significance of British Naval Missions to the Ottoman Empire, 1908–1914." *Middle Eastern Studies* 34, no. 1 (1998): 1–29.

San, Sabri Özcan. *Rusların Gümüşhane İlini İşgali*. Istanbul: Milli Eğitim Bakanlığı Yayınları, 1993.

Sanborn, Joshua A. "Unsettling the Empire: Violent Migrations and Social Disaster in Russia during World War I." *Journal of Modern History* 77, no. 2 (2005): 290–324.

Sarafian, Ara. "The Absorption of Armenian Women and Children into Muslim Households as a Structural Component of the Armenian Genocide." In *In God's Name: Genocide and Religion in the Twentieth Century*, edited by Omer Bartov and Phyllis Mack, 209–21. New York: Berghahn Books, 2001.

Sarısaman, Sadık. *Birinci Dünya Savaşı'nda Türk Cephelerinde Beyannamelerle Psikolojik Harp*. Ankara: Genelkurmay Askeri Tarih ve Stratejik Etüt Başkanlığı Yayınları, 1999.

———. "Birinci Ordu Birinci Kadın İşçi Taburu." *Atatürk Araştırma Merkezi Dergisi* 39 (1997): 695–723.

Schilcher, L. Schatkowski. "The Famine of 1915–1918 in Greater Syria." In *Problems of the Modern Middle East in Historical Perspective: Essays in Honour of Albert Hourani*, edited by John P. Spagnolo, 229–58. Reading, England: Ithaca Press, 1992.

Seikaly, Samir M. "Unequal Fortunes: The Arabs of Palestine and the Jews during World War I." In *Studia Arabica et Islamica: Festschrift for Ihsan Abbas on his Sixtieth Birthday*, edited by Wadad al-Qadi, 399–406. Beirut: American University of Beirut Press, 1981.

Selçuk, Mustafa. *Çanakkale Seferberliği: Savaş, Eğitim, Cephe Gerisi*. Istanbul: Kitap Yayınevi, 2016.

Sevinçli, Efdal. "Seferberlik Üstüne ve Bir Seferberlik Ağıtı." *Türk Folklor Araştırmaları* 358 (1979): 8659–61.

Shaw, Stanford J. *The Ottoman Empire in World War I*. Vol. 1, *Prelude to War*. Ankara: Türk Tarih Kurumu, 2006.

———. "Resettlement of Refugees in Anatolia, 1918–1923." *Turkish Studies Association Bulletin* 22 (1998): 58–90.

Shilo, Margalit. *Princess or Prisoner? Jewish Women in Jerusalem, 1840–1914*. Waltham, MA: Brandeis University Press, 2005.

———. "Women as Victims of War: The British Conquest (1917) and the Blight of Prostitution in the Holy City." *Nashim* 6 (2003): 72–83.

Simon, Reeva Spector. "The View from Baghdad." In *The Creation of Iraq, 1914–1922*, edited by Reeva Spector Simon and Eleanor H. Tejirian, 36–49. New York: Columbia University Press, 2004.

Showalter, Dennis. "'It All Goes Wrong!': German, French, and British Approaches to Mastering the Western Front." In *Warfare and Belligerence: Perspectives in First World War Studies*, edited by Pierre Purseigle, 39–72. Leiden: Brill, 2005.

Sluglett, Peter. "Aspects of Economy and Society in the Syrian Provinces: Aleppo in Transition, 1880–1925." In *Modernity and Culture: From the Mediterranean to the Indian Ocean*, edited by Leila Tarazi Fawaz and C. A. Bayly, 144–57. New York: Columbia University Press, 2002.

Somakian, Manoug Joseph. *Empires in Conflict: Armenia and the Great Powers, 1895–1920*. London: I. B. Tauris, 1995.

Sondhaus, Lawrence. *The Great War at Sea: A Naval History of the First World War*. Cambridge: Cambridge University Press, 2014.

———. *World War One: The Global Revolution*. Cambridge: Cambridge University Press, 2011.

Stanley, William R. "Review of Turkish Asiatic Railways to 1918: Some Political-Military Considerations." *Journal of Transport History* 7 (1966): 189–204.

Strachan, Hew. "The First World War as a Global War." *First World War Studies* 1, no. 1 (2010): 3–14.

———. "On Total War and Modern War." *International History Review* 22, no. 2 (2000): 341–70.

Suny, Ronald Grigor. *"They Can Live in the Desert but Nowhere Else": A History of the Armenian Genocide.* Princeton, NJ: Princeton University Press, 2015.

Sürgevil, Sabri. *II. Meşrutiyet Döneminde İzmir.* Izmir: İzmir Büyükşehir Belediyesi Kültür Yayını, 2009.

Svazlian, Verjiné. *The Armenian Genocide and Historical Memory.* Translated by Tigran Tsulikian. Yerevan: "Gitutiun" Publishing House of National Academy of Sciences of the Republic of Armenia, 2004.

Swanson, Glen W. "A Note on the Ottoman Socio-Economic Structure and Its Response to the Balkan War of 1912." *Middle Eastern Studies* 14, no. 1 (1978): 116–26.

Tamari, Salim. "The Great War and the Erasure of Palestine's Ottoman Past." In *Transformed Landscapes: Essays on Palestine and the Middle East in Honor of Walid Khalidi*, edited by Camille Mansour and Leila Fawaz, 105–35. Cairo: American University in Cairo Press, 2009.

———, ed., *Year of the Locust: A Soldier's Diary and the Erasure of Palestine's Ottoman Past.* Berkeley: University of California Press, 2011.

Tanielian, Melanie S. "Feeding the City: The Beirut Municipality and the Politics of Food during World War I." *International Journal of Middle East Studies* 46, no. 4 (2014): 737–58.

———. "Politics of Wartime Relief in Ottoman Beirut, 1914–1918." *First World War Studies* 5, no. 1 (2014): 69–82.

———. "The War of Famine: Everyday Life in Wartime Beirut and Mount Lebanon, 1914–1918." PhD diss., University of California, Berkeley, 2012.

Tauber, Eliezer. *The Emergence of the Arab Movements.* London: Frank Cass, 1993.

Thomas, David S. "The First Arab Congress and the Committee of Union and Progress, 1913–1914." In *Essays on Islamic Civilization: Presented to Niyazi Berkes*, edited by Donald P. Little, 317–28. Leiden: Brill, 1976.

Thompson, Elizabeth. *Colonial Citizens: Republican Rights, Paternal Privilege, and Gender in French Syria and Lebanon.* New York: Columbia University Press, 2000.

Toprak, Zafer. "The Family, Feminism, and the State during the Young Turk Period, 1908–1918." In *Première rencontre internationale sur l'Empire ottoman et la Turquie moderne*, edited by Edhem Eldem, 441–52. Istanbul: Editions ISIS, 1991.

———. "İstanbul'da Fuhuş ve Zührevi Hastalıklar, 1914–1933." *Tarih ve Toplum* 39 (1987): 31–40.

———. *İttihat-Terakki ve Cihan Harbi: Savaş Ekonomisi ve Türkiye'de Devletçilik, 1914–1918.* Istanbul: Homer Yayınları, 2003.

———. "Osmanlı Devleti'nin Birinci Dünya Savaşı Finansmanı ve Para Politikası." *ODTÜ Gelişme Dergisi* (1979–1980): 205–38.

———. "Osmanlı Kadınları Çalıştırma Cemiyeti, Kadın Askerler ve Milli Aile." *Tarih ve Toplum* 51 (1988): 34–38.

Traboulsi, Fawwaz. *A History of Modern Lebanon*. London: Pluto Press, 2007.

Trumpener, Ulrich. *Germany and the Ottoman Empire, 1914–1918*. Princeton, NJ: Princeton University Press, 1968.

Tunaya, Tarık Zafer. *Türkiye'de Siyasal Partiler*. Vol. 1, *İkinci Meşrutiyet Dönemi, 1908–1918*. Istanbul: Hürriyet Vakfı Yayınları, 1988.

———. *Türkiye'de Siyasal Partiler*. Vol. 3, *İttihat ve Terakki: Bir Çağın, Bir Kuşağın, Bir Partinin Tarihi*. Istanbul: Hürriyet Vakfı Yayınları, 1989.

Turfan, M. Naim. *Rise of the Young Turks: Politics, the Military and the Ottoman Collapse*. London: I. B. Tauris, 2000.

Türkyılmaz, Yektan. "Devrim İçinde Devrim: Ermeni Örgütleri ve İttihat-Terakki İlişkileri, 1908–1915." In *1915: Siyaset, Tehcir, Soykırım*, edited by Fikret Adanır and Oktay Özel, 324–53. Istanbul: Tarih Vakfı Yurt Yayınları, 2015.

———. "Rethinking Genocide: Violence and Victimhood in Eastern Anatolia, 1913–1915." PhD diss., Duke University, 2011.

Ulrichsen, Kristian Coates. *The First World War in the Middle East*. London: Hurst, 2014.

———. *The Logistics and Politics of the British Campaigns in the Middle East, 1914–1922*. New York: Palgrave Macmillan, 2011.

Uyar, Mesut. "Osmanlı Askeri Rönesansı: Balkan Bozgunu ile Yüzleşmek." *Türkiye Günlüğü* 110 (2012): 65–74.

———. "Ottoman Strategy and War Aims during the First World War." In *The Purpose of the First World War: War Aims and Military Strategies*, edited by Holger Afflerbach, 163–85. Berlin: De Gruyter Oldenbourg, 2015.

Uyar, Mesut, and Edward J. Erickson. *A Military History of the Ottomans: From Osman to Atatürk*. Santa Barbara, CA: Praeger Security International / ABC-CLIO, 2009.

Üngör, Uğur Ümit. *The Making of Modern Turkey: Nation and State in Eastern Anatolia, 1913–1950*. Oxford: Oxford University Press, 2011.

———. "Orphans, Converts, and Prostitutes: Social Consequences of War and Persecution in the Ottoman Empire, 1914–1923." *War in History* 19, no. 2 (2012): 173–92.

Üngör, Uğur Ümit, and Mehmet Polatel. *Confiscation and Destruction: The Young Turk Seizure of Property*. London: Continuum, 2011.

Van Creveld, Martin. "World War I and the Revolution in Logistics." In *Great War, Total War: Combat and Mobilization on the Western Front, 1914–1918*, edited by Roger Chickering and Stig Förster, 57–72. Cambridge: Cambridge University Press, 2000.

Van der Dussen, W. J. "The Question of Armenian Reforms in 1913–1914." *Armenian Review* 39 (1986): 11–28.

Van Os, Nicole A. N. M. "Aiding the Poor Soldiers' Families: The Asker Ailelerine Yardımcı Hanımlar Cemiyeti." *İstanbul Üniversitesi Edebiyat Fakültesi Türkiyat Mecmuası* 21, no. 2 (2011): 255–89.

———. "Feminism, Philanthropy & Patriotism: Female Associational Life in the Ottoman Empire." PhD diss., Leiden University, 2013.

———. "Taking Care of Soldiers' Families: The Ottoman State and the *Muinsiz Aile Maaşı*." In *Arming the State: Military Conscription in the Middle East and Central Asia, 1775–1925*, edited by Erik J. Zürcher, 95–110. London: I. B. Tauris, 1999.

Von Hagen, Mark. "The Great War and the Mobilization of Ethnicity." In *Post-Soviet Political Order: Conflict and State-Building*, edited by Barnett Rubin and Jack Snyder, 34–57. London: Routledge, 1998.

Wallach, Jehuda L. *Anatomie einer Militärhilfe: Die preussisch-deutschen Militärmissionen in der Türkei, 1835–1919*. Düsseldorf: Droste, 1976.

Watenpaugh, Keith David. *Bread from Stones: The Middle East and the Making of Modern Humanitarianism*. Berkeley: University of California Press, 2015.

Webster, Donald Everett. *The Turkey of Atatürk: Social Process in the Turkish Transformation*. Philadelphia: American Academy of Political and Social Science, 1939.

Williams, Elizabeth. "Economy, Environment, and Famine: World War I from the Perspective of the Syrian Interior." In *Syria in World War I: Politics, Economy, and Society*, edited by M. Talha Çiçek, 150–68. London: Routledge, 2016.

Winter, Jay. "Propaganda and the Mobilization of Consent." In *The Oxford Illustrated History of the First World War*, edited by Hew Strachan, 216–26. Oxford: Oxford University Press, 1998.

Winter, Jay, and Jean-Louis Robert, eds. *Capital Cities at War: Paris, London, Berlin, 1914–1919*. 2 vols. Cambridge: Cambridge University Press, 1997–2007.

Yalgın, Ali Rıza. "Cihan Harbi ve Halk Türküleri." *Görüşler: Adana Halkevi Dergisi* 22 (1939): 18–23.

Yanıkdağ, Yücel. *Healing the Nation: Prisoners of War, Medicine and Nationalism in Turkey, 1914–1939*. Edinburgh: Edinburgh University Press, 2013.

Yılmaz, Seçil. "Love in the Time of Syphilis: Medicine and Sex in the Ottoman Empire, 1860–1922." PhD diss., City University of New York, 2016.

Zaken, Mordechai. *Jewish Subjects and Their Tribal Chieftains in Kurdistan: A Study in Survival*. Leiden: Brill, 2007.

Zürcher, Erik Jan. "Between Death and Desertion: The Experience of the Ottoman Soldier in World War I." *Turcica* 28 (1996): 235–58.

———, ed. *Jihad and Islam in World War I: Studies on the Ottoman Jihad on the Centenary of Snouck Hurgronje's "Holy War Made in Germany."* Leiden: Leiden University Press, 2016.

———. "Little Mehmet in the Desert: The Ottoman Soldier's Experience." In *Facing Armageddon: The First World War Experienced*, edited by Hugh Cecil and Peter H. Liddle, 230–241. London: Leo Cooper, 1996.

———. "The Ottoman Conscription System in Theory and Practice, 1844–1918." In *Arming the State: Military Conscription in the Middle East and Central Asia, 1775–1925*, edited by Erik J. Zürcher, 79–94. London: I. B. Tauris, 1999.

———. "Ottoman Labour Battalions in World War I." In *Der Völkermord an den Armeniern und die Shoah–The Armenian Genocide and the Shoah*, edited by Hans-Lukas Kieser and Dominik J. Schaller, 187–95. Zurich: Chronos, 2002.

———. *The Unionist Factor: The Role of the Committee of Union and Progress in the Turkish National Movement, 1905–1926*. Leiden: Brill, 1984.

———. "What Was Different about the Ottoman War." *Pera-Blätter* 27 (2014).

———. "The Young Turks: Children of the Borderlands?" *International Journal of Turkish Studies* 9, nos. 1–2 (2003): 275–86.

INDEX